CHARLES NORMAN NELSON
BALL STATE U
SUMMER 1983

Mainstreaming Students with Learning and Behavior Problems

Mainstreaming Students with Learning and Behavior Problems

Techniques for the Classroom Teacher

COLLEEN BLANKENSHIP
University of Illinois

M. STEPHEN LILLY
University of Illinois

HOLT, RINEHART AND WINSTON
New York   Chicago   San Francisco   Philadelphia
Montreal   Toronto   London   Sydney   Tokyo
Mexico City   Rio de Janeiro   Madrid

Library of Congress Cataloging in Publication Data

Blankenship, Colleen.
  Mainstreaming students with learning and behavior
problems.

  Includes index.
  1. Learning disabilities. 2. Mainstreaming
in education. 3. Problem children. I. Lilly, M.
Stephen, 1944–   joint author. II. Title.
LC4704.B58   371.9   81-302

ISBN 0-03-046051-4   AACR1

CBS COLLEGE PUBLISHING
Holt, Rinehart and Winston
The Dryden Press
Saunders College Publishing

Preface

For American educators mainstreaming is no longer an issue for the future; it is present reality. With increasing frequency students with mild academic, behavioral, physical, or sensory handicaps are being educated in regular classrooms. Mainstreaming programs, when well planned and implemented, can be of social and academic benefit for all students involved, both handicapped and nonhandicapped.

There are three sets of individuals in the schools who will, ultimately, determine the success of mainstreaming programs. The first is the set of building and district administrators, who establish the tone and direction for any innovations in school programs. The second is the set of special educators, who must often abandon an operating style that is designed to provide an alternative to the regular curriculum, and opt for a cooperative, supportive approach in which the classroom teacher retains primary responsibility for the educational progress of the student. The third is the set of classroom teachers. In the authors' opinion this is the most important group. The authors feel that traditional special education services have underestimated the ability *and* willingness of classroom teachers to teach students with learning and behavior problems. It is our experience that the majority of classroom teachers do not want to relinquish their teaching responsibilities to special educators. Rather we have observed that, justly, teachers are proud of their curriculum and want to teach the maximum number of students the skills and knowledge necessary for adult functioning in our society.

This book is for these teachers, who are dedicated to teaching all the children with whom they come in contact, but who want occasional special help and support. This book is based on the premise that the regular curriculum is appropriate for all students without severe and/or multiple handicaps. We believe that, whenever possible, students should learn with their peers, and that the regular classroom is the appropriate setting for the majority of those students who require special educational services during their school careers.

The purpose of this book is to help classroom teachers to provide individualized instruction for students with learning and behavior problems. Tangentially the book may help special education resource teachers to work cooperatively with classroom teachers. The instructional approaches presented here are intended to complement, not replace, the approaches currently used by most elementary and secondary teachers. Our focus is on defining problem behavior in specific terms, assessing performance *in relation to the standard curriculum*, and continuously monitoring student progress.

This book—and many of the examples cited in it—has grown out of four years' work with teachers-in-training at the University of Illinois and with inservice teachers in the Champaign-Urbana area. The senior author, Colleen Blankenship, is the Coordinator of the Specialized Instruction Program at the University of Illinois, a program which prepares classroom teachers to teach students with learning and behavior problems. As a part of this program, approximately thirty regular educators have received inservice course work and have implemented the procedures presented in this book in their own classrooms. In addition, approximately twenty-five preservice trainees graduate each year having learned and implemented these procedures in a practicum. Thus the approaches presented herein have been studied, adapted, and applied in a variety of classroom settings.

This book is organized in five major sections:

Section 1   Overview of Mainstreaming Issues
            Chapters 1, 2, 3
Section 2   Assessing Instructional Problems
            Chapters 4, 5
Section 3   Collecting and Using Student Performance Data
            Chapters 6, 7, 8
Section 4   Instructional Approaches for Learning and Behavior Problems
            Chapters 9, 10
Section 5   Mainstreaming Students with Physical and Sensory Impairments
            Chapter 11

This book deals primarily with *methods* for assessing, monitoring, and improving student performance in academic and behavioral areas. The assumption is that most teachers are concerned with *how* to do mainstreaming rather than *whether* to do it.

The three chapters which comprise Section 1 provide a definition of major mainstreaming issues and describe the context in which mainstreaming occurs. Chapter 1 provides a historical overview of the mainstreaming movement, as well as of some of the important issues involved in mainstreaming. Chapter 2 provides an overview of typical special-education placement and instructional-planning procedures, with suggestions for meaningful teacher involvement in the process. Chapter 3 outlines the classroom teacher's role in mainstreaming, and presents an instructional model which is effective in working with students who have learning and behavior problems.

Sections 2 through 4 of the book present detailed information on the instructional model presented in Chapter 2. Chapters 4 and 5 focus on assessment: Chapter 4 is a description of the traditional special education assessment model; Chapter 5 is a proposal of an alternative model for assessing students in relation to the curriculum used in the regular classroom.

Section 3 focuses on monitoring student performance in specific academic and social areas. Underlying all of Section 3 are these assumptions:

(1) that good teaching procedures change student performance, and (2) that this change must be monitored and documented. Chapter 6 is a description of methods for collecting student performance data in the classroom. Chapter 7 is a description of how to represent the data visually so that it is most useful to the teacher and the student. Chapter 8 is a discussion of the use of student performance data for making instructional decisions as well as for communicating with parents and other school personnel.

Section 4 of the book presents practical strategies for teaching students with learning and behavior problems. Within Section 4, Chapter 9 focuses on methods for use with students with social behavior problems, and Chapter 10 presents methods for remedying academic difficulties. Both chapters present case studies to illustrate the principles presented in them.

Finally Section 5 (Chapter 11) provides a brief overview of information concerning the integration into regular classrooms of students with visual, hearing, and orthopedic impairments. This chapter focuses on the nature of these handicaps and their possible implications for classroom instruction. The instructional principles presented in Sections 2 through 4 work for these students as well as for those discussed earlier.

We have attempted in Sections 2 through 4 of the book to present complete information, with the expectation that teachers will selectively use that information in dealing with individual students. To many readers, the instructional principles and procedures presented in these sections may seem somewhat overwhelming. In fact if a teacher were to attempt to implement all of the strategies presented in this book simultaneously, we could expect a rapid case of "teacher burn-out." The examples and case studies used throughout these chapters illustrate that teachers pick and choose from the many data-collection and instructional strategies presented and make their own applications and adaptations for classroom use. Readers of the book are encouraged to do the same.

In the interest of clarity we have attempted to keep technical language to a minimum. However, since some technical terms are essential, we have provided a glossary at the end of the book. Those words that are included in the glossary are printed in italics when they first appear in the text.

The authors wish to acknowledge the contributions of several groups of people in producing this book. First we must acknowledge the cooperating teachers and preservice students in the Specialized Instruction Program of the University of Illinois without whom it would have been impossible to write the book. Second we wish to thank our professional colleagues for their support and encouragement, particularly Ann Nevin, Deborah Smith, and Cathy Morsink. Third we acknowledge the efforts of Jo Mahannah in typing and retyping the manuscript. And, finally, we express our appreciation to our spouses, Tim Blankenship and Marilyn Lilly, who are not only constant supporters, but helpful critics as well.

Contents

SECTION 2

Assessing Instructional Problems   51

SECTION 3

Collecting and Using Student Performance Data   111

SECTION 4

Instructional Approaches for Learning and Behavior Problems   213

SECTION 5

Mainstreaming Students with Physical and Sensory Impairments 313

Mainstreaming Students with Learning and Behavior Problems

SECTION 1

Overview of Mainstreaming Issues

Current Perspectives on Mainstreaming

DEFINITION OF CONCEPTS

Ten professional educators using the term mainstreaming will generally mean ten different things by it. This section will define mainstreaming as it is used in this book, and will distinguish mainstreaming from the more generic (and often preferred) term, *least restrictive environment*. Also the categories of *special education* most often associated with the mainstreaming movement will be defined and discussed, stressing that categorical labels often hinder effective instruction.

It is difficult, if not impossible, to trace the origin of the term *mainstreaming*. It is clear, however, that from its beginnings the term was intended to connote a commonality of purpose and procedures in the education of students in elementary and secondary schools, including students labeled as *mildly handicapped*. For many of these students, it has been assumed that education should occur in *special classes* isolated from other students and teachers in the schoo!. Advocates of mainstreaming challenge this notion, pointing out that separate education can be inferior education and that special classes often result in education in which goals for students have been unnecessarily and arbitrarily limited. They also argue that placement in self-contained special classes tends to be permanent, since specialized curricula do not teach the content and study skills necessary for successful participation in the regular classroom (Lilly, 1979).

Another concept questioned by advocates of mainstreaming is that students who have been labeled mildly handicapped are *qualitatively different* from other students in the regular classroom setting. Many special education (and regular education) programs assume that students labeled mildly handicapped have no peers in the regular classroom with regard to academic instruction, and therefore must receive their academic program in a special setting. On the contrary it can be argued that the standard curriculum is appropriate for students with *learning and behavior problems*, and that appropriate academic groupings often exist for these stu-

3

dents in the regular classroom. Thus *remedial* work is often indicated rather than completely separate academic instruction.

In order to define mainstreaming, we must first define the broader concept, *education in the least restrictive environment.* Historically, special education has been located in settings separated from the general public and from standard educational programs. Early special education for students with **hearing impairments**, **visual impairments**, emotional disturbances, and mental retardation has taken place in residential centers. As public school programs developed, they tended to be established apart from the standard educational program. Districts often built separate schools for certain groups of students, most notably the moderately and severely retarded and the physically handicapped.

The net result of such special education has been the substantial separation of handicapped and nonhandicapped students, a separation often justified on the basis of tradition rather than the educational needs of individual students. Over the past decade, the educational community has increasingly recognized that continued separation of handicapped and nonhandicapped students might not be wise public policy. Through litigation and legislation, society has established that *all* students have a right to normal school experiences, and that students may be removed from the standard educational program *only* when it is impossible to meet their educational needs in that setting. Special education programs must be as close as possible to normal, while still meeting the students' educational needs. That is, it is the right of every student to receive an appropriate education in the least restrictive or most normal environment possible.

The concept of least restrictive environment has substantial implications for special education. Implicit in this concept is the principle that placement decisions should be *individualized*, that is, based on the unique needs of an individual student rather than the diagnostic category to which a student has been assigned. Thus the fact that a student is labeled trainable mentally retarded, or physically handicapped, is not sufficient reason for the student to be assigned to a special school and separated from normal students. Any time a student is removed further from the normal environment, or any time a decision is made to maintain a student in a separate setting, it must be demonstrated that the educational needs of that student cannot be met in a more integrated setting. The burden of proof for this falls on those who wish to separate the student. Decisions to remove students from standard settings must be based not on convenience or tradition, but on the needs of the student.

The concept of least restrictive environment has had a significant impact on educational systems designed to serve handicapped students. Many school systems have begun to question the need for special schools for students with moderate or severe sensory, physical, and mental impairments. These school systems are now offering moderately and severely handicapped students special class services in public schools. Such special classes offer increased opportunities for contact between handicapped and nonhandicapped students which can be beneficial to both groups. The concept of least restrictive environment applies to *all* handicapped students, regardless of severity of handicap, since it calls for as little removal from normal environments as is necessary to meet the needs of the student (Brown, Wilcox, Sontag, Vincent, Dodd, & Gruenwald, 1977; Sontag, Burke, & York, 1973).

Mainstreaming is a part of the least restrictive environment concept. It refers to the education of handicapped students in regular classrooms with assistance from special education *resource teachers*. Until the mid 1960s, nearly all special education occurred in self-contained special classes; there was little or no contact with the standard educational program. The vast majority of students who were in special classes started their school careers in regular classrooms. These students had been referred to special education by their classroom teachers because of problems of academic learning and/or social behavior in the classroom. The students were then *diagnosed* as handicapped and placed in special classes.

For reasons described later in this chapter, substantial concern arose in the 1960s over the effectiveness of special class services for many students with mild learning and behavior problems. It became apparent upon closer analysis that the rationale for placing students in special classes often came from traditional and organizational concerns more than from an analysis of individual students' unique educational needs. In many cases, for example, if a student was diagnosed as educable mentally retarded, he/she was almost automatically placed in a self-contained special class since this was the way such students were serviced by the school district.

Perhaps no issue is now more widely discussed in education circles than mainstreaming, the education of students with mild learning and/or behavior problems in the regular classroom. Mainstreaming is a movement which has developed gradually over the past fifteen years, although educators of the visually impaired have been successfully placing students in regular classrooms for the better part of a century. Widespread discussion of mainstreaming programs, however, has intensified in the last five years as a result of a combination of legislative mandates, judicial decrees, and professional developments.

This book is about mainstreaming. Most of the book focuses on methods of *assessment* and instruction for teaching students with learning and behavior problems. The purpose of this chapter is to provide background information concerning mainstreaming as it has developed in America's schools. The following questions are addressed in this chapter: What is mainstreaming? Who are the students involved? How did the mainstreaming movement come about? What are the underlying principles of the movement? What does mainstreaming mean for classroom teachers?

In the past ten to fifteen years, a different set of assumptions have begun to emerge which support the notion that students with learning and behavior problems can be educated in the regular classroom as long as special educators provide a wide range of supportive services for classroom teachers. This method has been called *educating students in the mainstream* or *mainstreaming*. The major beliefs which underlie placement of students with learning and behavior problems in regular classrooms are:

1. Students differ on a continuum of functional ability levels, so students referred by classroom teachers for special education services are more *like* than *different from* their peers.
2. Traditional special classes, with their separate curricula, tend to widen rather than narrow the differences between special education students and their regular class peers.
3. Special classes introduce students into an artificial atmosphere in which class size is smaller and expectations are often reduced. This makes later reintegration into the regular classroom increasingly difficult.
4. Special class services isolate students from their peers, either requiring attendance in other than one's neighborhood school or placing students in a room with a less than desirable reputation among other students in the school.
5. Special classes deprive regular students of opportunities to interact with students of lesser ability or skill. This allows prejudice to be fed by lack of contact.
6. In mainstreaming programs classroom teachers are encouraged to learn new techniques and approaches for working with learning and behavior problems, techniques which can be used with other students. This may help reduce the need for future referrals to special education (Lilly, 1979).

STUDENTS WHO ARE MAINSTREAMED

Obviously not all handicapped students are candidates for mainstreaming programs, since some students have **handicaps** so severe that they would receive only minimal benefit from exposure to the standard curriculum. For these students the principle of least restrictive environment applies and school districts should strive to provide maximum contact with non-handicapped students while using a modified curriculum in a special class setting.

Students with a wide variety of handicapping conditions, including the deaf, blind, and physically handicapped, have participated successfully in mainstreaming programs. Sensory and physical handicaps, as they relate to mainstreaming, are discussed in a later chapter of the book. Most of the book deals with the largest group of students who are candidates for main-streaming programs, students traditionally categorized as educable mentally retarded, learning disabled, and behavior disordered. The remainder of this section will provide a discussion of traditional definitions of these terms and will make a case for reducing the emphasis in schools on sorting students into these three distinct categories.

Mental retardation, according to the American Association on Mental Deficiency, refers to "significantly subaverage general intellectual functioning existing concurrently with deficits in adaptive behavior, and manifested during the developmental period" (Grossman, 1973, p. 11). *Educable mental retardation* refers to "those pupils who experienced so much difficulty progressing through general education because they developed intellectually at only about one-half to three-quarters the rate of average children. . . " (Dunn, 1973, p. 127). Generally it has been assumed that students labeled educable mentally retarded would develop functional academic skills, and would lead independent lives after leaving school. The term *educable* has been used in describing these students because they were assumed to be able to learn academic skills and thus to benefit from education in the traditional sense of the word. In general students have been labeled educable mentally retarded if their classroom teachers referred them for special education because of inadequate performance in the regular classroom and subsequently they obtained a low score on an individual test of intelligence. There are no standard *intelligence-test* cut-off scores for being labeled educable mentally retarded, and upper limits have varied between 70 and 85 in different school districts. There is a clear tendency, however, for a disproportionate number of boys, minorities, and students of low socioeconomic status to be labeled as educable mentally retarded (Chinn, Drew, & Logan, 1975; Dunn, 1973). This category, as well as learning disabilities and behavior disorders, is discussed further in a subsequent section of this chapter that deals with historical perspectives on mainstreaming.

Behavior disorder has been defined as "deviation from age-appropriate behavior which significantly interferes with (1) the child's own growth and development and/or (2) the lives of others" (Kirk, 1972, p. 389). Graubard (1973) defines behavioral disabilities as chronic deviant behavior which the observer perceives as inappropriate and wishes to see stopped. School districts have generally exercised considerable latitude in identifying students with behavior disorders, since there are few assessment instruments or clear criteria for identifying such disorders. Teacher and administrator judgment have been the primary criteria used in classifying students as behavior disordered. Here also a disproportionate number of boys, minorities, and low-socioeconomic-status students have been identified as behavior disordered.

Learning disabilities is a relatively new area of special education, having been formally established in most states in the latter half of the 1960s. Professionals have not been able to agree on an acceptable definition of learning disabilities, although nearly all definitions agree on three factors:

1. A discrepancy exists between ability to learn and actual achievement.
2. Other handicapping conditions must be ruled out before a problem can be defined as a learning disability.
3. Most definitions of learning disabilities exclude cultural disadvantage (Gearhart, 1973).

Wiederholt (1974) has pointed out that "the heterogeneity of children currently categorized and served as learning disabled defies a concise specific definition" (p. 146). The treatment of learning disabilities has evolved as a *category of special education services* designed to serve students who are not performing well in the regular classroom, but who do not meet the criteria for being labeled educable mentally retarded or behavior disordered. The field of learning disabilities is ripe with controversy, and space limitations do not permit a full explication of these controversies in this book. The interested reader is referred to Lilly (1979) for further discussion. It will suffice here to say that professionals have been unable to agree on acceptable definitions of learning disabilities, even though it has grown to be one of the largest areas of special education. As with educable mentally retarded and behavior disordered students, more boys than girls tend to be identified as learning disabled, although the racial and socioeconomic biases identified in the other areas do not exist here. In fact, learning disabilities has been called a middle-class phenomenon (Weintraub, 1975), and many middle-class and upper-middle-class students receive services for the learning disabled.

When a student is referred by a classroom teacher for special education, a diagnostic process occurs which is designed to accomplish two purposes: (1) assessment of learning and behavioral difficulties which led to the referral, and (2) *diagnosis*, or placement of the student in a category of special education services. The first of these purposes is necessary if the student's educational needs are to be met. As a rule this purpose is accomplished through analysis of a student's learning difficulties, observation in the classroom setting, and analysis of the total learning situation. Tests which are given for this purpose are educational in nature, and are designed to pinpoint areas of strength and weakness, as well as to generate the instructional goals and objectives for an individualized program for the student. In short this is an *educational* process which focuses on setting conditions for improvement of the student's performance in the regular classroom.

The second focus of the identification process, *diagnosis*, is done for administrative rather than instructional reasons. Local school districts receive funds for the provision of special education services from both the state and federal levels. These funds are generally distributed on a reimbursement basis after school districts demonstrate that the services have been provided. With federal and, with few exceptions, state funds, school districts are required to report students served *by category*, in order to receive program-support funds. Thus while few educators would argue that classifying students into the categories of educable mentally retarded, behavior disordered, and learning disabled is necessary for instructional purposes, such classification is done primarily to qualify for state and federal funds.

While the use of categories is necessary to secure funds, there is growing evidence that the three categories discussed thus far should be deemphasized for all but administrative purposes. The labeling controversy has existed for several years in special education, with many professionals calling for less reliance on traditional categories in defining and delivering special education services. Some of the more salient arguments against the use of categories are:

1. *The categories invite overgeneralization concerning individual students.* It has been argued that when a student carries a label, the label sets certain expectations in the minds of others, and that special education labels produce negative expectations. If these expectations are based on characteristics traditionally associated with the label, rather than actual characteristics of the student in question, then the label can be detrimental to the student. For many years this negative-*generalization* effect was assumed to be true although there was no empirical support in the research literature. This lack of supporting data led some educators to question the validity of attacks on using traditional labels and categories in special education (MacMillan, Jones, and Aloia, 1974). However recent research data has indicated that labels do have a negative effect on teachers' expectations of students. For example in a study conducted by Foster and Salvia (1977), teachers were shown videotapes of a fourth-grade boy engaged in academic work, and asked to rate the adequacy of his academic performance and the frequency of his undesirable social behavior. Although the boy on the tape was actually exhibiting age-appropriate and grade-appropriate behavior, some teachers were told the boy was learning disabled and others were told that he was normal. After viewing the same tape, the teachers who had been told the boy was learning disabled rated him less academically able and more socially disruptive than did the teachers who had been told he was normal. Thus in the face of the same behavior, the teachers reacted differently to labels attached to the behavior. This is but one of a series of studies which have investigated this phenomenon, with relatively consistent results.

2. *The assumption is that the problem is in the student.* When a student is referred for special education, there is substantial testing to determine "what is wrong with this student." Often, the problem is not solely the student's, but results from the interaction of several factors including the student, the classroom setting, and the teaching techniques used. Examples are common of students who do not learn well one year in school, but do well the following year with a different teacher, with different learning materials, and with a different classroom climate. A system which assumes that the cause of learning and behavior problems must be found in the student, an assumption special education systems often make, can represent a gross oversimplification of complex learning systems.

3. *Categories provide information which is most often irrelevant for instruction.* If a special education teacher receives a student who has been diagnosed as educable mentally retarded, behavior disordered, or learning disabled, the first thing the teacher generally does is to conduct an educational assessment for the purpose of planning an instructional program. The characteristics of students carrying these labels are so diverse that they are meaningless for instructional planning. The variation of skills and abilities within a given category is substantially greater than

the variation between categories (Forness, 1974; Reger, 1972). Our purpose as educators should be to group students for instructional purposes according to educational need. Categories are often less than helpful in this process. In fact they often hinder effective educational programming by limiting a school district's flexibility in organizing special education programs.

4. *Categories often make simple problems complex.* The diagnostic process in special education has been known to turn reading problems into dyslexia, poor handwriting into perceptual motor dysfunction, and moving around the room without permission into hyperkinesis. It sometimes appears that the goal of the diagnostic process is to assign confusing names to simple behavior. This naming process is damaging in at least two ways:

   a. It implies that the problem is too complex to be handled in the classroom, and must be assigned to experts.

   b. It implies that labeling is explaining and that a useful process has occurred when a label is applied to the problem.

The authors contend that the labeling process has contributed to the gulf between regular and special education, by adding a new vocabulary which needlessly separates the field.

These are but four objections to the labeling process which have been raised in the regular and special education literature. For a more complete discussion of labeling, the reader is referred to Lilly (1979). The point to be made, however, is that the labels are maintained for administrative purposes, even though there are substantial programmatic drawbacks in using them. It has been suggested that the categories be combined and that schools offer generic services for students with "learning and behavior problems" (Lilly, 1977b). Many school districts are discussing ways of providing services on a less categorical basis while still reporting necessary numbers to state and federal education agencies.

The remainder of this book will focus primarily on students with learning and behavior problems, children who have traditionally been labeled as educable mentally retarded, behavior disordered, or learning disabled. The focus of the book will be on the *functional* problems these children encounter in school, rather than on the labels given these students. When teachers refer students for special education services, the reasons for referral are almost invariably problems of academic learning or social behavior, or a combination of the two. This book will deal directly with these. The authors urge teachers to maintain a healthy skepticism in dealing with categorization systems currently used in most school systems.

MAINSTREAMING: A HISTORICAL PERSPECTIVE

For nearly all of history, education has been considered not a right, but a privilege extended to those deemed able to benefit sufficiently from it.

Not until the latter part of the nineteenth century did education come to be considered universal or compulsory in this or any other country. For practically all of the history of civilization, education has been for the elite, and educational practices have reflected an elitist orientation.

Education has undergone a major reorientation over the past 100 years. The advent of compulsory schooling introduced to the public schools students for whom a college-bound curriculum and traditional teaching approaches are less than adequate. As is evident from the difficulties encountered in areas such as racial and socioeconomic integration, the adjustment of the schools to an expanding clientele has been anything but routine.

Much of special education as we know it today has evolved from an orientation which stresses students' disabilities. In the early 1900s the only special education services available were for the deaf, the blind, and those with severe mental retardation or severe emotional disturbance. Two levels of mental retardation were recognized, known at that time as idiocy and imbecility. Nearly all special education took place in residential schools, with the students safely out of view and out of contact with "normal" school children.

In the late 1800s and early 1900s, a series of events occurred which was to change the nature and scope of special education. First compulsory schooling was adopted by an increasing number of states until it was the equivalent of national educational policy. This policy, in combination with child labor laws, brought students into the public schools who had, heretofore, not received formal education. This expansion of the school population introduced significant challenges with which most schools were not ready to cope.

In the early part of this century, another set of events occurred which, in combination with compulsory schooling, began to shape the growth of special education. This scenario began in France, where Alfred Binet was commissioned by the French government to develop a test to predict which children would fail in school. The test was developed and came to be called an intelligence test. The test was translated into English and standardized on various populations in the United States. It came to be known as the Stanford-Binet Intelligence Test. The test consisted of a series of motor and verbal tasks, and is still in use with relatively minor revisions.

The development of the Stanford-Binet Intelligence Test, it must be remembered, occurred soon after the schools had experienced an influx of new students, students for whom the traditional curriculum was not well suited. When these students did not do well, a common response of school personnel was: "What's wrong with him, that makes him unable to benefit from our instruction?" With the introduction of the Stanford-Binet Intelligence Test, many schools tested students who were not achieving, and found they did poorly on the test. This was not too surprising, since the items on the test closely resembled school work and contained racial and socioeconomic biases. Nonetheless for many students the school had found the answer: the student is unintelligent, or mentally retarded. Since the students were clearly not as retarded as those who had been until this time called idiots and imbeciles, a new category of mental retardation was established, and the students were called *morons*. These terms have evolved over the past seventy years through various stages of offensiveness, and the modern-day equivalent of moron is *educable mentally retarded*.

Once students were identified as morons, it was up to the school district whether any type of special education should be provided. Only a few states provided any support for special education; generally, the school districts were expected to handle it themselves. The preferred model of special education for these students was the self-contained special class. Here it was assumed that smaller class size, specially trained teachers, and carefully designed curriculum would result in significant increases in learning.

Perhaps the most important point to be made with regard to this era of special education is that when students and schools were mismatched, the students were called handicapped. These students had not been identified as handicapped before, since their problems were apparent primarily in the school setting. At the time these problems appeared, several responses would have been possible on the part of the schools, ranging from revision of the curriculum to formally labeling the students as unable-to-learn. The latter course was chosen, and special education began an expansion into new areas of "handicap" and new types of service, an expansion which would last into the mid-1960s.

The area of educable mental retardation grew slowly but steadily from the beginning of services through the 1950s. Beginning with the late 1950s, however, this area of special education experienced tremendous growth due to two major factors. First, the federal government established grant programs for research and teacher education in mental retardation, with a concomitant effort to increase national awareness of and commitment to services for the mentally retarded. Second, many states began to adopt legislative mandates which required all school districts to provide special education services for students identified as handicapped. It has been estimated that enrollment in programs for the educable mentally retarded increased tenfold from 1920 to 1960 (Kirk, 1964), and most of that growth took place during the decade of the 1950s.

Special education for the educable mentally retarded through the 1960s generally took a single form: the self-contained, special class. The assumption was made that regular education was not suited for such students, since they were presumably incapable of benefiting from education in the regular classroom. Universities prepared teachers of the mentally retarded, using curricula especially designed by special educators to be less challenging for and better suited to the mentally retarded population than the general school curriculum.

From the 1950s to the present, several sets of events have led to the reassessment of both the category of educable mental retardation and the use of special classes as the primary service delivery model. Some of these events are:

1. From the late 1940s through the mid-1960s, a series of research studies were completed to assess the effectiveness of special classes for the

educable mentally retarded. In general these studies compared students who were enrolled in educable mentally retarded classes with students of comparable measured intelligence who were still in regular classes. Performance was assessed in several areas, including academic achievement, social adjustment, popularity, personality, and self-concept. The results of these studies were not encouraging to advocates of special classes for the educable mentally retarded. In general the studies indicated that students enrolled in special classes were no better than their regular class peers in academic achievement, and only marginally better on social dimensions (Dunn, 1973; Smith & Neisworth, 1975). However many of these studies were criticized on methodological grounds; unless students of similar IQ levels are randomly assigned to regular and special classes, it can be argued that a systematic bias is at work in favor of students who are still in regular classrooms. Yet a well-designed, carefully executed study of special versus regular class placement for the educable mentally retarded, conducted through the University of Illinois, confirmed most major findings of earlier studies (Goldstein, Moss, & Jordan, 1965). In particular this study found that for students in the upper range of IQ level for mental retardation (the majority of students labeled educable mentally retarded), academic achievement was better in the regular classroom than in the special class. This series of efficacy studies raised serious questions concerning routine placement of these students in self-contained special classes. It also triggered examination of alternatives to the special class for provision of needed special education services.

2. A second set of events contributing to the reassessment of educable mental retardation concerns the labeling process itself. As services for the educable mentally retarded grew in the public schools, it became apparent to careful observers that the population of these students was not randomly distributed along racial and socioeconomic lines. Several studies have indicated that a disproportionate number of students labeled educable mentally retarded are minority and/or from low-socio-economic-status families (Franks, 1971; Prillaman, 1975). In addition the fact that students are labeled educable mentally retarded is of real significance for students in school, as is evidenced by a study demonstrating that many high school students enrolled in programs for the educable mentally retarded, when asked, lied about their class placement (Jones, 1972). Many court cases have challenged the placement of minority students in school programs for the educable mentally retarded, on the grounds that placement tests (including individual tests of intelligence) are racially and culturally discriminatory. In one such case in California, which is typical of litigation in this area, the court ordered the school district to reevaluate all Mexican-American and Chinese-American students in their native languages, and to return students to regular classrooms in cases where the original placement in special education was a result of inappropriate testing (*Diana* v. *State Board of Education*, 1970).

The factors just discussed have created considerable turmoil in special education, in particular the area of educable mental retardation, and provide a part of the backdrop for the mainstreaming movement which we see today.

The development of services for the educable mentally retarded in the public schools has been discussed in some detail, since it marked the beginning of special education services for the mildly handicapped and set the tone for establishment of other areas as well. Development of services in the area of behavior disorders closely paralleled services for the educable mentally retarded. Here also there was slow and gradual expansion through the 1940s and 1950s. Though the number of classes established was never as great as for the educable mentally retarded, the special-class model also was predominant in the area of behavior disorders. Effectiveness studies similar to those done on classes of educable mentally retarded students were completed in the area of behavior disorders, with no more encouraging results (Rubin, Simson, & Betwee, 1966).

Part of the origins of mainstreaming can be traced to the late 1960s, and the beginning of the learning disabilities movement in special education. With services for the educable mentally retarded and behavior disordered established and functioning, it was still clear that there was a group of students who were in need of special education services but not eligible under the existing categories. These were students who did not score low on intelligence tests, were not significant behavior problems (or lived in districts without services for the behavior disordered), but who were experiencing problems in one or more academic areas. In effect these students did not fit into any of the existing categories of exceptionality.

In the late 1960s some states began to respond to this need by adding the category learning disabled to their special education legislation, thus making school districts eligible for state funds when servicing students so labeled. In 1970 the area of learning disabilities received national recognition when it was added to the language of federal special education legislation.

The development of learning disabilities as an area of special education spawned several activities which have given impetus to the mainstreaming movement. First, the establishment of the learning disability category in special education stirred debate concerning the appropriateness of traditional categories, since definitions of learning disabilities tended to be numerous, conflicting, and nonspecific. Many special educators embraced the concept of learning disabilities not as a label for a new category of student, but as an organizing concept for all of special education. After all, learning problems are the sine qua non of special education, regardless of the category to which a student is assigned. Despite these pleas learning disabilities came to refer to a category of students, not an overall conceptual organizer for special education. However the vagueness of the term encouraged increasing attention to the generic problems of all students placed in special education.

Second, the establishment of the learning disabilities category has had significant impact on the service delivered students. Because of both the diverse problems exhibited by learning disabled students and the way these problems are frequently limited to one or two academic areas, the special class was not considered appropriate for these students. Rather many school districts turned to *resource rooms* as the primary means for serving learning disabled students. Such resource rooms provided instruction *supplementary* to that offered in the regular classroom. They were modeled after resource rooms already in operation for the visually and hearing impaired. Thus, the movement away from special classes for the education of students with learning and behavior problems represented the first major attempt to provide special education for these students in cooperation with, rather than apart from, regular education. The movement started to open long-closed channels of communication between regular and special educators in the public schools.

As a result of the efficacy studies mentioned earlier in the areas of educable mental retardation and behavior disorders, some experimentation had begun in the 1960s on the use of resource rooms with students labeled in either of these categories. With the advent of learning disabilities services, the frequency of resource rooms increased significantly, and it became apparent to many educators that students with different labels could often be served effectively by a single teacher. Thus better integrated service developed which placed less emphasis on categories.

As resource rooms developed they primarily used a procedure in which students were removed from their classrooms for a brief period and tutored in academic subjects. Sometimes this tutoring was supplementary to work being done in the regular classroom, but at other times it represented a student's basic instruction in a given academic area. At the secondary level students often receive all of their instruction for certain required subjects in the resource room, with the *resource teacher* assigning the grade for those subject areas.

In cases in which resource teachers provide *all* instruction in a given academic area, it can be argued that the resource room is in fact a quasi-special class, since no regular classroom instruction is provided in that area. There may be little or no communication between resource teachers and regular educators, a situation analogous to that observed with special classes. This has led to a concern that many resource rooms provided extra attention for students, but that this extra work was so dissimilar to regular classroom activities as to hinder the student's eventual reintegration into a regular class.

Concerns about the separation of resource programs from regular education has led to a conceptualization of a more normal special education service. This is designed to maximize contact between regular and special educators. This model has been called the *teacher-consultation approach*, and stresses that resource teachers must work not only with students but also with regular teachers to facilitate the solution of learning and behavior problems in the regular classroom (Lilly, 1971). The teacher-consultation model establishes cooperative working relationships between classroom teachers and special educators, so classroom teachers can refer students not to see them removed from the class, but so the teachers receive help with classroom problems. The teacher-consultation approach has been implemented in several states, the most complete program being in Vermont (Egner & Lates, 1975). Teacher-consultation models vary, but all stress close coordination between special educators and classroom teachers to assure that students with learning and behavior problems make progress in the classroom curriculum. Development of planned consultation between special educators and classroom teachers has also affected many resource and special class teachers, who now stress the importance of relating their services to students' performance in the regular classroom. Classroom teachers now have a right to expect that they will be consulted in development of programs for children referred for special education services. Equally important they have a right to expect that children can receive special education services without being removed from the regular classroom setting.

Thus far our discussion has focused on professional forces behind the mainstreaming movement. Any consideration of mainstreaming would not be complete, however, without at least a brief explication of legislative and litigative forces behind the mainstreaming movement. Special education has been a center of legal activity for the past decade, and courts have ruled on a range of issues from basic right to education, to due process and protection of students' rights in the placement process of special education. In cases concerned with students' rights to a free, appropriate public education, the concept of least restrictive environment has been an issue (*Pennsylvania Association for Retarded Children* v. *Commonwealth of Pennsylvania*, 1971; *Mills* v. *Board of Education of the District of Columbia*, 1972). In virtually all such cases, the courts have ruled that all handicapped children have the right to be educated in the least restrictive environment. While the plaintiffs in most of these cases were moderately to severely handicapped children who would not be appropriately served in regular classrooms, the court rulings apply to *all* students in special education. So the courts have been a powerful force in encouraging movement toward education of mildly handicapped students in regular classrooms.

Partly because of court rulings and partly because of professional factors, an increasing number of states have incorporated the concept of least restrictive environment into legislation and regulations governing special education. Likewise federal legislation on special education mandates education of all children in the least restrictive environment. The term *mainstreaming* will not be found in federal legislation, and is rarely, if ever, mentioned in either state legislation or regulations. Rather the more generic term *least restrictive environment* is used. As defined earlier, however, mainstreaming is a subset of least restrictive environment and thus is covered by the various laws and regulations.

In closing this section on historical factors contributing to the mainstreaming movement, special mention must be made of federal legislation. In particular **Public Law 94–142**, The Education for All Handicapped Children Act of 1975, will be discussed. Public Law 94–142 is the most significant federal legislation in the history of special education. At the present time the appropriation for Public Law 94–142 is approaching one billion dollars, and it will doubtless exceed this figure before the publication date of this book. Of equal importance to the funding aspects of Public Law 94–142, however, is the regulatory aspect. The law establishes the following principles as federal policy regarding special education, and requires assurances that state education agencies are abiding by and implementing these principles:

1. All handicapped students between the ages of five and eighteen are to receive a free, appropriate public education.
2. All handicapped students between the ages of three and four, and nineteen and twenty-one must receive a free, appropriate public education, unless this requirement is inconsistent with state law or court order.
3. Each student receiving special education services must have a written *individualized education program (IEP)* which defines present levels of educational performance, annual goals, short-term objectives, educational services to be provided, participation of the child in the regular education program, date for initiation of and anticipated duration of services, and procedures for evaluating progress toward instructional objectives.
4. Each student must receive education in the least restrictive environment.
5. *Due process procedures* must be established to assure that the rights of students and their parents are protected in the provision of special-education services.
6. Diagnostic and assessment procedures for special education must be nondiscriminatory, and free of racial and cultural bias.

Public Law 94–142 has been posited as the cause of many recent developments in special education. It has been both heralded as a panacea and attacked as a scapegoat by those supporting and opposed to changes in the field. The law is primarily reactive, however, in that it reflects principles already established in judicial decrees and many state laws. The primary value of the law is in focusing our attention on the principles enumerated above, and establishing these principles as benchmarks against which special education programs can be judged. While the law itself will not play a major role in this book, the principles embodied in the law underlie virtually all of what is presented herein.

SUMMARY

The purpose of this chapter has been to define mainstreaming and related concepts, identify the students most directly affected by the mainstreaming movement, and provide a historical perspective which describes how we have come to where we are. The mainstreaming movement is upon us, and there are reasonable indications that it is more than just another passing fad in education. There are many things happening in education under the guise of mainstreaming, some good and some bad. Mainstreaming has been used as an excuse for cutting budgets and eliminating needed special education programs; it has also been the force behind exciting, new programs in which responsibilities for special education are shared, and co-operative relationships between regular and special education reestablished. Mainstreaming is changing the traditional roles of regular and special educators. It can be viewed as either a challenge or a nuisance. This book clearly accepts mainstreaming as a welcome challenge and endeavors to provide information which will help regular educators be more effective participants in its exciting future.

Referral and Placement Procedures in Special Education

2

The purpose of this chapter is to describe how the placement and instructional planning systems for special education work in the public schools. Topics to be covered include *referral*, assessment, placement, development of individualized education programs, periodic review of progress, and due process procedures. The procedures described in this chapter represent an amalgamation of information from Public Law 94–142 regulations, as well as from selected rules and regulations issued by state education agencies. While the procedures described in this chapter are typical of those used in most states, actual rules and regulations vary from state to state. The authors strongly suggest that all classroom teachers become thoroughly familiar with regulations in the state in which they teach, since these regulations define the rules and standards which must be observed in providing special education services. While considerable stress has been placed on making teachers familiar with federal and state special education legislation, it is generally the state regulations which interpret these laws and set standards for school districts. State regulations typically define referral and assessment procedures, placement and review mechanisms, maximum timelines for each step in the placement process, maximum caseloads for special education teachers and their support personnel, and general principles (such as least restrictive environment) which must be observed in the provision of special education services. Regulations governing special education vary in their specificity from state to state, and they can be helpful allies in teachers' attempts to provide appropriate special education services for students. Typically copies of state rules and regulations can be obtained from one's local director of special education. If they are not available locally, the state education agency will generally provide copies on request.

The procedures to be described in this chapter pertain primarily to students with learning and behavior problems, students typically served under the categories of learning disabled, behavior disordered, and educable mentally retarded. Classroom teachers are particularly apt to be involved in referring these students. Most students with significant sensory or physical impairments, or severe levels of mental retardation or emotional disturbance, are identified prior to school entry, making teacher

19

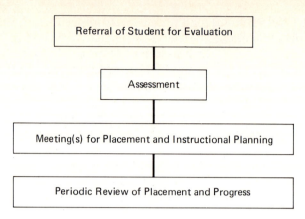

FIGURE 2–1 Steps in special education placement and instructional planning.

referral unnecessary. Of course many students with mild sensory impairments are referred originally by classroom teachers, based on observation of performance in everyday school work.

The steps involved in *special education placement* and instructional planning are presented in Figure 2–1. Each of these steps is discussed in detail in the remaining sections of this chapter. The final section deals with due process procedures available to parents and school district officials, procedures which can be invoked at several points in the system.

THE REFERRAL PROCESS

For most students in special education, the process begins with a referral by a classroom teacher. The teacher may observe that the student is not learning at a sufficient rate, or is engaging in socially disruptive or disturbing idiosyncratic behavior. Most school districts have a standard form for teachers who refer students for special help, and the forms range from simple, brief statements of the problem to rather complex descriptions of student performance. Typically the principal has referral forms for distribution to school faculty and receives completed referrals.

Teachers are not the only persons who can refer students for special education services. In most states referrals are accepted from parents, other professonals, and in some cases the student. The referral is meant to be an indication that a student *might* need special education services, not a guarantee that such services will be provided. Upon receiving a referral, a school district will investigate the problem further, often talking with the classroom teacher and observing the student at work in the classroom. No *formal* assessment can be done without obtaining parent permission. However samples of classroom work can be obtained which will aid in comparing the performance of the student to others in the classroom.

Based on informal information gathered after the referral, one of several actions can be taken. For example the problem may not be sufficient to warrant a full evaluation and assessment procedure. If this is the decision, the person making the referral is notified. If this person is the classroom teacher, there is often an attempt to provide some short-term assistance which will help the teacher cope successfully with the student in the classroom. This might take the form of a resource teacher or social worker spending time helping the teacher develop materials and/or approaches aimed at remedying the student's problem.

If the decision is made to conduct a full evaluation of the student in order to determine eligibility for special education, prior parental permission must be obtained. If parents refuse permission to have the student evaluated, the school district may request a hearing, chaired by an impartial hearing officer, in an attempt to override the parental refusal. The hearing procedures will be described in detail in a subsequent section of this chapter. It is sufficient here to note that both parents and the school district have the right to appeal certain decisions of the other party. In cases in which decisions are appealed, specific procedures for conducting impartial hearings are generally specified in the state regulations governing special education.

The only example of appeal cited above concerned parental refusal for permission to evaluate a student. The opposite can occur: the school district can receive a referral and decide not to conduct an evaluation and assessment, and, if the parents disagree, the parents can request a hearing in an attempt to force the school district to conduct the evaluation. Thus no one can unilaterally decide to short-circuit the referral process without being subject to appeal and hearing.

THE ASSESSMENT PROCESS

The purpose of this section is to describe the evaluation and assessment procedures used in special education and to explicate some of the assumptions and purposes underlying such assessment procedures. Specific tests and instruments for assessment will not be discussed in detail until Chapters 4 and 5.

Once parental permission for evaluation is obtained, the evaluation process is begun. State regulations vary widely in elements required for student evaluation. Many states mandate that the complexity of the evaluation process should vary in direct proportion to the complexity of the student's present problems. Thus students who are severely or profoundly handicapped, or who have significant sensory or physical problems, should be seen by a number of professionals representing a variety of disciplines. These multiple sources of information can then be combined in determining appropriate placement and educational programs for the student. On the other hand since nearly all students referred by classroom teachers exhibit problems of academic learning and/or social behavior, the assessment process should focus as much as possible on direct measurement of performance in the areas of teacher concern. With rare exceptions, there is little or no need to involve school nurses, physicians, physical therapists, occupational therapists, or psychometricians in evaluation of these students.

There are two major purposes for the evaluation and assessment process: (1) to determine a student's eligibility for special education services, and (2) to gather information which will be helpful in establishing an individualized education program (IEP) for the student. It is our contention that there is a tendency to overdo the evaluation process for students with mild learning and behavior problems. For example Gearhart (1973) calls for the following steps in conducting an assessment to determine whether a student is eligible for learning disabilities services:

1. Tests of vision and hearing.
2. Medical examination and medical history
3. Social history (usually by a social worker)
4. Educational history (including information on current levels of academic performance and social behavior)
5. Administration of an individual test of intelligence (usually the Revised Stanford-Binet or Wechsler Intelligence Scale for Children)
6. Administration of formal diagnostic instruments such as the Illinois Test of Psycholinguistic Abilities, Bender Visual Motor Gestalt Test, Frostig Developmental Test of Visual Perception, Wepman Auditory Discrimination Test, Psychoeducational Inventory of Basic Learning Abilities, and standardized tests of academic achievement such as the Wide Range Achievement Test and Metropolitan Achievement Test (The reader is referred to Chapter 4 and to Gearhart [1973] for further discussion of these and other tests.)

The approach to assessment suggested by Gearhart is very comprehensive and interdisciplinary. While interdisciplinary cooperation has been heavily stressed in education over the last decade, particularly in special education, many educators are questioning the value of involving so many diverse professionals in evaluating students with relatively mild problems. For example Smith & Neisworth (1975) reject the interdisciplinary team approach for three reasons:

1. It is very costly.
2. Educational decisions are not made by educators.
3. The emphasis is on specifying the weaknesses or their causes which are hypothetical and unverified. (p. 318)

It should be noted that in the steps outlined by Gearhart, five are related to diagnosis, or determining eligibility for services, while only one step (4) is focused on direct assessment of the student's academic and/or social behavior problems which likely prompted the referral to begin with. In short special education evaluation and assessment procedures tend to be complex and time consuming, with considerable emphasis on formalized evaluation procedures to aid in diagnosis of categories of exceptionality.

A standard part of nearly all evaluations for special education services is the fifth item in Gearhart's list, the administration of an individual test of intelligence. This step deserves special mention since it is the most commonly used and most specialized evaluation tool. The vast majority of school districts in the country require administration of an individual test of intelligence prior to placement of a student in services for the educable mentally retarded, learning disabled, or behavior disordered. Even school districts which have established cross-categorical or noncategorical programs for the mildly handicapped often require an individual intelligence test before a student is declared eligible for the program.

The primary reason for administering an intelligence test is diagnosis: to determine whether or not a student can be labeled mentally retarded. This decision is clouded, however, by several factors:

1. Intelligence tests are not precisely accurate or perfectly reliable. One must always be aware of the standard error of measurement of a test, and realize that a student's true score might be considerably different from the actual score obtained.
2. Intelligence tests are actually tests of achievement, in that they assess information and skills which are commonly learned in our culture. However for students with cross-cultural backgrounds, language differences, or limited contact with white middle-class culture, an intelligence test can be an invalid measure of intelligence.
3. Performance on intelligence tests can be affected by many idiosyncratic factors that are unrelated to one's intellectual ability, such as temporary physical ailments, intimidation in the testing situation, lack of attention to test details, or simply "having a bad day." While we can safely say that no one can surpass his/her potential on a given test, it is certainly possible for one's test performance to come up short of one's potential or, even, typical performance.

Even though intelligence tests have many shortcomings and have been frequently tested in court cases concerning special education placement, they continue to be widely used in the placement process. Aside from the professional issues discussed above, this reliance on intelligence testing causes logistical problems. One must be specifically trained and prepared in order to administer most individual tests of intelligence. Most school districts employ large numbers of school psychologists, many of whom spend a majority of their working hours administering, scoring, and interpreting individual intelligence tests. Traditionally these test results have weighed heavily in decisions about how students will be educated, so school psychologists have played a major role in determining whether students are eligible for special education services. The input of psychologists has often been minimal, however, in instructional planning, since the tests normally given by the psychologist have only limited relevance to the actual curriculum being used in a given classroom. Increasingly both regular teachers and special educators are stressing that diagnostic data coming from the regular classroom are the most important assessment data to be considered in the placement of students. In many school districts the primary role of the school psychologist in the assessment and placement process is being challenged, and the importance of data other than that obtained from formal standardized tests is being emphasized. Where this has occurred, teachers have generally begun to play a more vital role in the process.

This section has reviewed the primary procedural elements involved in assessing students for placement in special education. Most state regulations governing special education specify a maximum time limit for completing assessment procedures, generally between 45 and 60 school days from the time of referral. This means that it can easily be two or three months from the time of referral to initiation of needed special education services. In general it can be said that the less complex the evaluation procedures, and the fewer professionals involved, the quicker the assessment can be completed. This argues for focusing primarily on educationally relevant data in the decision-making process.

Once evaluation data are collected, placement in special education is determined in meetings involving parents and school personnel. The procedures involved in special education placement and instructional planning are discussed in the following section.

SPECIAL EDUCATION PLACEMENT AND INSTRUCTIONAL PLANNING

Placement of a student in special education is a two-step process. First based on assessment data and input from both professionals and the student's parents, it is determined that the student is eligible for special education. After eligibility is determined an individualized education program (IEP) is developed which contains the elements described earlier and establishes both the content and format of a student's special education program. *Without an already written and approved IEP, a student may not receive special education services.* The placement and instructional planning process is described in this following section, beginning with a discussion of eligibility decisions.

Determination that a student is eligible for special education services must be done at a meeting involving school personnel, parents and, when appropriate, the student. In this section we will treat as equivalent a determination that a student is eligible for special education, and placement of the student in an appropriate program, since federal and state laws require that all students who are in need of special education must be served. While some school districts still have waiting lists of students deemed eligible for special education, such waiting lists are not permitted in the laws and will not stand the test of legal or administrative challenge.

State regulations vary in prescribing who must participate in meetings to determine if a student is eligible for special education. However the regulations for Public Law 94–142 state that placement decisions must be made by a group of persons who are knowledgeable about the student, the meaning of the evaluation data, and the placement options. In addition the federal regulations require the following assurances regarding special education placement:

1. That it be based on input from a variety of sources.
2. That evaluation data be documented and carefully considered.
3. That placement be made in the least restrictive environment.
4. That an IEP be developed prior to initiation of services, with the placement based on the nature of the IEP.
5. That placement be reviewed and determined anew at least annually.
6. That placement be as close as possible to the student's home and, unless the IEP requires some other arrangement, in the student's neighborhood school.

A typical eligibility meeting in a public school will involve the school principal, the student's classroom teacher, the special educator who is most likely to serve the student, an administrative representative of the district special education program (such as the director of special education or an area supervisor), one or both parents, and other support professionals such as a social worker, school psychologist, or school nurse. It will be noticed that there is a potential for both the parent and the regular educator to feel overwhelmed in such a meeting, due to the preponderance of administrators and special education personnel. The meeting is usually chaired by either the principal or the special education administrative representative, although some districts designate social workers or school psychologists as meeting chairpersons. Eligibility meetings are called by different names, including multidisciplinary staff conferences, case study meetings, or simply *staffings*.

A staffing usually begins with the various professionals at the meeting being asked to summarize the information they have collected about the student. At this point it is very important for the classroom teacher to be included, to assure that data on student performance in the classroom setting is presented and taken into account in decision making. After the professionals make their presentations, the parents are usually asked for their input, as well as their reactions to information already presented. At this point the person chairing the meeting, or some other designated individual, summarizes the information and discussion begins to focus on decisions to be made. There are two necessary decisions, which must be made sequentially. First it must be determined whether the student is *eligible* for special education services. This decision most often focuses on diagnostic information and involves determination of the special education category under which the student will be served. If a student is eligible for services, the second decision relates to *placement* in a special education program. Placement decisions are made in the context of developing an individualized education program, and may or may not be made in the initial staffing at which eligibility is determined. In making placement decisions federal and most state regulations stipulate that the meeting participants should consider a variety of possible placements and choose the placement which is closest to normal while still assuring that the student's needs can be met. Students' placements should not be based solely or primarily on the category to which they have been assigned. For example it is inappropriate to assign a student to a special school because the decision has been made that the student is trainable mentally retarded. Likewise it should not be assumed that all students designated educable mentally retarded should be placed in self-contained special classes. Theoretically all possible placements should be considered for a given student in the meeting, and placement should be based on a choice among options rather than a predetermined decision rule.

Once a decision has been made concerning eligibility and placement, the parents are formally notified in writing of the proposed placement and given a chance to express any objections. If parents disagree with a labeling or placement decision, or question the adequacy of the assessment procedures, they may request a formal hearing for review of the decisions. The specifics of these hearings will be discussed in a subsequent section on due process. It is important to realize, for the purpose of this discussion, that if parents object and a hearing is requested, the student's present (prestaffing) situation is maintained until the hearings are concluded and the issue is settled. Thus if a student is in the regular classroom receiving no special education, either parental permission must be obtained or appeals must be settled before any special education services can be provided.

Development of Individualized Education Programs (IEPs)

As pointed out above placement decisions are made in the context of development of an IEP. The IEP is an instructional planning document, which must contain the following information:

1. Present levels of educational performance of the student;
2. Annual goals;
3. Short-term objectives;
4. Educational services provided;
5. Participation of the student in the regular education program;
6. Date for initiation of and anticipated duration of special education services;
7. Procedures for evaluating progress toward instructional objectives.

Every student receiving special education must have an IEP, which is completed prior to initiation of services. Individualized education programs are to be developed in meetings which, according to federal regulations, should include most of the participants in the decision about the student's eligibility for special education:

1. A representative of the school district who is qualified to provide, or supervise provision of special education services;
2. The student's teacher;
3. At least one parent;
4. When appropriate, the student;
5. Others at the discretion of the parent or school district.

Also if a student has been evaluated for special education services for the first time, someone familiar with the evaluation procedures used should be present at the IEP meeting.

IEP meetings are much more recent phenomena than staffings, and there is great variation between school systems in how they are conducted. Also since IEPs will vary greatly in complexity and length, depending on the severity of the student's problems, the format of meetings will not be consistent within a given district. In general the first topic dealt with in the IEP meeting is the present level of educational performance, and this discussion often carries over from the staffing at which eligibility was determined. Separate meetings need not be held to determine eligibility and to develop IEPs, but it is generally very difficult to accomplish both of these purposes in a single meeting without extensive preparation and considerable meeting time. Many school districts hold separate staffings and IEP meetings for students who are being placed in special education for the first time, and combine the meetings for students whose already existing placements and IEPs are being reviewed.

Even when eligibility and IEP development are handled in separate meetings, much of the information is carried over from prior discussion in the initial staffing. This may include information on educational performance, future special education and related services, and extent of participation in the regular education program. Additional topics which are brought forth for discussion and agreement at the IEP meeting involve development of annual goals, short-term instructional objectives, and criteria for evaluating whether instructional objectives are being achieved. While the number of goals will vary for each IEP, the tendency is for the number to increase as the amount of time the child spends in special education increases. Thus a student who spends 75 percent of the day in special education will have several subject areas represented in the IEP, with goals specified for each subject area. On the other hand a student who receives resource services in a single academic area, or a teacher-consultation program to deal with problems of social behavior, might have no more than one or two goals stated in the IEP, these focusing specifically on the problems which led to referral and provision of special education services.

The development of goals in an IEP meeting is relatively straightforward since these goals most often emanate from the referral process and the educationally relevant assessment data presented in the meeting. It is not so easy, however, to generate short-term instructional objectives. Although it is often preferable to have a student in special education services for a period of time before a full set of instructional objectives can be written, it is generally required that these objectives be in place prior to initiation of services. For example the *Illinois Primer on Individualized Education Programs* (1979), which sets the policy of the Illinois State Board of Education with regard to IEPs, states that school districts "cannot implement the placement of the child until short-term objectives have been written for each goal" (p. 63). This is often handled by preparing a limited number of short-term objectives at the IEP meeting, and completing the list during the first month of delivery of special education services.

While the development of individualized education programs might appear to be relatively straightforward, there are several areas in which difficulties have been encountered. First IEP meetings can be time consuming for both teachers and parents, and scheduling can be a problem.

Meetings must be scheduled at times convenient to parents, and this often necessitates holding meetings outside of normal school hours. Naturally, this draws less than positive comments from many teachers and teacher organizations. A second problem which has been encountered is that special educators often write IEPs rather independently, with little or no input from the classroom teachers who refer the students in the first place. This leads to many IEPs not reflecting the primary problems being encountered in the classroom, which in turn leads to less than effective special education services. Classroom teachers must be forceful in asserting their rights to be *active* participants in IEP development. Finally a third problem which has been encountered in IEP development relates to specification of services to be provided to the student. Often these services are determined by what is available in the school district, rather than by an analysis of the student's unique educational needs. Such determination of services can lead to a situation in which IEPs are program-based rather than student-based, a violation of the basic principles underlying the IEP requirement.

All of the problems listed above, as well as a number of others, have been encountered in implementing IEPs in the public schools. They are, however, procedural difficulties rather than problems rooted in the rationale upon which the IEP concept is built. With rare exceptions educators agree that students in special education deserve unique programs based on a thorough understanding of each student's individual strengths and weaknesses. The IEP has been established in federal law and state regulations in an attempt to assure that special education programs are personalized. IEPs *do not* demand individualized instruction; they *do* demand individualized attention and program planning. The IEP process is relatively new, and therefore at times difficult. With further implementation experience, the process will mature and procedures will be improved. In the meantime all contributors to the IEP process, and in particular regular educators, must be informed participants determined to reap the benefits of a new and exciting approach to provision of special services to students.

In this section, the authors have reviewed the placement and instructional planning process in special education. We have given particular attention to staffing meetings and IEP development. Once a student is placed in special education and services commence, the school system focuses on providing specialized instruction designed to maximize his/her progress. A discussion of the nature of this specialized instruction comprises the bulk of this book. Since this chapter deals with *procedural* aspects of special education, the next topic to be discussed relates to periodic reviews of both the placement and educational progress of students in special education.

PERIODIC REVIEW PROCEDURES

For many students placement in special education has been permanent, with little or no opportunity to return to complete participation in the regular education program. Gallagher (1972) estimated that in some school systems, less than 10 percent of students placed in special education ever return to a regular program. Federal and state regulations governing special education have begun to address this problem by requiring at least an annual review of students' educational placements and of progress on IEPs. In most states, regulations specify that parents must be notified prior to the beginning of each school year if a student is to continue to receive special education services. Included with this notice must be an explanation of the process by which parents can object to a proposed continuation of placement. If a school district wishes to change a student's participation in special education, either increasing or decreasing services or removing the student from special education altogether, a staffing involving parents and school personnel must generally be held.

IEPs must also be reviewed and revised at least annually. Goals are written for IEPs on a yearly basis, so it is assumed that new goals and objectives are written at each IEP review meeting, and substantially new IEPs are produced. IEP review meetings should involve, by and large, the same persons who attended the initial IEP meeting, although teachers in attendance will change as the student progresses from one grade placement or school year to another. School districts vary in terms of when they hold IEP review meetings, with some districts choosing to schedule meetings in the spring before the school year closes, and other districts holding the meetings in the fall, soon after school starts. If it is school district policy or practice to hold IEP review meetings in the spring, it is important that the student's probable regular classroom teacher for the *coming* school year be involved, since that is the educational setting for which the IEP is being written. Generally changes in IEPs involving only new or revised instructional objectives do not require that a meeting be held, while changes in goals or the nature of special education services being provided do require a meeting.

While annual review of placement and IEP is generally required, this is intended only to set minimum standards. More frequent review may be necessary. The parents, the classroom teacher, or anyone else empowered to refer students for special education can request, *at any time*, a review of the student's placement or individualized education program. Thus if a classroom teacher believes a student needs more intensive special education services, or that the time is right for increased reintegration of the student in the regular education program, a meeting can be requested to consider a change in placement. Likewise if parents want to seek a change in placement or a substantive change in a student's IEP, a staffing or IEP meeting can be requested. While the district can decide not to hold such requested meetings, this decision is subject to formal appeal.

The review process, then, is designed to assure that placements in special education are timely and based on students' *current* levels of education functioning. Also the review process helps to assure that students' IEPs reflect current needs and are not merely paper exercises. This review process is time-consuming, since the IEP review procedures require a meeting with parents at least annually and since the placement review procedures demand annual written communication with parents. However given the number of students who have been "lost" in special education programs in the past, the review procedures are necessary to assure that continual attention is given to the question of whether students are being educated in the least restrictive environment. The review procedures are intended to make education a dynamic system, and to focus our attention regularly on the extent to which students' needs are being met with the services provided.

DUE PROCESS PROCEDURES

Throughout this chapter reference has been made to parents' rights to appeal certain decisions of the school district and vice versa. Extended discussion of this appeal process has been limited to this section, since the process is generic and applies to all possible appeal situations. This section, then, will outline procedural due process requirements which must be available to both parents and school district personnel throughout the special education planning and implementation process.

In the process of providing special education services, there are several points at which parents and school district officials might disagree. In the past these disagreements might have resulted in loss of service or provision of inappropriate services to a student, since no procedures were specified for resolution of conflicts. If parents refused permission for placement in special education, or if the school district proposed a more restrictive placement than the parents thought was necessary, either a compromise was reached or an impasse existed which resulted in continuing hard feelings between parent and school. In many cases students suffered because of the lack of agreement.

Another factor which led to establishment of due process procedures was the lack of parental involvement in decisions concerned with special education placement and services. In many cases, the school district adopted a "we know best" approach, and proceeded to provide, or not provide, special education with as little parent awareness or involvement as possible. Parents were often seen as advocates for funds for special education programs, but not as codeterminers with school officials of the structure of those programs.

Due process procedures were introduced to special education through litigation which occurred in the early 1970s. In a classic right to education case (*Pennsylvania Association for Retarded Children* v. the *Commonwealth of Pennsylvania*, 1971), the judge specified detailed procedures for Pennsylvania schools to use in assuring parental involvement in the special education placement and planning process. These procedures were also included in a major suit in Washington, D.C. (*Mills* v. *Board of Education of the District of Columbia*, 1972), and have been included in most judgments in suits regarding special education identification and placement.

The due process procedures to be summarized in this section grew out of early court rulings, and are represented in federal regulations for

Public Law 94–142, and most state regulations governing special education.

Essentially the due process procedures are an attempt to assure that students are protected from less than adequate decision making on the part of either school personnel or parents. Due process procedures are *not* parent-protection oriented; they are student-protection oriented. Their basic purpose is to achieve impartial decision making in the best interest of the student.

At several points in this chapter, it was noted that either the parents or the school district could request a hearing in cases of significant disagreement with decisions that have been made. In general school districts can initiate a due process hearing under the following circumstances:

1. The district proposes that a student be evaluated to determine eligibility for special education services, and the parents withhold permission to conduct the evaluation.
2. In districts in which written parental permission is required before a student can be placed in special education, the district proposes a special education placement and the parents withhold permission to provide the services.

Parents can request a due process hearing in the following situations:

1. A student is referred for evaluation for special education services, and the district refuses to conduct an evaluation.
2. The district conducts an evaluation of the student which the parents consider to be inadequate and the parents seek an independent educational evaluation at the district's expense.
3. The school district proposes a special education placement, or denies special education placement, and the parents do not agree with either the type or quantity of special education services proposed by the district.
4. The district proposes a change in special education services currently being provided for a student, and the parents disagree with the proposed change.
5. The district proposes that a student receiving special education be returned to the regular school program, or graduate, with no additional special education services being provided, and the parents disagree with the decision to terminate services.
6. The district proposes a special education placement which the parents believe not to be in the least restrictive environment.
7. The district suspends or expels a student deemed eligible for special education services.
8. The parents believe that the school district has not complied with state regulations governing special education.

The remainder of this section will deal with the parent appeal process, since it contains all elements present in the school district appeal process.

If the parents of a student who either has been referred for or is receiving special education services have any of the concerns listed above, and if those concerns are of sufficient magnitude to lead the parent to challenge decisions made by the school district, a due process hearing may be requested. In general parents request a due process hearing by writing a letter to the superintendent of the school district, outlining the problem, and asking that a hearing officer be appointed and a hearing date set. School districts are usually required to include information on due process hearings any time they inform parents of new or continued special education placements, or of major changes in placement or instructional program. Thus it is the school district's obligation at least once a year to inform the parents of special education students of their rights to challenge placement or planning decisions.

If a parent writes a letter requesting a due process hearing, the school district generally has an opportunity to attempt to solve the problem through negotiation, without actually scheduling a formal hearing. Naturally informal solutions to problems are generally considered preferable to formal hearings, since they are less time-consuming and typically less combative. However if these informal attempts at solution are unsuccessful, the district must request that the state education agency appoint an informal hearing officer to conduct a hearing.

Appointment of hearing officers varies from state to state. Most states have a cadre of trained hearing officers who make themselves available to conduct hearings. With few exceptions, these are professionals or advocates who hold other jobs and serve as hearing officers on an occasional basis. Some states have begun to offer a list of names of possible hearing officers from which the school district and parents jointly choose one; other states assign hearing officers from the list of available and trained persons. In general persons cannot serve as hearing officers in cases involving a school district in which they are either employed or have substantial interest.

Once a hearing officer is chosen, a time for the hearing is set which is mutually convenient for parents and school district personnel. The school district may have in attendance at the hearing any school personnel who have significant information regarding the case, as well as legal counsel. The parents may bring to the meeting legal counsel and other representatives and advocates. In addition the parents may require the attendance of any relevant school personnel at the meeting.

The hearing is conducted with both sides presenting their cases and the impartial hearing officer questioning and acquiring further information as needed. The complexity of the testimony varies from case to case, and hearings may range in length from less than an hour to a full day. The school district is generally required to keep a verbatim record of the hearing by using either a court stenographer or a tape recorder.

Once the hearing is completed, the impartial hearing officer must render a decision. Sometimes the hearing officer will determine that more information is needed, and will request either additional evaluative information on the student or further explication of certain areas of testimony. Within a specified time (the time limits vary from state to state), the hearing officer issues findings and recommendations for resolution of the impasse.

If neither the parents nor the school district make a formal response to the report of the hearing officer, it is binding on all parties involved. The school district can respond to the hearing officer's report by accepting it or by rejecting the recommendations. In either case the parent must be satisfied with the school district's decision in relation to the report. If the parents are not satisfied with the school district's response to the hearing officer's report, or with the report itself, they may submit an appeal directly to the state education agency.

If an appeal is made by the parents to the state education agency, a state level hearing officer (or panel) is convened to study the content of the local hearing, as well as additional materials provided by the parents and school district. Generally the state panel can request further information from either or both parties, either in writing or in the form of oral testimony. The state hearing panel makes a recommendation to the chief state school officer (e.g., state superintendent of education), who makes a ruling which is binding on all parties involved. If either party does not wish to abide by the chief state school officer's decision, the only available recourse is litigation.

The due process hearing procedures outlined here are accurate with minor variations for all states. Obviously the procedures as outlined are cumbersome, highly technical, time-consuming, and expensive. Also they assume an adversarial relationship between school districts and parents who request hearings, a relationship which often endures far beyond the conclusion of the hearing process. Lilly (1979) has summarized the limitations of due process hearings as follows:

> While the aim of due process procedures is to guarantee that the rights of children and their parents are protected, it must be pointed out that such is not always the case. Impartial due process hearings are an imperfect mechanism for assuring positive parental involvement for four reasons. First, the process itself is complex and it generally takes a parent (or professional) who is relatively sophisticated and experienced in special education matters to understand the complexities of the process. Second, the entire system depends on parents being aware of its existence, a problem which is complicated in rural areas or areas where contact between homes and schools is infrequent and largely negative. Third, many parents who understand the due process procedures are hesitant to request a hearing because of the potentially enormous amount of time and energy required to prepare for a hearing. And fourth, many parents who request a hearing and receive a favorable ruling report that they have 'won the battle but lost the war,' due to the ill feelings created in the school district by the process, and the aftermath of these feelings (p. 53).

While due process requirements are not a perfect mechanism for assuring that appropriate decisions are made in the special education placement and planning process, they are a significant first step in more systematic parental involvement in decision making. Many school districts and state education agencies are currently experimenting with informal negotiation procedures which might be used to help mediate problems without necessitating formal hearings. Use of mediators has the potential for reducing the adversarial nature of parent-school interactions and encouraging consensus decision making rather than confrontation. Mediation or conciliation procedures are in the early stages of development, but they offer promise for helping to avoid protracted conflicts between home and school. Even where mediation procedures exist, it remains important for all teachers to have a thorough understanding of due process procedures used in their district, since they are likely to be either directly involved or vitally interested in one or more such hearings during their teaching careers.

SUMMARY

This chapter has outlined special education placement and instructional planning procedures. It is obvious from the materials presented here that regular classroom teachers are, or should be, centrally involved at all points in the process. Mainstreaming brings special education into the regular classroom, and classroom teachers are finding that it is more efficient and effective to be involved in the entire planning process than to be handed a set of expectations devised by others. In general traditional special education systems have not taken advantage of the unique and direct information about students which classroom teachers possess. This is changing and, increasingly, classroom teachers and special education resource teachers are working cooperatively to assure that relevant instructional information is brought to bear on placement and planning decisions. In some cases where the change is slow, progressive classroom teachers are asserting their rights to be centrally involved in the special education placement and planning process. This increased involvement of classroom teachers demands skills which are often not stressed in standard teacher education curricula, and is the basis for most of the information presented in this book. The next chapter presents an overview of skills which classroom teachers must possess if mainstreaming programs are to be successful.

The Classroom Teacher's Role in Educating Students with Special Needs

3

Thus far we have discussed the mainstreaming movement, provided a rationale and historical perspective for it, and described special education placement and planning procedures. In this chapter, we will focus specifically on the regular classroom teacher's role in provision of services to students with mild learning and behavior problems. This discussion will serve as the basis for much of the content presented in the remainder of the book, and will provide a perspective on the multifaceted nature of the teacher's role in the education process.

The role of the classroom teacher in educating students with learning and behavior problems can be conceptualized along four dimensions. First, the teacher functions as an education team member in helping to make the instructional placement and planning decisions discussed in Chapter 2. Second, the teacher helps to plan and implement instructional programs for students experiencing academic difficulties. Third, the teacher establishes positive classroom behavior by reducing the occurrence of socially inappropriate behavior and increasing occurrence of socially appropriate behavior. And finally, the teacher acts as an advocate for students throughout the education process (Blankenship & Lilly, 1977). Each of these four roles is discussed in a subsequent section of this chapter. In the section on planning and implementing instructional programs, an instructional model is presented which relates well to the IEP process and is supportive of mainstreaming efforts. This model of instruction, called data-based instruction (DBI), serves as the basic organizer for much of the remainder of the book.

THE TEACHER AS AN EDUCATION TEAM MEMBER

The teacher's role as an education team member begins with his/her knowledge of the types of special education programs available in one's school and school district, as well as placement and planning procedures used in the district. A wide variety of special education services are generally offered within a given school district, and a teacher who is knowledgeable about what is available can obtain substantial help for students who are in need of special services.

In general a teacher's participation as a team member is focused in four areas:

1. The teacher acts as a referral agent in recommending students for assessment who are not functioning adequately in the classroom.
2. The teacher collects assessment data regarding student performance in the classroom.
3. The teacher actively participates in staffings and IEP development.
4. The teacher maintains contact with parents and other team members as planned programs are implemented.

In most school situations the teacher is the most important referral agent, in that the vast majority of referrals for special education are made by classroom teachers. Referral patterns vary tremendously among teachers, with some refusing to refer students at all, others making only occasional referrals, and still others referring inordinately large numbers of students for special education services. How does a teacher decide to refer a student? How does a teacher differentiate between students who should be referred and students who should not? These are important questions to address, since a referral of a student for assessment for special education is a significant event in the life of both the student and the teacher making the referral.

As a basic principle teachers should refer students when two conditions exist: (1) the student is experiencing significant difficulty in the classroom, and (2) the teacher is unsuccessful in solving the problem as it exists. Many students experience difficulty in learning and not all should be referred for special education. Individual teachers have strengths in dealing with certain types of learning and behavior problems, and are confident that they can handle these problems as they occur. *If a teacher is handling a problem successfully, the student should not be referred.*

In the case that a teacher is having some difficulty dealing with a situation, the following types of problems might lead a teacher to refer a student for special education.

1. A student is significantly below grade level in one or more academic areas, and appears to be falling further behind despite attempts at successful instructional grouping in the classroom.
2. A student performs accurately in one or more academic areas, but the *rate* of performance is insufficient to allow the student to keep pace with others in the classroom.
3. A student lacks study skills necessary to consistently finish required work in the classroom.
4. A student displays frequent and consistent inappropriate, acting-out behavior which prevents the student and/or others in the room from completing necessary work.

5. A student displays withdrawn, isolated behavior to such an extent that acceptable levels of social interactions are not observed.
6. The teacher observes student performance which leads the teacher to believe that the student might have significant visual, hearing, or other health-related problems.

Once a teacher has referred a student for assessment for special education, the teacher should begin to collect systematic classroom data which will help to define the problem in precise terms. For example if a student is referred because of reading problems, the teacher might want to determine the student's correct and incorrect reading rates in a variety of classroom materials, as well as information on the student's reading comprehension. This information is most helpful if the teacher is able to compare the referred student's performance to two or three average students in the room. Likewise if a student is referred for acting-out behavior problems, the teacher should choose predetermined times of the day and systematically record the frequency of the behaviors which led to referral. Details on assessment and classroom data collection will not be presented here, since these are topics discussed in subsequent chapters. However teachers must realize that without classroom assessment data, they are not apt to be active participants in decisions concerning placement and instructional planning.

If teachers enter a staffing or an IEP meeting with objective data on classroom performance, they can be assertive in seeking equal time with other assessment personnel in presenting information relevant to decisions to be made at the meeting. In some school districts teachers are included in these meetings because it is a requirement of federal or state regulations. In these cases an active role is often not defined, for the teacher who is subsequently relegated to the role of an observer. Many special educators assume that classroom teachers do not want to be involved in placement and instructional planning conferences, since it takes additional time for which teachers are rarely paid. Most teachers do want to be involved, however, since they realize that both they and the students will benefit from close coordination between special and regular education programs. The best way to insure this involvement is for the teacher to collect classroom assessment data and make known the desire to present these data in the appropriate meetings.

Once decisions are made and IEPs are in place, the need for close communication between classroom teachers and other team members (including special educators, support personnel, and parents) intensifies. IEPs are developed prior to initiation of services, and the best-laid plans often do not work out in practice. Behavior management schemes which are successful with one student may not have any effect with another. Instructional plans that seem appropriate in a meeting may turn out to be impractical in the classroom. Decisions made in IEP meetings must always be subject to change based on actual experience. Continued communications between teachers and other team members helps to assure that such changes occur promptly and effectively.

In addition to solving implementation problems, close cooperation between team members can allow regular reporting of successes and encourage a focus on student progress rather than student failure. Communication between classroom teachers and parents, in particular, is often negative in nature, since parental contacts are usually initiated to share problems, not accomplishments. Regular contact with parents after the IEP meeting can focus on the student's progress in relation to problem areas discussed at the meeting, and can result in increased parental attention to appropriate behavior on the part of the student.

To summarize a recurring theme in this section on the classroom teacher as an education team member, teachers must often be assertive in determining their role on the planning team. In the past teachers' roles have tended to be passive, consisting of responses to inquiries, concurrence with decisions, and the implementation of appropriate parts of an instructional program. Teachers can and should play a more active, vigorous role in the decision-making processes by presenting relevant classroom performance data, suggesting special education services which can be provided to the teacher as well as the student, and advocating appropriate services for the student in the least restrictive environment. Teachers will be active team members when they insist on their importance in the decision-making process. When this happens the relevance of special education programs to what is happening in the regular classroom will increase significantly.

THE TEACHER AS AN INSTRUCTIONAL MANAGER*

There are several distinct and different modes for providing mainstream special education services. Perhaps the most common model for mainstreaming is the resource room, in which students remain in the regular classroom for a majority of the school day and receive instruction in the resource room for specified periods. This instruction typically focuses on selected academic areas, and may either *supplement* or *replace* regular classroom instruction for those subjects.

In cases in which resource room instruction *replaces* regular classroom instruction for a given subject area, the classroom teacher's role as an instructional manager is usurped since the teacher relinquishes all responsibility for teaching the student that subject matter. This model for resource room services is less than optimal since instructional expectations in the resource room may or may not be compatible with classroom requirements for success. Thus if the resource room teacher focuses on skills not critical for classroom success, or uses teaching techniques which do not resemble, and perhaps even contradict, those used in the regular classroom, the student's chances for successful reintegration into total classroom activities may actually be diminished.

* Substantial portions of this section are excerpted, with minor modifications, from the following text: Lilly, M. S. *Children with exceptional needs: A survey of special education*, New York: Holt, Rinehart and Winston, 1979, pp. 105–112.

On the other hand if resource room instruction is *supplementary* to classroom instruction, the importance of close coordination between the resource teacher and the classroom teacher becomes apparent. In this case the goals of the regular classroom become the goals of special education, and the focus of the special educator is directed towards better performance in the classroom. Thus Chapter 5 of this book focuses on **curriculum-based assessment**, and describes evaluation procedures which use as a starting point the regular classroom curriculum.

Even in supplementary resource room programs, there is a tendency on the part of many special educators to define instructional problems in terms irrelevant to regular classroom functioning, and to use teaching techniques which bear little or no resemblance to those used by classroom teachers. A variety of instructional models have developed in special education, and in particular in the area of learning disabilities. These instructional models can be categorized into two types:

1. *Basic-ability* instructional models place a major focus on finding underlying causes of learning problems. Instruction is targeted more toward these causes than toward remediation of observable skill deficits. Advocates of basic-ability instructional models have posited that learning problems are the result of deficits in such basic processes as perceptual-motor function (Cratty, 1969; Kephart, 1960), visual-perception skills (Frostig, Lefever, & Whittlesey, 1964), learning modalities (Mills, 1964), and psycholinguistic functioning (Kirk, McCarthy, Kirk, 1968). Advocates of a basic-ability approach assert that the student is not learning because of some underlying deficit which must be corrected. These advocates further contend that it is fruitless to attempt to directly remediate learning problems without attending to these deficits in the processes of learning, and that once the basic learning disorders are corrected, students' actual skill deficits will be alleviated. Most proponents of basic-ability approaches have devised tests to measure these learning processes, as well as remedial materials to correct student weaknesses as shown by the tests. Obviously the critical test of basic-ability instructional models must be actual improvement in performance in academic skill areas, since remedial programs which increase basic ability test scores but do not affect academic performance are of limited value to students and their teachers.

2. A second instructional model which has been used with children exhibiting learning and behavior problems rejects the notion that learning processes can be assessed, and focuses on direct remediation of learning problems as they exist in the regular classroom. Thus when a student is writing letters or numbers incorrectly, rather than testing for visual-perception problems and designing remediation programs based on weaknesses exhibited on the test, advocates of a *direct-skill* instructional model would devise a program to teach correct production of letters and numbers. Similarly reading problems would be remediated through direct work on inadequate reading skills, not through searches for perceptual-motor deficits, psycholinguistic deficits, or optional teaching

modalities. Proponents of a direct-skill instructional model adopt the attitude that "what you see is what it is," and attempt the shortest and most direct route to the solution of the problem.

This book advocates and operationalizes the direct-skill approach to remediation of learning problems. Basic-ability approaches are not presented here because they do not enjoy a great deal of support in the special education research literature, and because they tend to define instructional problems in a way which does not relate well to students' functioning in the regular classroom. Lilly (1979) has summarized the current status of basic-ability instructional models as follows:

> The "basic abilities" approach to instructional programming for children labeled learning disabled has been under increasing attack during the past decade. Research on "basic ability" approaches has tended to yield either negative or equivocal results . . . a good deal of research has been done on perceptual-motor approaches and visual perception models, testing the assumption that increasing skills in these "basic ability" areas will have resulting effects on academic performance. Reviews of these studies (Mann, 1970; Hammill, 1972; Goodman and Hammill, 1973; Larsen and Hammill, 1975) indicate that while intervention procedures can improve performance on perceptual-motor and visual perception measures, it is not at all clear that such improvement results in better academic performances. Likewise, reviews of research on aptitude-treatment interaction (Bracht, 1970; Arter and Jenkins, 1977) and on the Illinois Test of Psycholinguistic Abilities (Hammill and Larsen, 1974) indicate that the promise of such "basic ability" approaches has not been fulfilled in current practice. For this reason, many special educators are placing primary emphasis on development of instructional interventions designed to directly remediate the academic and/or behavioral problems of concern, rather than searching for underlying causes of those problems and initiating instruction a "step removed" from the performance of primary importance. (p. 88)

A Model for Instruction

In this section a direct skill model of instruction will be described, a model that is functional in orientation and focuses on direct and continuous measurement of pupil progress toward stated instructional objectives. This model, hereafter called data-based instruction (DBI), will be presented as the preferred model of instruction for students with learning and behavior problems for the following reasons:

1. DBI focuses on the specific behavior of concern, and essentially ignores the underlying causes of the behavior. This focus on observable behavior makes coordination between special and regular education an easier task, since both sides are talking the same language.
2. DBI avoids categorical labels, since the focus is on definition of academic and social problems in behavioral terms, thus leading to direct measurement and instructional intervention without necessity of further labeling.

3. DBI emphasizes functional assessment within the instructional setting as contrasted with norm-referenced measurement which only incidentally relates to the problems being encountered by an individual student and his/her teacher.
4. DBI emphasizes the use of specific instructional objectives as the basis for teaching, which means that instruction is well focused and expected outcomes can be agreed upon by parents, teachers, and other school officials.
5. DBI does not rely on a specific teaching methodology, but rather provides for evaluation of instructional effectiveness in each individual case. A teaching approach is not good or bad in a general sense, but might work with one student and not with another. These decisions are made not on the basis of subjective teacher judgment, but rather from data on student progress. Arguments over which teaching technique is best are rendered obsolete.
6. DBI is an individualized instruction model which operates on the basis of individualized instructional objectives and progress monitoring, but not necessarily one-on-one teaching. Instruction can be in groups, if it is effective in moving students toward stated instructional objectives.
7. DBI stresses collection of continuous data on student progress, so that teachers need not wait six weeks, two months, or an academic year to determine whether an instructional intervention is a success or failure.
8. If a student does not achieve an *instructional objective*, DBI focuses the teacher's attention on inadequacies in the instructional program, not inadequacies in the student.
9. DBI fits perfectly with the IEP requirements of Public Law 94–142, in that any teacher who has implemented DBI will have readily available all required instructional elements of the IEP.

Since Chapters 5 through 10 provide detailed information on elements of data-based instruction, only an overview is given here. A data-based instructional model has eight essential steps which are listed below and discussed individually:

1. Statement of problem in behavioral terms.
2. Collection of *baseline data*.
3. Statement of instructional objectives.
4. Analysis of instructional objectives into teachable components (if necessary due to the complexity of objective).
5. Determination of teaching-learning procedure and initiation of instruction.
6. Continuous measurement of student progress toward objective.
7. Charting student progress data.
8. Instructional decision-making concerning adequacy of intervention.

Statement of Problem in Behavioral Terms

The first step in a data-based instructional model, as for that matter in any adequate instructional model, is to define the instructional problem in precise, behavioral terms. The need for precise behavioral descriptions of instructural problems has been discussed as follows (Lilly, 1977a):

> No performance can be measured unless it can be reliably observed, and reliable observation depends on behavioral descriptions of problems. If a teacher's objective is to decrease a child's hyperactivity, for example, it is impossible to present unambiguous data in support of progress toward this objective, since hyperactivity in the classroom would not lend itself to direct and unambiguous measurement. However, if the objective is to decrease the frequency of inappropriate talk-outs, or leaving the seat without permission, then direct, reliable assessment is possible. Likewise, improvement of a child's performance in reading is too general to measure, while decreasing the error rate in oral reading or increasing the percentage of comprehension questions answered correctly represent objectives amenable to reliable measurement. (p. 28)

Behavioral descriptions of problems prevent educators from implicitly blaming students for inadequate performance by using terms such as obstinate, aggressive, or dyslexic. Problems should be described in *solvable* terms. Also behavioral problem descriptions help to narrow the focus of instruction: while it is impossible to solve a problem of hyperactivity, leaving one's seat without permission is more amenable to intervention. The key to knowing whether a problem is defined in behavioral terms is whether two people observing the behavior as described would agree on what they saw. For example two observers would tend to disagree on when a student is aggressive, but would be much more consistent in recording when the same student hit a classmate on the playground. Definition of problems in behavioral terms is the first, and most important, step in any feasible model of instruction.

Collection of Baseline Data

After problems have been defined behaviorally, the next step in DBI is to assess the present level of the problem. For example if some students are constantly talking out, how many times do they talk out in a thirty-minute period? If the problem is not completing worksheets independently, what percent of the problems are done correctly in the allotted time? If the problem is not knowing how to borrow in subtraction, what percentage of subtraction problems involving borrowing does a student get correct?

Baseline data must establish with some consistency the student's performance before intervention in areas of concern, and this usually involves collection of three to five instances of baseline data for each behavior. Three instances of baseline data are sufficient if the performance is relatively stable, for example, out of seat ten times in twenty minutes one day, twelve times the next day, nine times the third day. One need go beyond three instances of baseline data only when the data are inconsistent, for example, 20 percent correct the first day, 80 percent the second day, 40 percent the third day. Again the purpose of collecting baseline data is to provide a picture of the student's performance prior to intervention, to serve as a basis for later determination of progress.

Measurement of individual students' performance in the classroom is both essential and demanding. Teachers must be careful in selecting procedures for collecting baseline data, since the same procedures must be used to gather progress data after instruction has been initiated. Thus measurement systems must be chosen, taking into account both the nature of the behavior to be observed and the feasibility of the continued use of the system in the classroom. Techniques for data collection are presented in detail in Chapter 6.

Statement of Instructional Objective

Based on the behavioral problem description and baseline data, the next step in DBI is to specify one or more instructional objectives which serve as a statement of intended outcomes. Several well-known texts are available on writing instructional objectives (for example, Mager, 1962; Wheeler & Fox, 1972) and the information will not be repeated here in detail. Suffice it to say that an objective must contain (1) the expected behavior, (2) the criterion for successful performance, and (3) the conditions in which the student is expected to perform. For example an instructional objective in reading might be: "Given a list of 20 two or three syllable, phonetically regular words, the student will pronounce the words correctly with 90 percent accuracy, taking no more than five seconds per word." Obviously, this objective is amenable to measurement, and the specification of terms is clear and unambiguous.

Analysis of Instructional Objective into Teachable Components

Some instructional objectives are simple, and can be achieved in a single teaching step. For example, the objective may be that the student will not talk out more than two times during the independent work period for three consecutive days. Other objectives, however, are more complex and require a number of instructional steps. For example if a student cannot count to sixty by five's and cannot tell time to the nearest hour, then an objective calling for the student to tell time to the nearest five minutes is a complex multi-step objective. In this case the objective to tell time to the nearest five minutes is a *long-range instructional objective*. It must be broken down into smaller, individually teachable components. Doing so yields a sequence of enabling objectives which, when successfully completed, will culminate in the student performing the *terminal objective* successfully. Teachers are continually breaking down tasks into smaller, more readily teachable steps, and this process often takes on added importance in working with students who have learning problems.

Determination of Teaching-Learning Procedures

The search for instructional strategies has occupied a great deal of teacher time over the course of history, and educational researchers have invested considerable effort in searching for the best teaching methods. Data-based instruction, however, minimizes attention to teaching methodology by accepting as valid any teaching procedure that produces progress toward the stated instructional objectives. In DBI, good teaching is good outcomes, and as long as teaching procedures are humane and not derogatory or damaging to students, they are judged only in relation to student progress. This is especially important in bridging the gap between special and regular education, since it means that teachers need not necessarily learn a complete new set of instructional strategies previously associated only with special education, but rather can use their favorite procedures and see if they work.

One note of caution must be sounded with regard to teaching-learning procedures. In education there is a tendency to base instructional objectives on the materials used. For example, reading objectives might be taken from the basal reading series chosen for use with the entire class. In DBI however, the order of events is reversed. First instructional objectives are determined, and then instructional techniques (including materials) are chosen in relation to those objectives. While this might seem to be a minor point, it is essential to the very concept of individualized educational programming.

Continuous Measurement of Student Progress

Once instruction has been initiated, progress data must be collected on a continuous basis to determine whether the instructional intervention is successful. Some advocates of DBI suggest daily measurement of student progress (Lovitt, 1977), while others call for measurement at least twice a week (Lilly, 1977a). In general measurement of progress must be consistent and continuous. The more often such data can be collected, the better. Progress data must be of the same nature as baseline data if any conclusions concerning student learning are to be made. This means that the teacher must take care in choosing baseline data collection techniques that can be maintained through the intervention period.

Charting of Student Progress Data*

If a teacher has data on the instructional objectives, the data must be maintained in such a way that they can be used both for instructional decision making and for evidence of whether an objective has or has not been reached. Perhaps the most efficient and effective means of keeping student performance data is through charting procedures that provide a visual display of data over time. While various charting protocols are available, the most important aim is to choose a procedure that will allow quick and easily readable data displays that can be readily understood by other teachers and parents.

* This section is adapted from the following work: Lilly, M. S. Evaluating Individualized Education Programs. In. S. Torres (ed.) *A primer on individualized education programs for handicapped children*. Reston, VA: Council for Exceptional Children, 1977, pp. 26–30.

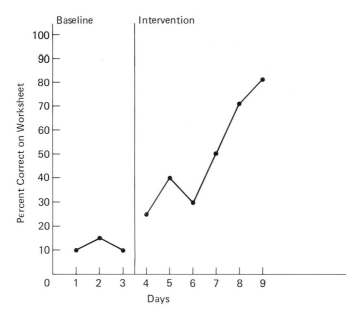

FIGURE 3–1 Example chart showing student progress in long division.

Figure 3–1 is a sample *chart* showing data on percent correct for long-division problems. The chart clearly displays data for three days of baseline and six days of instruction. The vertical line designates baseline data collection and the beginning of instruction; the horizontal dotted line represents the criterion level for successful performance as stated in the instructional objective.

This is by far the simplest of a number of charting protocols available. It is the most straightforward for teacher use. Other, more complex charting procedures might be more satisfactory to individual teachers. Any charting procedure can be used, as long as it serves its major purpose: to provide a visual display of student progress over time. More information on charting is provided in Chapter 7.

Instructional Decision Making

The only reason for collecting data on student performance in relation to specific objectives is to enable the teacher to make decisions concerning the adequacy of instructional interventions. While no infallible models exist for making these instructional decisions, the following guidelines apply:

1. Allow enough time for an instructional procedure to have an effect.
2. Do not allow a student to continue more than one week without making progress.
3. When progress does not occur, blame the instructional program, not the student.

4. When progress does occur celebrate with everyone involved.
5. Use progress charts in discussing school programs with parents.

The following questions must be asked in making instructional decisions (Lilly, 1977a):

1. Is progress sufficient to justify continuation of the present instructional procedures?
2. Do progress data indicate that the instructional objective and/or methodology is appropriate or inappropriate for the student?
3. Is the criterion level appropriate for the instructional objective?
4. If the objective is reached, what is the appropriate next step?

In summary the data-based instructional model just described provides a system for instruction that is noncategorical in nature, geared toward problems of concern for the regular classroom teacher, and sensitive to continuous measures of student progress. Obviously teachers should not expect to use DBI with all students in all subject areas. Typically students learn adequately without the use of DBI techniques. The authors recommend that DBI be used with students who are having significant learning and/or behavior problems in the classroom, students for whom less systematic and more standard instructional approaches have not been effective. The DBI concepts presented here serve as the basis for much of the information presented in the remainder of this book.

The authors believe that it is important that classroom teachers assume strong instructional roles in working with students who exhibit learning and behavior problems. Further we assert that choice of an instructional model is an important decision in working with these students, since some instructional models are more usable than others in mainstreaming programs. We recommend a data-based instructional model as summarized here and discussed in subsequent chapters, since it (1) employs a direct-instruction approach, (2) minimizes the difference in focus between regular and special educators, and (3) requires direct and frequent measures of student progress. A DBI approach clearly makes the teacher the most important person in the educational process, and provides a strong base of support for the classroom teacher's role as an instructional manager.

THE TEACHER AS A BEHAVIOR MANAGER

Perhaps no topic is of more consistent concern to classroom teachers than discipline, or control of inappropriate social behavior. Every teacher encounters behavior problems which must be dealt with successfully in order to create a proper learning environment in the classroom. Furthermore these behavior problems must be solved in the classroom, as opposed to the resource room, since behavioral gains made in resource rooms often do not carry over into the regular classroom setting.

While acting-out behavior is the most common concern of classroom teachers, it is not the only area in which teachers must assume the role of behavior manager. In the course of teaching students with learning and behavior problems (and, for that matter, all students), the teacher can expect to be pursuing at least the following goals:

1. Decreasing the frequency of inappropriate behavior with an individual student.
2. Decreasing the frequency of inappropriate behavior with a group of students.
3. Increasing the frequency of desired behavior (such as interacting with other students) with an individual student.
4. Arranging classroom variables such as space and schedule to establish a positive learning environment.
5. Increasing the study skills of individual students, such as independent work in the classroom and completion of assigned tasks.

As with the area of instructional management discussed in the previous section, a variety of intervention models are used in dealing with behavioral difficulties of students. Some of these intervention models focus primarily on identification and solution of inner conflicts which underlie the behavioral symptoms, and are comparable to the basic-ability approaches to academic problems discussed earlier. The method of intervention most closely associated with these psychodynamic approaches to behavior problems is individual or group counseling, which is not a classroom-based intervention and is generally not used in schools due to the expense involved and questions concerning effectiveness.

Far more popular in schools is the *behavioral* approach to solution of behavior management problems in the classroom. Most behavioral approaches to changing inappropriate social behavior closely adhere to the data-based instructional model presented in the previous section. One of the examples presented in the overview of DBI relates to modification of inappropriate acting-out behavior. Of primary importance in a behavioral approach is definition of the problem in a specific, observable form. This is especially important with social behavior problems, since emotion sometimes takes over and students are described as lazy, aggressive, hyperactive, or disruptive. While it is very difficult to bring about change in these supposed inner states of students, it is altogether possible to change the outward behaviors which lead us to describe students in these terms. Further once the outward behaviors are changed, the inner states seem to change as well.

One final approach to dealing with behavior problems must be mentioned, since it is often espoused by school personnel. This approach, which has been titled the *learning disability strategy* (Kirk, 1972), posits that learning problems underlie many behavioral difficulties which occur in school. The learning disabilities strategy focuses most heavily on acceleration of academic performance, on the assumption that students who are learning well will improve their social behavior. There is considerable truth to the contention that most students with behavior problems are experiencing learning problems as well, and many students do improve in social behavior as they experience academic gains. The learning disability strategy is useful for some students whose behavior is not extremely disruptive in the classroom. However for the majority of students with behavior problems, it is necessary to work simultaneously on academic instruction and behavioral difficulties, since the nature of the inappropriate social behavior often makes teaching academic skills very difficult.

In summary the classroom teacher's role as a manager of behavior is a complex one, and is certainly not limited to special education students who have been mainstreamed into the regular classroom. Every teacher faces behavior problems on a regular basis, and these problems must be dealt with in the classroom, where they are occurring. This section has provided an overview of the types of problems apt to be encountered by classroom teachers, as well as various models for intervention. All of the information presented in the previous section with regard to data-based instruction is directly applicable to behavior management, and DBI is recommended as the preferred approach to remedying social behavior and study problems in the regular classroom. An extended discussion of teaching strategies for behavior problems is presented in Chapter 9.

THE TEACHER AS A STUDENT AND PROGRAM ADVOCATE

The classroom teacher occupies a unique role in being able to advocate for appropriate services for students with learning and behavior problems. It is often assumed that when a teacher refers a student for special education, the teacher's goal is to have the student removed from the classroom. If, instead, a teacher argues for placement of the student in the least restrictive environment and for provision of services to help the student succeed in the regular classroom, this argument should carry considerable weight in the placement decision. Several times in this and previous chapters, it has been mentioned that classroom teachers must be assertive in assuming an active role in the special education placement and planning process. It is equally true that classroom teachers must be assertive in seeking placement of students in the least restrictive environment. In many school districts placement decisions are made on the basis of available services. Special education consultative services to classroom teachers are not well developed in most districts. Thus the tendency in some districts is to place students in full time special classes or for extended time in resource rooms, even when it is not clear that such intensity of service is necessary. Also there is often a tendency to place students with behavior problems in resource rooms, even though there is little likelihood of behavioral gains in the resource room carrying over to the regular classroom. In short some special educators will not advocate placement of students in the least restrictive environment. In these cases, the advocacy of the classroom teacher assumes major importance.

The advocacy role of classroom teachers must be conceptualized along two dimensions. First teachers must be advocates for individual students. This role can best be served by being an effective education team member. As pointed out earlier, teachers have a right to present classroom-based assessment data and to question the relevance of diagnostic information presented by other professionals. In addition teachers can resist unnecessary removal of students from the regular classroom and can request specific services which will enable the student to make progress in the classroom. In order to function as a student advocate, the teacher must be thoroughly knowledgable of: (1) special education programs available in the district in which he/she works, and (2) additional programs and services which are needed. In addition to the advocacy role at the time of placement and IEP planning, the teacher also must follow closely the progress of the student in special education, so as to be able to recommend increased integration of students who have been removed from the classroom for all or part of the school day. Again the tendency of some special education programs is to keep students permanently, and teachers can help bring periodic attention to the possible reintegration of students into regular education.

The second facet of teacher advocacy relates not to decisions concerning individual students, but to the overall configuration of special education programs in a school district. As pointed out earlier many districts do not offer a full configuration of special education programs; the level of service most often lacking is provision of direct support for teachers serving students in the regular classroom. Many districts offer largely separate resource room and special class programs, but do not provide quality consultative services to classroom teachers. If these services are not a part of a total special education program, it is more difficult for classroom teachers *or* special educators to advocate for placement of individual students in the least restrictive environment. Teachers and teacher organizations can be important forces in convincing school districts to expand special education services to include consultative help in the classroom. Presentations to school boards and frequent and continuous conferences with special education administrators and teachers can result in substantive program changes and additions. Program advocacy at this level can reap substantial benefits when the time comes to advocate placement of students in the least restrictive environment.

The mainstreaming movement has often been conceptualized as a special education versus regular education issue, with special educators arguing for increased integration of students with learning and behavior problems. Regular educators are often seen as resisting this integration. The authors have not found either characterization to be accurate. Some special educators do *not* advocate placement of students in the least restrictive environment, and are staunch defenders of traditional special education practices. On the other hand many regular educators have not accepted the argument that large numbers of students need to be removed from the classroom for special education services, and are active supporters of the mainstreaming movement. It is necessary that both regular *and* special educators serve as effective advocates for more integrated special education services, as well as for appropriate placement for individual students.

SUMMARY

This chapter has discussed the role of regular classroom teachers in educating students with learning and behavior problems, and has stressed that this role includes more than effective instruction. The classroom teacher has many opportunities to improve students' school experiences and must take advantage of all such opportunities. The next several chapters will deal with specific methods for carrying out the teacher's roles of instructional and behavior manager, they will also provide basic information which can be used in fulfilling the education team member and advocacy roles. As is evident thus far, it is a central theme of this book that teachers *can* make a difference, both in teaching children and in bringing about professional change. It is the hope of the authors that teachers will use their opportunities as change agents to bring closer to reality the goal of educating all students in the least restrictive environment.

SECTION 2

Assessing Instructional Problems

Traditional Practices in Educational Assessment

Educational assessment can be defined as a process in which a student's performance is measured for the purpose of making an educational decision. In order to understand assessment, it is important for teachers to realize that: (1) approaches to assessment vary, (2) assessments are conducted for different purposes, (3) there are several means by which measures of student performance can be collected, (4) all measures of student performance are based on varying sets of assumptions, and (5) the ability to make sound educational decisions depends upon obtaining relevant and accurate measures of student performance.

In this chapter we will examine the method most commonly used to assess the educational performance of students with mild learning and behavior problems. An overview of the traditional assessment method will be provided to acquaint the reader with the purposes of assessment, the general strategy of collecting assessment information, the types of measures used, the kinds of decisions which are based on those measures, and the assumptions which underlie the traditional approach to assessment.

The traditional assessment method will then be examined in detail with respect to its use in screening, diagnosis and placement, and instructional planning. Within each of these topics, emphasis will be placed on describing: (1) the purpose for the assessment, (2) the process one would use in conducting the assessment, (3) the kinds of tests one would administer, (4) the kinds of interpretations one would make based on the results of those tests, and (5) the assumptions which underlie the major types of tests used in the traditional assessment method. Throughout the chapter particular attention will be paid to evaluating the extent to which the traditional approach can provide educators with relevant and accurate information for making educational decisions.

TRADITIONAL EDUCATIONAL ASSESSMENT—AN OVERVIEW

Purposes

Assessments are conducted for different purposes, each designed to provide information which can serve as the basis for making an educational decision. Sometimes assessment takes the form of screening to identify students with physical, learning, and/or behavior problems. At other times assessments are conducted to diagnose handicapping conditions and to support educational placement decisions. Assessment information is also collected to plan instructional programs for students.

Assessment Strategy

Traditional educational assessment can be conceived as a series of steps which begins with a question regarding student performance and culminates in an educational decision. While the purpose of the assessment dictates the specific procedures to be used, the same general strategy is used to screen students for potential problems, to diagnose and place students in educational programs, and to plan instructional programs. For illustrative purposes we will examine the traditional educational assessment process as it applies to diagnosis and placement. In subsequent sections we will discuss the specific strategies associated with screening and instructional planning.

Traditional educational assessment for the purpose of diagnosis and placement can be thought of as a five-step process which is illustrated in Figure 4–1. The assessment process usually begins with a teacher observing a problem. Whether the problem observed concerns a student who squints while looking at the blackboard, or a student who is failing academically,

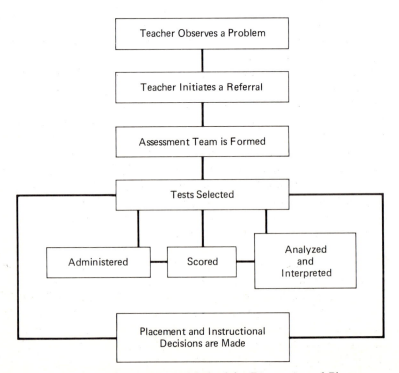

FIGURE 4–1 Traditional Assessment Method for Diagnosis and Placement.

or one who acts out in class, the student's behavior cues the teacher to begin to ask questions concerning the student's performance.

Typical questions a teacher might ask about a student with a suspected learning problem include: "Does the student understand my directions? Does he/she just need more practice? Is the student trying?" In many cases teachers can answer their own questions concerning a student's academic difficulties and take corrective steps. Sometimes due to the severity of the perceived problem or after exhausting all possible reasons to explain academic failure, a teacher may begin to ask other questions, such as: "Does the student have a hearing or vision problem? Is the student retarded? Could the student be learning disabled? Should I refer the student for evaluation?"

Once a teacher has referred a student for evaluation, the assessment process begins. An assessment team is formed which is usually comprised of a school psychologist, a special educator, and, when necessary, other related service personnel, such as a speech and language clinician. The school psychologist might assess the student's intellectual functioning by administering an intelligence test. Tests of language and visual-perceptual ability may also be given. The special educator might assess academic functioning by administering an achievement test or a battery of tests of academic skills. The student's behavior in the classroom may also be observed.

Following the administration of the tests, the results are analyzed and interpreted in an effort to obtain an answer to the question originally posed by the teacher. Finally a conference is arranged to discuss the results of the assessment with the student's parents, principal, and teacher. The assessment information is used to diagnose the presence of a handicapping condition, to determine an appropriate placement, and to plan an instructional program.

Types of Measures

The most common method of assessing student performance is through the use of standardized tests. Over 2,000 tests have been developed to measure different aspects of performance (Buros, 1973). A cadre of certified specialists have been trained whose primary responsibility is to administer tests and to interpret their results. Testing has become such an integral part of the traditional assessment method that the terms *testing*, *evaluation* and *assessment* are sometimes used synonymously.

There are two general types of formal tests—norm-referenced and criterion-referenced. *Norm-referenced tests* are so named because the scores of a particular student can be referenced or compared to the scores obtained by a similar sample of students on whom the test was standardized. Examples of norm-referenced tests include intelligence tests and achievement tests. The purpose of *criterion-referenced tests* is to measure a student's ability to perform a particular set of skills with reference to a stated level of performance, or criterion. The majority of criterion-referenced tests are in reading and arithmetic, and are used to pinpoint specific skills which a student has or has not mastered.

The purpose of the assessment dictates the type of tests which will be used. Several different types of tests have been developed. Among them are: screening tests for vision and hearing; screening tests for identifying students' potential learning and behavior problems; intelligence tests; tests of visual-perceptual, language, and auditory ability; tests of academic ability; and tests of social behavior. Depending upon the nature of the assessment, one or more of these types of tests will be used to make an educational decision.

Types of Decisions

Assessment information is used in the schools to make a variety of educational decisions. Some of the typical decisions which are made by school personnel include determining:

1. Which students are experiencing vision and hearing difficulties?
2. Which students are likely to experience learning and behavior problems?
3. Which students are eligible to receive special education services?
4. Which skills has a particular student mastered and which need to be acquired?

Many of the decisions made have a significant impact upon a student's educational program. Some of the most important decisions include the classification and placement of exceptional students, the formation of instructional groups, and the placement of students into curriculum materials. Errors in making these decisions can lead to negative consequences for students. Students may be misclassified resulting in faulty placement decisions. Some students may be placed in special classrooms when their needs could be met within regular classrooms, while others may not be found to be eligible to receive the special services they require. A student may be placed in an instructional group whose average member is functioning at a level which is markedly discrepant from his/her own. As a result a student may be given curriculum material which is either too easy or too difficult.

Due to the significance of the decisions, it is critical that assessment measures provide accurate and relevant information. It has already been noted in this text that the traditional assessment method relies heavily on the use of tests to make educational decisions. If student performance is to be measured by tests, then the assumptions underlying the use of a testing approach must be examined to discern the adequacy of the educational decisions which result from using them.

Assumptions

The assumptions of the traditional assessment method may be summarized as follows:

1. Tests are adequate for the purpose for which they were designed. Particular tests are seen as appropriate for measuring intelligence, achievement, and specific processes and/or abilities which are seen as related to academic achievement.

2. Differential diagnosis of students is possible through the appropriate selection and interpretation of test results, thereby allowing for the classification of mildly handicapped students as mentally retarded, learning disabled, or behaviorally disordered.
3. Test scores are reliable indicators of a student's performance. The results of a test, given according to the published directions in the test manual, are said to reflect a student's true ability within specified limits.
4. Instructional programs for students can be designed based on their performance on formal tests.
5. Educational assessment is best conducted by trained specialists who are skilled in selecting and administering tests, and in interpreting their results.

Later in this chapter these assumptions will be discussed. Serious questions will be raised concerning their validity and the ability of tests to provide educators with accurate and sufficient information to make educational decisions. For the present we will focus on how the traditional educational method is used to: (1) identify students with learning and behavior problems, (2) diagnose handicapping conditions and place students in special education programs, and (3) plan instructional programs for handicapped students.

SCREENING

The purpose of screening is to identify students who evidence problems which warrant further assessment. Screening programs are conducted to identify students with vision and hearing problems, to identify students in preschool and kindergarten who may later have learning problems, and to identify students of school age who display learning problems. All educational screening programs share some common characteristics. Namely screening is accomplished by testing student performance, though teacher ratings are sometimes used. Most screening tests are given by classroom teachers and can be administered in a brief amount of time. As such screening tests represent an efficient way for schools to sample the performance of a large number of students and to separate them into two groups—those who require further assessment and those who do not. We will now examine three common types of screening activities and consider the extent to which they achieve their purposes.

Vision and Hearing

A student's visual ability may be limited by poor acuity, restriction of the visual field, or imperfect color vision. Other aspects of visual functioning are sometimes assessed, for example, ability of the eyes to adjust to different distances and changes in intensity of light. The interested reader may consult Salvia and Ysseldyke (1978) to learn about tests which measure several different visual abilities. Visual-acuity screening is usually conducted by the school nurse using either the Standard Snellen Wall Chart or the adapted Snellen E Test for non-readers. Students who are thought to have poor visual acuity based on their performance on the Snellen Wall Chart are referred to a vision specialist for further evaluation.

Teachers need to be aware that a student's vision as measured by a Snellen Wall Chart indicates only far point visual acuity and is only a gross estimate. It is for that reason that teachers need to be alert to the possible visual problems of their students. Signs of eye problems may be indicated by a student's behavior (holding a book too close to the eyes), by the appearance of a student's eyes (red, inflamed), or by complaints that the eyes itch or burn. Other practical suggestions for spotting potential visual problems are provided by Ward (1979).

Many states require the routine screening of students' vision and hearing. Screening for hearing problems is usually conducted by a school nurse, a speech and language clinician, or a trained technician using an audiometer. The most commonly used type of measurement instrument is the pure-tone audiometer which produces tones at different frequencies. The screening test is individually administered to students who are requested to signal if they hear a tone as the examiner scans the various frequencies. If a student fails to hear a tone at a specified intensity level in one or both ears, a second screening is performed. If a student fails the second screening, a pure-tone threshold test is conducted to find the level at which a student can just barely hear the tone at each tested frequency (Salvia & Ysseldyke, 1978). Students who fail the pure-tone threshold test are usually referred to an audiologist or to an otologist for further evaluation.

As with vision, teachers need to be alert to their pupil's hearing problems. Signs of potential hearing problems may be indicated by: (1) a student's behavior (asks for frequent repetitions), (2) the presence of frequent colds, (3) the appearance of the ears (draining), or (4) complaints by the student of not being able to hear clearly.

Early Identification

There has been a tremendous emphasis in recent years on identifying potential learning problems as early as possible. The trend toward early detection of learning difficulties has received support from both federal and state governments who have encouraged the development of such screening programs as The Early & Periodic Screening, Diagnosis & Treatment Program (Reynolds & Birch, 1977) and Project Screen (Senf & Comrey, 1975).

Screening tests for the early identification of learning problems have been classified as single- or multiple-variable predictors (Jansky & de Hirsch, 1972). A number of single-variable predictors have been explored, ranging from the presence of hair swirls and the zinc content in student's hair to the more typical predictor variables noted by Wallace and Larsen (1978) which include: visual perception, visual-motor skills, auditory perception, oral language, chronological age, sex, intelligence and emotional status. Intelligence test scores have sometimes been used to predict later learning problems. Several educators have aptly pointed out the inadequacy of basing judgments concerning potential learning problems on intelligence test scores because of: (1) the instability of intelligence test scores, (2) the potential bias in using intelligence tests with non-white non-middle-class students and (3) the lack of precision in making an accurate prediction for a particular student based on an intelligence test score (Janky & de Hirsch, 1972; Keogh & Becker, 1973).

The Evanston Early Identification Scale (Landsman & Dillard, 1967) is an example of a test based on a single predictor variable, that is, the ability to draw a figure of a person. The test is intended for students between the ages of five and six years, and can be administered by a classroom teacher to individuals or to groups of students. A student's drawing is assigned points on a weighted scale based on the presence and position of body parts. A student is classified as either high, middle, or low risk based on his score. Only minimal reliability and validity data are presented for the Evanston Early Identification Scale. No information is provided on the extent to which the test does or does not identify students who later evidence learning problems.

The search for a simple single predictor of later learning difficulties has largely been abandoned by those interested in developing devices for the early detection of learning problems. The reasoning of many involved in this endeavor appears to be: "If a single variable is not useful, perhaps several single variables taken together will result in accurate predictions." This logic has resulted in administering several different single-predictor measures, for example, an intelligence test plus tests of visual perception, motor skills, and reading readiness and has led to the development of screening batteries which include several subtests designed to measure specific abilities.

The CIRCUS (Anderson, Bogatz, Draper, Jungleblut, Sidwell, Ward, & Yates, 1974) is an example of a multiple-predictor screening test. Some of the skills included on the CIRCUS are: comprehension of parts of speech, quantitative concepts, visual discrimination, copying letters and numbers, discriminating between capital and lower case letters, listening comprehension, and general knowledge. There are also three measures to be completed by the teacher consisting of an activities inventory (student's approach to classroom activities), a CIRCUS behavior inventory (student's reaction to the test), and a questionnaire describing the teacher's background and the class and school. Unfortunately no information is provided in the CIRCUS manual concerning the predictive validity of the test. Therefore there is no assurance that students who score poorly on the CIRCUS will actually experience learning problems later in school.

The search for early identification devices to detect learning problems brings up a number of interesting questions and poses some problems for educators.

1. The development of screening devices suggests that one can identify specific abilities associated with school success, that these abilities are

measurable, and that the lack of these abilities indicates later learning problems. The state of the art has not developed to a point where educators can make good predictions concerning future learning performance based on measures obtained in preschool. In commenting on the predictive validity of preschool screening tests, Keogh and Becker (1973) stated that based on "present evidence, it seems reasonable to conclude that relationships between single, specific preschool test findings and later school achievement are too low to allow definitive prediction about individual children" (p. 7).

2. In the traditional assessment model, screening is to be followed by further evaluation. It is implied that there are more extensive tests which are capable of really diagnosing a student's learning problem. We shall see that this is not a safe assumption when we consider the types of tests used to diagnose handicapping conditions.

3. The logic behind early identification programs is that the sooner a student is identified, the sooner intervention can begin. While this is practical for students with sensory impairments and severe handicapping conditions, problems arise in attempting to identify students in preschool who may later evidence mild learning and behavior problems. As Keogh and Becker stated "children who have not been exposed to a reading program cannot really be said to have reading problems; children who have not participated in a first grade program cannot be classified as first grade failures" (1973, p. 6).

4. Educators have expressed concern that early identification of students suspected of developing later learning problems may result in a self-fulfilling prophecy of failure (Keogh & Becker, 1973) or lead to students being negatively labeled (Reynolds & Birch, 1977).

5. Intervention programs for students considered high risk typically emphasize training students' weak abilities, those thought to be the underlying causes of learning problems. Proponents of ability training maintain that by strengthening certain abilities (visual-perceptual, auditory, psycholinguistic, or perceptual-motor) students' academic performance will improve. Reviews of research on the effectiveness of ability training on academic performance have been conducted by several educators (Arter & Jenkins, 1978; Hallahan & Cruickshank, 1973; Goodman & Hammill, 1973; Hammill & Larsen, 1974a). The consensus of opinion is that ability training does not always improve the specific ability trained, let alone improve academic performance. Many educators question the utility of identifying high risk students if this results in placing them in programs which are based on training methods which have failed to clearly demonstrate their effectiveness.

It should be pointed out that early education of the handicapped is a relatively new field and one which has been characterized as being "in a period of rapid growth" (Lilly, 1979, p. 122). Some of the most pressing problems facing the field concern developing valid identification procedures, determining effective intervention programs, and developing evaluation strategies to measure short- and long-term effects of preschool programs for students considered high risk.

The majority of students classified educable mentally retarded, learning disabled, or behavior disordered are identified not through screening but teacher referral. Even though teacher referral is the most common method of identifying students with mild learning and behavior problems, a number of screening tests have been developed for use with school-age children. We will focus our attention first on a general screening test and then on a behavior rating scale. Then we will discuss the use of group-administered achievement tests by teachers to document low academic performance or to support the need to refer students for further evaluation.

The Slingerland Screening Tests for Identifying Children with Specific Language Disabilities (Slingerland, 1970) is an example of a school-age screening device. The Slingerland contains eight subtests plus two supplementary auditory tests. The test is designed to be either individually or group administered by a classroom teacher. Four separate forms have been developed for use with first through fifth graders. While the content difficulty varies from form to form, the same types of skills are presented on each form. Some of the tasks included are: copying stories from a wall chart, copying words on a page from printed materials, and writing words dictated by the teacher. The two types of analyses which may be performed on student's responses are termed *quick analysis* (one score for each subtest and error analyses) and *detailed analysis* (error pattern groupings, for example, confusion of direction).

There are a number of difficulties associated with the use of the Slingerland. First there are no norms for the test; the author recommends that schools establish their own norms. Second no information is provided in the manual with respect to the reliability or validity of the test. These problems are not restricted to the Slingerland; rather they tend to characterize school-age screening devices.

The second type of screening device to be discussed is a rating scale. One such scale known as The Pupil Rating Scale: Screening for Learning Disabilities was developed by Myklebust (1971). The Pupil Rating Scale (PRS) was designed to allow classroom teachers to rate students' performance in five areas: auditory comprehension, spoken language, orientation, motor coordination, and personal-social behavior. The scale was developed for third and fourth grade students. As an aid in rating, sentence descriptions are provided which coincide with each point on a five-point scale. Teachers are asked to judge which description matches a student's behavior in each of the rated areas. A score of three in each area is considered to be average. The Pupil Rating Scale has been reviewed by Proeger (1973) who described the scale as impressive despite the lack of any reliability data and the rather small normative sample.

One of the most important considerations in evaluating a screening test is to determine the extent to which the test over- and under-identifies students with learning and/or behavior problems. By comparing the results of a screening test with the results of other tests, it is possible to determine the proportion of students whom the screening test failed to identify (false negatives) and the proportion of students who were incorrectly identified (false positives). Proeger (1973) analyzed data on the PRS collected by Myklebust, Boshes, Olson, and Cole (1969). Based on Proeger's report it appears that the proportion of false positives was one out of four and the proportion of false negatives was one out of five for subjects in the Myklebust *et al.* study.

One of the reservations in adopting a rating scale such as the PRS is the extent to which behaviors rated on the scale are correlated with learning problems. Many of the areas assessed on the test, for example, motor coordination and orientation, appear to have a dubious relationship to academic performance. As such they may be less than accurate predictors of success in school (Leydorf, 1970).

Group-administered achievement tests are routinely given by schools at periodic intervals. A low score on an achievement test may either alert a teacher that a student is experiencing difficulty or confirm a teacher's suspicions concerning a student's academic performance. Group-administered achievement tests can be regarded as screening devices when their results prompt a teacher to further assess a student's performance or when the results of an achievement test are used to support a teacher's request that a student be evaluated for special education services.

Some of the most commonly used group-administered achievement tests are the California Achievement Test (Tiegs & Clarke, 1970), the Metropitan Achievement Test (Durost, Bixler, Wrightstone, Prescott, & Balow, 1971), and the Stanford Achievement Test (Madden, Gardner, Rudman, Karlsen, & Merwin, 1973). All of these tests are norm-referenced with the exception of the Stanford Achievement Test which is considered to be both norm- and criterion-referenced. Using the Metropitan Achievement Test (MAT) as an example, we will examine the content of a typical group-administered achievement test.

The MAT has six levels appropriate for use with students in kindergarten through ninth grade. Depending on the level, there are tests of word knowledge, word analysis, reading, language, spelling, math computation, math concepts, math problem solving, science and social studies. The test can be given by a classroom teacher in from one to four-and-one-half hours depending on the grade level administered. One of the scores which can be derived from a subtest raw score is a grade equivalence score. Grade equivalence scores allow a comparison between the performance of a particular student and the performance of his/her peers. Students whose grade equivalence scores are markedly discrepant from the norm and from their peers in the classroom are usually referred for further evaluation.

The question to be asked is, "Can group-administered achievement tests be used to reliably screen students for learning problems?" Three problems exist in using group-administered achievement tests as screening devices. First most are timed tests which may serve to depress the scores of students who take a long time to complete test items. Second a student's score reflects ability on a given day, yet student performance is often variable. Third the content of the curriculum may not match the types of items contained on the test. Therefore a low score may represent nothing more than a mismatch between the content of a test and the skills which have been emphasized in the classroom.

Screening has been likened to a "rapid, rough selection process" (Anastasi, 1968, p. 153) which produces very little reliable or precise information (Reynolds & Birch, 1977). Screening is usually accomplished through tests which are viewed as rather crude indicators of performance. If screening tests are viewed with such disdain, why are they used? Perhaps they are used because they represent an efficient way for schools to scan the abilities of a large number of students and to identify easily those who may be in need of special attention.

Thus the traditional assessment model includes procedures to identify students with vision and hearing problems, those with potential learning problems, as well as those who evidence actual learning and behavior problems. The traditional assessment model prompts educators to select a certain type of test known as a screening test. Depending upon the nature of the assessment, one or more types of screening tests are selected for use. The purpose of the assessment usually dictates who conducts it. For example vision screening is typically conducted by a school nurse, whereas preschool and school-age screening devices are designed to be administered by classroom teachers. The particular test(s) selected dictates which aspect of behavior will be measured, how it will be measured, and how the test results should be interpreted.

Once a screening test is given, the results are analyzed and a decision is made. Here the decision is, "Is further assessment warranted based on the student's performance on the screening test?" If the answer is no the student is presumed to be functioning normally in the area assessed. If the answer is yes than further evaluation is recommended because of some doubt concerning the student's ability to see, hear, or progress either academically or socially.

Let us consider for a moment what can go wrong with screening programs. First screening tests may fail to discriminate between students who are and are not experiencing difficulty in the area assessed. Second screening tests may not measure relevant aspects of behavior. For example preschool screening devices often assess underlying abilities which have been shown to bear little or no relationship to academic performance. Third the technical adequacy of screening tests may severely restrict one's ability to obtain valid and reliable measures of an individual student's performance. In Chapter 5 we will discuss an alternative to screening. For the present we will continue our examination of the traditional assessment method as it applies to diagnosing mild handicapping conditions.

DIAGNOSIS AND PLACEMENT

Earlier it was mentioned that the majority of students with mild learning and behavior problems are referred for further evaluation by their classroom teachers. In this section we will discuss the nature of the evaluation procedures, the types of tests used, and the assumptions which underlie those tests.

Evaluation for special education services is influenced by three primary factors: federal and state law, definitions of handicapping conditions, and the theoretical orientation of members of the assessment team. Federal and state laws require schools to follow certain procedures in evaluating students referred for special education and related services. Briefly the federal rules and regulations for Public Law 94–142 as contained in the *Federal Register* (August 23, 1977) require the following:

1. Once a referral is made, parental permission must be obtained to evaluate the student.
2. Evaluation must be an individual evaluation which focuses on all areas related to a student's suspected disability.
3. The evaluation must be conducted by a multidisciplinary team.
4. Tests used in evaluation must be administered in the student's native language or other mode of communication, validated for the specific purpose for which they are used, and given by trained personnel.

State regulations often go considerably beyond the federal rules in requiring specific assessment measures.

Federal and state laws also influence the evaluation process by defining handicapping conditions. The way in which handicapping conditions are defined has direct implications for the types of tests which are used in evaluation. For example let us consider the federal definition for mental retardation. Mental retardation has been defined as,

> significantly subaverage general intellectual functioning existing concurrently with deficits in adaptive behavior and manifested during the developmental period which adversely affects a child's educational performance.
>
> (*Federal Register*, August 23, 1977, p. 42478)

To classify a student as mentally retarded according to the federal definition, one must assess a student's intellectual functioning, academic performance, and adaptive behavior. Functionally this often translates into administering an intelligence test, an achievement test, and a behavioral rating scale.

Similarly, in defining learning disabilities, certain types of tests are implied. A learning disability as defined by the Rules and Regulations for Public Law 94–142 means,

> A disorder in one or more of the basic psychological processes involved in understanding or in using language, spoken or written which may manifest itself in an imperfect ability to listen, think, speak, read, write, spell, or to do mathematic calculations. The term includes such conditions as perceptual handicaps, brain injury, minimal brain dysfunction, dyslexia, and developmental aphasia. The term does not include children who have learning problems which are primarily the result of visual, hearing or motor handicaps, of mental retardation, or of environmental, cultural, or economic disadvantage.
>
> (*Federal Register*, August 23, 1977, p. 42478)

In order to classify a student as learning disabled, measures of psychological processes as well as academic ability are often required. To discount the possibility that a sensory impairment may be negatively effecting a student's learning, several states recommend that a physician assess the student's vision, hearing, and motor abilities. To rule out the possibility that a student is mentally retarded rather than learning disabled, a measure of the student's intelligence is usually obtained by administering an intelligence test. The common types of tests used in classifying students as learning disabled include intelligence tests, achievement measures, and tests of abilities which are thought to be related to learning. These latter types of tests include visual, auditory, psycholinguistic, and perceptual-motor abilities.

The theoretical orientation of members of the assessment team may also predispose them to select certain types of tests. For example, practitioners who believe in differential diagnosis and diagnostic-prescriptive teaching tend to assess underlying abilities which are thought to be associated with learning problems. Remediation then takes one of two forms, either weak abilities are strengthened directly, or "instructional programs are devised that capitalize upon the child's pattern of underlying strengths and weaknesses, as identified in the course of diagnosis" (Arter & Jenkins, 1978, p. 3). The Differential-Diagnosis-Prescriptive Teaching (DD-PT) approach is consistent with the traditional assessment model as previously described. Adherents of the DD-PT approach, a term coined by Arter and Jenkins (1978), include Marianne Frostig (visual-perceptual abilities), Samuel Kirk (psycholinguistic abilities) and followers of Newell Kephart (perceptual-motor abilities). In this section, we will examine the types of tests used in the traditional assessment model by advocates of the DD-PT approach to diagnose students with mild learning and behavior problems.

Intellectual Functioning

Intellectual functioning is assessed by administering an intelligence test. Intelligence tests can be categorized into two global types—those which are administered to individuals and those which are administered to groups of students. Intelligence tests can be further subdivided into tests of general intelligence, picture vocabulary tests, and tests for special populations, for example, the hearing impaired. In this section, only individual tests of general intelligence will be considered as these are the tests which are commonly used in diagnosing and classifying students with mild handicapping conditions.

The two most commonly used tests of general intelligence are the Wechsler Intelligence Scale for Children-Revised (WISC-R) (Wechsler, 1974), and the Revised Stanford-Binet (RS-B) (Terman & Merrill, 1973). For discussion purposes, we will consider the WISC-R as an example of an individual intelligence test.

The WISC-R is designed to be used with students from four to sixteen-and-one-half years of age. The test contains twelve subtests designed to measure the following abilities: recall of factual information, understanding directions, identifying similarities between verbal stimuli, solving arithmetic application problems, defining words, recalling orally presented digits, identifying missing parts of pictures, sequencing pictures to produce a story, manipulating blocks to match a design, joining puzzle pieces to form objects, associating symbols and copying them on paper, and tracing a path through mazes.

The WISC-R must be administered by a certified psychologist. After scoring the test, the raw scores are used to derive three scaled scores—verbal, performance, and full-scale IQs. A student whose full-scale IQ score is two or more standard deviations below the mean (a score of 70 on the WISC-R) would be considered to have significantly subaverage general intelligence and would fit the impaired intelligence criterion contained in the federal definition of mental retardation. If the student's adaptive behavior was also impaired, the student could be considered to be mentally retarded according to the federal definition. As Lilly (1979) pointed out, various states have set different cut off limits for defining impaired intelligence. Scores typically range from 70 to 85. Therefore, a student might be considered to be mentally retarded in one state but not in another.

Intelligence tests and the use of IQ scores have stirred up a great deal of controversy in recent years. Many educators have questioned the use of intelligence tests with non-white, non-middle-class students stating that intelligence tests are culturally biased (Mercer, 1974). Court cases have also had an impact. In *Diana* v. *State Board of Education* (1970), the court ordered the school district to reevaluate all Mexican-American and Chinese-American students in their native language and to change any misplacements made on the basis of inappropriate testing. In *Larry P.* v. *Riles* (1972) the court ruled that the school district could no longer use IQ test scores as the sole criterion for placing students in classes for the educable mentally retarded. Public Law 94–142 contains specific provisions to protect students in evaluation procedures. Students are to be individually evaluated in their native language and no test can be used as the sole determinant of placement.

What should a classroom teacher's response be toward intelligence tests and intelligence test scores? The following factors must be taken into account in interpreting IQ scores:

1. Intelligence tests are merely samples of behavior and very restricted samples at that.
2. An intelligence test score represents a student's performance on a particular day.
3. Some educators maintain that intelligence tests are really measures of achievement, that is, they measure what students have learned rather than their potential. Not all students have had an equal opportunity to learn and their scores may be depressed due to lack of experience. Hobbs (1975) pointed out that the equal opportunity condition cannot be assumed when intelligence tests are used with students from cultural groups who differ from those on whom the test was standardized.
4. Intelligence tests are not excellent predictors of school performance. Hobbs stated that "not more than 50% of academic achievement is associated with IQ, even in the best of circumstances" (1975, p. 46).

5. The technical adequacy of intelligence tests administered to students referred for special education and related services must be examined. In the case of the WISC-R, Salvia and Ysseldyke (1978) consider the test to be technically adequate, but they caution examiners to go beyond the scores provided and to evaluate students' performance on specific subtests.
6. School psychologists should be asked to elaborate on the educational implications of the test results, bearing in mind that no educational decision should be overly influenced by a student's IQ score.

Visual-Perceptual Abilities

Some DD-PT advocates stress one ability more than another. The leading proponent of visual-perceptual skill assessment and training is Marianne Frostig, who believes that many students experience learning problems due to their inability to process visual-perceptual information. Frostig et al. (1964) developed the Development Test of Visual Perception (DTVP). The DTVP contains five subjects, each designed to measure a different type of visual-perceptual ability including eye-motor coordination, figure-ground discrimination, form constancy and shape, and spatial relations.

The DTVP can be administered by a teacher or by any specialist trained in the use of the test. The test is intended for students between the ages of three and nine. The DTVP can be administered in about forty minutes to small groups of students or to individual students. Each subtest yields a raw score which can be converted into perceptual age scores and scaled scores, the sums of which are used to derive a perceptual quotient. A perceptual quotient of ninety or less for kindergarten students is taken as an indication that the student should receive special training. Any student who is ten years of age or older, who fails to receive the maximum age equivalent score in any of the five areas tested, is presumed to be deficient in that aspect of visual perception (Salvia & Ysseldyke, 1978). Frostig and Horne (1964) have developed a training program designed to improve specific areas of visual-perceptual functioning.

The DTVP and Frostig & Horne's training program have prompted a great deal of research which has been reviewed by Hammill & Wiederholt (1973). These reviewers reached the following conclusions:

1. The test was standardized on over 2,000 white middle-class students from three to nine years of age. The test is often used with special populations, yet no one has demonstrated that the DTVP is either valid or reliable with students from these groups.
2. The subtest reliabilities are too low to be used to accurately identify students' visual-perceptual deficits.
3. The test does not appear to tap five discrete visual-perceptual skills, but rather one or two skills.
4. Frostig & Horne's training program "has no effect on reading and it has a questionable effect on school readiness and perception itself" (p. 44).

In commenting further on the technical adequacy of the DTVP, Salvia

& Ysseldyke questioned the way in which scores are derived and concluded by saying that the scores "absolutely must not be used in making diagnostic decisions" (1978, p. 311). Still, the DTVP is used in the schools despite serious criticisms concerning its validity and reliability. Furthermore, low test scores on the DTVP are interpreted to mean that students have particular visual-perceptual deficits, which if not remedied will serve to impede their learning. Training specific visual-perceptual skills is advocated to correct the deficit areas and enhance academic performance. As we have seen in this section, the following points must be taken into account when interpreting assessment information in the area of visual-perception: (1) research fails to support a relationship between visual-perceptual skills and academic performance; (2) the DTVP does not tap five discrete areas, thereby making differential diagnosis of visual-perceptual skills impossible; and (3) efforts to train visual-perceptual abilities do not reliably result in increasing visual-perceptual skills, let alone in improved academic performance.

Auditory Abilities

Some advocates of the DD-PT approach stress auditory skills such as auditory-visual integration, sound blending, auditory memory, phonetic auditory discrimination and nonphonetic auditory discrimination (Arter & Jenkins, 1978). Specific tests of auditory abilities include the Goldman-Fristoe-Woodcock Test of Auditory Discrimination (Goldman, Fristoe, & Woodcock, 1970), the Screening Test for Auditory Perception (Kimmell & Wahl, 1969), and the Auditory Discrimination Test (Wepman, 1973). Auditory abilities can also be assessed by using certain subtests of other tests such as the Illinois Test of Psycholinguistic Abilities (Kirk, McCarthy, & Kirk, 1968), and the WISC-R (Wechsler, 1974).

In assessing auditory skills, one makes the following assumptions: (1) auditory skills are discrete abilities which can be reliably measured; (2) auditory abilities are related to academic skills, e.g. reading; and (3) it is possible to train auditory skills and thereby enhance academic functioning as well as auditory abilities. In general test-retest reliabilities are higher for auditory perceptual tests than for visual perceptual tests. However as Arter and Jenkins (1978) stated "no activity can be considered a pure measure of an isolated ability" (p. 51). The relationship of auditory skills to academic abilities has been investigated by Hammill (1972), Hammill and Larsen (1974b) and Sabatino (1973). In Hammill and Larsen's (1974b) review of correlation studies of auditory skills and reading ability, the majority of coefficients were nonsignificant and no auditory skill correlated greater than 0.35 with reading.

Some of the parts of auditory tests may fail to discriminate between normal and impaired learners. Larsen, Rogers, and Sowell (1976) compared the performance of normal and learning disabled students on the Auditory Discrimination Test (Wepman, 1973) and found no significant difference between the groups. In summarizing the effectiveness of auditory training on reading and general achievement, Arter and Jenkins (1978) concluded that out of thirty-three studies, 36 percent of them (excluding studies with methodological flaws) reported significant differences between trained and untrained groups. The success rate would lead one to be less optimistic in training auditory skills in the hopes of improving academic performance.

Psycholinguistic Abilities

The Illinois Test of Psycholinguistic Abilities (Kirk, McCarthy, & Kirk, 1968) is the most commonly used test in diagnosing learning disabilities. The Illinois Test of Psycholinguistic Abilities (ITPA) is an individually administered test used with students from age two through ten years. The ITPA consists of twelve subtests, each designed to assess abilities in understanding, processing and producing verbal and nonverbal language. Specific skills presented on the ITPA include: auditory and visual reception; auditory and visual association; verbal and manual expression; visual, auditory, and grammatic closure; sound blending; and auditory and visual sequential memory.

The types of scores derived from raw scores on the ITPA include scaled scores, psycholinguistic ages and psycholinguistic quotients. The psycholinguistic age scores are plotted on a Profile of Abilities which enable the examiner to visually interpret a student's strengths and weaknesses on the various subtests. Students who do poorly on the ITPA are assumed to have deficits which must be remedied. While no specific training materials exist, psycholinguistic activities have been described by Kirk and Kirk (1971) in a training manual.

At the time of its development, the ITPA was heralded as *the* test capable of determining intra-individual differences with respect to underlying processes used in understanding, processing and producing language. In recent years, the ITPA has come under criticism. The ITPA model assumes that there are discrete psycholinguistic processes which can be measured. One of the explicit assumptions of the ITPA is that psycholinguistic training will improve those abilities as well as academic performance. The ITPA has stimulated a great deal of research since the experimental edition was published in 1961. Much of the research has been summarized by Sedlak and Weener (1973) and Hammill and Larsen (1974a). Thus the test's ability to measure discrete skills is unsupported, thereby making it a questionable practice to attempt to differentially diagnose language disabilities based on ITPA subtest scores.

Attempts to train psycholinguistic processes have been largely ineffective. Hammill and Larsen (1974a) reported that with the exception of verbal expression, other abilities such as visual sequential memory and grammatic closure have been unresponsive to training in over 70 percent of the studies they reviewed. Sedlak and Weener (1973) concluded on the basis of their review, that psycholinguistic training has little or no effect on school achievement. The ITPA has also been criticized on technical grounds by Salvia and Ysseldyke (1978) who maintain that "the norms appear inadequate; the validity's unestablished; and the reliability of the subtests is adequate only for experimental work" (p. 357).

ITPA test results can be used to plot a student's strengths and weaknesses with respect to psycholinguistic skills measured on the ITPA. Based on an ITPA profile, a student is described as an "auditory learner," "visual learner," or "kinesthetic learner." Several advocates of the DD-PT approach (Johnson & Myklebust, 1967; Lerner, 1971) advocate providing instruction through the strong channel or modality. Several studies have examined the effectiveness of matching students to instructional programs based on their modality strengths and weaknesses. In these studies some students receive instruction in their strong modality while others are provided with instruction in their weak modality. Arter and Jenkins (1977) reviewed fifteen modality studies. In commenting on their review, the authors stated that in fourteen of the fifteen studies "matching instruction with modality strength failed to produce differential improvement; children learned equally well whether or not instruction was matched to their strong modality" (Arter & Jenkins, 1978, p. 49).

One must seriously question the use of the ITPA as a diagnostic device and as a basis for planning instructional programs in light of the test's inadequacies and the failure of training programs to increase student's academic performance.

Perceptual-Motor Abilities

Some theorists, such as Newell Kephart (1960), have suggested that perceptual-motor ability and academic achievement are related. Perceptual-motor ability is sometimes assessed by using the Purdue Perceptual Motor Survey (Roach & Kephart, 1966). The Purdue Perceptual Motor Survey (PPMS) may be individually administered by classroom teachers to students of all ages. However, norms are available only for students between the ages of six and ten years. The PPMS contains subtests which are designed to measure the following perceptual-motor skills: balance and posture, body image and differentiation, perceptual-motor match, ocular control, and form perception. There are a total of twenty-two scorable items contained on the test. The teacher rates a student's ability to perform the tasks by selecting from the statements provided in the manual, the one which most closely describes the student's performance. Students who score poorly on the PPMS are considered to have perceptual-motor problems and it is recommended that they receive perceptual-motor training in deficit areas. Perceptual-motor training programs range from stressing only perceptual-motor skills to including activities designed to improve perceptual-motor functioning while continuing to teach academic subjects.

In reviewing the PPMS Salvia and Ysseldyke (1978) stated that the normative sample was limited and that the validity of the scale is questionable. In light of the fact that a relationship between perceptual-motor abilities and academic achievement has not been demonstrated, classroom teachers can rightfully question the utility of assessing perceptual-motor abilities. Further, attempts to remediate perceptual-motor skills have yielded far from satisfactory results in improving academic performance (Goodman & Hammill, 1973).

The most common way to measure academic ability is through the use of achievement tests. As previously noted, achievement tests can be either norm-referenced or criterion-referenced. Some tests are group-administered, whereas others are designed to be individually administered. Group-administered achievement tests, discussed previously, are used in screening. Individual norm-referenced achievement tests are used in diagnosis to establish a discrepancy between a student's actual performance (based on an achievement test) expected level (based on grade placement) and potential level (based on an IQ score). Although classroom teachers may administer individual achievement tests, they are usually administered by a special educator or by a school psychologist as are other tests used in diagnosing handicapping conditions.

Two of the most frequently used individually administered achievement tests are the Wide Range Achievement Test (WRAT) (Jastak & Jastak, 1965) and the Peabody Individual Achievement Test (PIAT) (Dunn & Markwardt, 1970). For discussion purposes we will examine the WRAT. The WRAT has two levels, Level 1 for ages 5 to 11 and Level 2 for ages 12 and over. The WRAT consists of three subtests, one in reading, one in spelling, and one in arithmetic. Subtest names can be very misleading, and for that reason the subtests of the WRAT will be described. The reading subtest measures saying words in isolation. The spelling test assesses the ability to write words from dictation, and the arithmetic subtest measures counting, reading numerals, computing arithmetic problems and solving orally presented word problems.

Three types of scores may be computed based on raw scores on the WRAT subtests: grade equivalence scores, percentile ranks, and standard scores. Usually in placement and planning conferences, the special education or school psychologist will report a student's grade equivalence scores. For example the examiner might indicate that a student scored 2.1 in reading, 2.5 in spelling, and 3.0 in arithmetic on the WRAT. If the student were a fourth grader, the grade equivalence scores would be used to support his/her eligibility for special education. If the student's IQ was within the normal range, the student would usually be classified as learning disabled. If the student's IQ was 70 or below, the student would be apt to be classified as mentally retarded.

In reviewing the WRAT, Salvia and Ysseldyke (1978) pointed out several flaws: (1) the normative sample was limited, (2) subtests sample very few behaviors, (3) the uses of the test are not validated, and (4) no test-retest reliabilities are reported. These problems are not restricted to the WRAT; rather they tend to characterize achievement tests. One of the most serious concerns regarding achievement tests deals with content validity. A test must measure skills similar to those presented in the curriculum used in the classroom, to have high content validity. In order to understand the importance of content validity and its effect upon placement decisions, let us examine the results of a study conducted by Jenkins and Pany (1978).

Jenkins and Pany (1978) investigated whether grade equivalence scores could be biased for or against different reading series simply because of the amount of overlap between words taught in the reading series and words presented on the test. They compared the amount of overlap between words contained in reading achievement tests and the words presented in five basal reading series. The achievement tests which were examined included the Wide Range Achievement Test (WRAT) (Jastak & Jastak, 1965); the Metropolitan Achievement Test (MAT) (Durost, Bixler, Wrightstone, Prescott, & Balow, 1971); the Slosson Oral Reading Test (SORT) (Slosson, 1963); and the Peabody Individual Achievement Test (PIAT) (Dunn & Markwardt, 1970).

Jenkins and Pany's analysis revealed that grade equivalence scores are substantially biased by the content of the curriculum. Some hypothetical illustrative examples cited by the authors revealed the following:

> A child who has learned the content words of *Keys to Reading* would, by the end of grade two, gain one year and three months according to the PIAT, gain four months in Word Knowledge (MAT), lose two months in Word Analysis (MAT), but gain eight months according to the SORT and the WRAT.
>
> A second grade teacher using SRA might "produce" a child reading at or above grade level by the end of the second grade merely by selecting the *WRAT* or *PIAT* instead of the *MAT*. If dramatic "growth" is desired, s/he could use the SORT and obtain nineteen months gain from the end of first to the end of second grade. (p. 451)

The results of Jenkins and Pany's analysis should serve to make educators leery of making placement decisions or evaluating pupil progress solely on the basis of achievement test results.

The use of achievement tests has come under increasing criticism in recent years. Among the critics are Salvia and Ysseldyke (1978) who summarize their impressions of some achievement tests by saying:

> We cannot understand how any examiner can select a norm-referenced device to aid in placement decisions when the authors of that device do not even describe the normative sample for the test.
>
> We cannot understand how any examiner can use a norm-referenced device as an aid in placement decisions when the test authors present no information regarding reliability—or so little information that a standard error of measurement cannot be computed or when measurement error accounts for more than half of the total variance in test scores.
>
> We cannot understand how an examiner can use a device as an aid in placement decisions when the test authors present either inadequate evidence or no evidence regarding the validity of the measure. (pp. 462-463)

Despite their inadequacies, achievement test results are one of the primary sources of data used to determine a student's eligibility to receive special education services. The result of this reliance upon achievement tests is that a student's daily work in the classroom is de-emphasized and undue importance is placed upon the results of a single test whose items may bear little resemblance to skills taught in the classroom. Many educators have become disenchanted with achievement tests due to their inability to provide accurate and sufficient information to make placement decisions, to plan instructional programs, and to evaluate pupil progress. What is needed is an alternative assessment strategy which will provide educators with data on which to make educational decisions. In Chapters 5 and 6, we will consider an alternative method of assessing and evaluating pupil progress.

Social Behavior

The assessment of social behavior has been problematic for educators. Rating scales represent one method of evaluating behavior. The reader will recall that in order to classify a student as mentally retarded, it must be demonstrated that the student's adaptive behavior is impaired. Several scales have been developed to assess adaptive behavior, among them are: (1) the AAMD Adaptive Behavior Scales (Nihiria, Foster, Shellhaas, & Leland, 1969), (2) the Vineland Social Maturity Scale (Doll, 1964), and (3) the Cain-Levine Social Competency Scale (Cain, Levine, & Elzey, 1963). None of the scales is designed to be administered to the student; rather, the examiner interviews a knowledgeable third person, such as the student's parents, about the behavior of the student being assessed.

Although there has been considerable interest in developing scales to measure adaptive behavior "measurement in this area is only beginning to attain a technical status warranting serious consideration" (Robinson & Robinson, 1976, p. 362). When careful attention is paid to evaluating the social behavior of students referred for special education services, considerable emphasis is placed upon the clinical judgment of the school psychologist.

In some school districts the referring classroom teacher may play a role in assessing a student's social behavior. A teacher may be asked to: (1) note comments concerning the student's behavior on a referral form, (2) indicate the behavioral characteristics of a student using a checklist, or (3) judge the extent to which a student displays various inappropriate behaviors on a scale ranging from "never" to "always." Teacher observations of a student's classroom behavior are sometimes used alone or in combination with the evaluations of other members of a student's assessment team. In some school districts it is common practice for a member of the assessment team (usually a special educator or school psychologist), to directly observe the behavior of the referred student on one or more occasions in the student's classroom. School social workers sometimes conduct home visits to observe the referred student's behavior in that setting.

Summary

In this section the various types of tests which are used to diagnose handicapping conditions and to place students in special education programs have been examined. Both the technical adequacy of specific tests as well as the ability of certain types of tests to provide educators with accurate information on which to base placement decisions have been questioned. The authors believe that the traditional assessment method tends to narrow the evaluation to those aspects of behaviors which are easily measured by currently available tests. Testing is far from an exact science, yet test results weigh heavily in making placement decisions. Oftentimes testing is conducted by specialists outside of the classroom. This practice tends to de-emphasize a student's classroom performance and to limit the teacher's role in the assessment process. In Chapters 5 and 6 we will discuss an alternative assessment strategy which emphasizes the role of the teacher in assessing the academic and social behavior of students within the classroom.

INSTRUCTIONAL PLANNING

There are a variety of tests available which are used to plan instructional programs for students; among them are: achievements tests, diagnostic tests, published informal inventories, and placement tests which accompany some curriculum materials. In addition teachers frequently construct their own assessment tests. It is possible to classify most tests into two general categories—norm-referenced and criterion-referenced. The reader will recall that earlier in this chapter, norm-referenced tests were defined as those which allow one to compare a particular student's score to the scores obtained by a sample of students of the same age or grade. Criterion-referenced tests are those which measure a student's level of mastery in a particular skill area relative to a set standard of performance. Criterion-referenced tests do not allow comparisons between students; rather, they assess whether or not a student can perform certain skills. For our purposes a test will be considered to be criterion-referenced if it contains items which are directly related to a series of instructional objectives and if performance is evaluated in terms of an established criterion or level of mastery. Using these definitions it is possible to classify a test as being either norm-referenced or criterion-referenced, or both, or neither.

In order to evaluate the usefulness of the various types of tests used to plan instructional programs, it is necessary to determine some criteria by which assessments can be evaluated. One way to determine these standards would be to ask a series of questions, including:

1. Does the test provide a direct measure of performance?
2. To what extent does the test measure performance on skills taught in the curriculum used in the classroom?
3. Are a sufficient number of examples included to measure performance on each skill?
4. Is the test timed?
5. Is the test organized in such a manner as to allow a teacher to easily determine specific skills which a student has and has not mastered?
6. How reliably does the test measure a student's performance?
7. Does the test lend itself to analyzing a student's errors?
8. Are there forms which allow a teacher to scan the performance of an entire class in order to form instructional groups?

These standards imply that the most useful information is obtained from assessment devices which: (1) directly measure performance on skills taught in the classroom, (2) contain a sufficient number of items to determine which skills a student has and has not mastered, (3) provide a reliable measure of performance, (4) lend themselves to diagnosing errors, and (5) allow teachers to form instructional groups or to individualize instruction based on the results of the assessment data.

Norm-Referenced Tests

Achievement tests and some diagnostic tests are norm-referenced. These two types of tests differ with respect to: (1) content, (2) number and types of items included, (3) type of repsonse required, and (4) length of time to respond. In general, achievement tests cover a wide range of academic subjects, whereas diagnostic tests focus on a specific academic area such as reading. Achievement tests contain fewer items per skill than diagnostic tests. Achievement tests are timed whereas diagnostic tests usually are not. A multiple-choice type of format is used on achievement tests whereas diagnostic tests allow a free response.

Diagnostic tests provide teachers with more information to plan instructional programs than do achievement tests. According to the criteria mentioned earlier, diagnostic tests are superior to achievement tests because they sample a number of skills in an academic area, are not timed, and allow a student to freely respond to test items. Using the results of a diagnostic test, classroom teachers are better able to pinpoint a student's strengths and weaknesses and to analyze a student's errors.

Despite their inadequacies, achievement tests are often used to place students in curriculum materials. The adequacy of this practice was investigated by Eaton and Lovitt (1972). These authors compared the results of placing children into readers based on the results of the Wide Range Achievement Test (WRAT) (Jastak & Jastak, 1965), the Metropolitan Achievement Test (MAT) (Durost, Bixler, Wrightstone, Prescott, & Balow, 1971), and a curriculum-based assessment (CBA) of the student's oral reading performance in the reader to be used for instruction. The study was conducted with thirteen learning disabled students in two classes over a two-year period. The CBA consisted of measuring individual student's oral reading performance in selected passages over a five-day period in the basal reader used in the classroom. Following the CBA, direct and daily measures of each student's oral reading performance were obtained in the reader in which the student was placed according to the results of the CBA. Lovitt and Eaton's findings showed that the results of the two achievement tests did not agree; the WRAT scores were consistently higher than the MAT. If either the WRAT or the MAT had been used to place children in readers, in almost every case the pupils would have been placed too high, according to the daily measures which showed that the students were unable to read at the higher levels indicated on the achievement tests.

Performance on achievement tests is often variable as Eaton and Lovitt (1972) noted when they analyzed the performance of students on three administrations of certain subtests of the MAT over a period of four weeks. They reported that the student's performance ranged from $-.7$ to $.5$ months on word knowledge and from $-.8$ to $.7$ on word discrimination. Contrary to what one might expect, the student's scores did not reliably increase from the first to the last administration of the test. These discrepancies speak to the reliability of a test. If a test's reliability is low then a teacher cannot be assured that the results of the test represent a student's typical performance.

In summarizing the ability of achievement and diagnostic tests to provide teachers with sufficient information to plan instructional programs, one can say:

1. Behavior is measured only indirectly (Eaton & Lovitt, 1972). For example, the Wide Range Achievement Test measures oral reading of words in isolation. The behavior required in the classroom may well include oral and silent reading in context and will surely stress comprehension.
2. Behavior is measured only infrequently (Eaton & Lovitt, 1972). Rarely are achievement or diagnostic tests given more than once a year.
3. The content of the curriculum used in the classroom may not match the skills assessed on the test (Eaton & Lovitt, 1972; Jenkins & Pany, 1978).
4. Too few items may be presented on an achievement test to assess a student's ability to perform a particular skill.
5. Timed tests may preclude a teacher's ability to determine which skills a student can and cannot perform.
6. It may be difficult to analyze a student's error patterns due to the way the test is organized.
7. While achievement and diagnostic tests often provide forms to record the results of an entire class, scores are reported rather than individual student's performance on skills, thereby making it difficult to form instructional groups based on skills acquired and those which need to be learned.

Criterion-Referenced Tests

Criterion-referenced tests are relatively new and are designed to measure an individual student's strengths and weaknesses in an academic area. As Popham (1978) noted, many tests which are labeled as criterion-referenced tests are so in name only. A good criterion-referenced test, according to Popham, should include: a brief description of the behaviors to be tested (sometimes referred to as objectives), a sample item for each behavior, a series of statements which describe the stimulus materials, and a series of statements which either define the student's response options or explain how responses will be evaluated.

The strength of criterion-referenced tests lies in their ability to sample a number of related skills, thereby making it possible for a teacher to distinguish between skills which have and have not been mastered. Often forms are provided which allow a teacher to group students for instruction according to the skills which they have and have not mastered. Error analysis is facilitated by the sequential design of criterion-referenced tests. For these reasons criterion-referenced tests have several advantages over achievement and diagnostic tests for instructional planning purposes.

Like norm-referenced tests, criterion-referenced tests are also based on some assumptions. According to Prescott (1971) two of these assumptions are: "mastery is a reasonable criterion" and "a definite hierarchy of skills and knowledge exists in any skill or content area" (pp. 350-351). Prescott has rightly questioned the existence of a hierarchial sequence of skills in many academic subjects. It is not possible, based on current knowledge, to conclude for example, that performance is facilitated when students learn vowel sounds in a particular order. Still, students learn their sounds in some order and it is difficult to argue with assessing skills in a logical order from the simplest to the seemingly more complex. Even if skills are assessed in a particular order, teachers are not bound to provide instruction in the same order or to focus instruction on a single skill at one time. As Prescott pointed out, mastery is a reasonable criterion only when it can be shown that mastery is prerequisite to learning other skills. Research evidence is lacking to support this notion. Until this area is investigated, teachers might gain some useful information to plan programs by experimenting with different levels of mastery and varying the order to skills presented while measuring pupil performance on a number of related skills.

Some criterion-referenced tests can provide valuable information to the extent that they: (1) assess generic skills (e.g. letter sounds, blending, or basic computational skills) which have a high probability of being included in the curriculum used in the classroom; and (2) possess a high degree of reliability. Although criterion-referenced tests are more suitable for diagnosing students' academic difficulties than achievement or diagnostic tests, they still have their drawbacks. First the content of the test may not match the content of the curriculum used in the classroom. If the objectives of the test are clearly stated, however, teachers could judge the degree to which the items on the test are reflected in their classroom materials. Second, most criterion-referenced tests are given only once, or at best in a pre/posttest fashion. Some tests do not provide information on test-retest reliability, or the reliability score may be so low that a teacher may either overestimate or underestimate a student's true ability.

In recent years, publishers of curriculum materials have begun to develop their own placement tests. Some of these, like the one accompanying the SRA Mathematics Learning System (Science Research Associates, 1978) are criterion-referenced tests. For this particular series there are both level placement tests and chapter placement tests. A student's score on the level placement test indicates whether or not the student is ready to work at, below, or above grade level. Once the appropriate level is selected, a chapter placement test may be given. A management system is also available which allows teachers to record performance for each student as well as for the entire class.

Criterion-referenced placement tests which accompany curriculum materials are preferred over informal inventories. Often, informal reading inventories such as the Sucher-Allred Placement Inventory specifically recommended that teachers use "graded basal readers other than those intended for regular classroom instruction" (Sucher & Allred, 1973, p. 16). When using such an informal reading inventory one cannot be sure that there is a good match between the items on the inventory and the skills presented in the curriculum used in the classroom.

There are two potential difficulties associated with criterion-referenced tests which accompany curriculum materials. First, too few items may be presented to adequately assess a student's performance. For example the level 4 placement test for the SRA math series (1978) contains sixteen items. The chapter placement tests contain ten to fifteen items per chapter, and may give a better indication of a student's performance than the level placement tests. Second performance on similar skills is not assessed over a period of days. Considering the variability of some student's performance, this practice could lead to incorrect placement decisions. In chapter 5 we will present a method teachers can use to develop their own assessment devices based on the curricula used in their classrooms which will hopefully overcome these difficulties.

SUMMARY

In this chapter the authors have examined the traditional assessment method as it relates to screening, diagnosis and placement, and instructional planning. They have seen that the use of the traditional assessment method governs the aspects of behavior measured; how it is measured; who conducts the assessment; and very often, who is involved in making a decision based on the assessment information.

The traditional assessment method is a test-based approach. We have questioned the ability of norm-referenced tests to provide accurate or sufficient information to make educational decisions. In so doing we have questioned the assumptions underlying the traditional assessment method. Use of this method tends to lock one into selecting a particular kind of test in order to gain information about some aspect of a student's performance. Often assessments are conducted by specialists outside the classroom. This practice tends to de-emphasize a student's daily work in the classroom and often places teachers in the role of consumers rather than contributors to the assessment process. Many teachers find that information provided by norm-referenced tests is not directly relevant to planning instructional programs. Assessment personnel must then attempt to translate the results of tests into educational prescriptions for the classroom teacher. The benefits of this practice can be questioned because tests used in assessment may not measure skills which are taught in the classroom.

Considering that classroom teachers spend more time with students referred for evaluation than do assessment personnel, teachers are in the best position to assess students' academic and social behaviors. The authors contend that teachers can become full partners in the assessment process by systematically assessing the social and academic performance of the students in their classrooms. In Chapters 5 and 6 we will outline a method which teachers can use to assess the performance of their students.

Curriculum-Based Assessment

5

Curriculum-based assessment can be defined as the practice of obtaining direct and frequent measures of a student's performance on a series of sequentially arranged objectives derived from the curriculum used in the classroom. The concept of curriculum-based assessment originated with Eaton and Lovitt (1972) who recommended that teachers place students in readers according to their daily performance in the reading series used in the classroom. The reading-placement inventory developed by Eaton and Lovitt (1972) was later refined by Lovitt and Hansen (1976). While some general suggestions for developing them have been made (Haring, Lovitt, Eaton, & Hansen, 1978) a detailed outline of how to develop and use curriculum-based assessments in regular classrooms is needed to assist teachers in assessing the academic performance of their students.

In this chapter we describe how teachers can develop and use curriculum-based assessments (CBAs) in their classrooms. An overview of the method is provided following the same format as was used to describe the traditional-educational-assessment method in Chapter 4. An outline of the steps one would use to develop a CBA, as well as two sample CBAs, are provided. In a summary section the teacher's role in assessing the academic performance of students referred for special education services is discussed. Guidelines are presented to assist teachers in assessing information collected by others as well as in participating in the academic assessment of students evaluated for special education services.

AN OVERVIEW OF CURRICULUM-BASED ASSESSMENT

Purposes

A CBA can be developed for any academic subject a teacher desires, with separate CBAs developed for each area a teacher wishes to assess. For example one could develop one CBA for reading, another for arithmetic, and a third for spelling. CBAs are usually administered at the beginning of a school year, to determine each student's level of functioning in relation to the skills presented in the curriculum used in the classroom. The results of a CBA can be used to determine which skills each student has and has not mastered. By analyzing the performance of all students in the class on the specific skills assessed on a CBA, a teacher can place students in curriculum materials, form instructional groups, and, when necessary, plan individualized programs.

All or part of a CBA could be given at the beginning of a school year. A teacher could choose to administer part of a CBA at the beginning of the year and then administer other parts just prior to introducing new units. For example a teacher who had developed an arithmetic CBA might assess students' computational skills and wait to assess performance on measurement problems until students master the computational skills required to compute the measurement problems.

CBAs can also be used to measure progress and to determine the extent to which students have maintained their skills. For example a reading CBA could be administered at the beginning of the school year. The results of the CBA could be used to place students in appropriate readers. By periodically readministering the CBA a teacher could monitor pupil progress and restructure instructional groups according to each student's present level of performance.

The results of a CBA also provide useful information concerning the academic performance of students referred for special education. By administering a CBA prior to making a referral, a teacher can provide specific information concerning which skills a student has and has not mastered. By comparing a referred student's performance to others in the class, it is possible to determine the extent to which the referred student's performance differs from the other students'. The results of a CBA can also be used in placement and planning conferences to summarize a student's present levels of academic performance and to identify appropriate goals and objectives.

CBAs serve another function in addition to those mentioned. The results of a CBA can be used to communicate to both students and parents exactly which skills have been acquired and which need to be learned. Teachers who use CBAs often comment that the information is invaluable at parent-teacher conferences.

Assessment Strategy

Curriculum-based assessment is a strategy which enables teachers to measure the performance of an entire class with respect to the skills presented in the curriculum used in the classroom. The assessment process can be conceptualized as a series of steps as shown in Figure 5–1. Once a particular curriculum series is chosen, such as a basal reading or math series, the teacher selects the particular level or text recommended for students in that grade. After carefully analyzing the types and sequence of skills presented in the grade-level text, the teacher develops a CBA. The specific steps one follows in developing a CBA are outlined later in this chapter. The CBA is then administered to the entire class over a period of a few

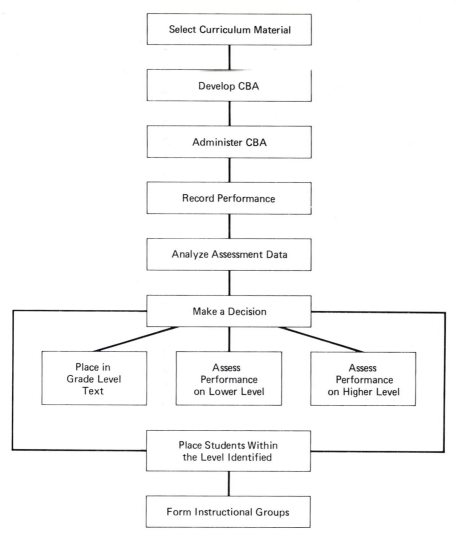

FIGURE 5–1 Curriculum-Based Assessment Method.

days. Performance is measured on more than one occasion to insure that the results represent each student's typical performance.

Following the administration of a CBA, performance is recorded in a way that allows the teacher to scan the performance of the class, noting which skills individual students have and have not mastered. Assessment data for individual pupils is analyzed and a decision is made either to place a student in the grade level text, or to assess performance on a lower or higher level. Once an appropriate level has been determined, an instructional starting point within the chosen level is identified. Instructional groups are then formed consisting of students who are placed at or very near the same point in a particular level.

Once students are placed in an instructional material which is consistent with their level of performance, the main purpose of the CBA has been achieved. For those students who place in the grade-level text or higher, the CBA can be readministered periodically throughout the school year. In so doing, one can monitor progress through the curriculum and check for maintenance of acquired skills. For those students who place in a lower-than-grade-level text, assessment needs to be more continuous. Therefore there are two kinds of assessment. The first is curriculum-based assessment which applies equally well to all students in a class as it is designed to yield data which allows teachers to form instructional groups. The second type of assessment is known as *direct and frequent measurement*. Direct means "the behavior taught is the one measured" (Haring, Lovitt, Eaton, & Hansen, 1978, p. 8). For example, if the desired behavior is to have a student correctly spell words in writing, one would measure a student's ability to write words when they are dictated rather than to circle which out of four words is misspelled. Direct measures are collected daily or at least frequently (Haring, Lovitt, Eaton, and Hansen, 1978). Direct and frequent measurement allows teachers to continuously evaluate student performance throughout the school year. Direct measurement is discussed in detail in Chapter 6.

Types of Measures

It has already been stated that one directly measures performance when assessing students' academic skills using a CBA. Direct measurement can take many forms depending upon the types of skills a teacher wishes to assess. For example in reading, a teacher might ask a student to read graded passages orally and then verbally respond to comprehension questions. The teacher might record: (1) the length of time a student took to read the passage, (2) the types of errors a student made, and (3) the number of comprehension questions a student answered correctly and incorrectly. In arithmetic, a teacher might present a page of all 100 multiplication facts and ask students to write their answers to each problem. The teacher might choose to assess student's accuracy as well as speed. This could be accomplished by: (1) asking the students to compute their problems row by row, (2) timing the class for two minutes, (3) asking them to circle the last problem worked when directed to stop (or collecting the papers), and (4) requiring them to complete any remaining problems after the time period was up. These examples demonstrate that teachers assess performance based on either oral or written responses, depending upon the type of skill to be assessed, and elect to measure accuracy and/or speed of response.

In most instances items contained on a CBA require a free response rather than the selection of the right answer from a series of choices. This practice is in keeping with the notion of direct measurement and facilitates the analysis of a student's errors.

Types of Decisions

The results of a curriculum-based assessment can be used to make a variety of instructional decisions. Specifically, CBA data assists teachers in determining:

1. The specific skills a student has and has not mastered
2. The level at which a student should be placed within the curriculum
3. Progress through the curriculum
4. The extent to which an individual student's performance is discrepant from the average class member.

Thus CBA data allows teachers to plan instructional programs, to monitor progress, and to judge the appropriateness of referring a student for special education. In order for teachers to evaluate the adequacy of making decisions based on the results of a CBA, we must examine the assumptions which underlie this approach.

Assumptions

Curriculum-based assessment is based on the following assumptions:

1. The best measure of a student's ability is obtained by directly measuring the student's performance in the *curriculum used for instruction*.
2. The most accurate indication of a student's ability is obtained by measuring a student's performance on the same skills on two or more occasions.
3. By analyzing a student's performance on a CBA, a teacher can: (1) pinpoint deficit skills, (2) identify error patterns, and (3) place students at an appropriate level in the curriculum.
4. For the majority of students, progress can be evaluated by periodically readministering a CBA throughout the school year. Direct and frequent measurement is needed, however, to guide the instruction of students who evidence learning problems.
5. Teachers can acquire the skills to develop, administer, and interpret the results of CBAs and to use those results to plan instructional programs for students.

In a later section of this chapter, we will present some evidence which supports these assumptions, and discuss a way that teachers can determine whether or not the CBA approach provides them with accurate and sufficient information to make instructional decisions.

DEVELOPING A CBA

A CBA can be developed for any type of curriculum material whether it be published or teacher-made. Curriculum materials may be classified into one of two types. The first type is known as single-strand because it focuses on one primary skill area. Examples of single-strand materials include phonics workbooks and handwriting programs. The second type of curriculum materials are called multi-strand because they emphasize several related skills. For example, basal readers contain several strands, including decoding, comprehension, language usage, and study skills. Similarly, basal math texts stress a variety of strands including computation, word problems, measurement, and money.

While it is easier to develop a CBA for single-strand material, one proceeds in essentially the same manner to develop a CBA for multi-strand material. The only difference is that with multi-strand material, one selects which strand or strands to assess and then assesses each separately. For example in developing a CBA for a basal math series, a teacher might initially develop an assessment just for computational skills. At a later time other strands could be added to the CBA, such as problem solving or measurement. The most important consideration in developing a CBA for multi-strand material is to select *the* most significant strand and then add other strands. This practice is recommended for three reasons:

1. When initially developing a CBA for multi-strand material, it is easy to become overwhelmed by the sheer number of skills presented. Rather than tackle an entire curriculum, one should pare down the task to a manageable size.
2. By focusing on the most critical strand one is assured of obtaining useful information to make instructional decisions. For example in assessing reading one could elect to measure oral and silent reading, comprehension, and the skills presented in the accompanying reading workbook. Rather than assessing skills presented in the workbook, one might elect to measure oral reading in context, and silent and oral reading comprehension, since this information would be the most useful in making decisions regarding placement of students into readers.
3. By proceeding strand by strand, one has the opportunity to develop and then try out the assessment device. The information gained can be of use in the development of subsequent strands a teacher might wish to assess.

The procedure for developing a CBA can be conceptualized as a series of eight steps which begins with an analysis of skills presented in a curriculum and culminates in the development of an assessment device to measure performance on those skills. The steps one would follow in developing a CBA are presented in Figure 5–2. In our discussion we will proceed step-by-step through the development of a CBA. Two sample CBAs are presented. An arithmetic CBA will be presented first, followed by a reading CBA. The reader will note some minor differences between the development of a CBA for an arithmetic and for a reading series. The arithmetic CBA presents the more general case, as the same steps could be used to develop a CBA in the following areas: phonics, spelling, handwriting, grammar. The reading CBA focuses on two particular skills, namely, oral reading in context and comprehension. The slight differences in the development of the two CBAs will be highlighted in the examples.

Step 1: Analyze Skills Presented in Curriculum

Using the level recommended for a particular grade, one first identifies which strand or strands to include on the CBA. Multi-strand materials

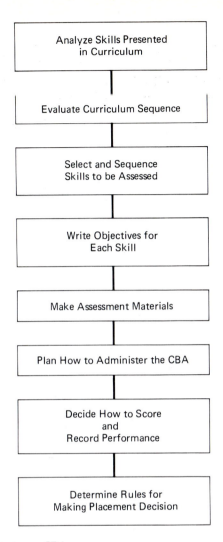

FIGURE 5–2 Developing a CBA.

consist of a half-dozen or so strands. Basal readers include several strands, such as decoding, comprehension, language usage, and study skills. Similarly, arithmetic series contain strands focusing on computation, measurement, and word problems, as well as other related topics.

Each strand consists of several major skill areas. For example, decoding is a strand which can be divided into several major skills such as decoding vowels, consonants, and endings. Similarly, in arithmetic one can identify major skills presented in the computational strand, namely, addition, substraction, multiplication, and division. Each major skill area can be further divided into a set of related skills. Decoding vowels, a major skill area in reading, can be broken down into decoding long *a*, short *u*, long *i*, etc. Similarly addition, which is a major skill in a computational arithmetic strand, can be divided into a number of different skills based on the complexity of the problems.

Once a particular strand has been identified, such as writing words from dictation in a spelling program, one identifies the major skill areas presented in the curriculum for that strand. Scope-and-sequence charts are of some assistance in identifying major skill areas; however, a more in-depth analysis is needed to determine the specific skills included under each major skill area. For example scope-and-sequence charts for spelling series usually list the sound(s) which are stressed in each unit. Thus it would be possible to determine the major skill areas presented from the scope-and-sequence charts. The exact number of words presented for each sound, or the number of words appearing in the unit which do *not* contain the targeted sound(s) would not be apparent from inspecting the scope-and-sequence chart. Although such charts are occasionally helpful, it is often easier to scan each page in the curriculum which is part of the strand one is analyzing.

One proceeds by drawing a form similar to the one shown in Table 5–1. As one flips through each page, one quickly notes whether the material on the page includes work on the strand one is analyzing. If not, one flips to the next page. When items are presented which deal with the strand one is analyzing, one notes the first major skill area by writing it in the left-hand column. Attention is then focused on identifying the specific skill or skills presented on that page. In the second column of the form, shown in Table 5–1, one lists the skill(s) presented on that page in the order in which they appear. Skills are listed directly under one another. If desired, an example of each skill can be written in the third column of the form. In the fourth column one jots down the page number and puts the number of items presented in parentheses.

When one finishes scanning a page, the process is repeated on the next page. If a new major skill area is introduced for the strand one is analyzing, one lists the next major skill on a new page. The end result of this process is a "skeleton" of the skills presented in the curriculum.

Although the process may initially seem complicated, the example for Step 1 should clarify for the reader that the aim is simply to produce an orderly list of the skills presented as they appear in the curriculum.

TABLE 5–1 Sample Analysis of Skills Form
Name of Curriculum Material

Major Skill Areas	Sequence of Skills	Example	Page Number (Number of items)	Total

Example for Step 1: Analyze Skills

Curriculum intended
for instruction:

Level 4 of SRA Mathematics: Learning System Text (DeVault, Frehmeyer, Greenberg, and Bezuszka, 1978)

Strand Selected:

Computational Skills. For the purposes of this example, only the major skill area of addition will be presented.

Procedure:

Prior to beginning the analysis, the following code was adopted to enable the teacher to distinguish one type of addition problem from another:

nn 2-digits-by-1-digit, no renaming, e.g.
$$\begin{array}{r} nn \\ +\,n \\ \hline \end{array} \qquad \begin{array}{r} 37 \\ +\,2 \\ \hline \end{array}$$

nc 2-digits-by-1-digit, renaming in the one's place, e.g.
$$\begin{array}{r} nc \\ +\,n \\ \hline \end{array} \qquad \begin{array}{r} 57 \\ +\,9 \\ \hline \end{array}$$

nno 3-digits-by-1-digit, zero in the addend, e.g.
$$\begin{array}{r} nno \\ +\,n \\ \hline \end{array} \qquad \begin{array}{r} 530 \\ +\,9 \\ \hline \end{array}$$

Beginning with the first page of the teacher's edition, the teacher scanned each page noting the occurrence of addition problems. When the first addition problem was encountered, the teacher coded the problem on a form similar to the one shown in Table 5–2. The teacher then recorded the page number in another column on the form and noted the number of problems of that type which appeared on that particular page. This same procedure was repeated for each new problem type which the teacher encountered as she scanned the pages in the text. Whenever a particular problem type reappeared, the teacher noted the page number and number of problems of that type next to the appropriate skill on the sequence of skills.

After completing the analysis, the teacher counted the total number of problems of each type which appeared in the text and entered that number on the form as shown in Table 5–2. The analysis for addition skills took one and one-half hours to complete.

Step 2: Evaluate the Curriculum Sequence

This step is necessitated by the fact that one bases the assessment on the types and sequence of skills presented in the curriculum selected for instruction. In order to base the assessment on the curriculum, one must be satisfied that the curriculum contains all the major skill areas one wishes to teach and presents skills in a logical sequence. To evaluate the curriculum one inspects the completed analysis of skills.

The analysis of skills can be used for a variety of purposes. First it aids in identifying the skills which should be presented on the CBA. Second it alerts the teacher to the possibility that certain skills are missing, or that they are presented in the wrong order, or that too few examples are pre-

**TABLE 5–2 Analysis of Computational Skills
SRA Mathematics, Level 4**

Major Skill Area	Sequence of Skills	Example	Page Number (Number of Problems)	Total
Addition	n +n	3 +2	p. 22(30)	30
	no +nn	30 +22	p. 23(4), p. 27(6)	10
	nn +nn	32 +22	p. 23(4), p. 27(6), p. 45(1), p. 164(2), p. 315(1)	14
	nc +nn	39 +22	p. 23(4), p. 24(21), p. 27(6), p. 41(2), p. 45(3), p. 315(2)	38
	cc +nn	79 +34	p. 27(20), p. 41(3), p. 45(3), p. 315(1)	27
	nnc +nnn	239 +445	p. 27(7), p. 31(3), p. 32(1), p. 39(1)	12
	ncn +nnn	263 +394	p. 27(8), p. 32(1), p. 39(2), p. 41(1)	12
	noc +nnn	507 +329	p. 27(4), p. 39(1)	5
	nco +nnn	360 +395	p. 27(2), p. 32(1)	3
	ncc +nnn	378 +246	p. 29(1), p. 31(2), p. 32(5), p. 39(3), p. 45(1), p. 165(1)	13
	ccc +nnn	784 +968	p. 29(6), p. 31(2), p. 32(2), p. 188(2), p. 315(1)	13

sented to insure sufficient practice and review. With this knowledge a teacher can make provisions for adapting the curriculum by adding and deleting skills, or by changing their order. Third the analysis reveals which skills are presented on which page. This information makes it easy to place children in instructional materials and to provide practice on particular skills.

With a completed analysis of skills in hand, a teacher can ask the following types of evaluative questions:

1. Are all important major skill areas included?
2. Does the order of major skill areas coincide with the order in which they will be taught?
3. Are all important skills covered under each major skill area?
4. Does the sequence of skills presented match the order in which each will be taught?

5. Are there an adequate number of tasks presented for each skill?
6. Do skills reappear throughout the curriculum to insure sufficient practice?

The answers to some of these questions have implications for instruction as well as for assessment. For example if a major skill area is not included in the curriculum, then supplementary materials would have to be used. Naturally one would assess performance on that major skill area based on the series of skills presented in the supplementary material. Fortunately this rarely occurs as most curriculum materials address the major skill areas one wishes to teach. Other problems are more common, such as: the order of major skill areas presented may not match the instructional sequence, or certain skills may be missing or appear out of order. If the order of major skill areas or skills presented does not coincide with the teacher's intended instructional sequence, then one must change the order in which they will be assessed to match the instructional sequence. If certain skills are missing then one must identify those skills and include them on the assessment. For example an analysis of a phonic workbook revealed that regular *-ing* endings were never presented, even though adding *-ing* endings to words which required doubling consonants was included. In that case, the teacher inserted regular *-ing* endings on her analysis-of-skills form to remind her to assess that skill and to provide supplementary materials to teach that skill.

As a teacher scans the analysis-of-skills form, it becomes obvious if too few tasks are presented when a skill is introduced or if they fail to appear often enough to insure sufficient practice. While neither of these outcomes has important implications for assessment, they should prompt teachers either to reevaluate their decision to use that particular curriculum or to be prepared to use supplementary materials to provide for sufficient practice.

Example for Step 2: Evaluate Curriculum Sequence

The complete analysis of addition skills presented in *Level 4 of SRA Mathematics* revealed the following:

1. In total, 92 different types of addition problems were presented.
2. The total number of problems per type varied from 1 to 38. For example, only one problem of the type $\begin{array}{r} noo \\ +noo \end{array}$ or $\begin{array}{r} 200 \\ +300 \end{array}$ appeared, whereas 38 problems of the type $\begin{array}{r} nc \\ +nn \end{array}$ or $\begin{array}{r} 37 \\ +29 \end{array}$ appeared.
3. Some skills appeared to be out of order. For example, several types of problems requiring renaming were presented prior to the introduction of other problem types which did not require renaming.

This particular series included a Level Placement Test and a Chapter Placement Test. These tests were evaluated to determine the extent to which they assessed the addition skills presented in the curriculum. The

Level Placement Test included one addition problem and the Chapter Placement Test included a total of nine addition problems, all of which required renaming. Due to the fact that neither test assessed a representative sample of the addition skills presented in the curriculum, the teacher decided not to adapt the test but to develop her own assessment.

Step 3: Select and Sequence Skills to be Assessed

Once a teacher has evaluated the sequence of skills presented in the curriculum it is time to select those skills which will be assessed on the CBA. In order to determine the number and types of skills to assess under each major skill area, one must consider the results of the evaluation completed in Step 2. For example, the analysis of addition skills presented in our example revealed that ninety-two different types of addition problems were presented which ranged in difficulty from basic facts to 4-digit-by-3-digit column-addition problems requiring renaming.

With respect to our example, one might ask, "How many addition skills must I measure to determine if a student has mastered addition?" Certainly if a student computed two addition facts correctly, one would not be convinced that the student had mastered addition facts; too few items were included to properly assess performance. One would want to sample that particular behavior more widely before concluding that the student really had mastered addition facts. While one might want to sample all addition facts, one must restrict the sampling of more complex skills. Instead of presenting several problems of each of the ninety-two problem types contained in the series, one should select representative types of problems such as those which do and do not require renaming. For example a teacher might assess performance on five types of problems of varying difficulty which do not require renaming and five types of problems which do.

Once the skills have been identified, the next step is to sequence the skills in some order. If the assessment sequence parallels the instructional sequence it is much easier to identify the point at which a student fails to perform a skill. Also if skills are grouped together on the assessment device, it is easier to analyze error patterns.

Step 3 is directly concerned with sequencing skills; yet, in reality, there are limited data to suggest that one sequence is preferable to another. We simply do not know, for example, if long *a* should be taught before long *i*, or whether it even makes a difference. Even though empirically derived sequences of instruction are lacking, sequencing makes sense for several reasons. First some skills require knowledge of a number of other skills. For example to divide, a student must be able to subtract and multiply. Second some materials are arranged in order of difficulty. We may not know whether it is better to group certain cursive letters for instruction based on beginning stroke, or to teach isolated letters in random order. Yet teachers would agree that instruction on isolated letters should precede instruction on whole words. Similarly if a child could not write a single cursive letter, we wouldn't expect the student to produce cursive letters in connected writing. Therefore, production of isolated letters would be assessed prior to assessing production of whole words. Third skills are always taught in some sequence whether the sequence is based on logic or happenstance. Why not apply logic to test our notions about sequencing and then base our decisions on pupil performance?

Example for Step 3: Select and Sequence Skills to be Assessed

For the purpose of our arithmetic example, the sequence of addition skills to be assessed on the CBA is shown in Table 5–3.

Step 4: Write Objectives for Each Skill to be Assessed

Once a teacher has identified and sequenced the skills to be assessed, behavioral objectives are written for each skill. A precise behavioral objective specifies the *conditions* under which a student will perform an *observable behavior* and also states the *criteria* by which performance will be evaluated.

Conditions specify what the student will or will not be given as he performs the behavior identified in the objective. Common condition statements include: "Given a worksheet containing *x* number of *x* types of problems." "Given a 200-word passage on the 3.2 level." "Given *x* number of words dictated by the teacher."

Every objective must also include an observable behavior to allow a teacher to accurately assess performance. Verbs used to describe behavior should be both observable and precise. For that reason verbs such as understand, believe, appreciate, know how, realize, or listen are *not* appropriate. Verbs such as write, point, or say are appropriate because they describe the behavior which a student must perform in observable and precise terms.

A behavioral objective must also contain a standard or criterion which specifies the minimal level a student must achieve to be considered as having mastered a particular behavior or skill. Research has been less than helpful in assisting teachers in selecting criterion levels. We simply do not know what level of mastery a student should attain on a skill or what effect a certain level of mastery has on a student's ability to maintain or generalize his newly acquired skill. Similarly we do not know at what level a student should perform to make functional use of his skills. For example how fast should a student be able to compute multiplication facts? Or, at what rate can a student be considered to be a proficient reader? If we knew that attaining certain levels allowed students to make functional use of their skills, we could use those levels as criteria. Unfortunately we don't have these kinds of information and we must rely on other means to set criterion levels. Ways of identifying criterion levels include:

1. Assess the performance of several students and identify those who are doing well in a particular academic area. Their performance on lower-

TABLE 5–3 Addition Skills to Assess on CBA SRA Mathematics, Level 4

Major Skill Area	Sequence of Skills	Code	Example
Addition	Facts	n +n	3 +2
	No renaming	nn +n	32 +2
		nnn +n	424 +3
		nn +nn	52 +21
		nnn +nn	324 +25
		nnn +nnn	324 +123
		nn nn +nn	24 32 +13
		nnn nnn nnn +nnn	121 213 312 +132
	Renaming in one's only	nc +n	59 +7
		nnc +n	328 +9
		nc +nn	39 +22
		nnc +nn	328 +47
		nnc +nnn	349 +129

level skills can then be compared to their performance on higher-level skills, and some judgment can be made as to the level which should be attained to insure continued progress on later skills.

2. Vary the criteria for a number of students going through the same sequence and see if it makes any difference in terms of number of skills acquired, proficiency level attained, and the extent to which students were able to generalize and maintain their skills.

TABLE 5–3 (*Continued*)

95
*Developing
a CBA*

Major Skill Area	Sequence of Skills	Code	Example
Addition	Renaming in ten's only	c n + nn	82 + 91
		ncn + nn	382 + 93
		ncn + nnn	592 + 284
	Renaming in hundred's only	cnn + nnn	923 + 735
	Renaming in one's and ten's	c c + nn	89 + 76
		nc c + nn	396 + 84
		ncc + nnn	398 + 245
	Renaming in one's and hundred's	cnc + nnn	937 + 428
	Renaming in ten's and hundred's	ccn + nnn	843 + 791
	Renaming in one's, ten's, and hundred's	ccc + nnn	897 + 465
	Column addition with renaming	c c nn + nn	59 32 + 44
		ccc nnn nnn + nnn	324 578 132 + 187

3. Make use of research which suggests minimal levels of performance. For example, Starlin (1970) suggested that students should be able to read between 80 and 100 words per minute correctly with no more than three errors at 90 percent comprehension to be considered proficient readers.

One of the most important considerations in selecting a criterion is to choose one which matches the behavior to be demonstrated. When assessing a student's accuracy on a skill the criterion may be stated using percent, such as: "Given a worksheet containing 100 multiplication facts, the student will correctly write answers to 90 percent of the problems." If one wishes to assess speed as well as accuracy, the objective would be stated as "Given a worksheet containing 100 multiplication facts, the student will write answers at the rate of 50 per minute with no more than 5 errors per minute."

Example for Step 4: Write Objectives

When writing objectives, it is not necessary to state them in sentence form. The assessment objectives for the arithmetic CBA were stated quite briefly, as shown in Table 5–4. All that was necessary was to state the conditions, behavior, and criteria next to each skill to be assessed. As the reader can see by looking at Table 5–4, needless duplication was avoided in specifying the components of each objective as the skills were all to be measured and evaluated in a similar manner.

Step 5: Make Assessment Materials

Once the objectives have been written, it is time to develop the materials to be used. By looking at the condition statement in each objective, one can readily determine the type of material needed to assess performance. For a given objective, one might develop worksheets which present the skills to be measured on the CBA. If oral reading and comprehension are to be assessed, one might xerox and/or type selected passages from the curriculum and write comprehension questions. If spelling is to be assessed, one might tape record lists of spelling words.

In order to assess performance over a period of a few days, it is necessary to develop a set of materials which measure the same skills, using slightly different items each day. For example in assessing addition skills, one would not present exactly the same problems each day (with the exception of addition facts). Rather one would present the same types of problems each day, such as 46 but vary the numbers presented to include
                                       +9
36 and other problems of the same type. Similarly when assessing oral
+8
reading, one would not ask a student to read the same passage three times, but rather three separate passages of equal difficulty.

Example for Step 5: Make Assessment Materials

Continuing with our arithmetic example, one might develop worksheets containing all 100 addition facts. By arranging the problems in a different order, the teacher could develop three sheets of 100 addition facts. To assess performance on the more complex problem types, the teacher might develop worksheets such as the one shown in Figure 5–3. In order to assess students' abilities over a three-day period, the teacher would generate three sets of similar forms including each problem type to be presented on the assessment.

TABLE 5–4 Addition Objectives to Assess on CBA
SRA Mathematics, Level 4

Major Skill Area	Sequence of Skills	Code	Example	Condition	Behavior	Criteria
					Objectives	
Addition	Facts	n +n	3 +2	Given 100 problems in mixed order	Write answers	90% correct for 2 out of 3 days
	No renaming	nn +n	32 +2	Given 5 problems	"	80% correct for 2 out 3 days
		nnn +n	424 +3	"	"	"
		nn +nn	52 +21	"	"	"
		nnn +nn	324 +25	"	"	"
		nnn +nnn	324 +123	"	"	"
		nn nn +nn	24 32 +13	"	"	"
		nnn nnn nnn +nnn	121 213 312 +132	"	"	"
	Renaming in one's only	nc +n	59 +7	"	"	"
		nnc +n	328 +9	"	"	"
		nc +nn	39 +22	"	"	"
		nnc +nn	328 +47	"	"	"
		nnc +nnn	349 +129	"	"	"
	Renaming in ten's only	cn +nn	82 +91	"	"	"
		ncn +nn	382 +93	"	"	"
		ncn +nnn	592 +284	"	"	"

TABLE 5–4 (*Continued*)

Major Skill Area	Sequence of Skills	Code	Example	Condition	Behavior	Criteria
					Objectives	
Addition			Given 5 problems	"	80% correct for 2 out 3 days	
	Renaming in hundred's only	cnn +nnn	923 +735	"	"	"
	Renaming in one's and ten's	cc +nn	89 +76	"	"	"
		ncc +nn	396 +84	"	"	"
		ncc +nnn	398 +245	"	"	"
	Renaming in one's and hundred's	cnc +nnn	937 +428	"	"	"
	Renaming in ten's and hundred's	ccn +nnn	843 +791	"	"	"
	Renaming in one's, ten's, and hundred's	ccc +nnn	897 +465	"	"	"
	Column addition with renaming	cc nn +nn	59 32 +44	"	"	"
		ccc nnn nnn +nnn	324 578 132 +187	"	"	"

Step 6: Plan How to Administer the CBA

One of the most common misconceptions concerning assessment is that it is too time consuming to be done in regular classrooms. By using some ingenuity assessment such as that described in this chapter is possible. While some students are completing an arithmetic assessment at their desks, others can be working on a spelling assessment with the aid of a tape recorder. The aim should be to design CBAs as teacher-free as possible. The overriding question in determining how to administer a CBA should be "What is the easiest way to collect the information I want?" Many assessments can be given to large groups of students, for example, penmanship, arithmetic, spelling, silent reading, and comprehension. Other assessments, such as oral reading, can be conducted with small groups of students by moving around the group and listening to one student read a section of a story at a time. Relatively few assessments require a teacher's undivided attention in a one-to-one situation.

Time should be taken to plan the logistics of conducting a CBA. Some of the decisions which need to be made include:

1. Over how many days will the assessment be given?
2. How much time per day will be devoted to assessment?
3. What directions will be given to the students?
4. Will all or part of the assessment be timed?
5. How will the assessment materials be presented—by the teacher, on paper, tape recorded, or by a peer or aide?

Once these decisions have been made, the teacher should have a clear idea of how much time assessment will take and the manner in which it will be conducted. Then plans can be made to schedule the assessment into the day's activities at the beginning of the school year, and at other times throughout the school year when it becomes necessary to place students into instructional groups.

Example for Step 6: Plan How to Administer the CBA

In our arithmetic example, it was decided that performance is assessed over a three-day period. On the first day the student is presented with a worksheet containing 100 addition facts. The following directions are given.

1. "This is *not* a test. I just want to see which problems you can and cannot do so I can tell what you need to learn and what you already know how to do."
2. "Please do these problems row by row."
3. "Work as fast, but as accurately as you can."
4. "Begin when I say 'start working' and stop when I call 'time'."
5. "After I call 'time,' circle the last problem you completed, then finish the problems on the page."

After the students complete the facts, each student is given a set of complex addition problems like the ones shown in Figure 5–3. As the students complete the pages, the teacher moves among them and notes whether students rely on their fingers to find the answers or use incorrect procedures, such as starting on the left side of a problem. After twenty minutes the teacher collects completed sets of worksheets and encourages

Addition: Set 1a

Name _____

Date _____

nn +n	21 +4	34 +2	67 +2	85 +3	60 +6

nnn +n	567 +2	485 +3	943 +2	304 +3	422 +6

nn +nn	23 +34	70 +22	42 +54	11 +23	45 +32

nnn +nn	302 +24	531 +12	712 +17	622 +12	411 +13

nnn +nnn	532 +264	336 +261	440 +323	354 +431	802 +134

FIGURE 5–3 Addition Worksheet

those who have not finished to work a few problems in their spare moments throughout the day.

Step 7: Plan How to Score and Record Performance

In order to evaluate performance, one must be able to distinguish between correct and incorrect responses. For example when assessing oral reading, one has to decide whether to count only mispronunciations as errors, or to include omissions, additions, and hesitations as well.

Student performance can be recorded on a raw data sheet. The aim should be to develop a sheet which contains all the information needed to determine which students met the criterion level specified for each objective assessed on the CBA.

Example for Step 7: Plan How to Score and Record Performance

For the purposes of our example, students' responses to addition problems were defined as follows:

> Correct—an answer written under a problem which corresponds exactly to the number one would derive from the computation presented in the problem.
>
> Incorrect—a written answer which does not match the correct answer, or one which is illegible.
>
> No attempt—no answer written under the problem.

Each day during the assessment period, the teacher collects the students' answers to the addition fact problems. The teacher counts the total number of problems each student solved correctly and incorrectly, and enters that information on the raw data sheet as shown in Figure 5–4. In order to determine each student's computational speed, the teacher counts the number of problems computed correctly and incorrectly (including only those problems computed in the two-minute period as indicated by the circled problem on a student's page). The total number of correctly and incorrectly computed problems is divided by two (minutes) to obtain each student's correct and incorrect rate per minute. Each student's data is entered on the raw data sheet as shown in Figure 5–5.

Each student's answers to the more complex types of addition problems is recorded under the appropriate box on the raw data sheet as shown in Figure 5–4. The number of correct, incorrect, and not-attempted problems is recorded as follows: 3(correct) /2(incorrect) /1(no attempt).

Step 8: Determine Rules for Making Placement Decisions

As experienced teachers know, there are no steadfast rules for making placement decisions. Some teachers place students in readers based on a word accuracy score of 90 percent or more, and a comprehension score of at least 80 percent. Other teachers prefer to place students in slightly more difficult materials. There is very little empirical data to guide teachers in determining where to place students in curriculum materials based on performance. Still some decision must be made before instruction can begin.

Placement-decision rules can be based on the extent to which a student meets the criterion specified for each objective assessed on the CBA. Since CBAs assess skills in a sequence from least to most complex, a general decision rule might be as follows:

> Instruction will focus on the lowest level objective or skill on which the student fails to meet the established criterion level on two out of three days.

Example for Step 8: Determine Rules for Making Placement Decisions

For the purpose of our addition example, the following rules were developed:

1. A student has acquired the ability to compute addition facts if on two out of three days the student correctly answers 90 percent of the problems presented. Students who score less than 90 percent correct will receive instruction on addition facts.

2. A student is proficient in computing addition facts if on two out of three days the student's rate equals or exceeds fifty problems per minute with four or fewer errors per minute. Students who do not meet these rates will receive instruction to improve their speed on computing answers to addition facts.

3. Each addition skill on which a student scores four out of five correct on

Student	Date	Facts				No Renaming							Renaming				
		n +n				nn +n	nnn +n	nn +nn	nnn +nn	nnn +nnn	nn nn +nn	nnn nnn +nnn	nc +n	nnc +n	nc +nn	nnc +nn	nnc +nnn
		#C	#I	CR	IR												
Susan	9/1	96	4	48	2	5/0/0	4/1/0	5/0/0	4/0/1	5/0/0	5/0/0	5/0/0	0/5/0	0/5/0	0/5/0	0/4/1	0/5/0

FIGURE 5–4 Addition Raw Data Sheet.

two out of three days will be considered to be mastered. Those students whose accuracy on addition facts is at least 90 percent but who fail to meet criterion on one or more of the complex skills will begin instruction on the lowest-level skill on which they fail to meet the criterion.

Using these decision rules the teacher examines the class raw data sheet and circles those students' scores which did not meet criteria. In that way the teacher can see at a glance exactly which students have and have not mastered the skills assessed on the CBA. This information can be used to group students according to those who need to work on improving their accuracy on facts, those who need to increase their speed, and those experiencing difficulties with the more complex types of addition problems.

SAMPLE READING CBA

Now that the reader is familiar with the basic steps for developing a CBA, a sample reading CBA will be presented. There are some differences between developing an oral-reading CBA versus developing a CBA in arithmetic. The reason is that an oral-reading CBA focuses on two strands—reading in context and comprehension. Rather than analyzing each decoding skill in the curriculum, one selects passages of varying levels of difficulty. Similarly rather than analyzing each type of comprehension skill presented, one selects certain types of comprehension skills to assess. Comprehension questions are then extracted from those following the selected passages, or are written to assess the desired types of comprehension skills.

In many ways the sample reading CBA is similar to published informal reading inventories. There are some important differences between the two methods. First some informal reading inventories (IRIs), such as the Sucher-Allred (1973), specifically recommend that students read from *other than* the basal text which will be used for instruction. In direct contrast the CBA approach requires one to measure performance in the curriculum to be used for instruction. In this way possible mismatches in difficulty or style between the assessment passages and the stories in the curriculum are avoided. Second most IRIs are designed to be individually administered. Many teachers find it difficult to do a thorough assessment of each student's oral reading at the beginning of a year. Those that do so may collect one sample of a student's performance in a few levels, and then monitor progress closely for the first few weeks. With the CBA approach it is possible to measure the oral-reading performance of small groups of students at one time. Third, most IRIs are administered on one occasion. Oral-reading CBAs are given over a period of a few days to insure that the results reflect a student's typical performance.

The sample is based on an oral-reading CBA originally described by Lovitt and Hansen (1976). Their CBA has been adapted to allow teachers to assess the performance of small groups of students. Although the CBA is based on a particular reader, the procedures would apply equally well to any basal reading series.

Example for Step 1: Analyze Skills

The CBA is based on *The New Macmillan Reading Program, Series r* (Smith & Wardhaugh, 1975). This CBA was developed to assess oral reading and comprehension at the third-grade level, therefore examples will refer to Levels 15–18.

As the series is comprised of levels of graduated difficulty, a formal analysis of skills was not necessary. With respect to comprehension, the teacher's editions for Levels 15–16 (Douglas, 1975) and Levels 17–18 (Maccarone, 1975) of *The New Macmillan Reading Program, Series r* include seventeen types of comprehension questions. Each story is followed by a series of one or more types of comprehension questions. The types of questions vary from story to story. In order to be consistent in the type of questions asked, only recall and interpretation questions were selected. The questions following each story served as a resource for writing comprehension questions to accompany each passage included on the CBA.

Example for Step 2: Evaluate Curriculum Sequence

The most appropriate way to evaluate the curriculum sequence was to verify the readability levels of a sample of the passages selected using the Fry (1977) readability formula. The passages when arranged in order of difficulty corresponded to Levels 15–18 of the reading series.

Example for Steps 3 and 4: Select and Sequence Skills to be Assessed; Write Objectives

The sequence of oral reading and comprehension skills as well as the assessment objectives are shown in Table 5–5.

Example for Step 5: Make Assessment Materials

The assessment materials consist of the following: (1) the student's texts from Levels 15–18 of *The New Macmillan Reading Program, Series r*, (2) a series of typed 100-word passages selected from the beginning, middle, and end of three stories at each level, and (3) a set of six typed comprehension questions to accompany each 100-word passage.

Within each level, three stories are selected which contain at least 500 words. The first 500 words in each story is marked off in 100-word segments. If the hundredth word does not appear at the end of a sentence, a slash is placed at the end of every hundredth word and a bracket is placed at the end of the sentence containing the hundredth word. This system allows a teacher to take data on five students reading 100-word passages in succession without asking a student to stop in the middle of a sentence.

Each 100-word passage from one of the 500-word stories is typed on a separate ditto page. Six comprehension questions are developed for each 100-word passage and typed underneath each passage as shown in Figure 5–5. This procedure enables a teacher to follow along as each student reads and to record each student's errors.

Example for Step 6: Plan How to Administer the CBA

On Day 1, the teacher places students into groups of five students using any performance indicators, such as school records, which are available. The teacher calls the first group of five students to the reading corner and explains the purpose of the assessment. The students are told the following: (1) they will be asked to orally read a short passage, (2) they should read as accurately and as fast as they can, (3) they should stop reading when asked to do so, and (4) they will be asked questions on the passage right after they read it. The teacher begins to assess the student's reading at grade level, which in this case is Level 15. The teacher directs the students to open their texts to the first story contained on the assessment.

TABLE 5–5 Assessment Objectives
The New Macmillan Reading Program, Series r, **Level 15–18**

Major Skill Area	Sequence of Skills	Condition	Evaluation Behavior	Criteria
Oral reading in context	Orally read passages Level 15	Given 3 100-word passages	Orally read	45–60 words correct per minute, 8 or fewer errors per minute
	Level 16	"	"	"
	Level 17	"	"	"
	Level 18	"	"	"
Comprehension	Answer recall and interpretation questions accompanying passages Level 15	Given 3 recall and 3 interpretation questions read orally by the teacher following each 100-word passage	Say answer	At least 3 out of 6 correct
	Level 16	"	"	"
	Level 17	"	"	"
	Level 18	"	"	"

Each student in turn reads a 100-word passage and responds to the accompanying comprehension questions. As each student reads, the teacher notes the following information on the ditto copy of the passage: (1) the student's name, (2) the date, (3) the time taken to read the passage, (4) the types of errors made, and (5) the student's answers to comprehension questions.

Depending upon the time a teacher wishes to devote to assessment per day, each group of students can read one or two passages at the level being assessed. This same procedure is repeated with the remaining groups of students until each student has read three passages in the beginning-grade-level reader. After the teacher has scored and recorded each student's performance on the first three passages, a decision is made to either assess a student's reading on the next lower or next higher level depending upon performance.

Student's Name _____

Date _____

The New MacMillan Reading Program
Level 15, p. 24
Passage 1 (words 1–100)

The Aquanauts

The astronaut flies far away from earth to explore space, the moon, and —maybe someday—other worlds. The aquanaut goes to the floor of the sea to explore places just as wonderful and strange as the astronaut's.

You may have seen some of the beautiful fish that swim in the ocean. If you were an aquanaut, you could go far under water and stay there long enough to see many unusual creatures. You would find things you never even dreamed of.

The only way you can stay under water for more than a short time is by using special gear/—the kind of gear used by aquanauts.]

No. Correct _____

No. Incorrect _____

Time _____

Correct Rate _____

Incorrect Rate _____

1. Where does an aquanaut explore?

2. What does an aquanaut see when he explores?

3. What does an aquanaut need in order to stay under water for a long time?

4. Why does an aquanaut need special gear to stay under the water for a long time?

5. Why would an aquanaut want to explore the sea?

6. Why would an aquanaut want to stay under water for a long time?

FIGURE 5–5 Sample Passage.

Example for Step 7: Plan How to Score and Record
Performance Scoring and Recording Procedure

107

Sample
Reading
CBA

As each student reads, the teacher records errors on the ditto copy of the passage. The following marking system suggested by Hansen and Eaton (1978, p. 53) is used to record errors.

Omission	Circle word omitted
Insertion	Write the word above the line where insertion occurred
Mispronunciation or Substitution	Write the observed word above the correct word
Hesitation of +4 seconds	Write 'H' above word
Don't Know	Write 'DK' above word

In Hansen and Eaton's system "don't know" meant that a student *said* he didn't know how to say a particular word. The teacher supplied the word if a student hesitated or said he didn't know the word. Also, in their system, errors on proper names or places, repetitions, and self-corrections were not counted as errors.

Performance is recorded on a raw data sheet similar to the one shown in Figure 5–6. If desired, a separate form could be used to record each

The New Macmillan Reader, Series r, Level _____

Student	Date	Passage Number	Oral Reading						Comprehension				Percent Correct
			Number of Words		Time	Rate		Recall		Interp.			
			C	I		CR	IR	C	I	C	I		
Average													
Average													
Average													
Average													

FIGURE 5–6 Raw Data Sheet. ORAL Reading and Comprehension.

student's performance at the various levels assessed. Following each day's assessment, the teacher enters the following information onto the raw data sheet: date, passage number, number of words read correctly and incorrectly, time taken to read the passage, number of recall and interpretation questions answered correctly and incorrectly, and percent of comprehension questions answered correctly. Using the following formulas, the teacher computes each student's correct and incorrect reading rates.

$$\text{Correct Rate} = \frac{\text{Number of words read correctly}}{\text{Total number of seconds}} \times 60$$

$$\text{Example: } \frac{83 \text{ (correct words)}}{105 \text{ (total seconds)}} \times 60 = 47.4 \text{ wpm correct}$$

$$\text{Incorrect Rate} = \frac{\text{Number of words read incorrectly}}{\text{Total number of seconds}} \times 60$$

$$\text{Example: } \frac{17 \text{ (incorrect words)}}{105 \text{ (total seconds)}} \times 60 = 9.7 \text{ wpm incorrect}$$

After each student has had the opportunity to read three passages from the beginning-grade-level reader, the student's average correct and incorrect reading rates and percent correct comprehension scores would be computed and entered on the raw data sheet.

Example for Step 8: Make Placement-Decision Rules

The teacher inspects each student's average rates and comprehension scores, and determines which students should be assessed on a higher or lower level. The placement-decision rule recommended by Hansen and Eaton (1978) consisted of placing a student in the highest level reader in which the student's average oral-reading rates ranged from 45 to 60 wpm correct, 8 or fewer wpm incorrect, and average comprehension scores ranged from 50 to 75 percent correct. If upon inspection a student's performance exceeded the specified range on all three measures, the teacher assesses the student's performance on the next higher level. If, on the other hand, a student's performance falls below the criterion level, the teacher assesses the student's performance on the next lower level. The assessment and evaluation process continues until each student had been placed in a reader according to the previously described decision rules.

SUMMARY

Curriculum-based assessment is one alternative which teachers can use to measure the academic performance of their students. The intent of curriculum-based assessment is not to compare one student's performance to another, but to determine each student's level of functioning in relation to what needs to be learned. Very often what needs to be learned is determined by the skills presented in the textbooks used in the classroom. The skills presented in those published curricula provide a natural source of assessment information. CBAs are really nothing more than a systematic method of assessing skills which are presented in the curriculum materials used in the classroom.

In this chapter we have described how teachers can develop CBAs. A step-by-step outline of how to proceed has been provided and two sample CBAs were presented. To be sure the assessment method described in this chapter takes time. Time is needed to analyze skills contained in the curriculum; to plan how to administer, score and record performance; and to make the assessment materials. Many teachers have found ways to develop CBAs without spending an inordinate amount of time. For example teachers using the same level of a curriculum have worked together to analyze the skills presented in their materials. Other teachers have enlisted the aid of student teachers in analyzing and sequencing skills. Sometimes groups of teachers have worked together to produce a CBA for several levels of the same curriculum.

When initially developing a CBA it is best to pare the task down to a manageable size. Rather than trying to assess performance on all strands contained in a material, for example in a sixth-grade math series, one might begin by targeting a specific area such as fractions. At a later time other strands could be analyzed and included on the CBA.

Once a teacher, or a group of teachers, has developed a CBA it can be used for as long as the curriculum is in use in the classroom. Thus a CBA can be used in succeeding years to assess the performance of new classes of students. Teachers who have developed CBAs find that the advantages far outweight the disadvantages in that they are provided with the kind of information which is helpful in planning instructional programs.

The CBA approach avoids many of the pitfalls associated with traditional educational assessments. First the skills assessed on a CBA are selected from the skills contained in the curriculum used in the classroom. Hence there is no possibility for a mismatch to occur between skills tested and what is taught in the classroom. Second assessment is conducted over a period of a few days rather than on one occasion as is the case with standardized tests. Therefore there is a greater chance that results on a CBA will indicate a student's typical performance. Hence one should be able to make better instructional decisions based on the results of a CBA than on a standardized test. Third CBAs are administered by classroom teachers to their students. In so doing the teacher has the opportunity to both ask and answer his/her own questions concerning student performance. The teacher can then make decisions regarding each student's performance and tailor instruction to meet the needs of each student by grouping students together for instruction, or planning individualized programs when necessary.

In the event that a teacher desires to refer a student for evaluation for special education services, the teacher can use the CBA data as a basis for the referral. The position of the authors is that classroom teachers can and should become active participants in the assessment process of students referred for special education services. No other member of a student's evaluation team has more opportunity than does a classroom teacher to observe and assess a student's performance. In order to become an active participant, it is necessary for classroom teachers to collect assessment information and to interpret the assessment information of others. The following guidelines are suggested:

1. Describe the behavior of a referred student in observable terms.
2. Observe and record the occurrence of a student's behavior problems prior to making a referral (except in extreme cases where the student could physically harm himself or others). Use the data you have collected as the basis for your referral. Specific methods for collecting social behavior data will be explained in Chapter 6.
3. Using the results of your CBA, review the student's progress to date in academic subjects and summarize his/her performance in areas of concern on the referral form.
4. Continue to obtain measures of the student's social and academic behaviors in the interim period between making a referral and the placement and planning conference.
5. Summarize the CBA data and social behavior observations in writing to use as a guide during the conference and for inclusion in the student's evaluation report.
6. Request that a member of the student's evaluation team (school psychologist or special educator) supply the names of the tests to be given and inform you of other procedures which will be used to evaluate the student. Inform the team of your efforts and work cooperatively with them. Request that a member of the student's team observe the referred student's behavior in the classroom on more than one occasion.
7. Examine the tests to be used by obtaining sample tests from a member of the evaluation team. Familiarize yourself with the items contained on the tests and read reviews of the tests in *Mental Measurement Yearbooks* (Buros, 1972) or in texts such as *Assessment in Special and Remedial Education* (Salvia & Ysseldyke, 1978)
8. Arrange with a member of the student's evaluation team to examine the referred student's completed test protocols. Determine the extent to which the test taps those skills that have been taught in the classroom. Analyze the student's performance on the tests with the results of your CBA and the student's daily work.
9. Express an interest in attending the student's placement and planning conference. During the meeting listen attentively to others and present the information you have collected. Do not hesitate to ask other evaluators to support their opinions with data or to elaborate on the educational implications of their findings.
10. At the placement and planning conference, summarize the student's present levels of performance based on the results of your CBA data and observations of the student's classroom behavior. State clearly the type of special education service you are requesting and use your data to support your request.

SECTION 3

Collecting and Using Student Performance Data

Observing and Measuring Behavior in the Classroom 6

Teachers are confronted with many different types of learning and behavior problems. One student may be frequently out of his/her seat. Another may flit from one activity to another. A third may be chronically late for class. Still another may fail to complete assignments. All of these behavior problems interfere with teaching and learning. Some students also evidence academic difficulties. One student may read very slowly. Another may have poor comprehension. Still another may frequently substitute words while reading. The presence of such academic difficulties provide continual challenges to classroom teachers.

Learning implies change, for without some change in behavior we cannot be assured that learning has taken place. One of the roles of a classroom teacher is to bring about behavioral changes which result in learning. In order to demonstrate behavior change, one must be able to define behavior in observable terms, to accurately measure and to reliably record its occurrence. These abilities are central to instructional decision making, for without them teaching may be guided more by intuition and past experience than by direct assessment of pupil performance.

Few teachers would characterize their approach as including systematic methods to observe, measure, and record the behavior of their students. Yet teachers are often asked to provide information regarding classroom behavior and academic performance. In both placement and parent conferences teachers are expected to share their observations of a pupil's behavior and to summarize a student's academic performance. Many teachers rely on anecdotal reports and the results of standardized tests. Though convinced of neither they may continue to use them due to their unfamiliarity with other ways of collecting and reporting information on pupil performance. Teachers often supplement the results of tests with samples of a student's daily work. While these provide a more direct measure of classroom performance than tests, it is difficult to gain a complete picture of a student's academic performance by examining several completed workbook assignments in different subject areas.

Another way that teachers communicate their observations of pupil behavior is through report cards. Grades are based on teacher observations which theoretically reflect the actual behavior of students. Yet grades are

113

one step removed from reporting the actual skills a student has or has not mastered.

There are three reasons why teachers need a systematic method of observing, measuring, and recording behavior:

1. Teachers are often asked to share their observations of pupil performance with others.
2. Teachers are expected to assess and remediate social and academic behavior problems as well as to teach new skills. Precise measures of performance are needed to pinpoint learning and behavior problems and to plan remedial strategies. When data are used as the basis for instruction, teachers can pinpoint a student's difficulties, apply a teaching technique, and measure the impact of the chosen technique upon performance.
3. In this age of accountability, teachers are being asked to demonstrate the effectiveness of their teaching. By using a data-based instructional approach, teachers not only have an efficient means of improving the academic and social behavior of their students, and a way of communicating progress, but they also have a ready means of documenting the effectiveness of their teaching in terms of the progress made by their students.

In this chapter we will present the characteristics of data-based observation followed by a discussion of the three types of observational systems. For the two most commonly used systems, descriptions will be provided of the various types of measurement techniques one could use. In discussing the different types of measurement techniques, emphasis will be placed on describing: (1) the conditions under which one would use a particular measurement technique, (2) how one would observe and record behavior when using a specific measurement technique, and (3) the advantages and disadvantages of each measurement technique. The practicality of using certain types of measurement techniques will be illustrated through the use of sample projects conducted in regular classrooms. Following the discussion of the various types of observational systems and measurement techniques, a step-by-step outline will be provided describing how classroom teachers can apply the techniques presented in this chapter to observe and measure the performance of their students.

CHARACTERISTICS OF DATA-BASED OBSERVATION

The observational systems to be described in this chapter share the following characteristics.

Only observable behaviors are measured

Behavior may be classified into two categories—overt and covert. Overt behaviors refer to: (1) actions which are observable, such as saying words or raising a hand, and (2) the products of behavior, such as written answers to comprehension questions. Covert behaviors include thoughts and feelings, which are detectable by the person experiencing them but cannot be observed by another individual. It is for this reason that observation is restricted to observable behaviors which can be defined and measured.

Behaviors are defined in specific terms prior to measuring their occurrence

It is common practice in education to describe the behavior of students in global terms, for example, distractible, hyperactive, dyslexic. While it is assumed that terms such as these adequately describe behavior, they actually necessitate further elaboration. What do we mean by distractible? What does a student *do* that leads us to believe that he's distractible? Does he look out the window, leave his desk, or only work on his assignments for a few minutes? Under what conditions does the student act that way— throughout the school day or only during instruction in certain subjects? Only when behaviors are defined in observable terms can they be measured. Once behaviors are stated in measurable terms, attention can be focused on changing behavior. Criteria for defining behavior in observable and measurable terms will be discussed later in this chapter.

Multiple measures of performance are collected prior to implementing an intervention

It is essential to observe a student's performance over a period of days prior to implementing an intervention. Data collected prior to intervention are known as *baseline data.* One of the main objectives of collecting baseline data is to obtain a reliable record of performance under the conditions which currently exist in the classroom. Many people assume that during a baseline period a teacher should provide no instructions or give no feedback on the behavior measured. While this is common practice in research studies, it is not always applicable in classroom situations. If, for example, a teacher is already providing instruction on a skill, it makes little sense to discontinue ongoing instruction to obtain a measure of a student's performance in the absence of instruction. Instead of creating an artificial situation, one should measure the student's performance under *typical classroom conditions* to determine if an instructional change is warranted. Similarly if a teacher was already reacting to the behavior of a student in some way, it would not be necessary to change that reaction in order to obtain a baseline of performance. For example a teacher may suspect that a student's out-of-seat behavior may be maintained by reprimands. Rather than immediately discontinuing reprimanding the student, the teacher can test this assumption by: (1) obtaining baseline data on the student's behavior under the present conditions, (2) changing conditions (for example, praising the student when she is in her seat and ignoring out-of-seat behavior, while continuing to collect data), and (3) comparing the student's performance during the baseline and intervention periods. In this way a teacher can use baseline data to describe a student's current performance and to determine if a change is warranted. Baseline data also serve as a standard by which change can be evaluated.

Baseline data provide teachers with a wealth of information for instruction. First baseline data serve to document whether a perceived problem is actually a problem. For example it may seem that a student is constantly talking out, but baseline data might reveal only a minor problem. Second by knowing the student's baseline level it is easy to specify a realistic aim. For example if a student only stays on task for an average of two minutes out of a thirty-minute period during baseline, it would be unwise to immediately require the child to stay on task for fifteen minutes. By using the information obtained during baseline, the aim could be gradually increased from the student's baseline level to the desired level. Third by taking the time to observe a student's behavior before trying to change it one may discern whether certain teacher instructions or instructional tasks appear to precipitate a behavior, or whether particular consequences, such as teacher attention appear to maintain a behavior. Armed with an educated guess as to what might be causing a behavior, a teacher is in a good position to select an effective teaching technique.

Steps are taken to assure the reliability of the data

All observations made by humans are subject to error. Observers may sometimes fail to measure behavior in the same way. If behavior is not reliably measured, the records obtained will not yield a valid indicator of performance nor can they be used to document a change in behavior following the application of a teaching technique. It is for these reasons that one attempts to assure that data are reliably observed and recorded.

The primary method for assuring the reliability of recorded observations is to have another person independently observe and record the behavior at the same time as the usual recorder. If the teacher is recording a particular behavior of a student, another person (for example, a resource teacher, student teacher, parent volunteer, or another student) may occasionally record along with the teacher. At the end of the observation period, the two records are compared and the extent of agreement between the two records is determined. The higher the agreement, the more faith one has that the data represents an accurate record of the student's behavior. Procedures for collecting reliability data will be presented later in this chapter.

OBSERVATIONAL SYSTEMS

Before collecting baseline data, one must first identify the behavior(s) to be changed and describe them in observable and measurable terms. The way one defines a behavior is directly related to the type of observation system and measurement technique one selects to record the behavior. For that reason we will delay our discussion of defining behavior and, first, focus our attention on describing the various types of observational systems and measurement techniques.

The two primary observation systems for use in classrooms are *observational recording* and direct measurement of permanent products.

These systems can be viewed as being at opposite ends of a continuum. At one end there is observational recording which is used to measure such classroom behavior problems as talking out, and being out-of-seat. These behaviors are transitory in nature and must be measured as they occur if one is to obtain a record of their occurrence. At the opposite end of the continuum is direct measurement of permanent products. The measurement system is used to measure "products" of behavior. The most common "product" measured in the classroom is written answers, for example, written answers to math problems, written lists of spelling words. The main difference between observational recording and direct measurement of permanent products is that the former leaves no lasting record of its occurrence, whereas the latter results in a "product" which can be measured after the behavior has occurred. In this text we will define permanent product data quite broadly so as to include: (1) written work, (2) tape-recorded answers, such as student's responses to words presented on a language master, or tape recordings of a student reading orally, and (3) other tangible products which are the result of some behavior, such as an answer displayed on an abacus, or a completed puzzle.

There is a third type of observational system known as **automatic recording** which relies on the use of a mechanical apparatus to record a subject's responses as they occur. Automatic-recording devices are frequently used in medicine and in behavior research with animals. Automatic recording has been used to measure the sound level in classrooms (Schmidt & Ulrich, 1969).

Computer-assisted instruction (CAI) represents another use of an automatic-recording device used in classroom settings. Computer-assisted instructional programs such as some of those contained in the PLATO system (Smith & Sherwood, 1976) present information and instructional tasks to students at their own pace. Feedback on performance is provided and, when necessary, further exercises are presented to correct a student's errors. A student's responses are automatically scored and recorded in a way which allows teachers to retrieve data on individual performance.

While automatic-recording devices are very sensitive and may free teachers from directly observing and recording behavior, they cannot be considered as a realistic alternative measurement system for classroom use. First most behavior of interest to teachers is not amenable to automatic recording. Second many automatic-recording devices are expensive and are not readily available. Because automatic recordings are seldom used in classrooms, they will not be discussed further. Instead we will focus our attention on observational systems and measurement techniques which are applicable to regular classroom settings.

MEASUREMENT TECHNIQUES
FOR OBSERVATIONAL RECORDING

There are six types of measurement techniques one can use when doing observational recording: (1) event, (2) duration, (3) latency, (4) time sampling, (5) interval, and (6) continuous recording. Each measurement technique will be described in detail followed by an example of its use in a classroom setting. The advantages and disadvantages of each system will be discussed, particularly in regard to the suitability of each given the constraints of the regular classroom. Adaptations to the basic measurement techniques will be suggested with the aim of making measuring and recording of behavior more manageable for classroom teachers. Finally an alternative measurement technique will be described which contains elements of more than one of the six basic measurement techniques in observational recording.

Event Recording

Event recording is used to count the frequency of behavior as it occurs. Event recording can only be used to count discrete behaviors, those with a definite beginning and end. Discrete behaviors include such inappropriate classroom behaviors as out-of-seats and talk-outs, both of which lend themselves to a simple tally of their occurrence. Frequency can be used to count either number of responses or number of correct and incorrect responses. Some behaviors such as hits or cries cannot be classified as correct or incorrect. In these instances one can only measure the frequency or number of responses which occur. Other behaviors can be classified as correct or incorrect, such as words read correctly and incorrectly. When responses can be classified as correct or incorrect, the frequency of each is measured.

One of the easiest ways to count events is to make a tally mark each time the behavior occurs. Some teachers keep their counts on index cards, others prefer to put masking tape on one of their cuffs and mark with a felt pen each time the behavior to be measured occurs. There are also several mechanical aids which can be used to count behaviors, including wrist golf counters and supermarket counters for recording purchases. The interested reader can consult Cooper (1974) for pictures and descriptions of several commercially available counters. When selecting a device to count behavior, one consideration should be to use something that is easily transportable from place to place within the classroom, whether it be poker chips that can be transferred from one pocket to another, or the fanciest counter available. A second consideration is to select a device which is as unobtrusive as possible so as not to call undue attention to the fact that one is observing a student's behavior.

Once a teacher has decided to use event recording to measure the occurrence of a particular behavior, a decision must be made concerning the length of the observation period. Not all classroom behavior problems occur at equal frequencies throughout the school day. This may be because of several factors. Students may attend more during certain academic subjects than others, thus decreasing the amount of time they engage in inappropriate behaviors. Some behaviors are more likely to occur at certain times—fighting is more likely on the playground than in the classroom; talking-out is more likely to occur during seatwork than when a student is close to the teacher. In cases where a *target behavior* occurs most fre-quently during a certain time period, such as coming into class, observation can be restricted to that time period. Behavior problems sometimes occur throughout the school day. In that case a teacher can either measure the behavior throughout the school day, or measure the behavior daily during a certain time period and every few days also measure its occurrence at other times of the day.

The following is an example of event recording.

Classroom Application of Event Recording
(Vollrath, F., & Clark, M., 1971)

Number of Students
    16 fifth graders

Setting
    Regular classroom

Target Behavior/Aim
    The aim was to reduce the number of times students talked out in a slow reading group to five or fewer times during the forty-five-minute reading period.

Definition of Target Behavior
    A tally was made each time a student talked to another person without teacher permission at any time during the reading period. A reply by a student to another student was also recorded as an instance of talking-out.

Observation System and Measurement Technique
    Daily data were collected by the teacher throughout the forty-five-minute reading period. The teacher used paper and pencil to tally the number of times the students talked out.

Procedures
    During baseline, the teacher counted the number of times students talked out. The first intervention consisted of telling the students that they could earn a special privilege during the last five minutes of the reading period provided that they talked out five or fewer times. The privileges suggested by the students in-cluded games, snacks, and free time to read or draw.
    During the first intervention the teacher tallied the times students talked out on the board. A return-to-baseline period was implemented to determine the ef-fectiveness of the privileges on the student's behavior. During this time, privileges for not talking out were withdrawn.
    A new intervention phase was then arranged during which the students once again earned privileges on days in which they talked out five or fewer times. Fol-lowing the second intervention, the students were told that they were doing so well that they no longer needed a treat each day. Thereafter the students never knew if on any given day their low rates of talking out would earn them privileges until the last five minutes of class.

Reliability
    The teacher enlisted the aid of a student who was not in the group to collect reliability data. The student also kept track of the number of talk-outs during each

phase of the project. The teacher and student's records showed that agreement scores ranged from 82 to 100 percent.

Results

The data presented in Figure 6–1 clearly show the effectiveness of the intervention on the students' talk-outs. During baseline, the students talked out an average of 33 times. When the intervention was applied the students never exceeded the limit of five. When the intervention was discontinued, talk-outs increased to near the original baseline level. When the intervention was reinstated, talk-outs decreased to an average of two per day. During the last phase, when low talk-out rates were occasionally reinforced by privileges, the students maintained their performance.

In the sample study conducted by Vollrath and Clark (1971), the data obtained through event recording were expressed in terms of frequency or number of times the students talked out. Although one always *measures* the frequency of a behavior when using event recording, it is often necessary to transform the data for reporting purposes. It is appropriate to *measure* and *report* the frequency of a behavior only when time and opportunity to respond are held constant. The reasoning behind this con-

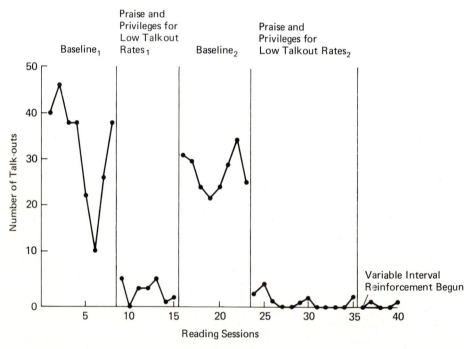

FIGURE 6–1 Number of talk-outs made by a fifth-grade reading class. (From F. Vollrath and M. Clark, Effects of reinforcement procedures on talking frequency in a slow-reading group, in R.V. Hall, *Managing behavior, Part 3: Applications in school and home.* Lawrence, KS: H & H Enterprises, 1971b, p. 14. By permission of the publishers.)

vention can be illustrated by an example. Suppose a teacher wished to count the number of words a student read correctly and incorrectly during oral reading. If the length of the passage varied from day to day neither opportunity to respond or time would be constant. Similarly if passages of equal length were assigned each day but the student was allowed two minutes to read one day and three minutes to read a similar passage the next day, time would not be constant. In neither case would it be appro priate to compare the student's oral reading performance across days in terms of frequency of words read correctly and incorrectly.

In the oral-reading example, the teacher could control for either: (1) opportunity to respond, by presenting passages of equal length, or (2) time, by sampling performance for an equal number of minutes each time data were collected on oral reading. If the teacher held the opportunity to respond constant and allowed time to vary, the student's reading performance would be expressed as number of words read correctly and incorrectly per minute (rate). On the other hand, if the teacher held time constant and allowed opportunity to respond to vary, the teacher could choose to report the student's performance either in terms of percent of words read correctly or rate of words read correctly and incorrectly. If the teacher only wanted information on the student's accuracy, percent would be the measure of choice. However, if the teacher wished to have information on accuracy as well as speed, reading rate data would be reported. The computational formulas for percent and rate are shown in Table 6–1 along with an explanation of how one can determine a student's accuracy based on rate data.

Teachers seldom *measure* and *report* data in terms of frequency as it is rare that both time and opportunity to respond are constant. There are instances, however, in which time is held constant and opportunity to respond is considered to be constant. For example a teacher might count the number of times a student talked out during a particular half-hour period in which the student was completing an assignment at his desk. One would assume that the student's opportunity to talk out would be constant, provided that the student was working on a similar assignment and that this behavior was measured during the same half-hour period each day. In this case, one could report the data as either the number of times the student talked out (frequency) or the number of talk-outs per minute (rate).

In most cases, when teachers measure the frequency of a behavior, they find it necessary to translate frequency data into percent or rate because of the difficulty in arranging situations in which both time and opportunity to respond can be kept constant. Table 6–2 illustrates when it is necessary to report frequency data in terms of percent or rate.

As shown in Table 6–2, it is appropriate to record behavior in terms of frequency only when time and opportunity to respond are both constant. For example one could record the number of times a student talked out if the observation period remained constant from day to day. If the length of the observation period varied, rate would be the appropriate measure. Similarly if opportunity to respond varies, one would record percent or

TABLE 6–1 Relationship Between Percent and Rate

Example: A child reads 117 words correctly and 9 words incorrectly in 2 minutes and 14 seconds.

1. *Percent of Words Read Correctly*

$$\frac{\text{Number of words read correctly}}{\text{Total number of words read}} \times 100$$

Example: $\frac{117}{126} \times 100 = 92.9\%$

2. *Number of Words Read Correctly and Incorrectly Per Minute*

$$\text{Correct Rate} = \frac{\text{Number of words read correctly}}{\text{Total number of seconds}} \times 60$$

Example: $\frac{117}{2(60) + 14} = \frac{117}{134} \times 60 = 52.4 \text{ WPM}^*$

$$\text{Incorrect Rate} = \frac{\text{Number of words read incorrectly}}{\text{Total number of seconds}} \times 60$$

Example: $\frac{9}{2(60) + 14} = \frac{9}{134} \times 60 = 4.0 \text{ WPM}^*$

3. *Computing Percent Based on Rate Data*

$$\text{Percent Correct} = \frac{\text{Correct rate}}{\text{Correct} + \text{incorrect rate}} \times 100$$

Example: $\frac{52.4}{52.4 + 4.0} = \frac{52.4}{56.4} \times 100 = 92.9\%$

* WPM = words per minute.

TABLE 6–2 Reporting Frequency Data

123

*Measurement
Techniques for
Observational
Recording*

rate data. For example if a student was given ten math problems to solve one day, fifteen problems the next day, and eighteen problems on another day, a teacher could elect to record either percent of problems computed correctly, or number of problems computed correctly and incorrectly per minute (rate). In cases where opportunity to respond is constant (such as when a student is given a worksheet containing the same number of items each day and asked to complete it) but time varies, performance is recorded in terms of number of items answered correctly and incorrectly per minute (rate).

Duration Recording

Duration refers to the amount of time a behavior lasts. Duration recording may be used in the classroom to measure the amount of time a student engages in a behavior. For example a teacher might wish to measure the amount of time a student takes to complete a task. After giving a student an assignment and asking her to begin working, the teacher would note the time the student began by either glancing at a wristwatch, a wall clock, or turning on a stopwatch. When the student finished the assignment, the teacher would note the elapsed time. The student's performance would be recorded in terms of total number of minutes spent completing the task.

For those students who rarely complete their assignments on time, data on the length of time they require to complete various types of assignments can be used to set realistic individual aims for them to meet. For example a student might take an average of fifteen minutes to complete a grammar exercise while the majority of his classmates take five minutes. At first the pupil might be required to complete the assignment in a little less time than his average performance. Gradually the time alloted can be reduced, over a period of days, provided that the student meets each aim the teacher establishes. Eventually the student will achieve the terminal goal which is to complete the assignment at the average time taken by his classmates. Care should be taken to make sure that a student is appropriately placed in the curriculum material before trying to reduce the amount of time the student requires to complete a task.

Duration can be expressed as either total amount of time engaged in a behavior, such as completing a task, or percent of time spent engaged in a behavior. Duration is expressed as percent of time when a teacher wishes to know the amount of time a student engages in a specific behavior during a certain time period. For example a student may frequently leave her desk during a thirty-minute seatwork period and spend several minutes wandering about the room. A teacher could turn on a stopwatch when the student left her seat and turn if off when the student returned to her seat. The percentage of time the student was out of her seat would be calculated as follows:

$$\frac{\text{total elapsed time on stopwatch}}{\text{total time during observation period}} \times 100 \quad \text{Example: } \frac{18}{30} \times \frac{100}{1} = 60\%$$

Additional information about this student's out-of-seat behavior could be obtained by combining a frequency count with duration recording. In that case when the student left her seat, a stopwatch would be turned on until she returned to her seat, just as in duration recording. However each time the stopwatch was turned off the elapsed time would be noted and recorded, perhaps on a 3 × 5 card. Each time the student left and returned the process would be repeated. At the end of the observation period, the teacher would have a column of elapsed times which could easily be counted to obtain the frequency of times the student left her seat. The average length of time spent out of seat would be obtained by adding all the elapsed times and dividing by the total number of times the student was out of her seat.

A classroom teacher related an instance in which she measured duration under unusual circumstances. A student announced that he was walking out of the classroom. As the student hurried out the door, the classroom teacher considered chasing the student through the halls. Luckily the teacher had the presence of mind to turn on a stopwatch and tell the student for every minute he was gone he would spend two minutes after school. The student's excursion was of relatively brief duration and within three minutes he was back in the classroom. The teacher thanked him for returning, reminded him he would spend six minutes after school, and then continued to conduct the lesson, being sure to praise the student for working well.

Fortunately for this teacher, the student never again left the classroom without permission. If he had the teacher probably would not have continued to take duration data on the amount of time he spent out of the classroom, both for the student's welfare and because of possible legal ramifications. In the instance cited, when the behavior had never occurred before and when the teacher dared not let it occur, the teacher chose to intervene immediately rather than just measure the occurrence of the behavior without applying some consequence.

Latency Recording

Latency may be viewed as a "special case of duration" referring "to the time between the onset of a stimulus and the beginning of a response"

(Reese & Johnson, 1976, p. 21). Latency measures are easily collected. After defining what the beginning of the desired behavior looks like and deciding on a signal such as a verbal command, one simply records with some timing device the time between the end of the signal and the beginning of the desired behavior. Latency data are reported in terms of total elapsed time.

Problems with latency in the classroom sometimes arise when students are asked to put away materials, to come in from recess, to switch from one learning center to the other, or to begin working on an assignment. Often when a teacher gives an instruction, such as "Please put away the art materials," the teacher's request is accompanied by groans from the students. Some students persist in using the materials long after the teacher has requested that they be put away. Parents frequently encounter problems with latency, when in response to almost any request, their child answers "In a minute." Such was the case in the following study by Reimers and Hall (1971). Their study is included for three reasons. First it demonstrates that it is sometimes appropriate to measure two aspects of behavior at the same time. Second the study was conducted in the student's home with data being collected by members of the student's family. Third the study clearly illustrates the difference between latency and duration recording.

Application of Latency and Duration Recording
(Reimers, H. and Hall, R. V., 1971)

Number of Students
    Nine-year old girl, Christine

Setting
    Home

Target Behavior/Aims
    To decrease both the amount of time Christine took before drying the first dish and the amount of time spent drying dishes.

Definition of Target Behaviors
    Latency was defined as the time between when a family member put the first washed dish into the draining rack and the time when Christine began to dry the dishes. Duration was considered to be the amount of time Christine took from the time she "picked up the first dish to when she finished drying the last" (p. 25).

Observation System and Measurement Technique
    Christine's grandfather used a combination of latency and duration recording. He measured latency by recording the number of minutes which elapsed between the time he placed the first dish in the drying rack and the time Christine picked it up. Duration was measured by recording the total number of minutes Christine took to dry the dishes once she had begun. Timings were recorded to the nearest minute.

Procedures
    Following the baseline phase (during which presumably no special instruction or consequences were arranged) an intervention was introduced. Christine was

told that she could earn "Two minutes extra reading time at bedtime for each minute less than six that it took her to begin drying dishes, or 12 minutes if she began within one minute after the first dish was in the rack" (p. 25). After fourteen days the intervention was applied to both behaviors and Christine was told that she must begin drying dishes within six minutes and complete drying all the dishes within fifteen minutes. Following the intervention period, several post-checks were conducted during which time Christine no longer had the opportunity to earn extra reading time.

Reliability

Christine's mother simultaneously recorded both latency and duration during each condition. Her records were in 100 percent agreement with the records taken by Christine's grandfather.

Results

The charted data, presented in Figure 6–2 shows that when the intervention was applied to the latency measure, the amount of time taken before beginning to dry the dishes decreased. However there was no accompanying decrease in the amount of time Christine spent drying dishes. It was not until the intervention was focused on both the latency and duration measure that time spent drying dishes decreased. When the intervention was no longer in effect, Christine's behavior maintained up to three months following the behavior change program.

Time Sampling

Time sampling may be defined as measuring "the occurrence or nonoccurrence of behavior *immediately following* specified time intervals" (Cooper, 1974, p. 54). This measurement technique can be used to measure the presence or absence of either a discrete behavior such as talk-outs or a continuous behavior such as not doing what one is supposed to be doing (called *off-task behavior*). Time sampling should only be used when the behavior occurs often enough so that occasional sampling will produce a reliable indication of the occurrence of the behavior. If the behavior is infrequent (less than once in fifteen minutes), another measurement technique should be selected (Arrington, 1943, cited in Sulzer-Azaroff & Mayer, 1977).

After first defining the target behavior and specifying the length of the observation period, one must decide how often to observe within the chosen time period. Usually one elects to observe a student's behavior at the end of every *x* minutes within the time period. For example a student may appear to be spending little time on his work during a 25 minute period. The student's teacher could elect to observe the student's behavior at the end of every five minutes during the 25 minute period. The teacher might record the data on a sheet similar to the one shown in Figure 6–3. As each time interval ended, the teacher would determine if the student's behavior met the definition for being on-task. If the student was on-task a "+" would be recorded, if not a "−" would be reported in the block corresponding to the time the observation was made.

Some teachers use kitchen timers or parking meter timers to remind

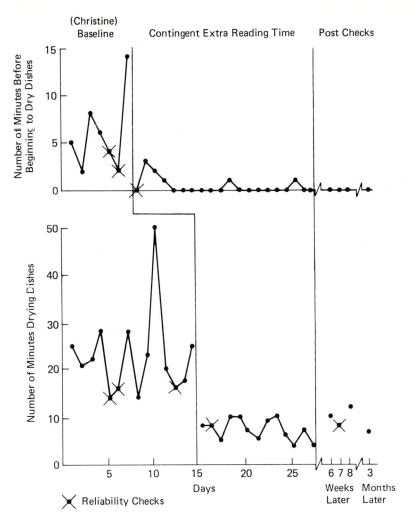

FIGURE 6–2 Number of minutes taken by Christine to begin drying dishes and to complete drying them once she had begun. (From H. Reimers and R.V. Hall, Reduction of nail-biting and increasing speed of doing dishes through reinforcement (experiment 2), in R.V. Hall, *Managing behavior, Part 3: Applications in school and home*. Lawrence KS: H & H Enterprises, 1971b, p. 24. By permission of the publishers.)

themselves to observe at the time they have selected. These devices work well unless the target student catches on to the fact that his behavior is being observed. It becomes obvious that a student has caught on when he behaves appropriately only upon hearing the bell or near the end of an interval. When this situation arises a teacher has two choices, either discontinue using the audible timer and rely on a wristwatch or wall clock, or vary the observation times.

If the decision is to vary the time of the observations then one must have some way to predetermine the exact time of each observation. Unless

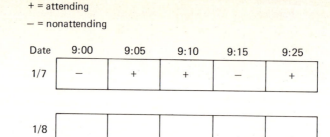

FIGURE 6–3 Sample Data Recording Sheet for Time Sample Data.

observation times are selected beforehand, there is a tendency to observe the student only when he is misbehaving. In that case one might as well use event recording if each instance of an inappropriate behavior is to be recorded.

There are many methods one could use to select variable observation times. Two ways of choosing observation times which vary are as follows: Given that a teacher wishes to observe a student five times during a 30 minute period to determine if the student is on-task, the teacher could:

1. Select five numbers from one to five to determine the number of minutes between each observation. For example, a teacher might select the following numbers: 3, 5, 4, 2, 5. If the observation period began at 9:00, the teacher would observe the student's behavior at 9:03, 9:08, 9:12, 9:14, and 9:19. Before the observation period began, the teacher would mark the recording sheet by noting the number of minutes between each observation above the corresponding time block. An audible timer could then be set to remind the teacher to observe the student at the predetermined times. This procedure would be repeated each day the teacher planned to observe the student's behavior.

2. Pre-mark instructional materials which will be in use by the teacher during the time a student's behavior will be observed. If the teacher was involved in a reading group at the time when a student's on-task behavior at his desk was to be observed, five marks could be randomly placed in the teacher's copy of the story. As the teacher follows along in the reader as one of the students in the group reads, the teacher

could glance at the target student each time one of the marks in the story was encountered. The teacher might also choose to record the exact time of the observation by glancing at the wall clock following each observation.

Three things should be kept in mind when using time sampling. First the length of the observation period and the number of observations made should remain constant from day to day. Second time sampling only provides an estimate of the frequency of a behavior. When using time sampling only one mark is made in each time block. It is impossible to determine the frequency of a behavior based on time sample data because all that is recorded is whether or not the behaviour was occurring at the time each observation was made. The more frequently one observes, the better one can estimate the frequency of the behavior. Third although time sampling does not provide an exact count of behavior, what it loses in precision is more than made up for in efficiency and applicability in the classroom. Time sampling can be used to measure the behavior of an individual student or an entire class. For example a teacher could use this method to determine whether a particular student was in her seat as each time interval ended; or, whether anyone in the class was out-of-seat, off-task, or talking out immediately following each time interval.

When reporting performance based on time sampling, one uses percentage of occurrence. The procedure one would follow in computing percentage of occurrence for time sample data is shown in Table 6–3.

**Classroom Application of Time Sampling
(Hendricks, G., 1979)**

Number of Students
        Seven-year-old boy, Bill

Setting
        Second-grade classroom

Target Behavior
        Increase number of assignments completed during the morning to three for six days and increase amount of time spent on-task.

Definition of Target Behavior
        Three assignments were given each morning, one page each of handwriting, phonics, and reading. An assignment was considered to be complete if it contained written answers to all required items on a page. On-task was defined as the student being in his seat, looking at or writing on his assignment, or raising his hand.

Observation System and Measurement Technique
        During the 45 minute period, the teacher used a time-sampling procedure to measure the student's on-task behavior. At the end of every five minutes, the teacher observed the student and noted whether or not he was on-task. The teacher recorded the data on a 3 × 5 card using a "+" to indicate on-task and a "−" to indicate off-task behavior.

TABLE 6–3 Computing Percentage of Occurrence for Time Sample Data

Example: A student's on-task behavior was observed during a twenty-five-minute
period at the end of every five minutes.

+ = on-task
− = off-task

DATE	9:05	9:10	9:15	9:20	9:25	Percent of Time On-task
1/7	−	+	−	−	+	40%

Each time block accounts for 20 percent of the total. The student received 2
plus signs signifying she was on-task at the end of two intervals and 3 minus signs
indicating she was off-task at the end of three intervals.

The student's percentage of on-task behavior could be computed each day
by following these three steps:

Step 1: Count the total number of observations, for example 5.

Step 2: Count the total number of plus signs scored, for example 2.

Step 3: Divide the total number of plus signs by the total number of observations
and multiply by 100

$$\frac{\text{Total number of plus signs}}{\text{Total number of observations}} \times 100 \qquad \text{Example:} \quad \frac{2}{5} \times \frac{100}{1} = 40\%$$

Permanent product recording was used to measure the number of assignments the student completed. Using a raw data form, the teacher recorded the
number and type of assignments given, the number and type of assignments completed, and the student's average accuracy on each day's completed assignments.

During baseline the teacher noted that accuracy was not a problem. Therefore
the teacher decided to record the student's average accuracy on a raw data sheet
rather than chart that information. The teacher charted number of assignments
completed and percent of time spent on-task.

Procedures

During baseline the teacher observed Bill's on-task behavior as previously
described. As no contingency was in effect, Bill was free to go to recess whether
his work was completed or not. While he was at recess, the teacher checked his
work and recorded the information on the raw data sheet.

During the intervention, the teacher placed an assignment sheet containing
three boxes corresponding to the number of assignments given per day. The sheet
contained enough boxes for one week. The teacher told Bill that she would check
on his work before recess. A smiling face was placed in each box on the assignment
sheet for each page Bill had completed. Bill was told that if he earned three smiling
faces, indicating that he had completed all of his assignments, he could go to recess.
During the intervention, the teacher continued to measure Bill's on-task behavior
as before. However, at the end of every five-minute period, the teacher praised
Bill provided that he was working on his assignments.

Four maintenance checks were collected during the week following the intervention. During this time the smiling faces were discontinued and Bill was allowed to go to recess provided he had finished his work. Bill's on-task behavior was only occasionally praised during this time.

Results

During baseline Bill spent an average of 55.6 percent of his time on-task. Although his work was accurate, he failed to complete more than one assignment. As shown in Figure 6–4, Bill's on-task behavior increased to 91.4 percent during the intervention. By the fourth day of the intervention, he was completing all of his assignments. Bill's performance maintained on the four post-checks collected during the week following the intervention.

Interval Recording

Interval recording is similar to time sampling, but it requires the teacher to observe a student's behavior *continuously* during a specific period of time. For that reason interval recording is seldom used by classroom teach-

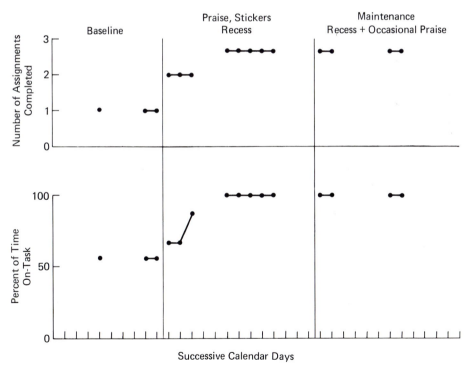

FIGURE 6–4 Number of assignments completed and percent of time spent on-task. (Adapted from Gloria J. Hendricks, *Increasing the percent of time on task and completion of assignments.* Unpublished manuscript, University of Illinois, 1979. By permission of the author.)

ers because they simply cannot observe a student continuously and teach at the same time. Interval recording will be discussed briefly for the sake of completeness, and because there are other individuals such as resource teachers, school psychologists, or volunteers who can assist teachers by collecting interval data.

Interval recording is appropriate for measuring either discrete or continuous behaviors. Like time sampling, interval recording is especially appropriate for behaviors which occur at high rates. In most cases interval recording will produce a more accurate estimate of the occurrence of a behavior than time sampling because the student's behavior is being observed continuously rather than just at the end of a specified interval. Like time sampling, interval recording is used to measure the occurrence or nonoccurrence of a specified behavior.

When using interval recording one uses a recording sheet similar to the one presented in Figure 6–5. With the aid of a stopwatch or some other mechanical cueing device, the observer can record either: (1) whether the target behavior did or did not occur at any time during the interval, or (2) whether the target behavior occurred throughout the *entire* interval. The first technique will be referred to as *partial-interval recording* and the second as *whole-interval recording*.

In using the partial-interval method to observe the "attending" behavior of a student, a "+" would be recorded if at any time within the interval to be scored, the student met the definitional requirements for "attending." If, on the other hand, one chose to use the whole-interval method, then a "+" would only be recorded if the student displayed "attending" behavior throughout the entire interval to be scored. When using either method, the teacher reports data as percent of time.

When using interval recording it is possible to observe and record the presence or absence of several behaviors of a single student, or to record the occurrence or nonoccurrence of a specified behavior for a number of students. As interval recording is seldom used in regular classrooms, fur-

+ = Attending

= − Nonattending

FIGURE 6–5 Sample Data Recording Sheet for Inverval Data.

ther examples of the technique will not be provided. The interested reader may consult Cooper (1974) to learn of some modifications which would be of use in training an observer to collect interval data.

Continuous Recording

Continuous recording is sometimes referred to as anecdotal or narrative recording. When using continuous recording one attempts to write down all of the behaviors exhibited by a student within a certain period of time. Attention is paid to noting events that occur both before and after each behavior.

Continuous recording can be used "before one has decided which classes of behavior are important and how they will be defined and measured" (Reese & Johnson, 1976, p. 14). For example, a teacher may be concerned about the types of activities a student engages in during a free-time activity with peers. By keeping continuous records over a period of days it would be possible to determine whether the student initiates any interactions, joins in and plays with others when asked, as well as what types of toys or games the student chooses.

There are relatively few examples of continuous records in the educational or behavioral literature, perhaps due to the demands the system places on the observer. The interested reader may consult Bijou, Peterson, and Ault (1968) who present a sample continuous record and explain the procedure in detail.

The primary advantage of continuous recording is that it allows one to determine the range of behavior displayed by a student. Based on a continuous record, a teacher can list the behaviors a student can perform and identify others which he/she may need to learn. By noting the types of events which occur before or after a behavior, it is possible to determine which events seem to set off a behavior and which might be maintaining a student's behavior.

Continuous recording requires the undivided attention of an observer and is therefore not practical for classroom teachers. Teachers who desire the type of information provided by continuous recording must usually rely on others to do the actual observations. Because teachers do not have the time to keep formal continuous records, an abbreviated version of the technique can be used. For example prior to implementing a behavioral change program, a teacher might jot down what happens immediately before and after a student displays an inappropriate behavior. In this way the teacher can make an educated guess as to the events which may precipitate or maintain a behavior. This information can then be used to select an intervention to remedy a behavior problem.

An Alternative Measurement Technique

Of the measurement techniques which are applicable to classroom settings, two are commonly used to measure the behavior of a group of students.

These measurement techniques are: *event recording* and *time sampling*. Event recording can be used to count the number of behaviors such as talk-outs made by a class of students. Similarly one could use time sampling to measure whether a group of students or an entire class were on-task at the end of an interval. Sometimes a teacher desires other information about the performance of a group of students, such as the number engaged in an educational activity. When a teacher wishes to know the number of students who are and are not engaged in some assigned activity, a measurement technique known as *PLA-check* or Planned Activity Check (Risley, 1972) can be used.

The steps one would follow in using PLA-check are:

1. The observer scientifically defines the behavior (planned activity) he wishes to record in a group of children.
2. At given intervals (e.g., each ten minutes) the observer counts as quickly as possible how many individuals are engaged in the behavior, recording the total.
3. The observer then counts and records as quickly as possible how many individuals are present in the area of the activity.
4. The number of pupils present can then be divided into the number of pupils engaged in the behavior. By multiplying the result by 100, the observer finds the percent of those engaged in the behavior at that particular time. (Hall, 1971a, p. 4)

PLA-check can be used to scan the behavior of a large group of students and is especially appropriate to use when the teacher is involved with small group instruction and must somehow maintain control over students working at their desks or in other areas of the classroom. PLA-check is similar to time sampling as it is only necessary to observe at the end of certain specified time periods. It varies from time sampling though, because one counts the number of students engaged in a behavior. (It may be faster to count the number who are *not* engaged in the activity and subtract that sum from the total to obtain the number who are engaged in the desired activity.)

Though the identity of individual students who are and are not engaged in a particular activity are not recorded, it would be possible to adapt the PLA-check technique to record that information. For example one could list students' last names in alphabetical order in a column. The time of each observation could be noted in columns next to the student's name. As each observation is made, one could quickly scan the group and place a check next to the names of those students who are not engaged in a particular activity. In this way it would be possible to record the percentage of students who are engaged in the activity as well as to determine if certain students are consistently not engaged in the desired activity. If a problem exists with only a certain group of students, then an intervention could be planned which would focus on improving their behavior and maintaining the appropriate behavior of other students.

The second type of observation system to be discussed concerns the direct measurement of permanent products. The reader will recall that permanent products were defined earlier in this chapter as including: (1) written work, (2) tape-recorded answers, and (3) other tangible products which are the result of some behavior on the part of a student.

Permanent product data are the most common data collected in the classroom. Teachers routinely correct student's written assignments and return them scattered with marks indicating correct and incorrect responses. In so doing teachers provide students with feedback on the frequency of correct and incorrect answers on their assignments. Spelling papers are commonly corrected and returned with the percent correct score noted on top of the page. Occasionally timed drills are given on arithmetic facts, and students are told the number of problems they solved correctly and incorrectly per minute. Thus, teachers express performance on permanent products using a variety of measures.

Knowing the conditions under which performance should be expressed in terms of frequency, percent, or rate of response is essential. In the previous section we discussed the conditions under which it is necessary to transform frequency data into permanent product data, that is, unless time and opportunity are constant, one cannot report frequency and must use either percent or rate. In selecting which response measure to use, one must consider the previously discussed rules as well as the instructional aim. There are three types of instructional aims for academic behaviors which include increasing: (1) frequency, (2) accuracy, and (3) speed.

Common classroom behaviors that result in permanent products and which teachers often wish to increase include: number of assignments completed, number of book reports written, and number of science experiments conducted. In cases such as these, if opportunity varies but time is constant, one would report percent of assignments completed or percent of experiments conducted. If speed was a concern, one would report performance in terms of rate such as number of book reports completed per week.

Most often instructional aims are focused on increasing accuracy and speed. When accuracy is the chief concern, performance can either be expressed in terms of frequency of correct and incorrect responses (if time and opportunity are constant), percent (if opportunity varies), or rate (if time varies). When speed is the primary concern, such as increasing the number of problems computed correctly per minute, the measure to be used is rate. Rate measures can be collected regardless of whether opportunity or time varies.

In order to illustrate the application of frequency, percent and rate measures to academic behavior problems, each response measure will be discussed briefly and followed by a sample project.

Frequency with Permanent Products

Frequency has been defined as the number of times a behavior occurs. Frequency counts can be taken on either the total number of behaviors which occur, such as number of assignments completed, or number of items completed correctly and incorrectly.

The following project demonstrates how a teacher used frequency to record the number of assignments a student completed per day. In this instance the number of assignments given per day did not vary. Therefore, it was appropriate to record the student's behavior in terms of frequency.

**Classroom Application of Measuring Frequency
(Clark, M. 1978)**

Number of Students
    Third-grade boy, Edwin

Setting
    Regular classroom

Target Behavior/Aim
    To increase the number of assignments Edwin completed per day.

Definition of Target Behavior
    An assignment was considered to be completed if all items were answered.

Observation System and Measurement Technique
    The classroom teacher recorded the number of completed assignments turned in by the student by the end of the day.

Procedures
    During baseline the teacher recorded the number of assignments Edwin turned in. No instructions or consequences were arranged. Prior to the first intervention, the teacher spoke with Edwin's parents. They indicated that they would like to try giving Edwin more encouragement and praise at home. The teacher monitored the effectiveness of the parent's home pep talks on Edwin's behavior. While the teacher appreciated the parents' cooperation, it soon became apparent that pep talks alone would not produce the desired result. The teacher spoke with Edwin and learned that he was worried about his backlog of assignments. The teacher suggested that all former assignments that possibly could be forgotten would be, provided that he could keep up with his daily work. During the second intervention Edwin's efforts were praised by the teacher each day he completed all of his assignments. If he failed to complete an assignment, it was to be completed the next day.

Results
    As can be seen in Figure 6–6, during baseline Edwin typically completed only one out of six assignments per day. During the first intervention, when Edwin's parents were encouraging him at home, his behavior improved but soon leveled off. During the second intervention, the student completed all of his assignments on eight out of eleven days. The teacher is continuing to record Edwin's scores.

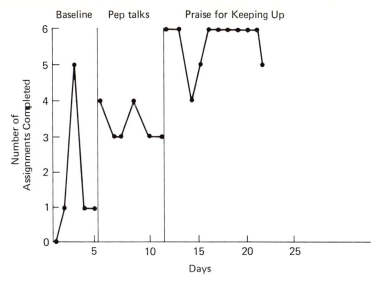

FIGURE 6–6 Number of assignments completed by Edwin. (Adapted from Marcia Clark, *Reinforcing task completion*. Unpublished manuscript, University of Illinois, 1978. By permission of the author.)

Percent with Permanent Products

Percent data provide information about the accuracy of a student's responses. Often teachers are concerned with improving students' accuracy and they choose to measure performance by computing and recording percent correct scores. Percent is the preferred measure when the instructional aim is to improve accuracy and one is not concerned with speed.

In the following project the practicing teacher was concerned about a student's low accuracy in completing workbook assignments in reading. The teacher chose to record performance in terms of percent of items completed correctly as the number of items presented on the assignments varied from page to page.

Classroom Application of Percent
(Paulsen, S. S., 1978)

Number of Students
    Fifth-grade boy, Jay

Setting
    Regular classroom

Target Behavior/Aim
    The aim was to have Jay complete his reading assignment with at least 90 percent accuracy.

Definition of Target Behavior

An assignment was considered to be completed if all items were answered. Correct answers were those which corresponded exactly to those presented in the teacher's edition of the workbooks.

Materials

Jay read daily from *The Magic Word* reader from the Macmillan (Smith & Wardaugh, 1975) basal series. Data were taken on the student's performance in the workbook which accompanied the reader.

Observation System and Measurement Technique

Following the half-hour reading workbook period, the practicing teacher corrected Jay's assignment. The student's percent correct score was then graphed.

Procedures

During baseline no special instructions or consequences were arranged. The practicing teacher simply recorded Jay's accuracy on a graph. During the intervention period Jay was allowed to play a football game. The game consisted of a football field made out of construction paper. Jay was told that each day he completed his assignment he could move the football ahead five yards. The student was also told that he would be given two days to reach 60 percent, one day to reach 70 percent, and two days each to reach 80 percent and 90 percent. Each time the student met the aim for the day he could move the football ahead another five yards. If he received a lower score one day than he had on the previous day, he was penalized five yards.

The goal was to constantly progress until 90 percent was achieved and then remain at that point until a touchdown was made. Jay moved the football himself and also filled in a bar graph. When he made a touchdown, he was given a paper award. When two touchdowns were made, he received a plastic football.

Following the intervention a maintenance condition was scheduled. The game was discontinued and instead Jay was given a piece of paper with blocks for each day of the week. If he scored 80 percent, he could place an Illinois football pennant sticker in that space. If he failed to score 80 percent, no sticker was given.

Results

The data in Figure 6–7 show that during baseline Jay's accuracy averaged 39 percent. On the first day of the intervention period, Jay surprised his teacher by immediately scoring 90 percent rather than progressing gradually. His high score meant he would have to score 90 percent each day to advance the football. His average accuracy during the intervention was 86 percent.

Jay maintained his accuracy after the game was discontinued and he was receiving stickers based on attaining a score of 80 percent correct. In this case no long-term follow-up data were taken as the practicing teacher completed her practicum experience.

Rate with Permanent Product

Rate is one of the most precise measures one can obtain. It provides more information than does a simple frequency count or a percent correct score. For example knowing that a student computed 97 add facts correctly out

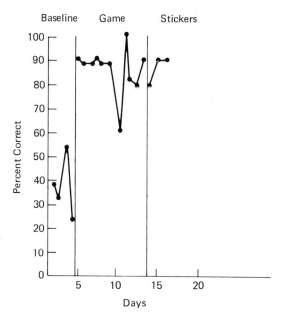

FIGURE 6–7 Jay's percent correct scores on reading assignments. (Adapted from Sandra S. Paulsen, *Improving accuracy on reading assignments*. Unpublished manuscript, University of Illinois, 1978. By permission of the author.)

of 100 does not provide as much information as knowing that a student computed the problem in two minutes, thereby making the student's correct rate 48.5 problems per minute (ppm) and the incorrect rate 1.5 ppm. When rate data are collected one can make statements concerning duration as well as speed and accuracy.

Rate is appropriate for measuring discrete behaviors and it is the measure of choice when one is concerned with speed. Rate is also one of the most overlooked measures, which is unfortunate because it is sensitive to small changes in behavior and is easy to collect. Some teachers time the performance of groups of students by glancing at the second hand of a wall clock. Others prefer to record tones on a tape at predetermined intervals to signal students to start and stop working. Even young students become quite adept at using and reading stopwatches. Many students enjoy timing themselves and are eager to beat their own rate.

**Classroom Application of Rate
(Fantasia, K., personal communication, February 3, 1980)**

Number of Students
Seven students participated in the project; however, data are shown for only one student. Mike was a ten-year-old boy.

Setting
Summer school program for students classified as learning disabled.

Target Behavior/Aim

Increase number of multiplication facts computed correctly per minute. The aim was 50 problems per minute (ppm) correct and zero problems incorrect for two out of three days.

Definition of Target Behaviors

Correct answers were written responses to multiplication facts which were computed accurately. Incorrect responses were written answers which were not computed correctly. Problems not attempted were not counted as either correct or incorrect.

Materials

Five random forms were developed which contained all 100 multiplication facts.

Procedures

During baseline each student was given a worksheet containing all 100 multiplication facts. The students were told the instructional aim and encouraged to work the problems as fast and as accurately as they could. The teacher timed the students performances for two minutes. After completing the worksheet the students corrected them using an answer sheet. The teacher then computed the student's rates and returned the pages to each student with his/her rates at the top of the page. The students then charted their own data.

During the intervention period the students were given five minutes to practice their multiplication facts on the Digitor, an electronic math teaching device. After practicing the students took their two-minute timing. Feedback was provided in the same way as during the baseline period.

Results

During baseline Mike computed an average of 22.7 problems correctly per minute and 1.1 problems incorrectly per minute. While his error rate was low and stable, his correct rate varied from approximately 12 to over 30 problems per minute. During the last four days of baseline his correct rate decreased each day. The data in Figure 6–8 indicate that when Mike practiced his facts on the Digitor his computational performance improved. During the intervention period Mike's average correct rate was 32.4 ppm and his error rate was 0.68 ppm. Due to the summer session ending, no maintenance data could be collected.

DEFINING BEHAVIOR

Before a behavior can be measured it must first be defined in observable terms so that its occurrence can be reliably recorded. Defining behavior can be thought of as a series of steps which begins by identifying the behavior to be measured and results in a written description of the behavior. The steps in defining a behavior are discussed in the following paragraphs and illustrated in Figure 6–9.

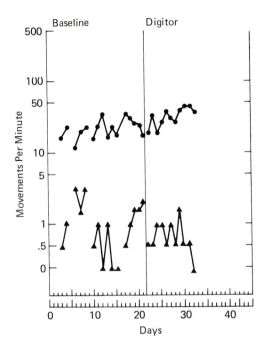

FIGURE 6–8 Mike's computational rate on multiplication facts. (From T.C. Lovitt, Arithmetic, in N.G. Haring, T.C. Lovitt, M.D. Eaton, & C.L. Hansen [Eds.], *The fourth R: Research in the classroom.* Columbus, OH.: Charles E. Merrill, 1978, p. 209. By permission of the publishers.)

Step 1: Identify the Target Behavior

The target behavior is the "behavior to be changed" (Sulzer-Azaroff & Mayer, 1977, p. 524). Another name for a target behavior is the behavior which will be counted or measured. The target behavior is identified by labeling it or by giving it a name. It is best to use short descriptive labels. Some commonly used labels for social behavior targets are: on-task, out-of-seat, and talk-outs. Common labels for academic behavior targets include descriptions such as words read orally or problems computed.

Step 2: Determine Instructional Aim

In addition to labeling the target behavior, it is important to indicate the *overall aim* of the behavior change program. Common target behaviors and instructional aims include: increased accuracy on writing answers to math problems, decreased number of talk-outs, increased amount of time on-task, and increased number of assignments completed. Overall aims indicate the *desired* direction of the behavior change. Although aims are stated broadly at first, they are stated more precisely prior to implementing an intervention. For example a global aim such as "increase speed and accuracy in writing answers to multiplication facts" might be refined to "in-

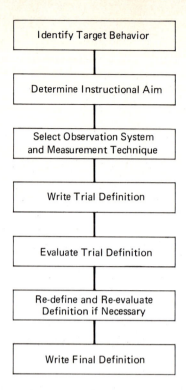

FIGURE 6–9 Steps in Defining a Behavior.

crease writing answers to multiplication facts to 50 per minute correct with zero errors for two days in a row." When possible, aims are stated in the positive, such as increasing time on-task rather than decreasing time off-task.

Step 3: Select Observation System and Measurement Technique

The target behavior determines the type of observation system which should be used. If the target behavior is transitory in nature, then observational recording is used. If the behavior produces a lasting product, then direct measurement of permanent products is used.

Once the observational system is determined one must select an appropriate technique to measure the target behavior. The various types of measurement techniques which can be used for observational and permanent product data are summarized in Tables 6–4 and 6–5, which illustrate the point that one chooses a measurement technique based on both the type of behavior to be measured and the instructional aim. The measurement technique one selects has implications for the way one defines a behavior as we shall see in the next section.

A definition can be thought of as a written statement which consists of a description of *who*, will do *what*, under *what conditions*. In writing a definition one must take into consideration the technique one will use to measure the behavior. This point can best be illustrated through the use of examples. A sample definition for in-seat behavior is as follows:

> In-seat means that Sam will be facing forward in his own desk, the chair and desk will be within two feet of each other and facing forward, his bottom will be in contact with the chair, and all four legs of the chair will be touching the floor. Sam is to be in his seat throughout the math period unless given permission by the teacher to leave the desk.

If one were to analyze the definition into its component parts, it might appear as follows:

Who: Sam

What: In-seat (Sam will be facing forward in own seat, chair and desk within two feet of each other and facing forward, his bottom on seat of chair, all four legs of chair touching floor.

What Conditions: Throughout the math period, unless given permission by teacher to leave his desk

Two points concerning this definition deserve comment. First the description of *what* includes the name of the target behavior as well as the specific criteria which Sam must meet in order to be considered in-seat. Second, the conditions are stated as the circumstances under which Sam is and is not expected to be in his chair.

The definition would be appropriate if one were using time sampling. At the end of every chosen interval, it would be a simple matter to observe Sam and determine if he met all the criteria for being in-seat. This definition would also be appropriate if one were using whole- or partial-interval recording. In the case of whole-interval recording Sam would have to meet all the criteria for being in-seat throughout an interval to be considered in-seat. Using partial-interval recording, Sam would be considered in-seat if at any time during the interval he met all the criteria listed for being in-seat.

If one wished to measure Sam's out-of-seat behavior using event recording, it would be necessary to specify when one out-of-seat ended and another started in order to obtain a frequency count. A sample definition for out-of-seat behavior might be as follows:

> An out-of-seat will be counted each time Sam gets up from a sitting position at his desk (bottom no longer in contact with his chair). Sam should be in his seat throughout the math period, unless given permission by the teacher to leave his desk.

This definition makes clear that one out-of-seat will be counted each time Sam leaves his desk. Another one cannot be counted until Sam returns to

TABLE 6–4 Measurement Techniques for Observational Recording

Instructional Aim	Measurement Technique	Method	Example	Reported As
Increase/decrease frequency	Event recording, p. 118	Tally the behavior after each occurrence.	Count the number of times a student is out-of-seat during a half-hour period.	Total number of times the behavior occurred
	Time sampling, p. 126	Observe only at the end of predetermined time periods and record whether the behavior did or did not occur.	Record whether a student was or was not "attending" at the end of every 5 minutes during a 30-minute period.	Percentage of time (or time blocks) in which the student engaged in the behavior can be expressed as either percent of time in- or out-of-seat (usually stated in positive terms).
	Partial interval recording, p. 131	Divide the observation period into intervals of equal length, e.g. 10 seconds. Continuously observe the student during each interval and record whether the behavior did or did not occur.	Record whether a student was or was not rocking in his/her chair at some time during each interval.	Percentage of time in which the student engaged in the behavior

	Whole interval recording, p. 131	Same as above, but record whether the behavior did or did not occur throughout an *entire* interval.	Record whether a student was or was not on-task.	Percentage of time in which the student engaged in the behavior
Increase/decrease duration	Duration recording, p. 123	Turn a stopwatch on when the student is engaging in the behavior and turn it off when the student is not engaging in the behavior. Repeat this process during length of the observation period or turn a stopwatch on when the student begins a task and turn it off when the task is completed.	Record the amount of times a student is out-of-seat. Record the amount of time a student took to complete an assignment.	Percentage of time in which the student engaged in a behavior during a specific period of time; total number of minutes taken to complete the assignment
Increase/decrease latency	Latency recording, p. 124	Turn a stopwatch on after a predetermined signal and turn it off when the student *begins* the desired behavior.	Record the amount of times a student takes to begin a task after being instructed to do so.	Total number of minutes between the signal (verbal request) and when the student began the task
Describe the full range of behavior displayed prior to pinpointing a target behavior	Continuous recording, p. 133	During a specified time period continuously record all behaviors displayed by the student.	Record behaviors displayed during free time.	Narrative report

TABLE 6–5 Measurement Techniques for Permanent Product Data

Instructional Aim	Measurement Technique	Method	Example	Reported As
Increase/decrease frequency	Frequency count, p. 136	Count the total number of items or tasks completed or count the total number of correct and incorrect responses.	Count the total number of pages completed or count the number of questions a student answered correctly and incorrectly on a written assignment.	Total number of items completed or total number of correct and incorrect answers
Increase accuracy	Percent, p. 137	Count the total number of correct responses, divide by the total number of items presented and multiply by 100.	Count the total number of words spelled correctly on a spelling test.	Percent correct
Increase/decrease speed	Rate, p. 138	Time the student's performance and count the total number of correct and incorrect responses. Then divide each by length of time taken.	Count the number of words a student pronounces correctly and incorrectly while reading orally.	Number of correct and incorrect responses per minute

his desk and again leaves his chair. This definition would be used to obtain a frequency count, or to measure duration or time spent out-of-seat. If duration recording were used, one could record the time which elapses between when Sam gets up from his chair and when he returns to it.

When defining responses which can be classified as either correct or incorrect, it is important to specify the criteria for counting a response as correct or incorrect. For example in defining oral reading one might state the definition as follows:

> Given a 200-word passage on the third grade level from the Ginn 360 series (Ginn, 1969), Susie will orally read the passage. One correct word will be recorded each time Susie correctly pronounces a word or corrects an error herself. One incorrect word will be counted each time Susie omits, adds, or substitutes a word, or if she hesitates on a word for more than four seconds. Errors will not be counted on common names and places or on foreign words.

Steps 5 to 8: Evaluate and Revise Definition

In evaluating a trial definition one might judge or ask others to judge the extent to which the definition includes observable behaviors which are clearly and completely described (Hawkins & Doebs, 1977). The only sufficient test to determine the adequacy of a definition for a transitory behavior is to have another person independently record the behavior at the same time as the teacher or usual observer. When the behavior to be measured results in a permanent product, another individual should independently score the student's work.

For data collected through observational recording, reliability checks are made by having another individual record the behavior along with the teacher. Individuals who could assist in obtaining reliability checks include resource teachers, student teachers, other students, and parent volunteers. At the end of the observation period, the records of the teacher and observer are compared. For example, a teacher may have recorded ten talk-outs and a parent volunteer may have recorded twelve talk-outs. The reliability score would be computed by dividing the lower score by the higher score and multiplying by 100, for example,

$$\frac{10 \text{ (talk-outs recorded by teacher)}}{12 \text{ (talk-outs recorded by parent)}} \times 100 = 83\%$$

This method of computing percent of agreement is appropriate for data obtained through event recording, duration recording, and direct measurement of permanent products (Hall, 1971a).

When computing reliability for data obtained through time sampling or interval recording, one uses the procedure shown in Figure 6–10. Reliability scores of 90 percent or above are "considered desirable, but 80 percent agreement or better is acceptable for many types of observational recording" (Hall, 1971a, p. 18).

If a high degree of agreement is obtained, one simply proceeds to

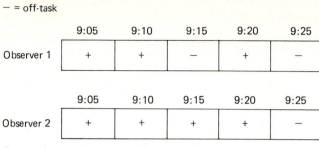

Step 1: Count the number of times each observer agreed with
the other that the behavior did or did not occur, for
example, the observers agreed 4 out of 5 times.

Step 2: Divide the total number of agreements by the total
number of time blocks and multiply by 100, for example:
$\frac{4}{5}$ × 100 = 80% agreement

FIGURE 6–10 Computing Reliability for Time Sample or Interval Data.

measure performance based on the behavioral descriptions contained in
the definition. On the other hand if reliability is low, then one must revise
the behavioral definition and evaluate its adequacy by continuing to make
reliability checks. Once a definition results in the collection of reliable data,
the final definition is written and behavior is recorded according to the
written description of the behavior contained in the definition.

SUMMARY

In this chapter, the reader has been introduced to a systematic method for
observing and measuring classroom behavior. Many teachers, upon learning of the uses of these observational methods and the effectiveness of
data-based instructional techniques, are impressed but unconvinced as to
the practicality of these methods in regular classrooms. Their comments
range from "That's fine for a special class teacher, but I don't have the
time," to "Show me how to do it with 30 kids!" It is no accident that
the measurement techniques described in this chapter were illustrated
through the use of sample projects, many of which were conducted by
preservice and inservice teachers in regular classrooms. The sample projects demonstrate that classroom teachers can successfully identify behavior problems, record their occurrence, and implement programs to change
students' behavior. Other individuals, such as resource-consulting teachers, school psychologists, school social workers, student teachers, and
parent volunteers, may also be able to assist teachers in collecting data.
However the tendency should not be to rely on outside help without considering ways that the teacher or another individual in the classroom, such
as a student teacher, could collect the desired data. Often resource-con-

sulting teachers can assist teachers in identifying practical ways to measure behavior and make suggestions for setting up programs to change behavior which the teacher can implement.

There are many advantages of using a data-based observational approach to solve classroom behavior problems. First it assists teachers in focusing on observable behaviors which can be changed. Second, it provides teachers with a variety of techniques which can be used to observe and measure a wide range of social and academic behavior problems. Third it helps teachers to verify whether a problem behavior really exists. Fourth it assists teachers in setting realistic aims for students to meet. Fifth it enables teachers to monitor the effects of their teaching techniques and to change techniques when necessary to improve pupil performance. Finally it allows teachers to document progress and to share that information with students, parents and other school personnel.

Charting Pupil Performance Data

7

In Chapter 6, a variety of techniques were presented which teachers can use to measure the behavior of students who display learning and/or behavior problems. Teachers who collect data often choose to record it on a graph. Graphs provide a visual display of pupil performance. Graphs also provide teachers with a ready means of documenting changes in pupil performance as well as communicating progress to students, parents and other school personnel.

Before one can use charted data to make instructional decisions, some basic charting techniques must be mastered. In this chapter the reader will be introduced to different types of graphs and raw data sheets. Emphasis will be placed on the mechanics of charting. We will delay our discussion of interpreting and evaluating charted data until the reader has had an opportunity to become familiar with basic charting conventions. In this chapter the reader will learn how to: (1) select an appropriate graph, (2) plot pupil performance data, and (3) design and record information on a raw data sheet.

METHODS OF RECORDING PUPIL PERFORMANCE

There are a variety of different types of graphs. Perhaps the most common type is the arithmetic line graph. These graphs can either be hand drawn using grid paper or purchased commercially. Due to the availability of published graphs, it is no longer necessary for teachers to draw their own graphs. Arithmetic line graphs, such as the Classroom Behavior Graph shown in Figure 7–1, have many uses. Using this type of graph paper the reader will learn how to plot both observational and permanent product data.

Although performance can always be plotted on a graph, there are times when teachers wish to record additional information. For example a teacher may choose to graph the percent of words a student spells correctly using an arithmetic line graph. If the teacher wishes to keep track of exactly which words a student spells correctly and incorrectly, it would be necessary to record that information on a raw data sheet. A sample raw data sheet for spelling is shown in Figure 7–2.

Raw data sheets can be designed to record precisely the information a teacher desires. Samples of several types of raw data sheets are included in this chapter to acquaint the reader with the many advantages they offer in recording pupil performance.

THE CLASSROOM BEHAVIOR GRAPH

Description

Arithmetic line graphs consist of several parts which can be simply diagramed as shown in Figure 7–3. Each part is briefly described and specific

CLASSROOM BEHAVIOR GRAPH

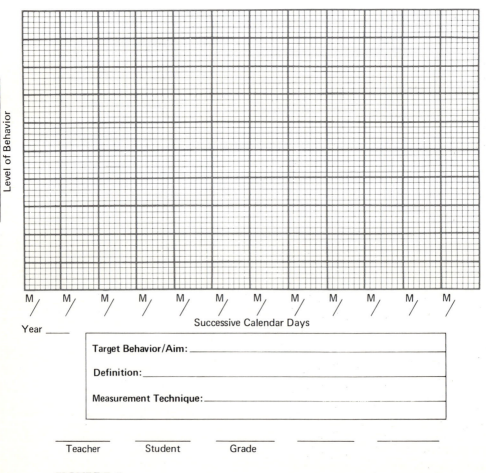

FIGURE 7–1

reference is made to the location of each part on the Classroom Behavior **153**
Graph shown in Figure 7–1.   *The Classroom*
Behavior Graph

The y-axis   The vertical line on an arithmetic line graph is called the y-axis. The y-axis is perpendicular to the x-axis (horizontal line) and has an origin of zero. The y-axis is used to denote the levels of behavior recorded on the graph.

On the Classroom Behavior Graph, one selects which values to use depending upon the behavior to be graphed. For example if one were graphing frequency of talk-outs and a student's talk-outs during baseline

Name _____

Day	Date	Condition	No. of Words C	No. of Words I	%C	across	under	between	over	side	front	among	around	through	back
M	9/1	Baseline	4	6	40	x	x	x	c	c	c	x	x	x	c
Tu	9/2	''	3	7	30	x	x	x	c	c	x	x	x	x	c
W	9/3	''	4	6	40	x	x	x	c	c	c	x	x	x	c
Th	9/4	Copy, cover compare	4	6	30	x	x	x	c	c	x	x	x	x	c
F	9/5	''	6	4	60	c	c	x	c	c	c	x	x	x	c
M	9/8	''	7	3	70	c	c	x	c	c	c	c	x	x	c
Tu	9/9														
W	9/10														
Th	9/11														
F	9/12														
M	9/15														
Tu	9/16														
W	9/17														
Th	9/18														
F	9/19														
M	9/22														
Tu	9/23														
W	9/24														
Th	9/25														
F	9/26														

FIGURE 7–2 Spelling Raw Data Sheet

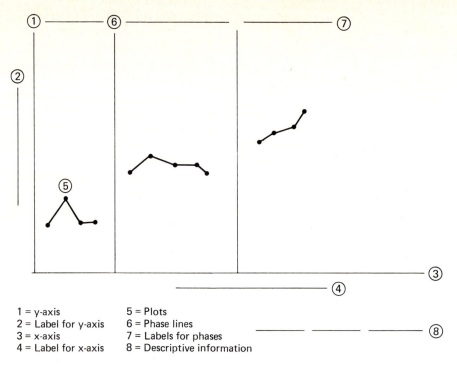

1 = y-axis   5 = Plots
2 = Label for y-axis   6 = Phase lines
3 = x-axis   7 = Labels for phases
4 = Label for x-axis   8 = Descriptive information

FIGURE 7–3 Parts of a Line Graph

ranged from ten to thirty, one might mark the increments as shown in Example 1 of Figure 7–4. If one wished to graph percent data, such as percent of problems computed correctly, one would mark the increments as shown in Example 2 of Figure 7–4. As the reader can easily determine, one has the option of marking in precisely those increments needed to record a particular behavior when using the Classroom Behavior Graph. Because the Classroom Behavior Graph is drawn on an arithmetic scale one must make sure that the values one marks on the *y*-axis are the same distance from one another.

Label for the *y*-axis The label indicates the type of data displayed on the graph. Labels necessarily vary depending upon the type of behavior to be graphed. Common descriptive phrases for observational and permanent product data are shown in Table 7–1. On the Classroom Behavior Graph one would write the appropriate label to describe the behavior graphed as shown in the examples in Figure 7–5.

The *x*-axis The *x*-axis or horizontal line is used to denote days. Some teachers prefer to include only school days on graphs they design themselves; others prefer to use graphs containing lines for each day in a calendar week. Graphs which include calendar days, such as the Classroom Behavior Graph, enable teachers to note the effect of weekends and holidays on performance.

The Classroom Behavior Graph allows one to record performance for a twelve-week period. In looking at Figure 7–6, one can see that each Sunday line is darker than the other day lines. Each Monday line is marked with an *M* and one records the appropriate month and date under each *M* or Monday on the graph as shown in Figure 7–6. The Classroom Behavior Graph also contains a line on which one can write the year in which the data were collected.

Label for x-axis If a teacher designs his or her own graph, the *x*-axis must be labeled. If the graph contains lines for each day of the week, one labels it "Successive Calendar Days." This label is printed on the Classroom Behavior Graph as it contains lines for each day in a calendar week. If one designs a graph with lines for Monday through Friday, then one labels the *x*-axis "Successive School Days."

Plots Plots on a line graph are made by either drawing a darkened circle freehand or using a template. If one is graphing a single behavior such as number of out-of-seats or percent of time studying, a dot is placed at the point at which the recorded value intersects the day on which the data were collected. For example, if a student scored 10 percent correct in spelling on Monday, September 1, one would graph it as shown in Figure 7–7. Since the graph in Figure 7–7 contains increments of two, one would have to plot odd-numbered scores such as 15 percent midway between even-

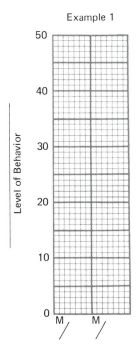

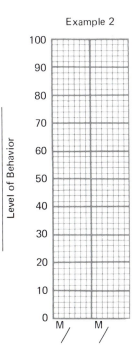

FIGURE 7–4 Marking the Y-Axis

TABLE 7–1 Common Labels for the Y-Axis on Arithmetic Line Graphs

Observational System	Measurement Technique	Data Collected	Labels	Examples
Observational recording	Event recording	Number of times a behavior occurs	Number of (behavior) or frequency of (behavior)	Number of talk-outs or frequency of talk-outs
	Duration recording	Number of minutes engaged in a behavior or percent of time engaged in a behavior	Number of minutes spent (behavior) or number of minutes to complete (behavior) or percent of time spent (behavior)	Number of minutes spent out-of-seat or number of minutes to complete math assignment or percent of time spent studying
	Latency	Number of minutes between a signal and beginning to engage in a behavior	Time taken before beginning to (behavior)	Time taken before beginning to put away materials
	Time sample	Percent of time engaged in a behavior	Percent of time (behavior)	Percent of time on-task

	Interval	Percent of time engaged in a behavior	Percent of time (behavior)	Percent of time interacting with peers
Direct measurement of permanent products	Frequency	Number of times a behavior occurs or number of correct and incorrect responses	Number of (behavior) or number of (responses)	Number of assignments completed or number of words spelled
	Percent	Percent of correct responses	Percent of (behavior) correctly	Percent of words spelled correctly
	Rate	Number of times a behavior occurs per unit of time or number of correct and incorrect responses per unit of time	Number of (responses) per minute or number of (correct/incorrect responses) per minute	Number of talk-outs per minute or number of words read correctly per minute

Example 1   Example 2

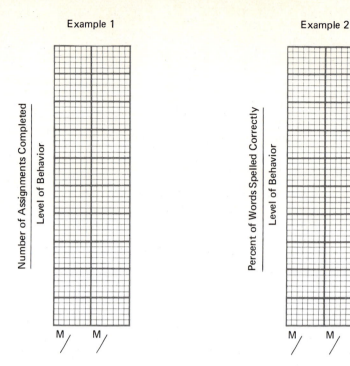

FIGURE 7–5 Labeling the Y-Axis

numbered scores. Thus one would graph a score of 15 percent on Tuesday, September 2, as shown in Figure 7–7.

Sometimes one wishes to graph both the number of correct and incorrect responses a student makes on an assignment. For example one might plot the number of correct and incorrect answers a student makes on an arithmetic worksheet. The reader will recall from Chapter 6 that the data can be plotted in terms of frequency only if the number and types of problems remain constant from day to day; otherwise, performance would have to be graphed as percent. If the assignment contained an equal number of problems per day, and the problems were similar, one could plot

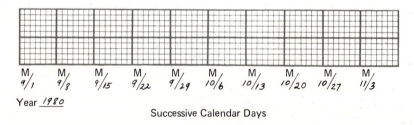

Year *1980*

Successive Calendar Days

FIGURE 7–6 Marking the X-Axis

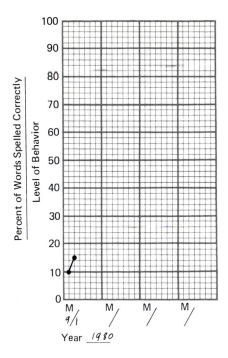

FIGURE 7–7 Plotting Performance

frequency data. In that case a dot could be used to indicate the number of correct problems and either an *x* or a triangle could be used to indicate the number of incorrect problems per day. It is usually faster to plot incorrect responses using *x's* rather than triangles. When using triangles to plot incorrect responses, the apex of the triangle should point to the number of incorrect responses. Both methods of graphing incorrect responses are shown in Figure 7–8.

Phase lines   *Phase lines* indicate the conditions under which the data are being collected have changed. For example a phase line would be drawn between data collected under baseline conditions and after each new teaching technique. Phase lines are made by drawing a solid vertical line from the top of the *y*-axis to the *x*-axis. The graph shown in Figure 7–9 has one phase line which is used to separate the data collected under baseline and the data collected under the first teaching technique used.

Labels for phase lines   Labels consist of short phrases which describe the conditions under which data were collected. For example after obtaining a baseline measure of a student's on-task behavior, a teacher might choose to praise the student at the end of each interval in which the student was observed to be on-task. The first condition would be labeled "Baseline" and the second would be labeled "Praise" as shown in Figure 7–9.

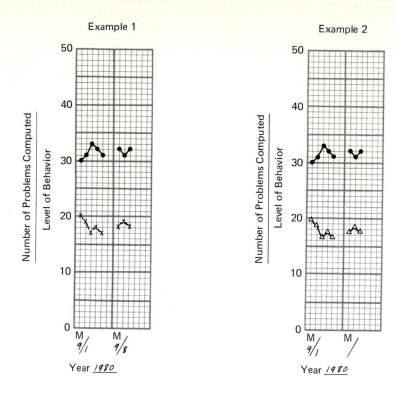

FIGURE 7–8 Plotting the Number of Correct and Incorrect Responses

Descriptive information Common descriptive information included on most commercially available graphs includes: teacher's name, student's name, grade, behavior charted, setting, and type of measurement technique used. As can be seen in Figure 7–9, the Classroom Behavior Graph includes spaces to write the following information: target behavior/aim, definition of target behavior, and measurement technique used. This information is included so that anyone viewing the graph can immediately determine the type of behavior being recorded, the instructional aim, how the behavior is defined, and how it is being measured. On the horizontal lines along the bottom of the graph one can write the teacher's name and the student's name and grade. The two additional lines can be used to record other desired information such as, the student's school and classroom, the name of a supervisor, or perhaps the name of a student teacher who is implementing the behavioral change program.

Graphing Conventions Graphs are used to record the effects of instructional techniques on student performance and to communicate pupil progress to others. In order to represent a student's actual performance and to make educational decisions based on charted data, one must be sure that the data recorded on the graph is accurate. By following certain graphing rules or conventions, teachers can be sure that they plot performance consistently. This practice aids them and others in interpreting charted data and making instructional decisions based on student performance.

Although conventions are arbitrary rules, some procedures have become fairly well accepted. When graphing data, one always uses a pencil so that corrections can easily be made. Two conventions described by White and Haring (1976) concern connecting points and phrase lines. Plots are connected by drawing a straight line from one plotted day to the next. Plots are *not* connected over weekends, holidays, absences or across instructional phases. Phase lines are made by drawing a solid vertical line from the top of the *y*-axis to the *x*-axis. Phase lines are placed one-half day before a new teaching technique is implemented. For example if a new technique is applied on Monday, the phase line would be drawn halfway between Sunday and Monday of the appropriate week. These charting conventions are illustrated in Figure 7–10.

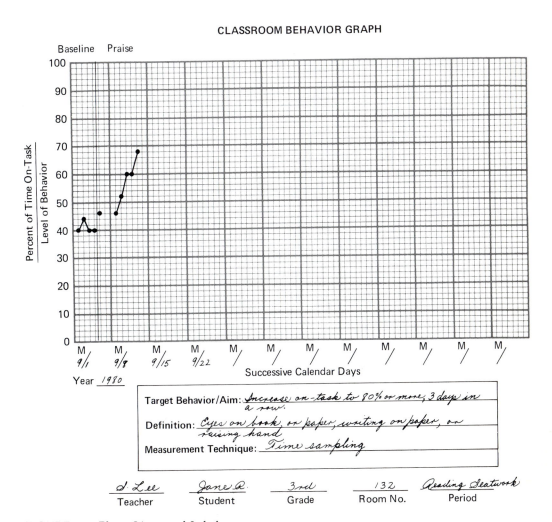

FIGURE 7–9 Phase Lines and Labels

PLOTTING PERFORMANCE ON THE CLASSROOM BEHAVIOR GRAPH

In Chapter 6 the reader was introduced to a variety of techniques to measure classroom behaviors. In this chapter we will explain how one records certain types of pupil performance data on the Classroom Behavior Graph. Hypothetical case studies as well as sample graphs and step-by-step directions are presented to illustrate how one plots the following types of data.

Observational Data

The following types of observational data can be plotted on the Classroom Behavior Graph: event, duration, latency, time sampling, and interval.

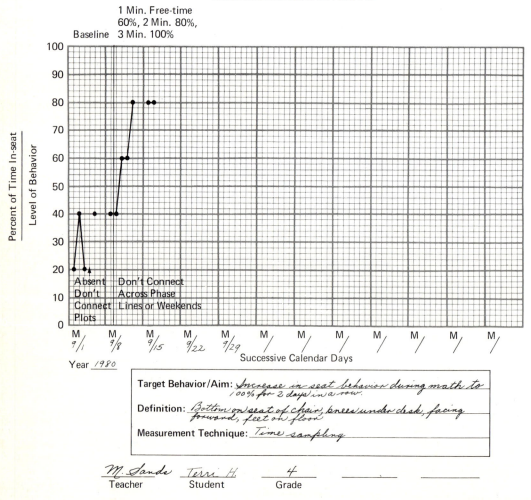

CLASSROOM BEHAVIOR GRAPH

FIGURE 7–10 Charting Conventions

Example for Event Recording

Number of Students
>Five-year-old girl, Stacy

Setting
>Kindergarten classroom

Target Behavior/Aim
>Decrease number of talk-outs per day to two or fewer and maintain at that level.

Definition of Target Behavior
>A talk-out was defined as any verbal sound made by Stacy which was audible to the teacher. Whenever Stacy paused for thirty seconds or more and then talked-out, another talk-out was recorded.

Measurement Technique
>The teacher took data throughout the school day in the classroom. Each time Stacy talked-out the teacher noted it by pushing the clicker on a supermarket counter which she kept in her pocket.

Procedures
>During baseline the teacher continued with her normal procedure for dealing with Stacy's talk-outs. Whenever Stacy began to talk-out the teacher directed her to go back to work, and carried on the lesson with the other students while ignoring Stacy's outbursts. During baseline the teacher noted that even though she was ignoring Stacy's inappropriate behavior, other members of the class were not.

>For the first intervention the teacher told Stacy that she could earn five minutes of free time at the end of each half hour in which she refrained from talking-out. The teacher asked the rest of the class to ignore Stacy's outbursts and praised them for working well whenever Stacy began to talk-out.

Hypothetical Data
>The teacher recorded the number of talk-outs Stacy had each day on the raw data sheet as shown in Figure 7–11.

		Student's Name *Stacy*	
Day	Date	Condition	No. of Talk-outs
M	9/1/80	Baseline	7
Tu	9/2	"	6
W	9/3	—	Absent
Th	9/4	"	8
F	9/5	Free time/praise others	4
M	9/8	"	3
Tu	9/9	"	1
W	9/10	"	1

FIGURE 7–11 Stacy's Raw Data Sheet

Steps in Graphing Performance

The following completed steps are shown in Figure 7–12.
1. Fill in descriptive information
2. Label the *y*-axis "Number of talk-outs"
3. Label *y*-axis from 0 to 10, marking each bold line in increments of 1
4. Write in appropriate dates and year
5. Label baseline phase
6. Plot baseline data
7. Draw phase change line one-half day before Friday, September 5
8. Label second phase "Free Time & Praise Others"
9. Plot data collected during second phase

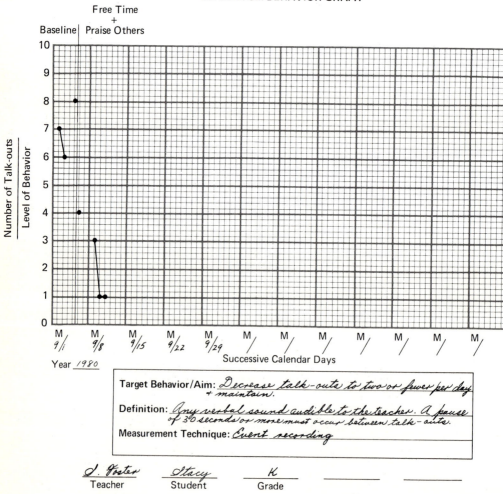

FIGURE 7–12 Stacy's Graph

Example for Duration Recording[1]

Number of Students

> Tenth grader, Alan

Setting

> Study hall

Target Behavior/Aim

Increase percent of time Alan spends studying to 80 percent or more for one week and maintain at or above this level throughout the semester.

Definition of Target Behavior

Studying was defined as: sitting in assigned seat, facing forward, eyes directed toward textbook or note paper, writing on note paper, or raising hand. Nonstudy behaviors included: talking without permission, laughing, throwing objects, leaving desk, turning around in desk, dropping books on floor.

Measurement Technique

The study hall teacher used a stopwatch to record the amount of time Alan actually spent studying during the fifty-minute study hall period. As the teacher was not involved in providing direct instruction to students in study hall, it was a simple matter to click the stopwatch on when Alan was studying and click it off when Alan engaged in other behaviors. The teacher began recording Alan's behavior as soon as he completed filling out the day's attendance form after requesting all students to sit down and begin working. The teacher noted the time he began to observe Alan. At the end of the first thirty-minute period, the teacher checked the elapsed time on the stopwatch and recorded the number of minutes Alan had been seen studying. He then quickly reset the stopwatch and began again to click it on when Alan was studying and off when Alan was not studying. When the bell rang, the teacher noted the time on the wall clock and turned the stopwatch off. He then checked the elapsed time and recorded the total number of minutes Alan had spent studying between the time he reset the watch and when the bell rang.

Procedures

During baseline the teacher recorded the total number of minutes Alan spent studying. No special consequences were arranged. Prior to implementing an intervention, the study hall teacher spoke with some of Alan's teachers. He learned that Alan was doing poorly in most subjects with the exception of mechanical drawing. Most of Alan's teachers believed that Alan was capable of doing better; he just rarely put in the effort required to do well in their courses. The study hall teacher and mechanical drawing instructor agreed that Alan would be allowed to spend Friday study hall period assisting the mechanical drawing teacher provided that he averaged at least 50 percent of his time studying during study hall on Monday through Thursday. The study hall teacher presented the option to Alan and he readily agreed. Each day after class the study hall teacher told Alan the percent of time he had spent studying.

---

[1] The reader will recall from Chapter 6 that there are two ways to measure the duration of a behavior. One example for duration is shown.

Hypothetical Data

The study hall teacher recorded Alan's study behavior on the raw data sheet shown in Figure 7–13. Alan's behavior was then charted on a graph as shown in Figure 7–14.

Steps in Graphing Performance
1. Fill in descriptive information
2. Label *y*-axis "Percent of Time Spent Studying"
3. Label *y*-axis from 0 to 100, marking each bold line in increments of 10
4. Write in appropriate dates and year
5. Label baseline phase
6. Plot baseline data according to data in last column on raw data sheet
7. Draw phase change line one-half day before Friday, November 7
8. Label second phase "Assist Mechanical Drawing Teacher"
9. Plot data collected during second phase

Example for Latency Recording
Number of students

Twenty-seven third graders

Setting

Playground and classroom

Target Behavior/Aim

Increase punctuality of entire class in returning to the room after morning recess. The aim was to reduce the length of time it took the class to return to the classroom to two minutes or less following the ringing of the recess bell.

Definition of Target Behavior

Punctuality was measured by recording the number of minutes which elapsed between the ringing of the recess bell and when the last student sat down.

Day	Date	Condition	Start Time	Number Minutes Spent Studying		Stop Time	Total Number Minutes Observed	Total Number Minutes Spent Studying	Percent of Time Studying
				First Half	Second Half				
Tu	11/4/80	Baseline	1:05	3:40	4:20	1:50	45:00	8:00	18
W	11/5	"	1:07	4:12	2:05	1:49	42:00	6:17	15
Th	11/6	"	1:04	2:17	2:30	1:50	46:00	4:47	10
F	11/7	Assist Teacher	1:05	15:43	16:32	1:49	44:00	32:15	73
M	11/10	"	1:04	18:25	19:00	1:50	46:00	37:25	81
Tu	11/11	"	1:06	25:03	15:17	1:49	43:00	40:20	93

FIGURE 7–13 Alan's Raw Data Sheet

Measurement Technique

As soon as the recess bell rang, the teacher glanced at the wall clock and noted the time to the nearest half minute. She then recorded the time on an index card. When the last student to enter the room sat down, the teacher again noted the time on the wall clock and recorded the information on the index card.

Procedures

Prior to implementing an intervention, the teacher collected baseline data. She recorded the data without saying anything to the students. On the first day of the intervention condition just before recess, the teacher announced that she had just received an exciting adventure story. The teacher then read a bit of the story out loud and told the students she would read some more of it after recess. When the recess bell rang the teacher noted the time. She then waited for two

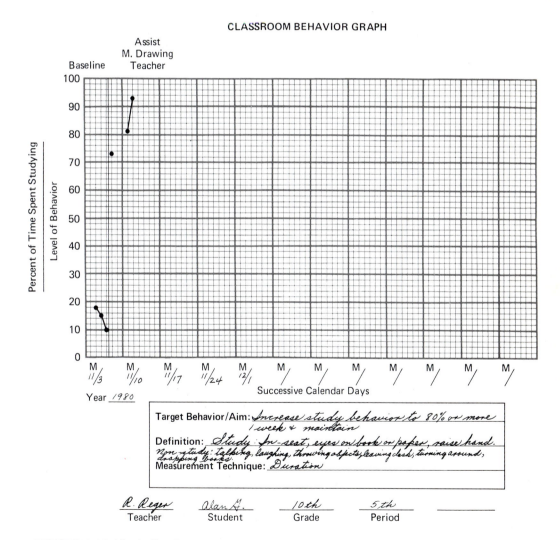

FIGURE 7–14 Alan's Graph

minutes, complimented the students who were on time, and began to read the story. When the last child returned to the class and sat down, the teacher noted the time on the index card.

Hypothetical Data

The teacher transferred each day's data from the index card to the raw data sheet which follows.

Steps in Graphing Performance
1. Fill in descriptive information
2. Label *y*-axis "Number Minutes Taken to Return to Class"
3. Label *y*-axis from 0 to 10 in increments of 1
4. Write in appropriate dates and year
5. Label baseline phase
6. Plot baseline data according to data shown in last column on raw data sheet
7. Draw phase change line one-half day before Tuesday, January 8
8. Label second phase "Read Story"
9. Plot data collected during second phase

Example for Time Sample Recording
Number of Students
Two first-grade girls, Cindy and Sue

Setting
Regular classroom

Target Behavior/Aim
Decrease the extent to which two girls visited with each other while the teacher was instructing other students in reading. The aim was to reduce the girls' visiting to zero during the first reading-group period.

Definition of Target Behavior
Visiting was defined as one girl talking to the other, looking at each other, one or both girls giggling, or passing notes to each other.

Measurement Technique
The teacher collected data during the first reading group, when both Cindy and Sue were to be working at their desks. The reading group met for twenty-five

Day	Date	Condition	Time Bell Rang	Time Last Student In-Seat	Elapsed Time
Th	1/3	Baseline	10:15	10:23	8 minutes
F	1/4	''	10:14	10:20	6 minutes
M	1/7	''	10:15	10:21	7 minutes
Tu	1/8	Read Story	10:14	10:19	5 minutes
W	1/9	''	10:15	10:20	5 minutes
Th	1/10	''	10:15	10:18	3 minutes
F	1/11	''	10:14	10:17	3 minutes

FIGURE 7–15 Raw Data Sheet for Class

minutes. At the end of every five minutes, on the average, the teacher looked at the two girls and determined whether or not they were visiting. Using an index card with five time blocks marked off, she recorded a " + " if they were visiting and a " – " if they were not. The teacher computed the percent of time the girls visited per day and transferred each day's data to a raw data sheet.

Procedures

During baseline the teacher simply recorded the data without letting on to the other students what she was doing. At the end of the baseline period, the teacher spoke with Cindy and Sue and told them that sitting next to each other was a privilege. She indicated that in order to keep their same seats, they would have to show the teacher that they could work quietly without visiting. The teacher encouraged them to try their best not to visit during classtime but to wait until free time or recess. After the end of the reading period, the teacher told the two girls

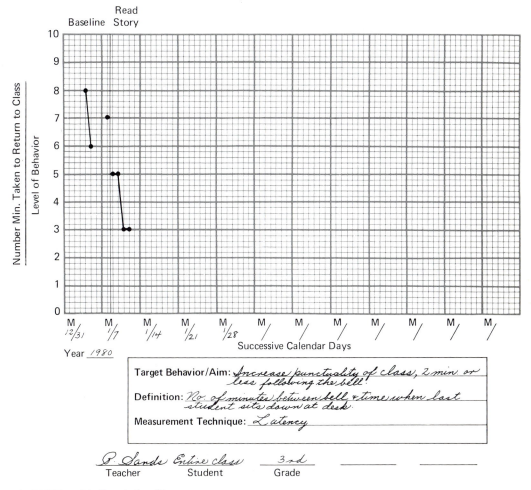

FIGURE 7–16 Graph for Class

whether she thought they had worked quietly or not. On days when the girls spent less than 60 percent of their time visiting, the teacher complimented them and encouraged them to try harder the next day. The lower the level of visiting, the more lavish the teacher became with her praise. Once the girls reached the aim, the teacher changed to a maintenance condition. The teacher decreased the frequency of her praise and told the girls they had proved to her they could work quietly and suggested they keep it up.

Hypothetical Data
        The teacher recorded the data on the raw data sheet shown in Figure 7–17.

Steps in Graphing Performance
 1. Fill in descriptive information
 2. Label *y*-axis "Percent of Time Visiting"
 3. Label *y*-axis from 0 to 100, making each bold line in increments of 10
 4. Write in appropriate dates and year
 5. Label baseline phase
 6. Plot baseline data
 7. Draw first phase change line one-half day before Friday, October 10
 8. Label second phase "Daily Praise"
 9. Plot data for second phase
10. Draw second phase change line one-half day before Friday, October 17
11. Label third phase "Occasional Praise"
12. Plot data for third phase

Example for Interval Recording
Number of Students
        Kindergarten boy, Ed

Setting
        Regular classroom

Day	Date	Condition	Percent of Time Visiting
M	10/6/80	Baseline	80
Tu	10/7	"	60
W	10/8	"	40
Th	10/9	"	80
F	10/10	Daily Praise	40
M	10/13	"	20
Tu	10/14	"	0
W	10/15	"	0
Th	10/16	"	0
F	10/17	Occasional Praise	0
M	10/20	"	20
Tu	10/21	"	0

FIGURE 7–17 Cindy's and Sue's Raw Data Sheet

Target Behavior/Aim
    Increase amount of time Ed interacts with other students during free time to 60 percent or more, and maintain at or above that level.

Definition of Target Behavior
    Interaction was defined as Ed being within three feet of another student and either looking at or talking to a student, exchanging materials, or playing a game.

Measurement Technique
    Because the teacher supervised free-time play, she asked her student teacher to do the observations. The student teacher observed Ed's behavior throughout the fifteen-minute free-time period. Using a ten-second observe, ten-second record procedure, the student teacher noted if at any time during an interval, Ed interacted with his classmates. A "+" was used to indicate that the student had interacted

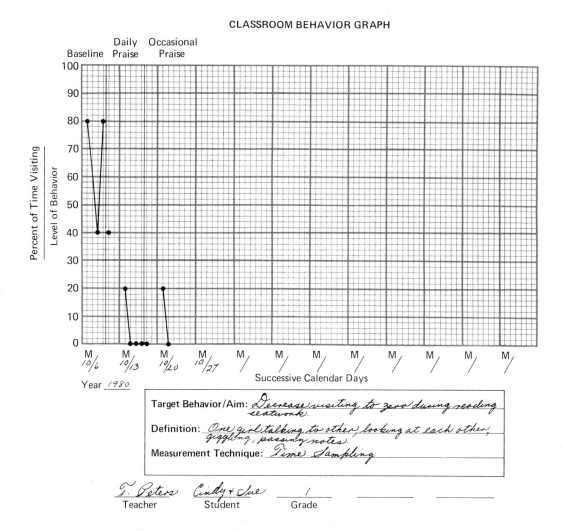

FIGURE 7–18 Cindy's and Sue's Graph

and a "−" was used to indicate that no interaction had taken place during the interval.

Procedures

During baseline, the teacher continued to supervise the student's free time as she had in the past. The student teacher observed Ed's behavior without commenting to the pupils what she was doing. After the baseline period the teacher began the following intervention. Whenever Ed was playing by himself, she encouraged him to join in with the group. The teacher stayed with the group for a brief time and then left. After a short time she returned to the group and complimented the students if they were playing together well. She particularly complimented Ed for joining in with the games.

Hypothetical Data

The student teacher recorded her data on the raw data sheet shown in Figure 7–19.

Steps in Graphing Performance
1. Fill in descriptive information
2. Label the y-axis "Percent of Time Interacting"
3. Label y-axis from 0 to 100, marking each bold line in increments of 10
4. Write in appropriate dates and year
5. Label baseline phase
6. Plot baseline data according to data shown in last column of raw data sheet
7. Draw phase change line one-half day before Friday, October 19
8. Label second phase "Coach and Praise"
9. Plot data collected during second phase

Permanent Product Data

Frequency, percent and rate data collected by the direct measurement of permanent products can be plotted on the Classroom Behavior Graph. The

| Day | Date | Condition | Number of Intervals | | | Percent of Time Interacting |
			Interacting	Not Interacting	Total	
M	10/15/80	Baseline	6	39	45	13
Tu	10/16	"	8	37	45	18
W	10/17	"	10	35	45	22
Th	10/18	"	7	38	45	16
F	10/19	Coach & Praise	15	30	45	33
M	10/22	"	20	25	45	44
Tu	10/23	"	25	20	45	56

FIGURE 7–19 Ed's Raw Data Sheet

reader will recall from Chapter 6 that frequency data can be collected by measuring either the number of times a behavior occurs, or the number of correct and incorrect responses. In our first example the latter type of frequency data is shown so that we can demonstrate how one plots both the number of correct and the number of incorrect responses on the same day.

Example for Frequency
Number of Students
   Third grader, Jim

Setting
   Regular classroom

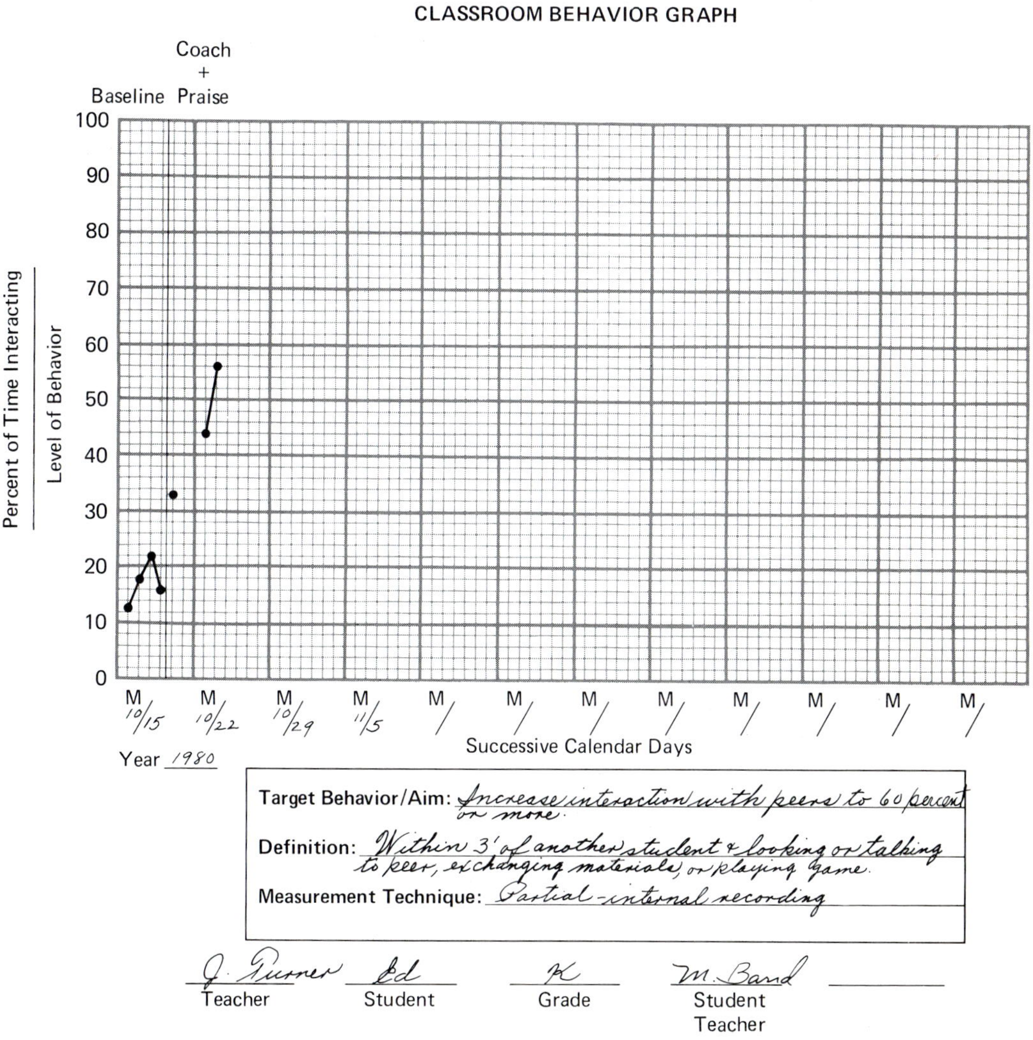

CLASSROOM BEHAVIOR GRAPH

FIGURE 7-20 Ed's Graph

Target Behavior/Aim

Increase number of correct answers to subtraction problems involving borrowing to twenty correct with zero errors for two days in a row.

Definition of Target Behavior

A correct response is a written answer which matches the sum one would obtain by subtracting the subtrahend from the minuend. Incorrect responses included wrong answers and problems not attempted.

Measurement Technique

Each day the teacher corrected Jim's worksheet containing twenty subtraction borrow problems and counted the number of correct and incorrect answers.

Procedures

During baseline Jim completed one of five pages of twenty subtraction borrow problems. No instruction or feedback was provided. On the first day of the intervention period, the teacher demonstrated how to compute four types of subtraction borrow problems contained on the student's worksheet. After the student completed the worksheet the teacher corrected it and told Jim the number of problems he answered correctly and incorrectly.

Hypothetical Data

The teacher recorded Jim's data on the raw data sheet shown in Figure 7–21.

Steps in Graphing Performance
1. Fill in descriptive information
2. Label the *y*-axis "Number of Problems Computed"
3. Label the *y*-axis from 0 to 20, marking each increment as 1
4. Write in appropriate dates and year
5. Label baseline phase
6. Plot baseline data using a dot for number of correct answers and an *x* for number of incorrect answers

Day	Date	Condition	Number Right	Number Wrong
M	11/3/80	Baseline	5	15
Tu	11/4	''	6	14
W	11/5	''	4	16
Th	11/6	Demonstration Plus Feedback	10	10
F	11/7	''	12	8
M	11/10	''	15	5
Tu	11/11	''	18	2

FIGURE 7–21 Jim's Raw Data Sheet

7. Draw phase change line one-half day before Thursday, November 12
8. Label second phase "Demonstration + Feedback"
9. Plot data collected under second phase

Example for Percent
Number of Students
      Sixth grader, Kim

Setting
      Regular classroom

Target Behavior/Aim
      Increase accuracy on circling correct answers to reading comprehension questions to 80 percent or more, and maintain at or above that level.

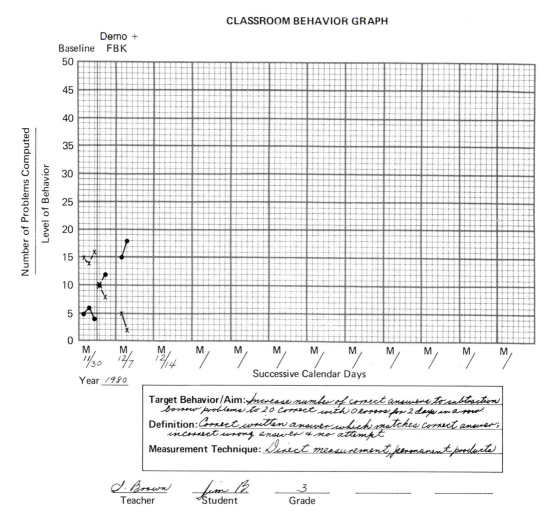

FIGURE 7–22 Jim's Graph

Definition of Target Behavior
    A correct answer was one which matched the multiple-choice answer given on the key.

Measurement Technique
    The teacher looked back through her records and graphed the student's accuracy on reading comprehension questions during the prior two-week period. During the intervention the student corrected her own work and graphed her daily accuracy.

Procedures
    During baseline the teacher corrected the student's assignments and marked the percentage correct at the top of the page. Prior to the intervention the student was shown her graph and asked if she would like to keep track of her own performance. During the intervention period the teacher requested to see the student's chart and praised her if her performance had improved.

Hypothetical Data
    The raw data sheet shown in Figure 7–23 was used to record performance.

Steps in Graphing Performance
1. Fill in descriptive information
2. Label the y-axis "Percent Correct Comprehension"
3. Label the y-axis from 0 to 100, marking each bold line in increments of 10
4. Write appropriate dates and year
5. Label baseline phase
6. Plot baseline data using data shown
7. Draw phase change line one-half day before Monday, February 18
8. Label second phase "Self-Graph"
9. Plot data collected during second phase

Day	Date	Condition	Reading Card Number	Number Right	Number Wrong	Percent Correct
M	2/4/80	Baseline	21	4	6	40
Tu	2/5	"	22	7	3	70
W	2/6	"	23	5	6	45
Th	2/7	"	24	8	3	73
F	2/8	"	25	4	7	36
M	2/11	"	26	6	6	50
Tu	2/12	"	27	3	7	30
W	2/13	"	28	6	4	60
Th	2/14	"	29	4	7	36
F	2/15	"	30	3	7	30
M	2/18	Self-graph	31	6	4	60
Tu	2/19	"	32	8	2	80
W	2/20	"	33	7	3	70

FIGURE 7–23 Kim's Raw Data Sheet

Example for Rate
Number of Students
    Fourth grader, Sam

Setting
    Regular classroom

Target Behavior/Aim
    Increase number of written answers to multiplication facts to fifty per minute correct with zero errors for two days in a row.

Definition of Target Behavior
    Correct answers were those which matched the answer one would obtain by multiplying the numbers presented. All other responses were counted as incorrect as were illegible answers. Problems not attempted were not counted as either correct or incorrect.

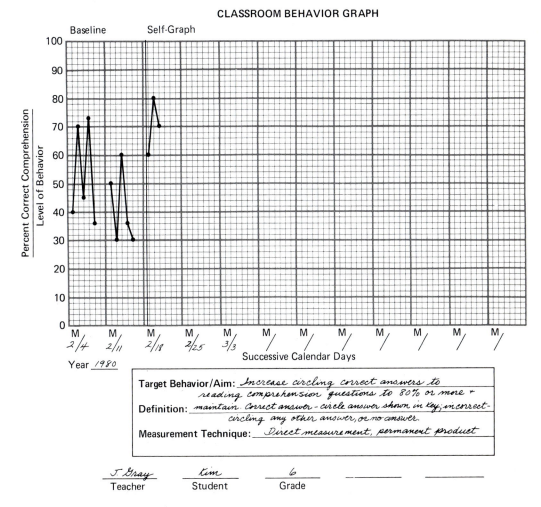

FIGURE 7-24 Kim's Graph

Measurement Technique

Each day during baseline the teacher presented Sam with five pages of 150 mixed multiplication problems and asked him to compute the problems as rapidly but as accurately as he could. She then set a timer for two minutes. Following the completion of the assignment, the teacher corrected Sam's paper and told him the number of problems he computed correctly and incorrectly per minute.

Procedures

During the first intervention, the teacher told Sam he could earn five minutes of free time each day he scored between forty and forty-nine problems per minute with one error or less, and ten minutes of free time if he could reach the aim of fifty correct problems per minute with zero errors.

Hypothetical Data

The teacher recorded Sam's arithmetic performance as shown in Figure 7–25.

Steps in Graphing Performance
1. Fill in descriptive information
2. Label the *y*-axis "Number of Problems per Minute"
3. Label the *y*-axis from 0 to 100, marking each bold line in increments of 10
4. Write in appropriate dates and year
5. Label baseline phase
6. Plot correct and incorrect rate data using a dot for number of correct answers per minute and an *x* for number of incorrect answers per minute
7. Draw phase change line one-half day before Monday, October 13
8. Label second phase "Free Time"
9. Plot data collected under second phase

Plotting Two or More Behaviors

In some instances it is desirable to plot two or more behaviors on the same graph. In these cases one might select a multiband graph such as the one shown in Figure 7–27 (DeBriere, Spellman & Aronhalt, 1975). Multi-Graphs

Day	Date	Condition	Number of Problems		Time	CR	IR
			C	I			
Tu	10/7/80	Baseline	50	8	2:00	25	4
W	10/8	"	70	10	2:00	35	5
Th	10/9	"	70	8	2:00	35	4
F	10/10	"	68	7	2:00	34	3.5
M	10/13	Free time	75	8	2:00	37.5	4
Tu	10/14	"	80	6	2:00	40	3
W	10/15	"	82	3	2:00	41	1.5
Th	10/16	"	85	2	2:00	42.5	1

FIGURE 7–25 Sam's Raw Data Sheet

can be used to record:

1. Two target behaviors for the same student, such as number of assignments completed and average percent correct score on assignments
2. A student's performance on a series of instructional objectives, or
3. The performance of a small group of students on the same objective, such as percent of reading comprehension questions answered correctly

Figure 7–27 shows how one would use Multi-Graph paper to plot a student's performance on three spelling lists.

The Multi-Graph shown in Figure 7–27 consists of two sides. One side contains five bands and the other contains three bands. Most of the information one records on the Multi-Graph is self-explanatory with the exception of the abbreviations on the right-hand side of the graph. The

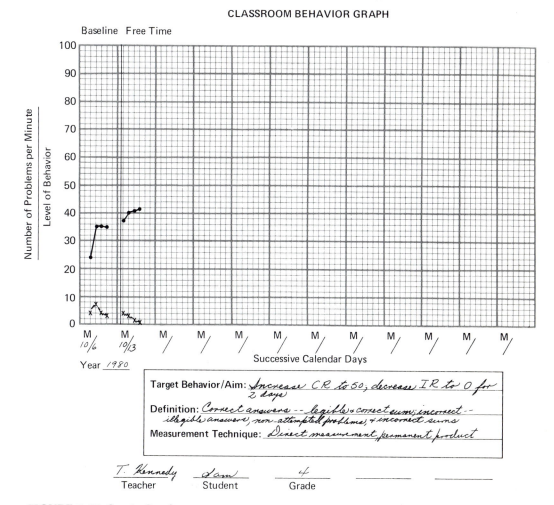

CLASSROOM BEHAVIOR GRAPH

FIGURE 7–26 Sam's Graph

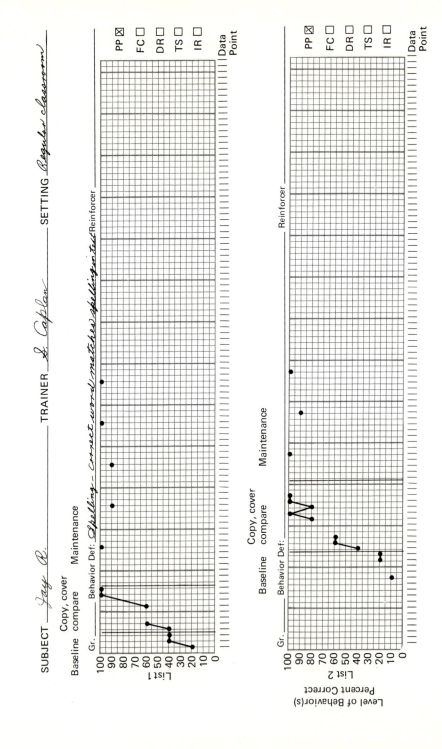

SUBJECT _Jay R._ _____ TRAINER _L. Caplan_ _____ SETTING _Regular classroom_

Behavior Def: _Spelling – Correct word matches spelling list_ Reinforcer

Baseline   Copy, cover   Maintenance
           compare

PP ☒
FC ☐
DR ☐
TS ☐
IR ☐

Data Point

Gr.

100 90 80 70 60 50 40 30 20 10 0

List 1

Behavior Def: _____ Reinforcer

Baseline   Copy, cover   Maintenance
           compare

PP ☒
FC ☐
DR ☐
TS ☐
IR ☐

Data Point

Gr.

100 90 80 70 60 50 40 30 20 10 0

List 2

Level of Behavior(s)
Percent Correct

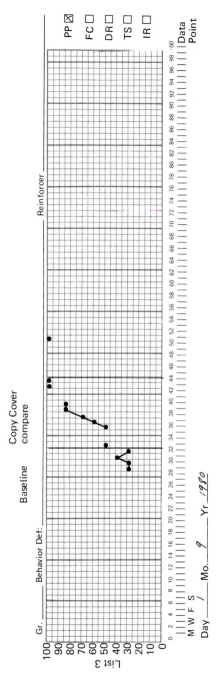

FIGURE 7–27 Data charted on Multi-Graph paper. (From T. DeBriere, C. Spellman, & R. Aronhalt, Multi-graph paper. H & H Enterprises, P.O. Box 1070, Lawrence, KS., 66044. By permission of the publishers.)

abbreviations stand for the following: PP (permanent product), FC (frequency count), DR (Duration recording), TS (time sampling), and IR (interval recording). When using Multi-Graph paper, one places an *x* in the box which describes the measurement system used in collecting the data displayed on each graph.

SUMMARY

In this chapter we have focused on the mechanics of charting. The reader has been introduced to plotting performance on arithmetic line graphs and recording data on raw data sheets. Arithmetic line graphs represent only one way of visually displaying pupil performance. Other types of charts such as The Standard Behavior Chart (White & Haring, 1976) have been developed especially for the recording of rate data. The interested reader may wish to consult White and Haring or Howell, Kaplan and O'Connell (1979) to learn more advanced charting techniques.

Although we have focused on how to chart, rather than providing a rationale for charting, there are many advantages to systematically recording pupil performance on graphs. First teachers encounter students who present various types of learning and behavior problems. Once these problems are carefully defined and their occurrence measured, a graph can be of assistance in interpreting a student's behavior. Second by graphing performance one can monitor a student's progress and make instructional decisions based on a student's actual performance. Third at a time when accountability in the schools is a concern, graphs provide a ready means of documenting pupil progress and communicating progress to others.

We would be remiss if we did not state that initially it takes time to become adept at charting pupil performance data. However with proper instruction, charting proficiency may be achieved in as few as ten practice sessions (O'Connell & McManman, 1977). Even without formal instruction many teachers become quite adept at graphing data and some even teach their students to chart. In consideration of all of the benefits charting provides, the few minutes devoted to charting per day is time well spent.

Using Data to Evaluate and Communicate Student Progress

8

Now that the reader is familiar with methods of collecting and graphing pupil performance data, we can focus on the uses of instructional data. As indicated in Chapter 7, teachers can use data to:

1. evaluate pupil performance and make instructional decisions,
2. communicate progress to students, parents, and other school personnel.

In this chapter we will address both uses of data, focusing first on using data to make instructional decisions. The preliminary steps of the data-based instructional model are reviewed followed by an overview of the remaining steps of the model. Then attention is focused on only those steps of the model which require one to evaluate pupil performance and make instructional decisions. The types of decisions which may be made at each decision-point in the model are discussed and a method for making those decisions is illustrated.

Later in the chapter attention is devoted to using data to describe pupil performance and to communicate progress. Situations in which teachers can use instructional data are discussed, and suggestions for summarizing and presenting charted data to others are provided.

THE DATA-BASED DECISION PROCESS

In this section the decision-making *process* is emphasized rather than methods for making instructional decisions. A method for evaluating data in order to make instructional decisions is discussed in the next section. Before focusing on the evaluation component of the data-based instructional model, we will review the preliminary steps of the model which set the stage for decision-making.

Review of Previous Steps in the DBI Model

In Chapters 6 and 7, the reader was introduced to several components of the DBI model, including procedures for identifying, defining, measuring

183

and charting behavior. The first five steps of the model are shown in Figure 8–1a. When using the data-based approach, one first pinpoints the behavior to be changed. This behavior, known as the target behavior, is then defined in observable terms. An appropriate measurement technique is then selected to record the occurrence of the identified target behavior.

Before beginning data collection, the teacher sets a desired level of performance or *aim* for the student to achieve. Prior to instituting any change, the student's performance is measured under present classroom conditions. These preintervention measures, known as baseline data, are then plotted on a graph.

Overview of Remaining Steps in the DBI Model

The remaining components of the model consist of six steps as shown in Figure 8–1b. Each of these steps is briefly described in this section, and discussed in detail in the remainder of this chapter, as well as in Chapters 9 and 10.

Following the collection of baseline data, the student's performance is evaluated as shown in Step 6 of Figure 8–1b. After inspecting the student's baseline data, the teacher decides whether an intervention is warranted. If, for example, a student is not performing at the desired aim and little if any progress is being made, the decision would be to begin an intervention. If, on the other hand, a student is making progress toward the desired aim, it would be unnecessary to intervene at that time.

When the decision has been made to begin an intervention, a teaching technique is selected and applied. Specific techniques to remediate social

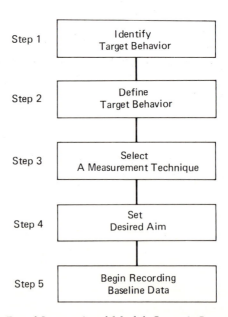

FIGURE 8–1a Data-Based Instructional Model: Steps 1–5

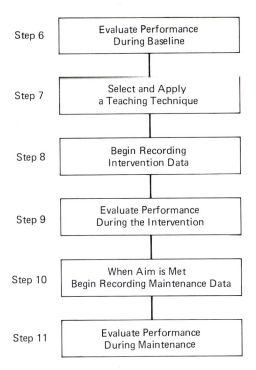

Step 6	Evaluate Performance During Baseline
Step 7	Select and Apply a Teaching Technique
Step 8	Begin Recording Intervention Data
Step 9	Evaluate Performance During the Intervention
Step 10	When Aim is Met Begin Recording Maintenance Data
Step 11	Evaluate Performance During Maintenance

FIGURE 8–1b Data-Based Instructional Model: Steps 6–11

and academic behavior problems are presented in Chapters 9 and 10. Throughout the first intervention, performance data are continuously measured and graphed. To determine the effectiveness of the intervention, a teacher inspects the student's data during the first intervention. Based on the student's performance during the intervention, the teacher must decide whether to continue with the same technique, change to another intervention, or proceed to more advanced instructional aims. If a student is making progress toward the aim, one would continue with the same technique and reevaluate performance in a few days. If, however, a student is making little if any progress, one would change to another intervention. The process of applying one teaching technique at a time while continuously measuring and evaluating performance is repeated until a student achieves the desired aim.

Once the desired aim has been met, attention is focused on maintaining behavior at or near the desired level. During maintenance the target behavior is measured progressively less frequently. For example during the first week following the attainment of an aim, the target behavior may be measured daily. During the second week the target behavior may be measured every other day. If performance is maintained weekly measures may be collected for a few weeks to insure that the behavior remains at or close to the desired level. Once a teacher is satisfied that the student is consistently performing at or near the desired level, data collection can be terminated for that behavior. If the problem behavior should ever reoccur, the process begins anew with the collection of baseline data under present classroom conditions.

MAKING DATA-BASED DECISIONS

Types of Decisions

In the process of changing behavior using the data-based approach, a number of decisions must be made. At the outset of a behavioral-change program, a teacher must decide how to define, measure and record the target behavior, as well as to determine an appropriate desired aim. The reader is already familiar with ways of making these preliminary decisions. Once data collection is underway, the following decisions must be made:

1. How many days of baseline data should be collected?
2. Is an intervention warranted?
3. Should the intervention continue or be changed?
4. When should maintenance begin?
5. Can maintenance be discontinued, or is it necessary to intervene again?

All of these decisions are based on a pupil's performance; teachers must have some way of systematically evaluating pupil performance. Methods of evaluating data are discussed in the next section.

Methods of Evaluating Data

A number of data-decision methods have been developed. Some are applicable to only certain types of data, and some are more complex than others. The interested reader may wish to consult Eaton (1978), White and Haring (1976), and White and Liberty (1976) to learn more advanced data-decision techniques than will be presented here. For the purposes of this text, we will limit our discussion to the most common method of evaluating charted data. This method, known as visual inspection, is applicable to all types of data, is easily learned and is efficient to use.

Decisions During Baseline

Once baseline data collection is underway, the first decision which must be made is:

> Decision 1:
> How many days of baseline data should be collected?

There can be no recommendation as to the exact number of days one should collect baseline data because the length of baseline is determined by the extent of variability in the data. A general rule for determining baseline

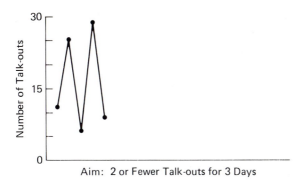

a. Variable

FIGURE 8–2 Variable Data

length is as follows:

Collect baseline data for five days initially. At the end of that time, inspect the student's baseline performance and determine if the data are:

If the data are variable, as shown in Figure 8–2, continue baseline for a few more days and re-evaluate performance.

If the data are stable, such as the data shown in Figure 8–3, baseline can be discontinued and intervention begun.

If the data are going in the direction of the desired aim, in other words, increasing when the aim is to accelerate a behavior or decreasing when the aim is to decelerate a behavior, such as the data shown in Figures 8–4 and 8–5, baseline should continue for a few more days.

When the data are going in the direction *opposite* of the desired aim, in other words, decreasing when the aim is to increase a behavior or increasing when the aim is to decrease a behavior, such as the data shown in Figures 8–6 and 8–7, baseline can be discontinued and intervention begun.

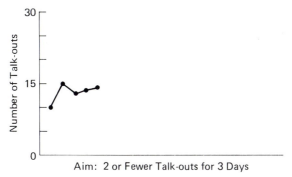

b. Stable

FIGURE 8–3 Stable Data

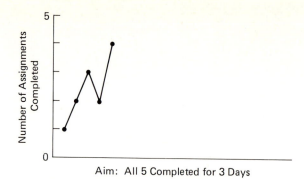

Aim: All 5 Completed for 3 Days

FIGURE 8–4 Data Going in Direction of Desired Aim

Let's examine each of the outcomes shown in Figures 8–2 through 8–7 and discuss the rationale for each decision.

Variable data.   If data are variable, such as the data shown in Figure 8–2, is is unwise to discontinue collecting baseline data because the student's behavior is *not* predictable. On the first day the student talked out 10 times; the next day, 24; then 5 times; and so on. The risk of beginning an intervention following such an unstable baseline is depicted in Example 1 of Figure 8–8.

In Example 1 it is difficult to evaluate the effects of the intervention because a clear pattern of responding was not established during baseline. Of course there is the possibility that the intervention will have an immediate and dramatic effect upon performance as shown in Example 2 of Figure 8–8. The effectiveness of the technique is easy to determine in Example 2 because of the magnitude of the change. As we cannot always hope for such dramatic changes in behavior, it is best to obtain a stable baseline before beginning an intervention.

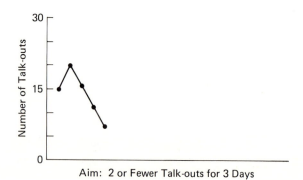

Aim: 2 or Fewer Talk-outs for 3 Days

FIGURE 8–5 Data Going in Direction of Desired Aim

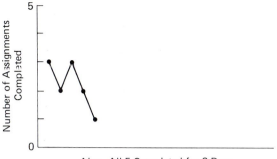

Aim: All 5 Completed for 3 Days

FIGURE 8–6 Data Going in Direction Opposite of Desired Aim

Stable data. When data are stable, such as the baseline data shown in Figure 8–9, one has a clear picture of the student's behavior. Stable data allow one to compare later changes in performance to performance during baseline. Thus decisions regarding the effectiveness of an instructional technique can easily be made as shown in Figure 8–9.

Baseline data may initially be variable and then become more stable as shown in Figure 8–10. The baseline data in Figure 8–10 were variable for the first three days, but by the seventh day performance had stabilized. Because of the stability of the last four days of data, it is possible to evaluate the student's change in behavior during the intervention.

Trend in the direction of the desired aim. It sometimes happens that a student's performance improves during baseline. For example if the aim is to decelerate an inappropriate behavior, the behavior may start to decrease during baseline as shown in Figure 8–11.
One reason which may account for such a decrease during baseline is that a student could have caught on to the fact that his behavior was being observed.

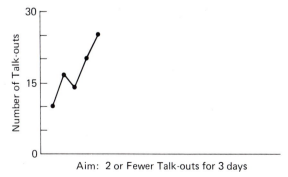

Aim: 2 or Fewer Talk-outs for 3 days

FIGURE 8–7 Data Going in Direction Opposite of Desired Aim

It sometimes happens that when the aim is to accelerate a behavior, the behavior begins to increase during baseline. An example of this is shown in Figure 8–12 where a student began to increase the number of problems computed correctly during baseline.

Sometimes increases during baseline can be explained because of an increased opportunity to practice a skill on a daily basis.

In both Figures 8–11 and 8–12, the behavior is going in the desired direction. As the students are making progress toward their aims, there is no reason to intervene at this time. Instead baseline should continue for a few more days. If at the end of that time, progress has deteriorated or leveled off it would be appropriate to intervene.

Trend opposite of the desired aim. As previously indicated baseline data need not be stable before a change is made if the trend is going in the direction *opposite* of the desired aim. To illustrate this point consider the baseline data presented in Examples 1 and 2 of Figure 8–13.

In Example 1 the aim was to decrease out-of-seat behavior. The student's frequency of out-of-seats was obviously increasing during baseline. In Example 2 the aim was to increase the number of assignments a student completed, The trend reveals a decrease in the number of assignments completed. In both cases a predictable pattern is apparent: the trend is going in the direction opposite of the desired aim. As shown in Figure 8–13 when such predictable patterns are apparent, it is easy to judge the effectiveness of an intervention by comparing the trend during baseline to performance during the intervention period.

Although the five-day minimum rule for baseline can be used as a general guideline, there is one exception to this rule. In cases where a student performs at or near zero for three days, it is best to intervene immediately because in all probability the student doesn't know how to perform the behavior. For example a student may fail to compute any math problems correctly for a three-day period. One would probably assume that the student lacked the necessary skills to compute the problems. Sim-

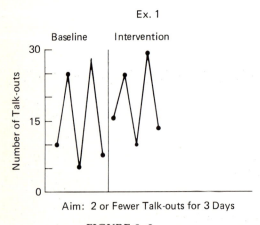

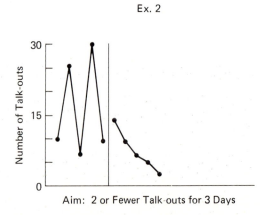

FIGURE 8–8

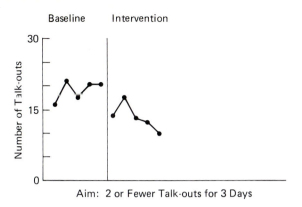

FIGURE 8–9

ilarly if a student spent 0 percent of his time on-task for three days, it is unlikely that his performance will improve until the teacher implements an intervention.

A few final comments about baseline length are in order. Many teachers initially doubt the importance of obtaining a stable or at least a predictable baseline. In their eagerness to change a student's behavior, many would prefer to skip collecting baseline data. The importance of collecting baseline data cannot be emphasized enough—without it one can neither precisely describe a student's current performance nor evaluate later progress.

In most projects conducted by classroom teachers which the authors have supervised, baseline data collection was accomplished in three to ten days. Usually within this time period teachers were able to obtain stable baselines. When one encounters a great deal of variability in performance during baseline, it is wise to have another person independently record the behavior along with the teacher. By performing a reliability check as described in Chapter 6, one can determine whether the variability in the data is due to errors in recording the behavior. If it is, it may be necessary

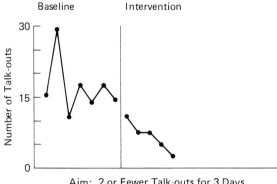

FIGURE 8–10

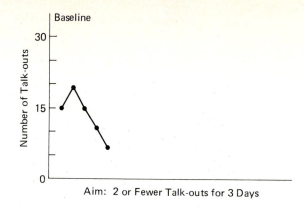

Baseline

Number of Talk-outs

Aim: 2 or Fewer Talk-outs for 3 Days

FIGURE 8–11

to define the behavior more precisely and/or become more consistent in recording the behavior.

Once an adequate baseline has been obtained, one must make the following decision:

Decision 2:
Is an intervention warranted?

In order to make this decision, one evaluates the student's baseline performance as shown in Step 6 of the DBI model presented in Figure 8–14. Depending upon the outcome of the evaluation of baseline performance, one of the decisions as shown in Step 6 of Figure 8–14 would be made. The authors will now consider each of the outcomes and determine the decision one would make in each instance.

After inspecting the baseline data, a teacher may determine that the student's performance is:

1. Not at the desired aim and little if any progress is being made
   This is perhaps the most likely outcome during baseline. After all a

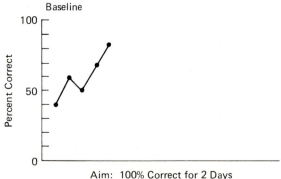

Baseline

Percent Correct

Aim: 100% Correct for 2 Days

FIGURE 8–12

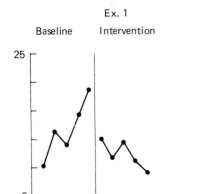

Ex. 1

Baseline   Intervention

Aim: 2 or Fewer for 3 Days

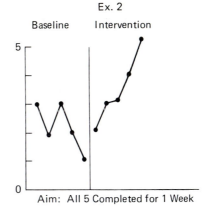

Ex. 2

Baseline   Intervention

Aim: All 5 Completed for 1 Week

FIGURE 8–13

teacher begins to collect baseline data to verify that a problem behavior exists. In Figure 8–15 the teacher's suspicions are confirmed by the baseline data showing that the student is making a high number of talk-outs.

In the next example shown in Figure 8–16, performance is going opposite of the desired direction. The decision in both cases would be to change to an intervention.

2. Not at the desired aim but continued progress is being made
   If the student is making sufficient progress toward the aim, as shown in Figure 8–17 or 8–18, there is no reason to intervene. Instead baseline should continue for a few more days and progress should be reevaluated. If at the end of that time performance has deteriorated or stabilized short of the desired aim, one would change to an intervention.

3. At the desired aim
   It sometimes happens, as mentioned previously, that once a teacher begins to measure a student's behavior, the supposed problem turns out not to be a problem at all. This usually happens for one of two reasons. First a teacher may overestimate the severity of a behavior. Second performance sometimes improves through practice. If, like the student in Figure 8–19, a student achieves the desired aim during baseline, one would check for the continued maintenance of the behavior. More will be said about measuring the maintenance of behavior later in the chapter.

Decisions During Intervention Periods

If following baseline a student's performance is not at the desired aim and little progress is being made, one proceeds to Step 7 of the DBI model as shown in Figure 8–20. Once a teaching technique has been selected, it must be consistently applied over a period of days to determine its effectiveness. Although one should inspect the data daily as it is graphed, it

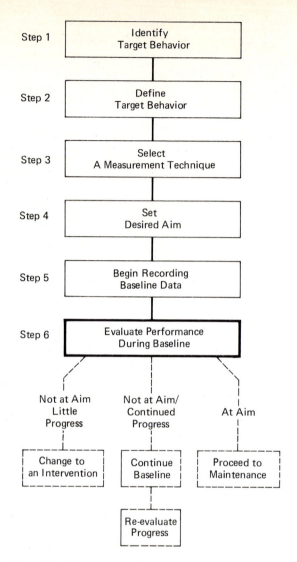

FIGURE 8–14 Data-Based Instructional Model: Steps 1–6

is best to withhold making a decision until the technique has been in effect for at least five days.

Usually after five to seven days, one can discern whether the data have stabilized or whether there is a predictable trend.

At the end of the five days, one inspects the trend of the data during the intervention. Using the same decision rules previously described for determining the length of baseline, one notes whether the data have stabilized or if there is a predictable trend. If the intervention data are variable, such as those shown in Figure 8–21, the intervention should continue until the data stabilize or a predictable trend develops.

When the data have stabilized or a predictable trend is noted, one

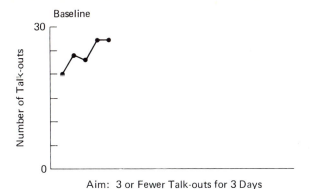

FIGURE 8–15

is ready to make the following decision:

Decision 3:
Should the intervention continue or be changed?

To make this decision one evaluates the student performance during the intervention as shown in Step 9 of the DBI model presented in Figure 8–22.

When evaluating a student's performance during an intervention, three outcomes are possible. Each leads to a different decision, as shown in Figure 8–22. As before let's consider each outcome and determine the decision one would make if the student's performance during the intervention is:

1. Not at the desired aim and little if any progress is being made
   This outcome suggests that the first teaching technique was not as effective as expected. Figure 8–23 provides an example of a technique which initially appeared to be effective but later proved not to be.
   Whenever a teaching technique does not result in the desired amount of progress, one should hypothesize possible reasons accounting for the failure of the technique. For example two possible reasons account-

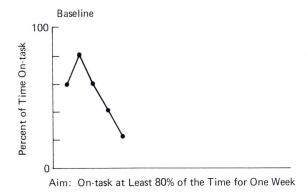

FIGURE 8–16

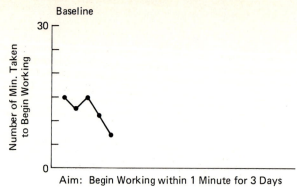

FIGURE 8–17

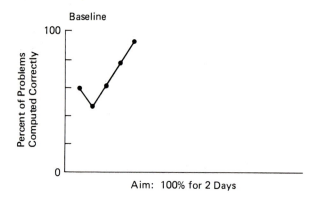

FIGURE 8–18

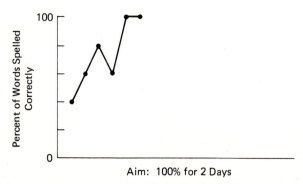

FIGURE 8–19

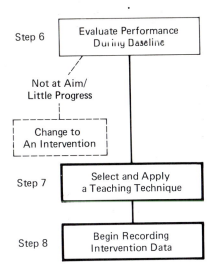

FIGURE 8–20 Data-Based Instructional Model: Steps 6–8

ing for the decrease in performance shown in Figure 8–23 may be that the student couldn't find anything interesting to do during free time or the aim was set too high. After one has identified the most probable reason, a new teaching technique is selected and applied. The process of implementing a technique, measuring performance continuously and evaluating the effectiveness of the intervention are repeated, as shown in Figure 8–22, until a student reaches the desired aim.

2. Not at the desired aim but continued progress is being made
   This outcome is positive because it indicates that performance is improving during the first intervention tried. As shown in Figure 8–24, performance under the first intervention indicates continued improvement toward the aim.
   In this case, one would continue with the same technique and reevaluate performance in a few days to insure that the student maintains his progress. If at the end of that time the student's performance has de-

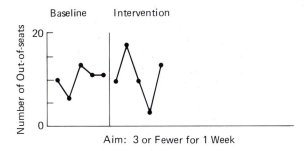

FIGURE 8–21

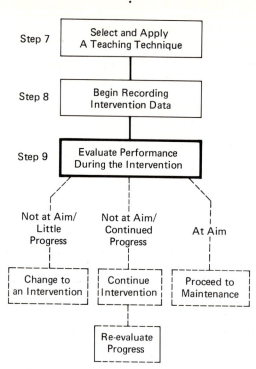

FIGURE 8–22 Data-Based Instructional Model: Steps 7–9

teriorated or has stabilized short of the aim, a new teaching technique would be selected and applied.

3. The desired aim

This of course is the most desirable outcome because it indicates that the first teaching technique was so successful that the student achieved the desired aim. An example of this instance is shown in Figure 8–25. In this case one would discontinue the intervention and proceed to maintenance.

As is evident from the latter example, the fourth decision is:

Decision 4:
When should maintenance begin?

The decision to proceed to maintenance is made immediately after the student has achieved the desired aim. Usually this decision is made following an intervention, although a student could meet the desired aim during baseline. For example if one had incorrectly identified a behavior as a problem, or if performance improved due to practice alone, a student could achieve the desired aim during the baseline period. Provided that one has correctly identified a problem behavior, it is far more likely that

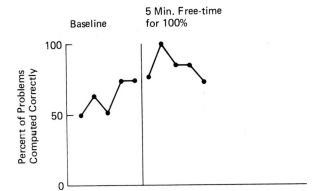

FIGURE 8–23

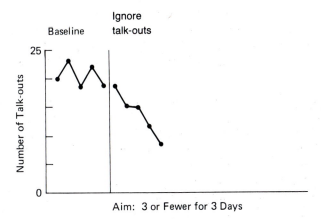

FIGURE 8–24

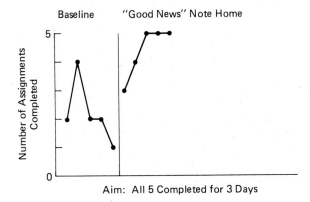

FIGURE 8–25

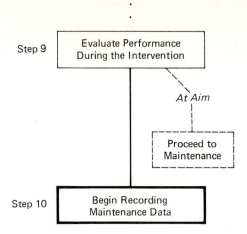

FIGURE 8–26 Data-Based Instructional Model: Steps 9 & 10

a student will reach the desired aim during an intervention than during baseline. As this decision commonly follows a successful intervention, the authors will examine how one proceeds to implement the few remaining steps in the data-based instructional model.

As shown in Figure 8–26, following a successful intervention in which a student has achieved the desired aim, one begins a maintenance phase. During maintenance the teaching technique is either discontinued or gradually withdrawn. More will be said about techniques to maintain behavior in Chapters 9 and 10. For now it is important for the reader to understand the purpose of collecting maintenance data and how one measures performance during the maintenance phase of a behavioral change program.

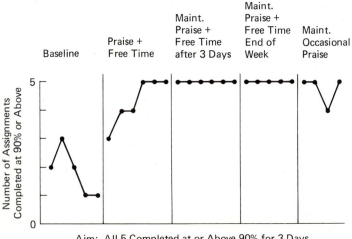

FIGURE 8–27

Maintenance data are collected to determine the durability of a behavioral change. To illustrate this point, consider the data shown in Figure 8–27. In this example the teacher implemented an intervention in which a student received praise plus an opportunity to earn one minute of free time for each assignment he completed at 90 percent or more correct. As shown in Figure 8–27, the student met the teacher's desired aim on the sixth day of the intervention. At this point the teacher is concerned with maintaining the student's behavior. Rather than immediately withdrawing the special privilege, the teacher gradually removes the extra privilege the student was earning, while continuing to praise his behavior. In this case maintenance might initially consist of telling the student that he can earn five minutes of free time after every third day in which he scores 90 percent

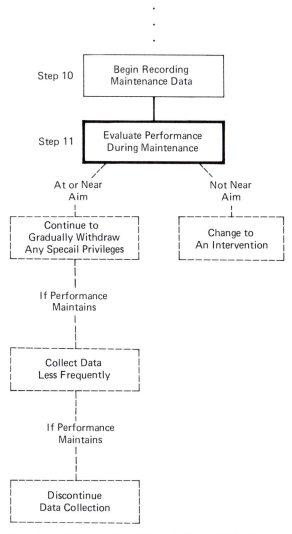

FIGURE 8–28 Data-Based Instructional Model: Steps 10 & 11

or more correct. If his performance is maintained, the opportunity to earn free time for this behavior is gradually withdrawn until the student is consistently performing the behavior with only the use of occasional praise.

Sometimes during maintenance the teaching technique is immediately withdrawn. An example might be when one has provided instruction on a skill, such as demonstrating how to compute a math problem. As the teacher's objective is to have the student compute the problems without prior instruction, maintenance may consist of withdrawing the demonstration while continuing to provide feedback on performance.

For the next five days following a successful intervention, a teacher should continue to collect daily data. After all special privileges or instructions have been withdrawn, and the behavior is being maintained by more natural consequences such as occasional praise or feedback, data collection can become less frequent. After the first five days of collecting maintenance data, the student's performance should be evaluated according to the previously discussed rules. Depending upon the student's performance, one of the decisions as shown in Step 11 of Figure 8–28 would be made.

Again, let's consider each outcome shown in Figure 8–28 and determine the decision one would make in each case. When evaluating performance during maintenance, a teacher may determine that the student:

1. Consistently performs at or near the desired aim

   If this is the case and all special privileges have been withdrawn, there is no need to collect daily measures of performance. For example in Figure 8–29, the student's accuracy is maintained after instruction was terminated. As there are no special privileges to withdraw and only feedback is being provided, one could collect data on this behavior every other day for perhaps a week. Provided that the student continues to maintain his performance at or near the desired level, one might collect weekly maintenance checks for a few weeks. If performance remains at or near the desired level, data collection for that behavior can be terminated.

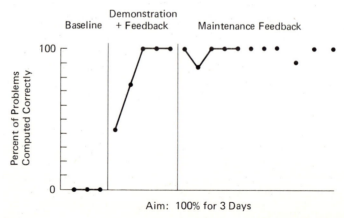

FIGURE 8–29

2. Consistently performs too far above or below the desired aim

If performance deteriorates during the first week of maintenance when data are still being collected daily, the maintenance data can serve as a new baseline. Provided that the maintenance data are stable or the trend is going opposite to the desired direction, another teaching technique can be immediately applied. An example of the necessity of changing to an intervention after the first week of maintenance is shown in Figure 8–30.

In the example shown in Figure 8–30, performance was not maintained when free time was discontinued and only praise was given. In this case the teacher might reinstate free time, couple it with praise and gradually discontinue the use of free time. For example at first free time may be given after the second day the student completed all assignments, then after every fourth day and eventually only once in awhile. Provided that performance was maintained, free time could eventually be discontinued and the teacher could return to occasionally praising the behavior.

It sometimes happens that performance is maintained during the first week of maintenance, but begins to deteriorate later on. For example the data in Figure 8–31 reveal that performance was maintained during the first and second week following the intervention. By the end of the second weekly maintenance check, however, performance had decreased to near the baseline level.

In cases where performance deteriorates during weekly postchecks, it is best to resume daily data collection under present conditions to determine if the behavior has once again become a problem. If it has the daily measures one has collected under maintenance conditions can serve as a new baseline. If the data are stable or a predictable trend is apparent, a new teaching technique can be applied. The process of implementing a technique and measuring and evaluating its effects continues until the student is able to maintain his/her performance at or near the desired aim once the intervention has been withdrawn.

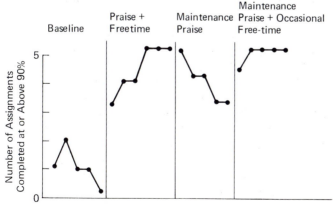

FIGURE 8–30

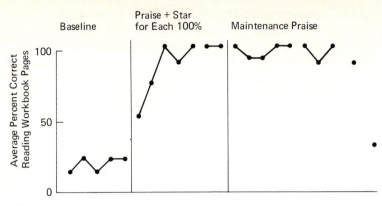

FIGURE 8–31

Summary

The authors have discussed how teachers can use visual inspection of charted data to make instructional decisions. In so doing the authors have stressed a number of points. First baseline data can be used to verify the existence of a problem behavior as well as serve as a standard by which later progress can be evaluated. Second decisions to continue or change techniques are based on pupil performance. By visually inspecting a student's data, one can determine whether to continue with the present technique or change to another intervention. Third teaching techniques are applied and evaluated one at a time until a student reaches the desired aim. Finally once the aim has been met, any special privileges or instructions are gradually withdrawn or discontinued to determine the durability of the behavioral change. Provided that a student's performance is maintained, the target behavior is measured progressively less frequently and eventually measurement is discontinued.

There are several advantages to using charted data to guide instruction:

1. Teachers are provided with continuous feedback concerning the effectiveness of their techniques on pupil performance.
2. By inspecting a student's graph, a teacher can tell at a glance whether a student is or is not making progress. If insufficient progress is being made, a teacher can readily change techniques to improve a student's performance.
3. A certain sense of pride in one's accomplishments can be derived from inspecting a student's graph and seeing that one's teaching skills were responsible for improving the student's performance.

It should be stressed that visual inspection is only one method of evaluating charted data. Other methods such as those described by White and Haring (1976) are particularly appropriate for evaluating rate data and providing teachers with precise information concerning the effectiveness of teaching techniques. The reader is encouraged to learn more advanced skills for analyzing and interpreting charted data by consulting the following texts: *Exceptional Teaching* by White and Haring (1976), *The Fourth R: Research in the Classroom* by Haring, Lovitt, Eaton, and Hanson (1978), and *Evaluating Exceptional Children: A Task Analysis Approach* by Howell, Kaplan, and O'Connell (1979).

205
*Using Data to
Describe
Student
Performance
and
Communicate
Progress*

USING DATA TO DESCRIBE STUDENT PERFORMANCE AND COMMUNICATE PROGRESS

Teachers encounter a variety of situations in which they are expected to provide information concerning a student's academic and social behavior. For example when making a referral for special education services, a teacher needs to document a student's skill deficits and describe academic and social behavior problems as precisely as possible. When participating in conferences to determine a student's eligibility to receive special education services, a teacher must present information in such a way as to indicate a student's need for specific services or, in some cases, the lack of need for special services. Similarly at meetings to develop a handicapped student's individualized education program (IEP), a teacher must be able to summarize the information he/she has collected on the student's performance in the classroom. In this case the teacher's data serve as the basis for developing goals and objectives for the student to achieve. For a handicapped student in a regular classroom who also receives instruction from a resource teacher, some means of ongoing communication must be maintained between the two teachers throughout the year. In addition teachers are expected to express students' progress to the students themselves, to parents and to other school personnel.

As the previous discussion demonstrates, there are a variety of situations in which teachers are expected to provide information on pupil performance. In each of these cases teachers can rely on the data they collect on a student's performance in the classroom. Specifically data can be used:

1. To describe a student's deficit skills, thereby serving as a basis for referring a student for special education services
2. To advocate appropriate services for handicapped children
3. To plan instructional programs
4. To communicate about student progress to students themselves, to parents and to other school personnel

In this part of the chapter, we will discuss how teachers can use data for each of these purposes.

Methods of Summarizing Data

The easiest and most effective way to communicate a student's progress is to share the student's graph with others. The graph contains complete information concerning the student's performance on a particular skill, and is useful for communicating with other teachers, assessment personnel and parents. While charted data are the most direct and useful method of communicating student's progress, it is sometimes necessary to summarize data for purposes of presentation. This section will describe methods for summarizing data on student performance.

When making a referral for a social behavior problem, one typically states what the behavior problem is in observable terms and reports the average number of times it occurs. Although a graph could be attached to the referral form, performance is usually summarized in a few words. There are also occasions on which one would like to supplement the charted data by summarizing a student's performance. For example at a meeting to review and revise a student's IEP, a teacher might wish to comment on the student's variability in performance, or describe the change in a student's performance from baseline to intervention. In these cases summary statistics such as the *range, mean* and *median* can be used to describe performance. Let's consider when each of these statistics might be appropriate to use.

Range. The range is used to indicate the variability of a student's performance. The range is found by inspecting the charted data and noting the lowest and highest scores. For example, the range for the baseline data shown in Figure 8–32 is from fifteen to twenty-one talk-outs per day.

The range is a useful statistic to report because it helps to describe the consistency of a student's behavior. For example contrast the impression one might have of a student whose scores in computing multiplication facts range from 90 to 100 percent versus a student whose scores ranged from 30 to 100 percent. One might choose to report the range in these situations:

1. When making a referral—The range of scores during baseline may be provided to indicate the variability of a student's performance.
2. When discussing progress—The range of scores during baseline and intervention can be compared to illustrate changes in a student's performance. For example the range for the baseline data shown in Figure

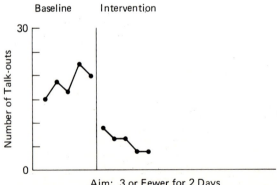

FIGURE 8–32

8–32 was from fifteen to twenty-one. During the intervention perform-ance was considerably less variable as the scores ranged from seven to three.

207
*Using Data to
Describe
Student
Performance
and
Communicate
Progress*

Mean. While the range is useful for expressing the amount of variability in performance, it is also important to report the student's average per-formance. To compute a student's average performance, or mean, one sums the value of each data plot and divides the sum by the number of plots. For example, to find the mean for the baseline data shown in Figure 8–32, one adds the values (15 + 18 + 16 + 21 + 19 = 89) and divides the sum by the number of plots or days (89 ÷ 5). The mean for the baseline data shown in Figure 8 –32 is 17.8 talk-outs per day.

Means can be used to describe a student's average performance. For example when making a referral one could report the average number of times a behavior problem occurred. By reporting the mean one can com-municate the severity of a student's academic or behavior problems. Means can also be helpful when discussing changes in a pupil's performance. When discussing progress with others, one might wish to compare a stu-dent's performance during baseline to his/her performance during an in-tervention. For example if one wished to summarize the change in the student's performance shown in Figure 8–33, one could call attention to the fact that during baseline the student completed an average of two assignments per day, while during the intervention the student completed an average of four assignments per day.

Means can sometimes be misleading. If a mean is calculated on ex-tremely variable data, the mean will present a distorted picture of the student's performance. As illustration of this point consider the baseline data shown in Figure 8–34. In this example the student computed an average of 34 percent of the problems correctly (10 + 15 + 90 + 35 + 20 = 170 ÷ 5 = 34). Although the mean indicates the student's average score, it does not represent the student's typical performance very well. When data are variable it is best to report a student's median score.

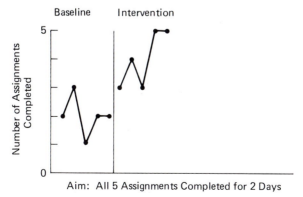

FIGURE 8–33

Median.   The median is the middle score in an array of scores ranked in order from lowest to highest. The steps for computing the median are shown in Table 8–1. The reader should note that the procedure for finding the median varies slightly depending upon whether there are an even or odd number of scores.

The median is not influenced as much by extremely high or low scores. To demonstrate this point consider the data shown in Figure 8–34. The mean in this example is 34, whereas the median is 20. In cases where performance is variable, it is best to report the median. Medians can be used like means to summarize a student's performance and to compare performance during baseline and intervention periods.

**TABLE 8–1 Calculating the Median
Procedure for Odd-Number of Data Points**

Step 1:   Rank order the scores from lowest to highest. For the data in Figure 8-34, the rank order would be as follows:

> 10
> 15
> 20
> 35
> 90

Step 2:   Find the middle score in the full array of scores. For the data in Figure 8-34, the third score is the halfway point or median.

> 10
> 15
> 20—median
> 35
> 90

Procedure for Even-Number of Data Points

Step 1:   Rank order the scores from lowest to highest. For example, if a student's baseline scores were 20, 15, 35, 90, 10, 70, the rank order would be as follows:

> 10
> 15
> 20
> 35 —Median lies between these scores
> 70
> 90

The middle score lies halfway between two scores. In our example the median lies halfway between the third and fourth score.

Step 2:   Add the two scores on either side of the midpoint (20 + 35 = 55) and divide by two (55 ÷ 2). In our example the median is 27.5.

209

*Using Data to
Describe
Student
Performance
and
Communicate
Progress*

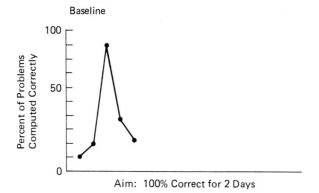

Baseline

Percent of Problems Computed Correctly

Aim: 100% Correct for 2 Days

FIGURE 8–34

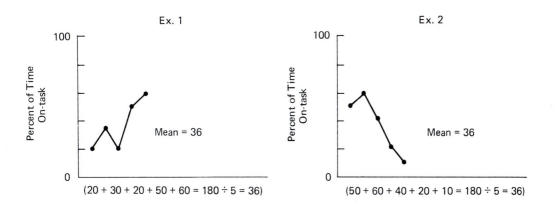

Ex. 1

Percent of Time On-task

Mean = 36

$(20 + 30 + 20 + 50 + 60 = 180 \div 5 = 36)$

Ex. 2

Percent of Time On-task

Mean = 36

$(50 + 60 + 40 + 20 + 10 = 180 \div 5 = 36)$

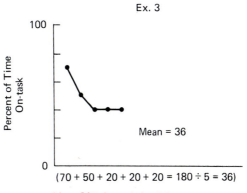

Ex. 3

Percent of Time On-task

Mean = 36

$(70 + 50 + 20 + 20 + 20 = 180 \div 5 = 36)$

Aim: 80% On-task for 3 Days

FIGURE 8–35

Trend. Although the mean and median describe a student's performance, they do not indicate progress very well. Consider, for example, the data shown in Figure 8–35.

All three examples have the same mean, yet in Example 1 the trend indicates that the behavior is increasing; whereas in Example 2 the behavior is decreasing and in Example 3 the behavior has leveled off. When describing a student's performance, it is a good idea to report the trend of the data as well as the range, and either the mean or median. For example when making a referral, one might mention that during a five-day period, a student was out of his/her seat between twelve and twenty times per day; his average was fifteen per day, and the number of times he/she was out of his/her seat appears to be increasing. Similarly when reporting changes in performance, one might compare the trend during baseline to the trend during intervention. For example if one were discussing the data shown in Figure 8–36, one would be sure to point out that performance during baseline was very low and stable, whereas performance continued to increase during the intervention when the desired aim was met.

Discussing Charted Data

As pointed out earlier the easiest and most effective way to communicate a student's progress to others is to show them the student's graph. When using a graph to describe a student's performance, it is important to:

1. tell what behavior the data represent
2. state the desired aim
3. describe how the behavior was measured
4. explain the conditions during baseline
5. discuss performance during baseline
6. explain each teaching technique used
7. discuss performance during each intervention
8. explain the conditions during maintenance
9. discuss performance during maintenance

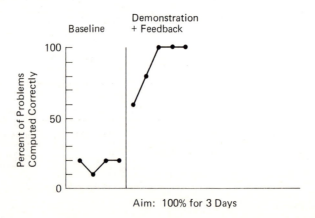

FIGURE 8–36

Charted data without summary statistics may be used in situations in which the teacher is presenting the information in person, and has ample time and opportunity to discuss the data. Charted data are often very helpful in staffing conferences, IEP meetings and parent conferences, where specific and detailed information is needed concerning the student's progress. As a general rule charted data should be used for communication purposes as often as possible, and summary statistics should be presented only when the complete charted data would be confusing, easily misunderstood or given less than full consideration.

USING DATA FOR COMMUNICATION

It is not unusual for teachers to be frustrated in their contacts with school administrative personnel and parents concerning appropriate programming for individual students. In meetings held to determine eligibility of a student for special education, or to develop IEPs, teachers frequently are called on only very briefly and are not directly involved in the decision-making process. In contacts with parents, most notably, parent conferences, teachers often find themselves talking in generalities and providing limited information concerning actual student progress. Teachers who chart pupil performance data discover that their ability to communicate meaningful information is increased and that parents react favorably to viewing their child's progress on a chart.

In staffing conferences and IEP meetings, teachers who have charted data on student performance can present information to corroborate or refute information provided by school psychologists and other assessment specialists. For example if the general feeling in a placement staffing is that a student should be placed in a special education classroom, and a regular classroom teacher presents data showing successful student performance in a normal setting, an overly restrictive placement decision might be averted. Likewise when instructional goals and objectives are being determined in an IEP meeting, data on current classroom performance can be a key factor in planning the nature and intensity of special programs, as well as the relationship of these programs to what is happening in the classroom.

In summary, the collection of systematic data on a student's performance in the classroom increases the likelihood that the teacher will have a voice in determining the student's needs and seeing that those needs are met. Of all school personnel no one knows more about a student's performance than the teacher who works with that student daily. However the knowledge is often ignored in the decision-making process, because a teacher's information is not specific or in a form in which it can be readily shared with others. Data-based instruction can help to assure that for students with learning and behavior problems, classroom teacher input into placement and planning decisions is expected and valued. Teachers must be assertive in assuming that as specialists present formal test data and case histories, final attention is focused on the matter of greatest concern, day-to-day performance in the classroom. Thus teachers must collect data on student performance not only to help in their own instructional decision making, but also to use in the all-important task of communicating with others concerning the student's progress and continuing needs.

SECTION 4

Instructional Approaches for Learning and Behavior Problems

Remediating Classroom Behavior Problems

9

Teachers are confronted with students who evidence a variety of behavior problems. Some of the most common behavior problems noted by classroom teachers include: not completing assignments, not attending, disruptive behaviors such as talking out, and verbally and physically aggressive behaviors. These types of behaviors, if not remedied, tend to interfere with a student's learning and/or disrupt other students. In order to facilitate instruction, teachers must be able to establish and maintain appropriate behaviors in the classroom.

The data-based instructional approach represents an effective strategy for maintaining appropriate behaviors and for dealing with classroom behavior problems. The reader has already been introduced to several components of the Data-Based Instructional (DBI) model, including procedures for identifying, defining, observing and charting behavior, as well as methods for making instructional decisions based on data. The only component of the model which has yet to be presented deals with selecting and applying teaching techniques to remediate behavior problems. Techniques to remediate social and academic behavior problems are presented in Chapters 9 and 10, respectively.

In this chapter the authors will discuss how the DBI model can be applied to remediate classroom behavior problems. Specifically we will examine procedures to increase appropriate behaviors and to decrease inappropriate behaviors. It should be stressed that the behavioral procedures discussed in this chapter have been extensively covered in other texts. In fact in recent years, a number of excellent texts have been published dealing with the use of behavior modification procedures in school settings (Axelrod, 1977; Kazdin, 1975; and Sulzer-Azaroff & Mayer, 1977). While many classroom teachers regard behavioral procedures as effective, they often question the practicality of using these techniques in regular classrooms. A frequent comment made by classroom teachers is, "Sure, those techniques work in special education classrooms, but I have thirty students!" The authors believe that there is a need to highlight those techniques which teachers have found to be both practical and effective in dealing with behavior problems in regular classrooms.

To illustrate the utility of using behavioral procedures in regular classrooms, we have included a number of projects conducted by preservice and inservice teachers, as well as a few research studies. In many cases the projects represent a teacher's first attempt to implement a data-based instructional approach. The projects are designed to serve a dual purpose. First they illustrate how one would apply the procedures discussed in the chapter. Second they provide a review of the entire data-based instructional process as each project contains a description of the procedures a teacher used to define, measure, record and evaluate behavior.

Following the discussion of teaching techniques, we will present some general guidelines for structuring the learning environment in such a way as to reduce the likelihood that behavior problems will occur.

GAINING A PERSPECTIVE ON BEHAVIOR PROBLEMS

Throughout the text the authors have stressed that the data-based approach represents the most direct and effective means of dealing with behavior problems. Rather than looking for supposed internal causes to explain a student's behavior problems, the data-based approach pares behavior problems down to a manageable size. Instead of trying to improve a student's self-concept, decrease his hyperactivity or improve his poor attitude, attention is focused on the observable behaviors which led one to describe a child as being hyperactive, or as having a poor attitude or poor self-concept.

The data-based approach maintains that once a behavior is defined, it can be measured, recorded and changed. Rather than attributing a student's behavior problems to a poor home life, or to other conditions beyond a teacher's control, attention is focused on events in the classroom which might be maintaining a student's inappropriate behavior. Hence remediation is directed toward changing conditions in the classroom which may precipitate or maintain inappropriate behaviors. Although there is no question that conditions outside the classroom can negatively effect a student's behavior, teachers are simply not in a position to remedy a student's home life or to counteract the effects of poverty or the limited educational experiences of a student's parents. Despite the negative effects such factors may have on a student's behavior, there is good reason to be optimistic! As the research literature and projects in this chapter demonstrate, teachers can bring about dramatic changes in students' behavior through the wise use of behavioral procedures.

THE NATURE OF REINFORCEMENT

There are certain behaviors teachers wish to maintain or increase such as completing assignments, following directions, working quietly, and participating in group discussions. In this section we will discuss the use of reinforcement procedures to maintain and increase appropriate behaviors in the classroom.

217

The Nature of Reinforcement

Positive Reinforcement

Positive reinforcement may be defined as a process in which the presentation of a consequence following a behavior serves to increase or maintain that behavior (Bushell and Burgess, 1969). Positive reinforcers are those objects or events which, when presented following a behavior, result in increasing or maintaining that behavior. There are many potentially reinforcing events available in the classroom, such as teacher praise, free time and privileges. Whether or not these consequences actually serve to positively reinforce behavior depends upon their effect upon a student's behavior. For example consider two students, John and Tom, who complete less than half of their daily assignments. In attempting to positively reinforce the students' behavior, the teacher may tell each boy that he can earn five minutes of free time if he completes his assignments. After trying this technique for a few days, the teacher inspects John's data and notes that he is beginning to increase the number of assignments he completes. In this case we would say that John's behavior is being positively reinforced because a consequence (free time) was presented following the completion of his assignments and his behavior (number of assignments completed) increased. When evaluating the effects of free time on Tom's performance, the teacher determined that his behavior had actually decreased. Even though a consequence (free time) was presented, it did *not* result in maintaining or increasing his behavior (number of assignments completed). Therefore one could not say that Tom's behavior had been positively reinforced.

When initially learning about positive reinforcement, some people tend to associate positive reinforcers with only desirable objects or activities, such as praise, stars, and recess. Actually, positive refers to the *presentation* or *addition* of a consequence rather than to its perceived desirability. To illustrate this point consider a student who spends a great deal of time away from her desk. Whenever the teacher sees the student wandering about the room, the teacher reprimands her and tells the student to get back to work. Although most of us would not consider such attention to be desirable, this consequence could actually serve to positively reinforce the student's inappropriate behavior. In order to test the notion that the student's behavior is being positively reinforced by teacher attention, the teacher may decide to ignore the student when she is out of her seat and praise her only when she is sitting at her desk. If the student begins to spend more time at her desk, the teacher may conclude that the student's previous behavior had been inadvertently reinforced by teacher attention.

Negative Reinforcement

Negative reinforcers are those objects or events which, when removed following a behavior, serve to increase or maintain that behavior (Bushell and Burgess, 1969). There are many naturally aversive consequences, such as excessive heat, cold and noise which people tend to avoid. For example we learn to avoid being drenched in a rainstorm by carrying an umbrella, to adjust the heat in our homes and to turn down the volume on a radio when it blares.

Both positive and *negative reinforcement* serve to increase or maintain behavior. To illustrate the difference between positive and negative reinforcement, consider the following example. A child may beg his parents to buy him snacks in the grocery store. In order to terminate the child's whining and begging, the parents may give in to the child's demands. If on future shopping trips, the child continues to nag his parents until they buy him treats, we may conclude that the child's whining and begging is being positively reinforced. The parent's behavior, however, is being negatively reinforced because they continue to buy their child treats in order to terminate or avoid their child's whining and begging.

Some other examples of negative reinforcement are as follows: A teacher may stare at John until he begins working. In order to avoid the teacher's gaze, John begins to work on his assignment. A mother may continually nag her son to pick up his room. If the mother's nagging is more aversive than the chore of cleaning his room, the son may learn that he can avoid his mother's nagging by cleaning his room. A student may be taunted by his peers on the playground for his inability to shoot baskets. In order to avoid being teased by his friends, the student may practice shooting baskets at home until he becomes quite good at it.

The major difficulty with using negative reinforcement is that some aversive consequence must be present which can be removed once a student engages in the desired behavior. The usual response to aversive consequences is escape and avoidance. Therefore the mother who nags her son to clean his room runs the risk of her son ignoring her. The child who was teased by his friends on the playground may learn that the best way to avoid being teased is to stop coming to school.

There are times when negative reinforcement procedures are justified. For example a teacher may have tried praise, free time and privileges to encourage a student to complete his assignments. If the student's behavior does not improve, the teacher may resort to a negative reinforcement procedure. For example the teacher may tell the student that he can avoid an extra homework assignment by completing all of his work in class. Whenever negative reinforcement is used, it is a good idea to combine it with positive reinforcement. Therefore in the previous example, the teacher would refrain from giving the student an extra homework assignment provided he completed his work and praise him for finishing his work in class.

Another drawback to using negative reinforcement is that the teacher may become associated with aversive consequences. While students may behave appropriately so as to avoid punitive consequences, they may also tend to avoid interacting with their teacher. Because of the effectiveness of positive reinforcement techniques, most teachers rarely find it necessary to resort to the use of negative reinforcement. Therefore this procedure will not be discussed further in this chapter.

Types of Positive Reinforcers

Positive reinforcers can be classified into a number of different types. For our purposes we will discuss four types of potentially reinforcing objects or events in order of their desirability.

Social Reinforcers   *Social reinforcers* include such things as smiles, compliments and a pat on the back. One of the advantages of using social reinforcers is that there is little danger of their losing their effectiveness. It is very difficult to imagine anyone saying, "Boy, I hope nobody praises me today!" People seemingly never tire of receiving compliments. When using social reinforcers such as praise, it is important to deliver the praise in a sincere manner and in a way which is consistent with one's teaching style. For example one teacher may use words like fantastic and super when complimenting students on their work. Another teacher may write excellent on top of a student's assignment and smile as she returns his paper. The type of social reinforcer one selects may vary from student to student. Some students may shrink away from pats on the head and prefer a simple compliment.

Social reinforcers such as praise are often referred to as natural reinforcers because many people at least occasionally praise a student's behavior in other settings. The same is true with other social reinforcers such as grades or positive written comments. Many teachers routinely deliver these consequences to their students. By using natural reinforcers to improve behavior, one enhances the possibility that other persons will react to the student's behavior in the same way. Thus it is likely that many individuals will at least occasionally reinforce a student's behavior. When a behavior is reinforced at least intermittently and in more than one setting, there is a greater chance that the behavior will be maintained and will spread to other settings.

Activities   The effectiveness of using classroom activities to reinforce behavior is well established (Sulzer-Azaroff & Mayer, 1977). Some activities which can be used to improve students' behavior are shown in Table 9-1. The list of activities is by no means exhaustive, but it should serve to provide the reader with an idea of the types of activities which can be used to reinforce behavior. When using activities to reinforce behavior, the activity must follow the behavior one wishes to increase. This simple tactic is sometimes known as "Gramma's Law." An example of Gramma's Law would be, "After you finish your dinner, you can have dessert." An academic example would be, "After you complete your reading assignment, you can color a picture."

When using activities to reinforce behavior, a teacher can allow a student to perform a specific activity such as running errands, playing a game or reading a favorite book. Of course there is a chance that when a single activity is used the student may tire of that activity. Hence the activity may lose its ability to reinforce behavior. To prevent that possibility teachers often allow students to earn minutes of free time during which they can engage in a variety of activities. By allowing students access to a wide range of activities such as playing games, reading and tutoring other students, one enhances the possibility that some activity will maintain its ability to reinforce behavior.

Tangible reinforcers   Many types of objects may serve to reinforce a student's behavior. Some teachers attach paper stickers or stars to perfect papers. Other teachers give students special certificates or send "Good News" notes home to a student's parents. These types of objects are commonly used by teachers to reward appropriate behavior and to commend students for their academic performance.

Small toys or school supplies are sometimes used to reinforce behavior. While this practice may be appropriate for students for whom praise or activities have not been effective, one should not rely strictly on the use of *tangible reinforcers* for the following reasons. First if too many tangible reinforcers are delivered, the student may tire of the objects and thereby the objects will lose their effectiveness to reinforce behavior. Second tangible reinforcers will not always be provided in other settings in which the student is expected to engage in a behavior. For example a resource teacher may allow a student to select an object from a grab bag provided that he has completed all of his work and behaved appropriately in the resource room. The student may well expect the same arrangement in the regular classroom. If the student does not receive trinkets in that setting, he may fail to complete his work or misbehave. Third parents usually take a dim view of providing objects to reinforce a student's behavior. Fourth the cost of dispensing such items quickly adds up.

It is best to try social and *activity reinforcers* first. If neither prove to be effective, one might elect to use the more natural types of tangible reinforcers such as paper stickers, certificates and "Good News" notes.

TABLE 9-1 List of Potentially Reinforcing Activities

Preschool	*Elementary*	*Junior & Senior High*
1. Listening to stories	1. Running errands	1. Listening to the radio
2. Playing games	2. Correcting papers	2. Working on crafts
3. Coloring, painting	3. Feeding animals	3. Playing checkers or chess
4. Building objects	4. Films	4. Looking at teen magazines
5. Extra recess	5. Reading comics	5. Tutoring younger students
6. Playing records	6. Helping the teacher	6. Working on a school play
7. Doing a puzzle	7. Tutoring other students	7. Helping in the library
8. Choosing a game	8. Writing on the blackboard	8. Working on the school paper
9. Playing with puppets	9. Typing	9. Watching films
10. Working with clay	10. Playing board games	10. Reading magazines

Naturally if none of these objects serve to reinforce a student's behavior, one might have to resort to the use of more exotic types of reinforcers such as colored pens or small toys. Whenever tangible reinforcers are delivered, the teacher should always pair them with praise. The reason being that by pairing desirable objects with praise, eventually praise alone will assume reinforcing properties. Using this method the objects can eventually be discontinued and praise can be used to maintain the behavior as well as to increase other behaviors.

Edible reinforcers   Perhaps the most famous *edible reinforcer* is "M & M" candies. In the past behavior modifiers commonly used candy to reinforce such behaviors as attending (Craig & Holland, 1970) and to decrease disruptive behaviors (Coleman, 1970). Unfortunately due to the overuse of edible reinforcers to demonstrate such principles as positive reinforcement, behavioral procedures became associated in the minds of many teachers with the use of edible reinforcers.

In some special classrooms today, it is not uncommon to see students receiving candy for completing their assignments, sitting quietly, coming to a reading lesson on time or giving a correct answer. When students receive candy in special settings, they may expect to be given candy for performing the same behaviors in their regular classrooms. If candy is not provided in the regular classroom, students may fail to generalize their behavior to that setting. Whenever students are receiving instruction in both special and regular classroom settings, one of the primary concerns must be to find ways to facilitate generalization to the regular classroom. Therefore in special settings, it is best to use natural reinforcers in order to promote generalization to the regular classroom.

Only when other more natural reinforcers such as praise, activities and tangible reinforcers have failed to bring about a desired change in behavior, should one even consider the use of edible reinforcers. Whenever it becomes necessary to use edible reinforcers to establish a behavior, one should always pair their delivery with praise. In this way after the behavior is established, the candy can be eventually withdrawn and the behavior can be maintained through the use of praise.

Selecting Positive Reinforcers

Each of us has likes and dislikes, which makes it difficult to predict whether a potential reinforcer will actually serve to increase or maintain a particular individual's behavior. There are some ways that teachers can heighten the chance of selecting effective reinforcers for students. First when deciding to use social reinforcement, consider whether reinforcers such as praise or some kind of teacher attention has served to increase or maintain other behaviors in the past. If so praise might very well serve to increase the behavior which is presently a concern. Second observe the types of activities a student chooses to engage in during free time. If for example a student chooses to color or play games with friends, these activities might serve as reinforcers. Third present the student with a variety of classroom privileges he could earn and allow the student to select his own reinforcing activity. Of course students sometimes select activities which fail to increase their behavior, but generally this method is an effective way of identifying reinforcers.

In selecting positive reinforcers care should be taken to select a reinforcer which is as natural as possible and which can be easily delivered. For example a teacher may determine that a student might like to earn parts of a model airplane for completing his work. While this reinforcer could be easily delivered, one would first select a more natural activity such as free time. There is no need to try more exotic reinforcers before exhausting the more natural types of reinforcers. Similarly when offering a choice of activities to a student, one need not suggest such things as a special field trip or watching film strips in the library. These types of activities will certainly be noticed by other class members who might wonder why they are not receiving such privileges. Instead keep the activities simple and begin by offering those privileges which are commonly given to other students in the classroom who are behaving well.

Using Reinforcement Effectively

In order to make reinforcement maximally effective, one should:

1. *Make the reinforcers contingent upon the desired behavior.*
   In other words the reinforcer must always follow the desired behavior. For example a student who frequently talks out during reading group might be given a few minutes of free time after his reading lesson, provided that he had not talked out more than two times. Under no circumstances would free time be given before reading group based on a promise by the student that he will refrain from talking out during the lesson.
2. *When initially establishing a behavior, reinforce each occurrence of the behavior.*
   When trying to reinforce a behavior, it is important to reinforce it each time it occurs. For example each day a student completes his homework and brings it to class, the teacher would compliment the student for finishing his work and remembering to bring it to school. By reinforcing a behavior each time it occurs, the behavior will increase more rapidly than if it had only been occasionally followed by reinforcement. Of course once a behavior has been established through the use of continuous reinforcement, the behavior will decrease if it is not followed by reinforcement. It is for this reason that one moves to a more intermittent schedule of reinforcement once a student is performing the behavior at the teacher's desired aim.
3. *Deliver the reinforcer immediately or as soon as possible after the desired behavior occurs.*
   Reinforcement is most effective when it is delivered immediately following the occurrence of a behavior. When attempting to reinforce a student for staying on-task during math, a teacher might initially reinforce the student's behavior at the end of every five minutes provided

he was on-task at that time. Once the student's behavior had become well established, reinforcement might be delivered at the end of every fifteen minutes; then only at the end of the math period.

4. *Restrict the availability of reinforcers.*

   When using reinforcers such as activities or tangible reinforcers, it is important to restrict their availability. If a teacher wishes to give a student a special privilege for engaging in an appropriate behavior, the student should not be able to earn that privilege in any other way. For example if a student is already earning free time for completing a reading assignment and a teacher wishes to use free time to reinforce the completion of his math assignment, free time would only be awarded for completing both assignments.

5. *Deliver an appropriate amount of reinforcement.*

   In general more or stronger reinforcers are required to increase behaviors which are hard for an individual to perform. For example consider a student who finds reading easy but who has difficulty in math. Reading may be maintained through the use of feedback, but feedback may prove to be a weak reinforcer when it is used to increase a student's accuracy in math. At first it may be necessary to pair feedback with a stronger reinforcer such as free time. As the student's accuracy improves, free time can be gradually withdrawn and the behavior may be maintained through the use of feedback.

   When initially attempting to reinforce behavior, there is a tendency to provide several reinforcers at once. For example a teacher might give a student a star for each assignment he completes, allow him to spend twenty minutes of free time per day and send a "Good News" note home to his parents provided that he has completed all of his assignments. If the student's behavior improves, the teacher will not be able to determine if the improvement is due to giving the student stars, the free time, the sending of the note home or a combination of these consequences. More important it may not have been necessary to deliver so many reinforcers to increase the student's behavior.

   When reinforcing a behavior it is best to start with a small amount of reinforcement. After delivering the reinforcer for a few days, one should inspect the student's data. If performance is not improving, the amount or type of reinforcement may be adjusted.

INCREASING APPROPRIATE BEHAVIOR

This section provides more detailed descriptions of some techniques using the principles outlined in the section on the nature of reinforcement. Each technique will first be briefly described. Then reference will be made to the types of classroom behaviors which have been increased through the use of each technique. Finally sample projects will be presented to illustrate how one would apply each technique to change behavior.

Praise

Teacher attention has proved to be a very strong reinforcer for many students. Praise has been used in regular classrooms to increase a variety of social and academic behaviors. Among them are: attending (Hall, Lund, & Jackson, 1968), raising hands before speaking (Hall, Fox, Willard, Goldsmith, Emerson, Owen, Davis, & Porcia, 1971), and following instructions (Schutte & Hopkins, 1970).

Whenever social reinforcers such as praise are used, it is important to focus the praise on the student's *behavior* rather than on the student himself, and to make reference to the *specific* behavior which is being praised. For example when praising John for working quietly at his desk, a teacher might say, "I like the way you're working quietly" rather than "You're a good boy." In this way, the student learns that it is his behavior which the teacher is rewarding and specifically, the behavior of sitting quietly at one's desk and working. By commenting on a student's behavior one avoids the possibility that the student will think he or she is "bad" if his teacher occasionally reacts with disapproval to some inappropriate behavior.

Praise may be used alone or in combination with other procedures. For example praise for appropriate behavior is often coupled with ignoring inappropriate behavior. The technique of positively reinforcing appropriate behavior, while extinguishing inappropriate behavior by withholding teacher attention, has proven to be a very effective technique. In the following project, we will see how a teacher was able to increase the amount of time a student spent on a task simply through the use of praise.

Classroom Application of Praise
(Lee, E., 1978)

Number of Students
Nine-year old girl, Susie

Setting
Fourth-grade classroom

Target Behavior/Aim
Increase amount of time spent on-task during English period to 100 percent for three days.

Definition of Target Behavior
On-task meant that the student was to be in her seat looking at her book or at the teacher while the teacher was giving directions. After the class was instructed to begin their assignment, Susie was considered to be on-task if she was looking at her book, writing on her paper or raising her hand.

Observation System and Measurement Technique
During the half-hour English period, the practicing teacher observed Susie's behavior at the end of every five minutes. The wall clock was used to remind the teacher of the time. The practicing teacher used an index card, which she carried around the room with her while assisting other students, to record Susie's behavior.

If at the end of a five-minute interval Susie was on-task, a "+" was recorded; if not, a "−" was recorded.

Procedures

During baseline the practicing teacher measured the behavior without attending to it in any way. After three days an intervention was applied which consisted of praising Susie's behavior at the end of each interval if she was on-task and encouraging her to work if she was off-task.

During maintenance praise was delivered on a more intermittent basis, in other words a maximum of three times following the end of an interval in which Susie was on-task. Following the first week of maintenance data were taken only once a week for two weeks during which time Susie's on-task behavior was occasionally praised by the practicing teacher.

Reliability

Reliability was taken by the practicing teacher's university supervisor. The records of the practicing teacher and supervisor agreed exactly.

Results

During baseline Susie was on-task less than 20 percent of the time as shown in Figure 9-1. Her on-task behavior improved dramatically during the intervention. When praise was delivered intermittently during maintenance, Susie's attending behavior maintained at 100 percent for two weeks.

Comment

The reader should note that Susie's performance improved dramatically during the intervention when praise was delivered on a fairly continuous basis for being on-task. During maintenance the teacher switched from a continuous schedule of reinforcement to a more intermittent one in which Susie's on-task behavior was only occasionally praised. The maintenance data suggest that Susie's behavior maintained very well even though praise was only occasionally delivered.

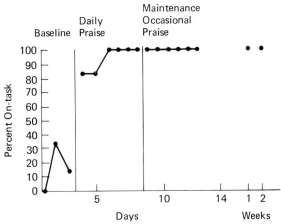

FIGURE 9–1 Percent of time Susie spent on-task during English period. (Adapted from Erin Lee, *Increasing the on-task behavior of a nine-year-old girl.* Unpublished manuscript, University of Illinois, 1978. By permission of the author.)

Premack Principle

The Premack Principle states that high frequency behaviors can be used to reinforce low frequency behaviors (Premack, 1959). All too often behaviors which occur at low frequencies such as completing assignments, working quietly and sitting at one's desk, are precisely those which teachers wish to increase or maintain.

When reinforcing behavior using the Premack Principle, one simply makes access to some activity which the student frequently engages in and seems to enjoy, such as free time activities, contingent upon the occurrence of the low frequency behavior. For example to reinforce in-seat behavior during math, a teacher might allow a student to earn five minutes of free time provided that he remained in his seat throughout the half-hour period.

The Premack Principle has been used in regular classrooms to increase behavior such as sitting quietly and paying attention (Homme, DeBaca, Devine, Steinhorst, & Rickert, 1963), writing legibly (Hopkins, Schutte, & Garton, 1971) and spelling words accurately (Lovitt, Guppy & Blatter, 1969). In the study by Hopkins, et al., students were allowed to go to a playroom as soon as their papers had been scored. Although no contingency was placed on rate or accuracy of printing, the majority of students wrote legibly. For the few students who hurried through their assignments in order to play sooner, the teacher simply changed the contingency and required those students to achieve a certain level of accuracy. If the students wrote legibly enough, they were allowed to go to the playroom; if not they copied over part of their assignment.

When using the Premack Principle, a teacher must first identify a high strength activity which can be used to reinforce the desired behavior. A teacher can select either one particular activity, allow a student to choose from several activities or give the student free time so that he can participate in a variety of activities. As students sometimes tire of one activity, it is wise to offer them a choice of several activities. In this way there is a good chance that some activity will maintain its ability to reinforce behavior. In the following project we will see how a teacher used the Premack Principle to increase the on-task behavior of two boys.

**Classroom Application of the Premack Principle
(Willerman, J., 1979)**

Number of Students
     Two fifth-grade boys, Eric and Mark

Setting
     Fifth-grade classroom

Target Behavior/Aim
     To increase amount of time both boys spent on-task to 80 percent for three consecutive days.

Definition of Target Behavior
     If the class was doing boardwork, the students were to be in their seats, looking at the board and not playing with their pencils or other objects, or talking

to each other. Once the assignment was given, the students were expected to be in their seats, looking at their work, writing answers or raising their hands to request assistance. Talking out and being out of one's seat were considered to be off-task behavior.

Observation System and Measurement Technique

The teacher used a separate 3 × 5 card to record each student's on-task behavior. At the end of every six minutes during the first 30 minutes of the 45 minute math period, the teacher glanced at each boy and recorded whether or not he was on-task. A " + " was used to record on-task behavior and a " − " was used to record off-task behavior.

Procedures

During baseline whenever the students were off-task, they were reprimanded and asked to stop whatever they were doing that the teacher felt was disruptive. Prior to the intervention, the teacher asked the students what they would like to do for fun during math. The students suggested working with multiplication flash cards. The teacher told each boy that he, the teacher and the other boy could spend five minutes working on flashcards provided that he was judged to be on-task at least four out of five times when the teacher checked.

During the two weeks following the intervention, the teacher conducted four maintenance checks. The students were unaware as to which days the teacher collected data. Both boys were told that if they kept up the good work they would occasionally be able to do the flashcards. During maintenance the students were allowed to do flashcards once per week provided that their on-task behavior remained at or above 80 percent.

Results

During baseline Mark spent 40 percent of his time on-task and Eric spent 28.6 percent of his time working. When the intervention was in effect, Mark and Eric both increased the amount of time they spent on-task to 60 percent. As shown in Figure 9-2, during the last three days of the intervention, both boys were spending 80 percent of their time on-task. The boys' average during maintenance was 85 percent.

Comment

This project demonstrates that an academic activity can be used to reinforce appropriate study behaviors. For Mark and Eric the opportunity to work with each other and the teacher on flashcards proved to be a high strength activity capable of reinforcing on-task behavior.

Shaping

Shaping refers to a procedure in which successive approximation to some terminal behavior is reinforced. When a student has seldom or never performed a behavior, one must shape the student's behavior by reinforcing small steps. For example if a student rarely spends more than five minutes in his seat during a twenty-minute period, one could begin by reinforcing the student after he had spent five minutes in his desk. Eventually reinforcement would be delivered after the student was sitting for eight minutes, then after ten minutes, fifteen minutes, and twenty minutes.

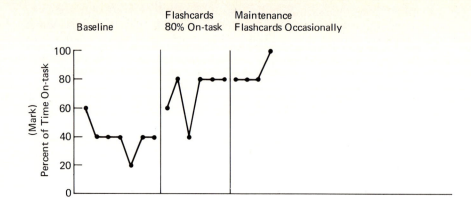

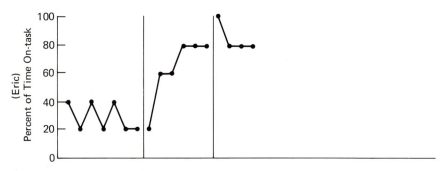

FIGURE 9–2 Percent of time Eric and Mark spent on-task. (Adapted from Janet Willerman, *The remediation of off-task behavior in the regular classroom*. Unpublished manuscript, University of Illinois, 1979. By permission of the author.)

By gradually increasing the difficulty of the task and by reinforcing successive improvements, behavior is shaped.

Shaping has been used extensively with moderately and severely handicapped students to teach them behaviors which they seldom or never exhibited, such as speaking (Lovaas, Berberich, Perlaff, & Schaeffer, 1966). Shaping has also been used with students in classrooms to increase behaviors which they perform at low levels, such as completing assignments and computing math problems (Hall & Fox, 1977). In the following project a teacher used shaping to increase the number of assignments a student completed.

**Classroom Application of Shaping
(Wooley, K., 1979)**

Number of Students
Seven-year old boy, Keith

Setting
Third-grade classroom

Target Behavior/Aim

Increase number of assignments completed in the morning to four assignments for five days and decrease amount of time taken to begin working to one minute or less.

Definition of Target Behavior

Each morning the student was given four worksheets, one each in vocabulary and phonics, and two reading worksheets. An assignment was considered to be complete if a written answer was provided for each item presented on a worksheet. The student was said to have begun working when he had written one answer on an assignment.

Observation System and Measurement Technique

The teacher used a combination of observational and permanent product recording. To measure the amount of time Keith took before beginning his assignment, the teacher recorded the number of minutes which elapsed between the time she placed the work on the student's desk and the time Keith wrote his first answer. At the end of the reading period the teacher collected Keith's work and counted the number of assignments he had completed.

Procedures

During baseline four assignments were assigned to be completed during the one and one-half hour reading period. Keith was given directions and asked to complete his assignments independently.

Following baseline the teacher assigned Keith one assignment to complete. Keith was told that he would receive a colorful sticker as soon as he had finished his assignment. When Keith handed his assignment to the teacher, she praised him verbally, shook his hand or gave him a pat on the back.

During the second intervention the teacher assigned Keith two workbook pages. Keith was told that if he completed both assignments for four days he could select the first game the class could play during game time on Friday. The third intervention consisted of giving the student three assignments to complete. During this intervention the student's behavior was occasionally praised. Finally during the fourth intervention, the student was given all four assignments to complete. As during the previous intervention, the student's behavior was occasionally praised.

During maintenance the teacher returned to baseline procedures and the student was asked to complete his assignments independently. The student received no more praise than was normally given by the teacher to other students who had completed their work.

Results

As can be seen in Figure 9-3, Keith rarely completed any assignments during baseline and he sometimes took as long as 39 minutes to begin working on his first assignment. Each time the teacher adjusted her aim, the student was able to complete the required number of assignments. While the first intervention was in effect, Keith began to take less time to begin working. Throughout the remaining intervention, Keith began working within one to three minutes after the teacher placed his assignments on his desk. During maintenance Keith consistently began working within one minute and completed all four of his assignments.

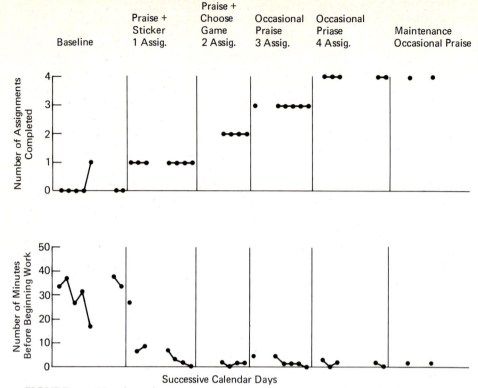

FIGURE 9–3 Number of assignments completed and time taken to begin working. (Adapted from Karen Wooley, *Remediating "off-task" behavior in the regular classroom.* Unpublished manuscript, University of Illinois, 1979. By permission of the author.)

Comment

One of the interesting aspects of this project is that the teacher measured two behaviors at the same time. Even though no contingency was placed on the amount of time Keith took to begin working, he clearly began to settle down to work within a few minutes. It should also be pointed out that the teacher used different reinforcers to shape completing the first two assignments. When using shaping one need not vary the reinforcer if it is effective, but simply require more and more behavior before delivering the reinforcer. In this instance however, the teacher began by combining praise with stickers to reinforce the completion of one assignment. Rather than continue using a tangible reinforcer, the teacher showed good judgment in changing first to an activity reinforcer and then to praise alone.

Self-Recording

So far, we have spoken about teachers measuring, recording, and changing the behavior of their students. It is also possible for students to take an active role in changing their own behavior. Although *self-recording* has not been investigated as extensively as some of the other techniques discussed, the effectiveness of this procedure has been demonstrated by Broden, Hall, and Mitts (1971). In their study two eighth-grade students were taught to record their own behavior. One eighth-grade girl recorded the amount of time she spent studying and one boy kept track of the number of times he talked out. Self-recording was clearly effective in increasing the amount of time the girl spent studying. While this same procedure was initially effective in reducing the boy's talk-outs, no long-term positive effects were noted. This discrepancy in results serves to illustrate an important point, that is a technique which works with one student may not work with another. Therefore one must measure and evaluate the effects of techniques on individual students.

The two sample projects which follow illustrate how teachers were able to increase the amount of work students completed by teaching them how to record their own behavior. The first project shows the effects of self-charting on a student's ability to accurately complete her reading assignments. The second project demonstrates how a resource teacher and five other teachers in a middle school banded together to increase the number of assignments a student completed.

Classroom Application 1 of Self-Recording
(Simon, E. A., 1979)

Number of Students
Twelve-year old girl, Toni

Setting
Sixth-grade classroom

Target Behavior/Aim
Increase percent of work completed to 100 percent and increase accuracy to 85 percent correct for two weeks.

Definition of Target Behavior
Each day the student was given between four and seven workbook pages to complete in addition to comprehension questions. As the number of pages varied from day to day, the teacher recorded the percentage of items completed correctly. An item was scored as completed if a written answer was provided. Completed items were scored as correct if they matched the answer(s) provided in the teacher's key.

Observation System and Measurement Technique
Permanent product recording was used. At the end of the reading period, the teacher counted the number of items completed correctly and incorrectly and then computed the percent of work completed and percent of items answered correctly.

Procedures
During baseline the teacher checked and recorded Toni's work at the end of the reading period. As with all students in the class, Toni was praised for the work she completed. During the intervention the teacher showed Toni her graph and told her that she would like her to complete all of her work with at least 75 percent accuracy. The teacher also told Toni that each day she would be able to chart her own performance. If Toni completed all of her work and scored 75 percent or better, the teacher praised her. After four days the teacher encouraged Toni to try to score

85 percent correct or higher. Toni was praised when she completed all of her work at or above the 85 percent level.

During maintenance Toni was told that occasionally the teacher would check her work and that Toni would be able to graph her performance. As during the intervention Toni was praised for completing all of her work at or above 85 percent correct.

Results

During baseline Toni completed an average of 74.1 percent of her assignments. Her average accuracy was 62.3 percent. As can be seen in Figure 9-4, her performance was quite variable. During the intervention Toni consistently completed all of her assignments at or above 80 percent correct. Data from the two weekly maintenance checks reveal that Toni continued to complete all of her assignments with a high degree of accuracy.

Comment

Although the teacher's usual procedure was to praise students for completing their work, this technique was simply not effective for Toni as indicated by her

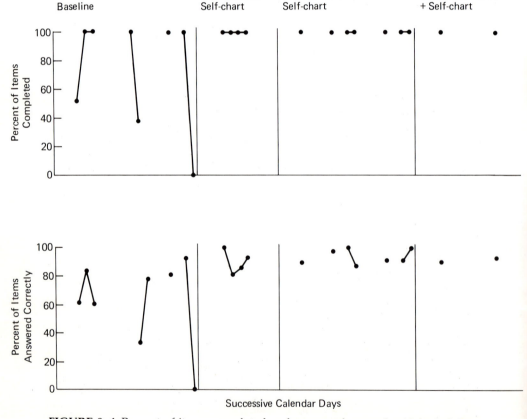

FIGURE 9–4 Percent of items completed and answered correctly. (Adapted from Ellen A. Simon, *Improving work completion and accuracy in the regular classroom.* Unpublished manuscript, University of Illinois, 1979. By permission of the author.)

baseline performance. When praise was coupled with charting her own performance, Toni increased the amount of work she completed and improved her accuracy.

Classroom Application 2 of Self-Recording
(Wolfson, D., 1979)

Number of Students
    Eleven-year old boy, David

Setting
    Middle school, five regular classes and resource room

Target Behavior/Aim
    Complete all daily classroom assignments in at least four of five classes for
two weeks.

Definition of Target Behavior
    The types of assignments varied from class to class. Generally the assign-
ments consisted of reading and writing activities, and participating in group projects. Before beginning the project the resource teacher and five other teachers met
to discuss criteria for completing assignments. Using these criteria each of the five
teachers was to determine whether David had completed his assignment. Assignments did not include work completed at home or in the resource room.

Observation System and Measurement Technique
    Permanent product recording was used to measure the percent of assign-
ments David completed. Prior to beginning the intervention, the teachers inspected
their daily grade books and noted the number of assignments David had completed
during the past week. Throughout the intervention David carried a checklist with
him to each of five classes. His teachers placed their initials next to their respective
subject area if he had completed his work. At the end of the day, David brought
his checklist to the resource room where he and his teacher recorded his performance on a graph.

Procedures
    No special contingencies were placed on David's performance during base-
line. Prior to the intervention, the teachers met and discussed how they would
implement their plan. It was agreed that the resource teacher would explain the
procedure to David. The teachers agreed to praise David for completing his assignments and to initial the daily checklist if he had finished his work. The resource
teacher showed David his baseline data and told him that his teachers were interested in helping him to complete all of his assignments. She then gave David
the checklist and told him to ask each of his teachers to initial it if he completed
his work or write a comment if he did not. Finally she told David that they would
plot his performance on his graph each day after school.
    During maintenance the teachers had planned to discontinue using the check-
list on a daily basis. However David liked it so much that he asked to continue
using it.

Results
    During baseline David rarely completed any assignments as shown in Figure
9-5. While the intervention was in effect on a daily basis David always completed

all of his assignments in at least four out of five classes. On each maintenance check, which occurred over a three-week period, David completed all of his assignments in all five classes.

Comment

This project clearly demonstrates that teachers can work together to improve a student's performance. The teachers undertook this project in the hope that by completing his assignments, David's grades would improve. David's mid-term progress report showed that his grades, as well as his study skills, had improved.

Contingency Contracts

A *contingency contract* is a "written signed agreement between a teacher and a student which specifies that the student will receive a stated amount of some privilege activity (or other reinforcer) after he satisfactorily completes a specific task" (Buckholt et al., 1975, p. 185). An example of a contingency contract is shown in Figure 9-6.

As shown in Figure 9-6, the contract specifies what the student will earn if he meets the contract as well as the penalty for failing to fulfill the contract. The reader should note that the penalty need not be the loss of some privilege; rather the penalty could be some sort of remedial work as indicated in the sample contract.

Contingency contracts were originally proposed by Homme (1966). Contacts have been used successfully by both parents and teachers (Cantrell, Cantrell, Huddleston, & Wooldridge, 1969). Homme (1966) used them with potential school dropouts to improve their performance on academic tasks.

Specific rules for developing contracts have been provided by Homme, Csanyi, Gonzales, & Rechs (1977). Briefly these rules are as

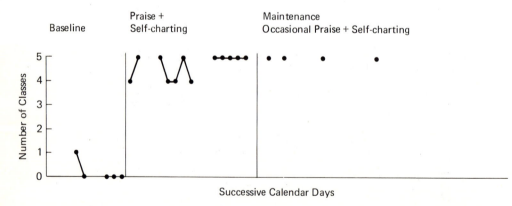

FIGURE 9–5 Number of classes in which David completed his work. (Adapted from Deborah Wolfson, *The use of a checklist to monitor a student's daily completion of in-class assignments in a middle school setting.* Unpublished manuscript, University of Illinois, 1979. By permission of the author.)

```
┌─────────────────────────────────────────────────────────────────────┐
│                                                                       │
│   Task:                 I will read one section (approximately 10      │
│   (What I must do)      pages) of my history book and answer the       │
│                         progress check at the end of the section.     │
│                                                                       │
│                                                                       │
│   Time:                 During history lesson.                        │
│   (When)                                                              │
│                                                                       │
│   Criteria:             Get at least 60 percent correct (6 or more     │
│   (How I must do it)    correct out of 10).                           │
│                                                                       │
│                                                                       │
│   Reinforcer:           10 minutes of free time in the social area.    │
│   (What I will get)                                                   │
│                                                                       │
│   Penalty Clause:       If I get less than 60 percent correct (5 or less│
│                         correct), see the teacher for a remedial unit. │
│                                                                       │
│                                                                       │
│                                                                       │
│                                                                       │
│              Signed _____                   │
│                                (student)                              │
│                     _____                   │
│                                (teacher)                              │
│                                                                       │
└─────────────────────────────────────────────────────────────────────┘
```

FIGURE 9–6 Contingency Contract. (Adapted from D. R. Buckholt, D. E. Ferritor, H. N. Sloane, G. M. Della-Piana, K. S. Rogers, & I. F. Coor. *Classroom & instructional management: A teacher training program in behavior analysis.* New York: CEMREL, 1975, p. 187. By permission of the publisher.)

follows:

1. The contract payoff (reward) should be immediate.
2. Initial contracts should call for and reward small approximations.
3. Reward frequently with small amounts.
4. The contract should call for and reward accomplishment rather than obedience.
5. Reward the performance after it occurs.
6. The contract must be fair.
7. The terms of the contract must be clear.
8. The contract must be honest.
9. The contract must be positive.
10. Contracting as a method must be used systematically.

In addition some excellent suggestions for negotiating contracts have been suggested by Shea, Whiteside, Beetner, & Lindsey (cited in Walker & Shea, 1980). Their suggestions are as follows:

1. Teacher begins by establishing rapport with the student.
2. Teacher explains the purpose of the meeting.
3. Teacher provides a simple definition of a contract.
4. Teacher explains that they are going to write a contract.

5. Teacher and student discuss task.
6. Teacher and student discuss reinforcers.
7. Teacher and student negotiate the ratio of task to reinforcer.
8. Teacher and student set time for task to be completed.
9. Teacher and student agree on standard to be achieved.
10. Teacher and student discuss how progress will be evaluated.
11. Teacher and student negotiate delivery of reinforcer.
12. Teacher and student agree on date contract will be renegotiated.
13. Teacher or student writes contract.
14. Teacher reads the contract as student looks at a copy of the contract.
15. Teacher and student verbally affirm to uphold the contract.
16. Teacher and student sign contract.
17. Teacher congratulates student for making the contract and wishes the student success.

Contingency contracts can provide students with a sense of responsibility as students are treated as partners in the negotiating process. Although contracts have been used with junior high and high school students, they have also been used successfully with younger children (Buckholt, Ferritor, Sloane, Della-Piana, Rogers, & Coor, 1975). In the following project contingency contracting was used to increase the amount of work completed and the accuracy of a sixth grader.

**Classroom Application of Contingency Contracting
(Schmidt, J., 1980)**

Number of Students
Eleven-year-old boy, Andy

Setting
Sixth-grade classroom

Target Behavior/Aim
Two target behaviors were measured: to increase the amount of work completed and the accuracy on reading workbook pages. The aim was to increase percent of items completed and accuracy to 100 percent for three consecutive days.

Definition of Target Behavior
An item was said to be completed if the student provided a written answer. Correct answers were those which matched those provided in the teacher's manual. Items which were left unanswered or did not match those given in the teacher's manual were scored as incorrect.

Observation System and Measurement Technique
Permanent product recording was used to measure work completion and accuracy on reading workbook pages. Because the number of pages assigned varied between three and four per day, the teacher chose to record percent of items completed. Both percent of items completed and percent correct scores were charted.

During baseline the practicing teacher asked the student to let her correct his workbook pages. If the student had completed any work, the teacher returned the workbook without comment.

Prior to the intervention the practicing teacher suggested to Andy that they might write a contract to help him complete his workbook pages. The original contract, which focused on work completion, is shown in Figure 9-7. Andy and the teacher negotiated the privileges which he could select provided he fulfilled his contract by completing 90 percent of his reading workbook assignment. The teacher also gave Andy a poster, similar to the one shown in Figure 9-8 to remind him of the privileges he could earn.

Prior to the second intervention, the teacher and Andy renegotiated the contract. In order to earn the same privileges, Andy now had to complete all of his workbook pages and score at least 90 percent correct.

Results

During baseline Andy failed to complete any of his workbook pages. As shown in Figure 9-9, within six days after the introduction of the contingency contract, Andy had met the teacher's initial aim of completing 90 percent of his assignments for three consecutive days. During the first intervention Andy's accuracy on assignments increased, even though he was receiving privileges for completing his work and not accuracy. During the second intervention when the contract was changed to include an accuracy criterion, Andy's accuracy increased. On the last three days on which the practicing teacher was in the classroom, Andy was completing all of his workbook pages with a high degree of accuracy.

THIS CONTRACT IS BETWEEN *Andy Smith* AND *Ms. Schmidt*
ABOUT *completing assignments.*

I, *Andy Smith* AGREE TO *Complete my reading workbook pages*

I, *Julie Schmidt* AGREE TO *allow Andy to select a privilege from his list each day he completes at least 90% of his reading workbook pages*

SIGNED *Andy Smith* DATE *3/12/80*
SIGNED *J. Schmidt* DATE *3/12/80*

FIGURE 9–7 Contract Agreement. (Adapted from J. A. Schmidt, *Using contingency contracts to increase work completion.* Unpublished manuscript, University of Illinois, 1980. By permission of the author.)

Comment
        In this project the teacher clearly demonstrated the effectiveness of using
contingency contracting to improve work completion and accuracy. The types of
privileges the teacher allowed the student to select illustrate the kinds of potential
reinforcers which are naturally available to classroom teachers.

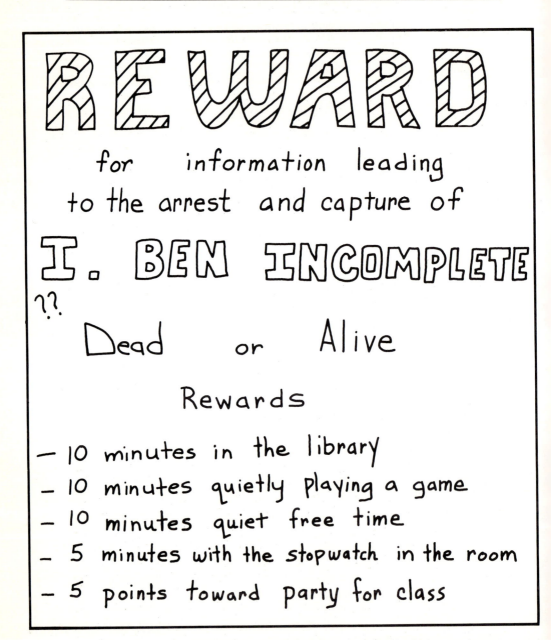

FIGURE 9–8 Sample Contract. (Adapted from J. A. Schmidt, *Using contingency*
contracts to increase work completion. Unpublished manuscript, University of Illinois,
1980. By the permission of the author.)

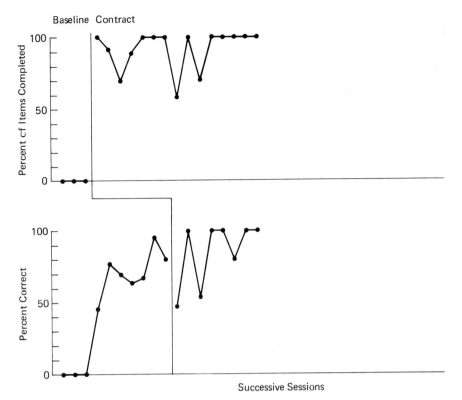

FIGURE 9–9 Percent of items completed and percent correct scores on workbook pages. (Adapted from Julia A. Schmidt, *Using contingency contracts to increase work completion.* Unpublished manuscript, University of Illinois, 1980. By permission of the author.)

Summary

Teachers can choose from a variety of techniques to increase and/or maintain appropriate behaviors in the classroom. All of the techniques presented in this section are based on the principle of positive reinforcement, which states that a behavior can be increased or maintained by presenting a consequence contingent upon behavior. Teachers can choose from a number of potential reinforcers, including: praise, classroom activities, certificates of achievement, self-charting and even formalized contracts. When selecting reinforcers, one should keep in mind that the simplest technique is usually best. Therefore if teacher attention appears to be a probable reinforcer, one would first use praise to reinforce a behavior. In the event that praise was not effective, other types of potential reinforcers such as activities, self-charting or contingency contracts could be tried. While all of the techniques presented in this chapter have proven effective, one should remember that students are individuals and that no technique is guaranteed to work with all students. Therefore one should use these techniques, adapt them to fit one's own needs, and make instructional decisions based on their effect on the performance of individual students.

Extinction

Many inappropriate behaviors are actually maintained by the consequences which they produce. For example a student may continue to shout out answers rather than raise his hand if his shouting results in the teacher calling on him. A classic example of inappropriate behavior being maintained by attention was provided by Williams (1959). The subject of that study was a twenty-one month-old boy who screamed and cried after being put to bed. In order to get the child to quiet down, his parents would often spend one-half to two hours each night in his bedroom until the boy went to sleep. To reduce the boy's tantrums the parents used *extinction* which is "a procedure in which behavior that has been reinforced previously is no longer reinforced" (Sulzer-Azaroff & Mayer, 1977, p. 147). Instead of attending to their son's tantrums, the parents simply put him to bed and left the door, closing the door behind them. At first the boy yelled and screamed for up to forty-five minutes. By the seventh night, however, the boy did not cry after his parents put him to bed.

Extinction has been used in classrooms to decrease disruptive behaviors (Thomas, Becker, & Armstrong, 1968), tantrums (Carlson, Arnold, Becker, & Madsen, 1968), and off-task behaviors (Thomas, et al., 1968). When using extinction to decrease behavior, the following points should be kept in mind. First if extinction is to be effective, one must withhold *all* reinforcement following the occurrence of an inappropriate behavior. For example a teacher may decide to ignore a student's talking out. This procedure would likely be effective unless other members of the class were also attending to the student's talking out. In cases where other students attend to a student's inappropriate behavior, one can reinforce them for ignoring inappropriate behavior (Carlson, Arnold, Becker & Madsen, 1968). Second extinction results in a gradual change in behavior. Therefore one must be able to put up with the behavior while it is being extinguished. For example in the study by Williams (1959) the parents had to put up with their son's crying for periods of up to forty-five minutes until his crying ceased. Third there is often a temporary increase in the inappropriate behavior when extinction is applied. Knowing this, one should not abandon the procedure if during the first few days the behavior actually gets worse. Eventually if all reinforcement is withheld, the behavior will decrease. Fourth extinction is most effective when used in combination with other procedures. For example when extinguishing talking out, a teacher would couple ignoring talking out with praising a student for raising his hand. A combination of ignoring inappropriate behavior and praising appropriate behavior was used in the following project.

Classroom Application of Extinction
(Hall, R. V., Fox, R., Willard, D., Goldsmith, L., Emerson, M., Owen, M., Davis, F., & Porcia, E., 1971)

Number of Students
    Fifteen-year-old boy, Mike

Setting
     Special education classroom

Target Behavior/Aim
     Reduce arguing behavior

Definition of Target Behavior
     An instance of disputing behavior was recorded "whenever Mike argued with the teacher, failed to comply with a teacher request within 10 sec, or shook his head in a negative manner during discussion of assignments" (p. 142).

Observation System and Measurement Technique
     The teacher used event recording to tally the number of disputes which occurred throughout the school day.

Procedures
     During baseline the teacher recorded the number of disputes which occurred. When the intervention began, the teacher walked away from Mike whenever he began to argue with her. The teacher also praised Mike whenever he began an assignment without arguing. During the return to baseline the teacher again attended to Mike whenever he began to argue with her and discontinued praising him for not arguing. Following this condition the teacher again ignored disputes and praised Mike for not arguing. This same arrangement was continued over a two-week maintenance period in which three postchecks were conducted.

Results
     As can be seen in Figure 9-10, during the initial baseline Mike's disputes ranged from five to nine per day. When the intervention was applied disputes decreased to zero on the last three days of the condition. During the return-to-baseline phase, disputes increased to an average of 5.4 per day. When disputes were again ignored and Mike was praised for not arguing, disputes averaged less

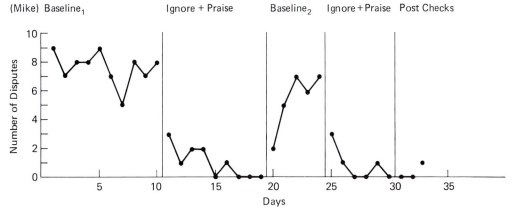

FIGURE 9–10 Number of disputes Mike had with his teacher. (From R. V. Hall, R. Fox, D. Willard, L. Goldsmith, M. Emerson, M. Owen, F. Davis, and E. Porcia, The teacher as observer and experimenter in the modification of disputing and talking-out behaviors, *Journal of Applied Behavior Analysis*, 1971, 4, p. 142. By permission of the publishers.)

than one per day. The follow-up data reveal that only one dispute occurred during postchecks taken on three different days, two weeks following the last intervention.

Comment
It should be pointed out that this project was a research study designed to show the relationship between teacher attention and disputing behavior. In order to demonstrate a functional relationship, the teacher returned to baseline following the first intervention and then reinstituted the teaching technique. Usually classroom teachers do not return to baseline conditions to verify the effectiveness of their procedures, as they are more concerned with maintaining behavior than proving functional relationships. Therefore after a successful intervention, teachers usually proceed to a maintenance condition.

Positive Reduction Procedures

Reinforcing incompatible behaviors   One of the most positive ways to deal with inappropriate behaviors is to reinforce an incompatible behavior. For example sitting on one's seat is incompatible with being out of one's seat. Therefore one could ignore out-of-seat behavior and praise a student when he is sitting at his desk. An example of this technique is provided in the following sample project.

**Classroom Application of Reinforcing an Incompatible Behavior
(Clasey, D. A., 1979)**

Number of Students
Seven-year-old girl, Linda

Setting
Combined first-second grade classroom

Target Behavior/Aim
Increase amount of time Linda spent in her seat during a ten-minute language arts period to 90 percent of the time for four days and maintain accuracy at or above 80 percent correct on language arts assignment.

Definition of Target Behavior/Aim
In-seat behavior was defined as "sitting in her own seat, with her bottom touching the seat of the chair; facing forward with her legs under her own desk; having no physical contact or talking out; and raising her hand if she had a question" (p. 1).

Observation System and Measurement Technique
The teacher used a combination of observational and permanent product recording. In-seat data were recorded by using a time-sampling procedure. At the end of every minute during the ten-minute seatwork period, the teacher observed Linda's behavior. Using a piece of paper with ten time blocks, the teacher recorded a "+" if Linda was in-seat and a "−" if she was out of her seat. At the end of the morning the teacher collected Linda's assignment and counted the number of items answered correctly and incorrectly. Items not attempted were counted as incorrect. The teacher then computed the percent of items Linda answered correctly. Each day the teacher graphed the percent of time Linda spent in her seat and the percent of items answered correctly.

Procedures

During baseline no special instructions or feedback were provided. When the intervention began, the teacher gave the student a list of in-seat behaviors to tape to her desk. The student was told that she would receive a star on a chart taped to her desk if she was following all the rules after every time the teacher checked to see if she was in her seat. The teacher told the student that if she earned at least four stars a day, she could color fifteen dotted sections of a picture at the end of the seatwork period. During the intervention period the teacher also praised Linda when she was in her seat.

A maintenance condition was instituted during which the picture completion activity was discontinued. Stars for being in-seat and praise were given occasionally.

Results

During baseline the student's mean percent score for in-seat behavior was 15 percent with a range of 0-40 percent. Average accuracy on her assignments during this time was 78 percent. As can be seen in Figure 9-11, in-seat behavior increased to an average of 82 percent and accuracy increased to 90 percent during the intervention. During maintenance in-seat behavior averaged 93 percent and accuracy rose to 97 percent.

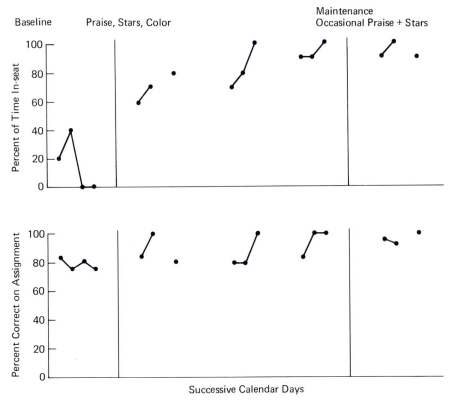

FIGURE 9–11 Percent of time Linda spent in-seat and percent correct scores on her assignment. (Adapted from Debra Ann Meislahn Clasey, *Contingent coloring as a reinforcer to improve in-seat behavior.* Unpublished manuscript, University of Illinois, 1979. By permission of the author.)

Comment

Rather than nagging Linda to return to her seat, the teacher reinforced in-seat behavior. Using a combination of praising in-seat behavior, dispensing stars for following rules and allowing the student to exchange stars to color, the teacher was able to increase Linda's in-seat behavior. Although accuracy on assignments was never directly reinforced, accuracy increased as well during the intervention period.

Differential reinforcement of low rates (DRL) of behavior

Sometimes teachers do not wish to reduce an inappropriate behavior to zero. For example one might be satisfied if a student only talked out a few times a day. When the aim is to reduce rather than to eliminate an inappropriate behavior, one can differentially reinforce low rates of a behavior. An example of this technique is provided in the following project.

**Classroom Application of DRL
(Knieriem, S., 1979)**

Number of Students

Six-year-old girl, Jenny

Setting

First-grade classroom

Target Behavior/Aim

Decrease talk-outs during reading period to two or fewer times.

Definition of Target Behavior

Talk-outs were defined as any audible sound made with her mouth such as clicking or whistling, or talking without teacher permission.

Observation System and Measurement Technique

Either the teacher or student teacher recorded Jenny's talk-outs by tallying them as they occurred using a pencil and a 3×5 card.

Procedures

During baseline the teacher continued with her usual procedure which consisted of verbally reprimanding Jenny whenever she talked out. During the first intervention the teacher ignored talk-outs and praised Jenny when she raised her hand before speaking. As Jenny rarely raised her hand, she had little opportunity to be reinforced. The teacher changed to another intervention in which Jenny was given a card like the one shown in Figure 9-12 to take home to her parents provided she talked out two or fewer times.

During maintenance the teacher phased out the daily note and instead told Jenny that if she could refrain from talking out more than two times each day for a week, the teacher would give her a note to take home. This procedure remained in effect for three weeks, after which the teacher reported that she planned to phase out the weekly notes and occasionally praise Jenny for remembering to raise her hand.

Results

The data in Figure 9-13 show that Jenny talked out between four and nine times per day during baseline. Her performance during the first intervention was

FIGURE 9–12 Daily Note. (Adapted from Susan Knieriem, *Remediating "talk-out" behavior in the regular classroom*. Unpublished manuscript, University of Illinois, 1980. By permission of the author.)

almost as variable as during baseline. When the teacher implemented the DRL procedure, Jenny's talking out decreased below the desired limit by the second day. By the end of the first week Jenny did not talk out at all during reading time. Jenny was also able to maintain her performance as she rarely talked out more than once per session following the intervention period.

Comment

In this case the teacher began by ignoring talk-outs and praising Jenny when she raised her hand. The teacher's data revealed that this procedure was not work-

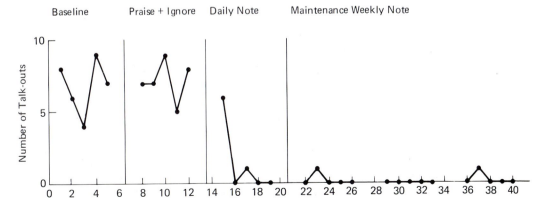

FIGURE 9–13 Number of talk-outs made by Jenny. (Adapted from Susan Knieriem, *Remediating "talk-out" behavior in the regular classroom*. Unpublished manuscript, University of Illinois, 1979. By permission of the author.)

ing, so the teacher changed techniques. At first Jenny received a note to take home every day. Eventually a note was sent home once a week. One of the advantages of sending "Good News" notes home is that parents are happy to learn of their child's progress and can provide further reinforcement.

Differential reinforcement of other behavior (DRO)

Differential reinforcement of other behavior is also known as omission training (Sulzer-Azaroff & Mayer, 1977). DRO has been defined as a procedure in which "reinforcement is delivered only if a particular behavior does *not* occur for a specified period of time" (Axelrod, 1977, p. 29). This procedure was used in the following project to reduce talk-outs.

**Classroom Application of DRO
(Hughes, F., & Gregerson, G., 1971)**

Number of Students
     Six-year-old boy, Kirk

Setting
     First-grade classroom

Target Behavior/Aim
     Reduce talk-outs

Definition of Target Behavior
     The teacher recorded a talk-out whenever Kirk talked out about something not related to the lesson.

Observation System and Measurement Technique
     Talk-outs were recorded simultaneously by the teacher and the student teacher.

Procedures
     During baseline talk-outs presumably did not lead to any particular consequence. When the intervention began the teacher showed Kirk his graph and told him she had been keeping track of the number of times he spoke out about something not related to his lesson. The teacher also gave Kirk a magic slate and told him that for every half hour he refrained from talking out he could play with the slate for five minutes. During the return-to-baseline phase, the teacher told Kirk that because he was doing so well, she would no longer keep track of his talking out, and he wouldn't be playing with the magic slate. When the intervention was reinstituted, playing with the magic slate was again made contingent upon not talking out.

Results
     The data in Figure 9-14 reveal that during baseline Kirk talked out an average of thirteen times per day. When playing with the magic slate was made contingent upon not talking out, Kirk's talk-outs decreased to two or three per day. During the return-to-baseline phase, Kirk's talk-outs increased to 9.5 per day. Talk-outs again decreased to fewer than three per day when Kirk was again allowed to play with the magic slate provided that he refrained from talking out during each half hour period.

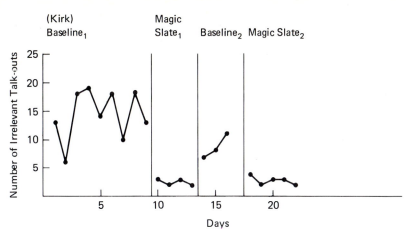

FIGURE 9–14 Number of talkouts made by Kirk. (From F. Hughes & G. Gregerson, Reducation of irrelevant talking-out in a first grader through the use of magic (slate). In R. V. Hall, *Managing behavior Part 3: Applications in school and home.* Lawrence, KS: H & H Enterprises, 1971b, p. 46. By permission of the publishers.)

Comment

In discussing this study, Hall (1977b) pointed out that the teacher decided to return-to-baseline to determine whether her attention, feedback or the magic slate was responsible for the behavior change. The data suggest that the opportunity to play with the magic slate was the important factor in controlling the child's talk-outs.

Group Contingencies

So far we have focused on increasing or decreasing the behavior of individual students. There are times, however, when a teacher wishes to modify the behavior of several students at once. Rather than arranging individual contingencies for each student, one can treat the students as a group.

Group contingencies have been defined as a procedure in which "the outcomes available to any individual are at least in part determined by the performance of others" (Wilcox & Pany, undated). Wilcox and Pany classified group contingencies into the following types:

1. The behavior of one individual determines the consequences available to a group of students.
2. The behavior of a selected subgroup of students determines the consequences available to a group of students.
3. The behavior of an entire group determines the consequences available to the whole group.

An example of the first type of group contingency was provided by Patterson (1965). The subject of that study was a nine-year-old boy named Earl who rarely completed his work, often talked out, and frequently engaged in disruptive behaviors. Earl's inappropriate behaviors were thought to be maintained by the attention he received from his classmates. In order to increase Earl's on-task behavior, his peers were told to ignore Earl's inappropriate behaviors. Earl was told that he could earn reinforcers for being on-task which he could share with his classmates. Thus the class was reinforced for not paying attention to Earl's off-task behavior. This technique effectively reduced Earl's inappropriate behavior. Teachers might consider using this approach in cases where attention by peers may be maintaining a student's inappropriate behavior.

The second type of group contingency, in which the behavior of a selected subgroup determines the consequences available to a group of students, was used by Jones and Kazdin (1975). In that study a daily reinforcer was available to a primary level class contingent upon the performance of four students. This procedure would be appropriate in cases where the behavior of a few students, sometimes called trouble-makers or ring leaders, seems to be maintained by the attention of other students or to encourage other members of the class to misbehave. By allowing the so-called trouble-makers to earn a privilege for the class based on their good behavior, classroom disruptions will likely decrease as all students will receive reinforcement either for continuing to behave appropriately or for refraining from attending to the inappropriate behaviors of others.

The third type of group contingency is when the behavior of an entire group determines the outcomes available to the group. This contingency is by far the most common (Wilcox & Pany, undated). Barrish, Saunders, and Wolf (1969) used such a group contingency to reduce talk-outs and out-of-seats in a regular fourth-grade classroom. In that study the teacher divided the class into two teams and explained that they were going to play a game. Each time a member of a team talked out or was out-of-seat, a mark was placed against his team on the board. The team that had the fewest rule violations at the end of the period won the game. Both teams could win provided that they had five or fewer rule violations. When using the *good behavior game*, it is important to arrange it so that both teams can win as one should reinforce each team for exhibiting low levels of inappropriate behavior.

The advantages of the good behavior game are that a teacher need not record the behavior of individual students or arrange individual contingencies. One possible disadvantage is that certain individuals will act up and cause their team to lose. In the Barrish and Saunders' study this problem arose with two students on one team. These students were placed on individual contingencies so that their inappropriate behavior would not effect their team's chance of winning the game. Another possible disadvantage of a group contingency, in which a teacher marks down rule violations, is that attention is focused on inappropriate behavior. To circumvent this problem, one might first define "on-task" behavior. Then one could use time sampling to record whether the entire class, or teams of students, were or were not on-task at the end of every five minutes during a period. Reinforcement could then be delivered based on the entire group of teams achieving a certain percentage of time on-task. Another option would be to use Placheck as described in Chapter 6. Using this system a teacher would look up at the end of every x minutes and record the number of students who were and were not on-task. Reinforcement could be based on the average number of students who were on-task during the period. For example reinforcement might be delivered if at least 28 out of 30 students were recorded as being on-task when the teacher observed their behavior.

An example of using a group contingency to reduce talk-outs and out-of-seats in a junior high math class is provided in the following sample project.

Classroom Application of a Group Contingency
(Willis, J. W., Hobbs, T. R., Kirkpatrick, D. G., & Manley, K. W., 1975)

Number of Students
   Twenty-seven seventh graders

Setting
   Math class

Target Behavior/Aim
   Reduce talk-outs and out-of-seat behavior

Definition of Target Behavior
   The student teacher recorded a talk-out whenever a student spoke out in class or spoke to another student at an inappropriate time. One out-of-seat was recorded whenever a student left his desk without permission.

Observation System and Measurement Technique
   The student teacher tallied the total number of talk-outs and out-of-seats which occurred during the math period.

Procedures
   During baseline the teacher responded to the students' inappropriate behavior in her usual manner. Prior to the intervention the teacher and guidance counselor met to discuss a program to change the students' behavior. During the intervention the teacher told the students that they could earn five minutes of free time at the end of class, provided that they did not talk out or leave their desk during the first fifteen minutes of class. After the first week the teacher increased the amount of time to twenty minutes, then thirty minutes, and finally forty minutes during the fourth week of intervention. The amount of free time remained the same.

   During the return-to-baseline phase, the students were no longer able to earn free time. When the contingency was again in effect, the students could earn five minutes of free time if they refrained from talking out or getting out of their seats during the forty-minute period. During the last intervention the teacher told the students that on some days they would receive their five minutes of free time provided they achieved the forty-minute criterion. The students, of course, were not told which day they would be allowed to earn free time. On the average, they received free time about once a week.

Results
   As can be seen in Figure 9-15, the students made between twenty-three and forty-four talk-outs and out-of-seats during baseline. When the group contingency

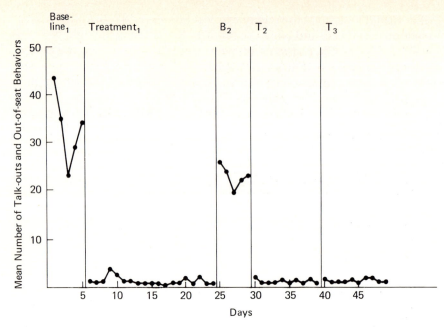

FIGURE 9–15 Mean number of talk-outs and out-of-seat behaviors. (From J. W. Willis, T. R. Hobbs, D. G. Kirkpatrick, & K. W. Manley, Training counselors as researchers in the natural environment. In E. Ramp & G. Semb (Eds.), *Behavior analysis: Areas of research and application*, Englewood Cliffs, NJ: Prentice-Hall, 1975, p. 180. By permission of the publisher.)

was in effect, inappropriate behaviors decreased to less than one per period. When the contingency was no longer in effect, inappropriate behavior increased to near baseline levels. When the group contingency was reapplied, talk-outs and out-of-seats decreased to near zero. Finally when the students were receiving free time on an intermittent basis, their inappropriate behaviors remained at low levels.

Comment

This study clearly demonstrates the effectiveness of a group contingency. It also illustrates the use of shaping as students were required to spend progressively longer periods of time not talking-out or being out-of-seat in order to receive free time. The maintenance procedure is one which is often effective as students cannot predict on which day they will receive reinforcement. Therefore they tend to behave appropriately so as not to miss the opportunity to earn a special privilege.

Negative Punishment

Negative punishment may be defined as a process in which the subtraction of a reinforcing object or activity following a behavior serves to decrease that behavior (Bushell & Burgess, 1969). Negative punishment can be thought of as punishment by loss. Examples of negative punishment in society include fines for speeding and docking workers if they are late. Perhaps the most common example of the use of negative punishment in school is depriving children of recess contingent upon their inappropriate behavior.

So far we have spoken of positive procedures to decrease inappropriate behaviors. In the event that procedures such as reinforcing incompatible behavior, ignoring inappropriate behaviors and praising appropriate behaviors, DRO, and DRL are not effective, one might consider the use of *response-cost* or *contingent observation*. Both of these procedures will now be discussed.

Response-cost   *Response-cost* has been defined as "a reductive procedure in which a specified amount of available reinforcers are contingently withdrawn following the response" (Sulzer-Azaroff & Mayer, 1977, p. 522). Usually, the *cost* of engaging in an inappropriate behavior results in the loss of points which can be exchanged for reinforcers or the loss of minutes of free time.

Response-cost has been used to decrease inappropriate behaviors of both individuals and groups of students. Hall, Axelrod, Foundopoulos, Shellman, Campbell, and Cranston (1971) used response-cost to decrease a student's crying, whining and complaining. In that study the student was given slips of paper with his name on them. Each time he cried, whined or complained the teacher took one slip of paper away. Even though the slips of paper could not be exchanged for any type of reward, their loss still served to reduce the student's inappropriate behavior.

The following study illustrates the use of response-cost to decelerate an inappropriate behavior of a group of students. Following the presentation of the sample project, we will discuss some considerations in using response-cost to decrease inappropriate behaviors.

Classroom Application of Response-Cost
(Sulzbacher, S. I., & Houser, J. E., 1968)

Number of Students
Fourteen students, ages six to ten years, classified as educable mentally retarded

Setting
Special classroom

Target Behavior/Aim
Decrease the use of the "naughty finger"

Definition of Target Behavior
The "naughty finger" was defined as raising one's fist with middle finger extended, verbal reference to it, and tattling or other comments made by members of the class when a student used the "naughty finger" (p. 88).

Observation System and Measurement Technique
Each time an instance of the "naughty finger" was observed, it was recorded by the teacher.

Procedures

During baseline the teacher kept track of the number of times the inappropriate behavior occurred. On the first day of the intervention, the teacher told the students that there would be a special ten-minute recess at the end of the day. The teacher then showed the students ten cards numbered one through ten which were arranged on a bracket similar to a daily desk calendar. The teacher told the students that each time she saw the "naughty finger" or heard about it, she would flip down one card which meant that the class would lose one minute of the special recess. During the return-to-baseline phase, the special recess was withdrawn.

Results

The data in Figure 9-16 reveal that during the baseline the frequency of the inappropriate behavior ranged from approximately twenty-one to eighteen. When the intervention was in effect, the frequency of the "naughty finger" decreased. When the contingency was withdrawn, the inappropriate behavior increased.

Comment

This study is considered to be one of the classics in behavior modification. It illustrates quite simply the effect that consequences can have on students' behavior. In this study the authors wanted to demonstrate a relationship between the inappropriate behavior and loss of recess time; therefore they returned to baseline conditions. It should be stressed that in applying a similar procedure in the classroom, one would proceed to a maintenance condition rather than return-to-baseline.

Response-cost is a negative procedure in that it focuses a teacher's attention on inappropriate behavior and it involves taking away reinforcers. Whenever special privileges or other reinforcers are taken away contingent upon inappropriate behavior, there is a possibility that students will engage in aggressive behavior or seek to avoid or escape the consequences. The authors are somewhat reluctant to mention this procedure as too often teachers elect to take something away from students when they misbehave, rather than praise appropriate behavior. It is the

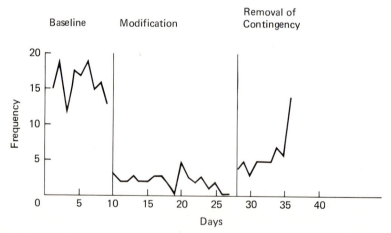

FIGURE 9–16 Number of times students displayed the "naughty finger." (From S. I. Sulzbacher & J. E. Houser, A tactic to eliminate disruptive behaviors in the classroom: Group contingent consequences. *American Journal of Mental Deficiency*, 1968, 73, p. 89.

hope of the authors that teachers will resort to using response-cost only after exhausting more positive approaches and will always combine the procedure with reinforcing appropriate behavior.

Contingent observation Contingent observation is a procedure whereby a student is placed a few feet away from others contingent upon some inappropriate behavior. In this way a student can observe the activities of other class members but cannot participate nor receive reinforcement for engaging in the activity. Contingent observation was originally used by Porterfield, Herbert-Jackson, and Risley (1976) to reduce disruptive behaviors of nursery school students. In that study whenever a student engaged in an inappropriate behavior, such as taking a toy from another student, the teacher pointed out the inappropriate behavior and told the student what the appropriate behavior would have been. The student was then moved to the periphery of the activity and told that he could watch but not participate. After the student sat quietly for a minute or two, he or she was allowed to return to the group.

Teachers commonly use a similar technique when they ask a student who has misbehaved to put his head down on his desk or to sit in a corner of the room. Contingent observation can be considered as a mild form of *time-out*. *Time-out* is a procedure in which access to reinforcement is removed for a particular period of time contingent upon an inappropriate behavior (Sulzer-Azaroff & Mayer, 1977). Time-out has been used to decrease severe acting-out behaviors and it usually involves sending students to a "time-out room" which is devoid of reinforcing objects. Great care must be taken in implementing a program using time-out as it can easily be mismanaged by those who fail (1) to use it only for specific behaviors, (2) to apply it consistently and for brief periods of time and (3) to take data on its effectiveness in reducing inappropriate behaviors. Due to the potential mismanagement of this procedure, it is best used by those who are highly skilled in behavioral procedures. Teachers would be well advised to seek additional training before considering implementing time-out. In cases where time-out is to be administered by someone else, the classroom teacher should monitor the student's data to insure that adequate records are being kept and that the data indicate that the technique is effectively reducing a student's inappropriate behavior.

While time-out is best administered by those who have had special training, classroom teachers may have an opportunity to use its milder form, *contingent observation*. The following project illustrates the use of contingent observation to decrease "monopolizing" the conversation during class discussion.

**Classroom Application of Contingent Observation
(Haffner, L., 1979)**

Number of Students
  Six-year-old girl, Susan

Setting
  First-grade classroom

Target Behavior/Aim

Decrease to zero the number of times Susan volunteered an answer without permission during group discussion.

Definition of Target Behavior

A talk-out was recorded each time Susan spoke out without permission during the forty-five-minute group discussion.

Observation System and Measurement Technique

Each day the teacher recorded the number of talk-outs Susan made during the group discussion period.

Procedures

During baseline the teacher continued with her usual procedure of allowing Susan to talk-out. After she did so the teacher reminded her to raise her hand. Occasionally the teacher would stop Susan before she had a chance to talk. The first intervention consisted of the teacher presenting a DUSO lesson (Dinkmeyer, 1970) which consisted of using hand puppets and posters to present four rules for group participation. Students who followed the rules were verbally praised. On each day of the intervention, the DUSO lesson was reviewed and students were praised for following the rules.

During the second intervention the DUSO lesson was discontinued. Whenever Susan spoke out, she was asked to put her head down for three minutes. Whenever she raised her hand and waited to be recognized, the teacher verbally praised her behavior. Although maintenance data are not available, the teacher indicated that she hoped to maintain Susan's behavior through the use of occasional praise.

Results

The data in Figure 9-17 show that during baseline Susan spoke out between thirteen and twenty-two times. The combination of the DUSO lesson and praising hand raising appears to have decreased Susan's talk-outs. As the first intervention did not reduce Susan's talk-outs to an acceptable level, the teacher combined con-

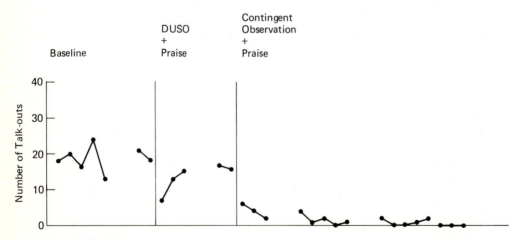

FIGURE 9–17 Number of talk-outs made by Susan during group discussion. (Adapted from Lois Haffner, *Using contingent observation to reduce "monopolizing" a conversation.* Unpublished manuscript, University of Illinois, 1979. By permission of the author.)

tingent observation with praising hand raising. When this intervention was applied, Susan decreased her talk-outs to three per period. On the last three days of the second intervention, Susan refrained from talking-out and continued to participate in the discussion, raising her hand to be called upon.

Comment

This project was undertaken by a classroom teacher under the direction of a behavioral disorder consultant who assisted the teacher in planning and carrying out the behavioral change program. This project illustrates the kind of cooperative relationship between special and regular educators which has been advocated in this text. In addition the project demonstrates the wise use of behavioral procedures in that the teacher initially tried rules and praise to encourage appropriate behavior before applying a reductive procedure. When contingent observation was used, the teacher was careful to pair this procedure with praising appropriate behavior.

Positive Punishment

Positive punishment is a procedure in which a behavior decreases due to the presentation of some consequence following the behavior (Bushell & Burgess, 1969). It is important that the reader be able to distinguish between the technical use of the term *punishment* and the layman's use of the term. Most people would probably say that a student has been punished if he's spanked after he misbehaves. While spanking was delivered as a consequence, technically we cannot say that the student's behavior was positively punished unless his inappropriate behavior decreases. As with positive reinforcement, *positive punishment* refers to the *addition* of a consequence following a behavior and has absolutely nothing to do with the desirability of the consequence. If a consequence is applied contingent upon a behavior and that behavior *increases*, the behavior has been *positively reinforced.* If, on the other hand, a consequence is applied contingent upon a behavior and the behavior *decreases*, the behavior has been *positively punished.* Therefore the only way to determine whether a behavior has been reinforced or punished is to evaluate its effect on that behavior.

Although regretably our society still condones corporal punishment in the schools, that practice shares little in common with the technical procedure known as positive punishment. Schools which use corporal punishment commonly specify the behaviors which result in punishment, who should administer the punishment, who should supervise it, as well as the number of times a student can be spanked. When positive punishment is used to decrease severe behavior problems such as self-injurious behavior, punishment is: (1) selected only after other more positive approaches have failed, (2) delivered contingent upon a specific behavior, (3) applied consistently, (4) delivered immediately following the occurrence of the inappropriate behavior, and (5) paired with reinforcing appropriate behavior. In addition data are recorded continuously and performance is evaluated to determine the effectiveness of the procedure.

Other types of punishers which are sometimes used in school include: yelling at students who are misbehaving, giving extra homework, and having a student write 100 times "I won't _____ anymore." Reprimands are often used to control students' behavior, yet reprimands have actually been found to increase inappropriate behavior (Madsen, Becker, Thomas, Koser,

& Plager, 1970). In the study by Madsen, et al., reprimands served to positively reinforce inappropriate behavior rather than suppress it. In another study (O'Leary, Kaufman, Kass, & Drabman, 1970) soft reprimands delivered privately to individual students were more effective than loud reprimands shouted across the room. Due to inconsistent effects, Kazdin (1975) has recommended that reprimands be used with great caution.

The authors would like to go one step further and recommend that positive punishment be used only for very serious types of behavior, and then only when other positive procedures have been ineffective or are deemed inappropriate by specialists skilled in the use of behavioral procedures. This recommendation is made in light of the effectiveness of reinforcement procedures and the possible side effects of punishment which include: escape, aggression and emotional behaviors. As punishment can produce behaviors which are incompatible with learning, its use cannot be justified for all but the most extreme types of behavior problems.

Summary

In this section we have discussed a number of procedures to decrease inappropriate behaviors. The intent of the authors has been to acquaint the reader with positive approaches for reducing inappropriate behaviors, such as ignoring inappropriate behavior and reinforcing appropriate behavior. It is our hope that teachers will try to "catch kids when they're good" and positively reinforce them for behaving appropriately. Our experience in working with classroom teachers has shown us that it is rarely necessary to resort to reductive procedures such as response-cost because other, more positive procedures such as reinforcing incompatible behaviors are so effective.

STRUCTURING THE CLASSROOM FOR SUCCESS

Until now the authors have spoken about ways to increase appropriate behaviors and to decrease inappropriate behaviors. The authors would like to turn our attention to techniques which teachers can use to reduce the likelihood that behavior problems will occur. Some suggestions for encouraging appropriate classroom behaviors are as follows:

1. *Make sure that students are correctly placed in curriculum materials.*
   It is not uncommon for students who are experiencing academic difficulties to act up in class. If students lack prerequisite skills to do their work, they often find other things to do such as disrupt other students.
2. *Establish and follow classroom rules.*
   In order to behave appropriately, students need to be aware of their teacher's expectations. At the beginning of the year, the teacher should discuss appropriate classroom rules. When making rules the emphasis should be on positive behaviors. Many teachers choose to post the rules

in the classroom to serve as a reminder to students. To be effective one must consistently reinforce students for following the rules.

3. *Make a habit of ignoring inappropriate behavior and praising appropriate behavior.*

   An easy check to determine how often one praises appropriate behavior as opposed to attending to inappropriate behavior is to count the number of positive and negative statements one makes. After keeping this count for a few days, one can easily judge the extent to which appropriate behaviors are being reinforced and inappropriate behaviors are being ignored. If there are few positive comments or several negative comments, one should strive to make more positive statements.

4. *Try to circumvent potential behavior problems before they occur.*

   Teachers are usually quite adept at pinpointing situations in which behavior problems are likely to occur. For example, many teachers find that talk-outs and out-of-seats occur more frequently during seatwork when the teacher is instructing a small group of students. When the teacher's attention is diverted, other students in the class may feel free to act up. Knowing that this is a frequent occurrence, a teacher may interrupt instruction when working with a small group of students to reinforce students who are working well at their desks. Another potential trouble spot occurs after students have finished their work. Instead of assigning more work, a teacher might allow students to engage in a quiet free time activity such as reading a favorite book. In this way students who finish early are reinforced for completing their assignments and are less likely to disturb other students.

5. *Arrange positive consequences for improvement on academic tasks.*

   Research has shown that disruptive behaviors can be decreased by reinforcing academic performance (Ayllon & Roberts, 1974). If students are reinforced for improving their academic skills, they are less likely to engage in inappropriate behaviors. One of the best ways to discourage behavior problems is to reward students for behaviors such as completing assignments, increasing the accuracy of work and mastering progressively more difficult tasks.

SUMMARY

In this chapter the authors have attempted to acquaint the reader with positive procedures for managing classroom behavior problems. To illustrate the effectiveness of the recommended techniques, the authors have presented a number of projects conducted by classroom teachers. The projects serve to document the effectiveness of the techniques as well as to demonstrate the ability of teachers to implement the data-based approach in regular classrooms. The authors hope that teachers will implement some of the procedures discussed, adapt them to fit their own needs and continue to learn more about applying behavioral procedures to remedy classroom behavior problems.

Remediating Academic Behavior Problems

10

Teachers encounter students who display a variety of academic behavior problems. For example some students may read very slowly; others may omit or mispronounce words; while still others may fail to comprehend what they have read. In math some students may lack accuracy, while others may be very accurate but compute their problems too slowly. Some students may compute their problems accurately one day, but not the next. Other students may have difficulty remembering how to compute certain types of problems from one week to the next. Still others may be able to acquire and maintain skills which have been directly taught, but fail to apply their newly acquired skills to solve other types of problems.

These kinds of difficulties are not specific to reading or math, but in fact represent general types of academic behavior problems. In this chapter we will focus on remediating the behavior of students whose performance indicates that they:

1. *"Can't"* perform a skill very *accurately*
2. *"Can"* but *won't* or *choose not to* perform a skill
3. *"Can"* but do so *too slowly*
4. *"Can't"* *maintain* a previously learned skill
5. *"Can't"* *apply* learned skills to new situations

Not all mildly handicapped students experience difficulties in acquiring, generalizing or maintaining skills. Also many "normal" students experience problems in these areas. These categories represent types of academic behavior problems which teachers can expect to encounter in the normal course of providing instruction to students. Therefore in this chapter the authors will discuss teaching techniques to: (1) improve accuracy, (2) increase consistency of performance, (3) increase speed, (4) enhance maintenance of previously learned skills, and (5) promote generalization of learned skills to different tasks and to other settings.

Before discussing specific teaching techniques, the DBI model will be reviewed to aid the reader in understanding how one proceeds from assessing to remediating academic behavior problems. Emphasis is then placed on using assessment data to pinpoint academic behavior problems and to determine instructional aims. Next attention is focused on describing general instructional strategies which can be used to improve academic performance. As in Chapter 9 sample projects are included to illustrate how one would apply the instructional strategies to improve students' accuracy, consistency, speed, and ability to maintain and generalize skills.

FROM ASSESSMENT TO REMEDIATION

Applying the DBI Model to Academic Behaviors

The DBI model was discussed in detail in Chapter 8. The model is presented in Figure 10–1 to aid the reader in understanding how one proceeds from assessing to remediating academic behavior problems.

As shown in Figure 10–1 one begins by identifying the behavior to be remediated. This behavior, known as the target behavior, will eventually become the focus of remediation. In order to identify appropriate academic target behaviors, one assesses a student's academic performance using a curriculum-based assessment (CBA). To review from Chapter 5, CBAs are used to assist teachers in identifying skills their students can and cannot perform. After analyzing and evaluating the skills presented in the curriculum, the teacher selects and then proceeds to measure students' performance on those skills. After measuring and recording performance for a few days, each student's performance is evaluated. Based on the results of the CBA, a teacher pinpoints academic behavior problems and identifies appropriate target behaviors for individual students. Procedures for pinpointing academic behavior problems will be discussed in a later section.

The first target behavior or skill a teacher wishes to focus on is then defined in observable terms. Prior to remediation the teacher collects baseline data on the identified target behavior. In order to collect these data, the teacher first selects a measurement technique and establishes a desired aim. Following the baseline period, the student's performance is evaluated in relation to the desired aim. Using the data-decision rules presented in Chapter 8, one decides whether an intervention is necessary. If it is, a teaching technique is selected and applied. Instructional strategies for remediating academic behavior problems will be presented later in this chapter. As when remediating social behavior problems, academic performance is continuously measured and evaluated. Decisions whether to change interventions or to proceed to maintenance are based on data.

PINPOINTING ACADEMIC BEHAVIOR PROBLEMS

Earlier in this chapter, we spoke of students whose performance indicates that they:

1. *"Can't"* perform a skill very *accurately*
2. *"Can"* but *won't* or *choose not* to perform a skill

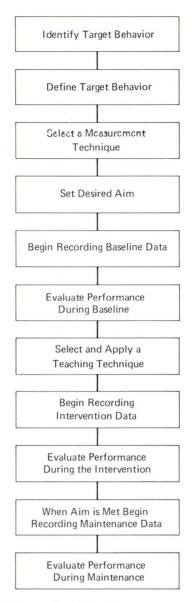

FIGURE 10–1 Data-Based Instructional Model.

3. *"Can"* but do so *too slowly*
4. *"Can't"* *maintain* a previously learned skill
5. *"Can't"* *apply* learned skills to new situations

In the following two sections, we will discuss how teachers can use CBA results and charted data to pinpoint these types of academic behavior problems.

Analyzing CBA Results

To pinpoint academic behavior problems using CBA data, one inspects the raw data sheet on which one has recorded the performance of individual students. A sample raw data sheet showing the hypothetical performance of four students on part of a math CBA is shown in Figure 10–2.

Sample CBA Results   In order to pinpoint the academic behavior problems of the students whose data are presented in Figure 10–2, one must evaluate each student's performance in relation to the following criterion levels which were specified by the teacher:

1. Accuracy on facts—90% to 100% on all 3 days.
2. Speed on facts—Correct rate (CR) equal to or greater than 45 problems per minute; incorrect rate (IR) equal to or less than 2 per minute on all 3 days.
3. Accuracy on other, problem types—At least 4 out of 5 correct on 2 out of 3 days.

An analysis of the students' performance indicates the following:

1. Tim is performing below criteria in two areas, speed on addition facts and accuracy on problems requiring renaming.
2. Rick's problem seems to be inconsistent performance on facts as well as on several other types of more advanced problems.
3. Sue's only difficulty appears to be in generalizing her renaming skills to problems requiring renaming in more than one column.
4. Tom is performing at criteria on all skills.

To check Tom's ability to maintain his addition skills, the teacher readministered the CBA to Tom a month later. Tom's performance on the second administration of the CBA is shown in Figure 10–3. According to the

Math CBA

Name	Date	#C	#I	%C	Time	CR	IR	nn +n	nn +nn	nnn +nn	nnn +nnn	nc +n	nc +nn	ncn +nn	ncc +nnn	ccc +nnn
Tim	3/1	90	10	90%	3:40	24.5	2.7	3/2	5/0	4/1	4/1	0/5	0/5	0/5	0/5	0/5
	3/2	95	5	95%	3:10	30.0	1.6	4/1	4/1	3/2	5/0	0/5	0/5	0/5	0/5	0/5
	3/3	98	2	98%	3:21	29.3	.60	4/1	5/0	4/1	4/1	0/5	0/5	0/5	0/5	0/5
Rick	3/1	43	57	43%	1:23	31.1	41.2	4/1	0/5	5/0	3/2	5/0	4/1	2/3	5/0	3/2
	3/2	82	18	82%	1:40	49.2	10.8	3/2	4/1	4/1	0/5	4/1	1/4	4/1	4/1	2/3
	3/3	58	42	58%	1:35	36.7	26.5	0/5	3/2	4/1	4/1	3/2	3/2	5/0	3/2	4/1
Sue	3/1	97	3	94%	1:45	55.4	1.7	5/0	5/0	5/0	5/0	5/0	4/1	5/0	0/5	0/5
	3/2	98	2	98%	1:30	65.3	.63	4/1	5/0	4/1	5/0	5/0	4/1	5/0	0/5	0/5
	3/3	99	1	99%	1:35	62.5	.63	5/0	5/0	5/0	4/1	5/0	5/0	4/1	0/5	0/5
Tom	3/1	98	2	98%	1:27	67.6	1.4	5/0	5/0	4/1	5/0	3/2	4/1	5/0	5/0	5/0
	3/2	100	0	100%	1:30	66.7	0.0	4/1	4/1	5/0	4/1	5/0	4/1	5/0	5/0	5/0
	3/3	99	1	99%	1:32	64.6	.65	5/0	4/1	5/0	5/0	5/0	5/0	4/1	4/1	5/0

FIGURE 10–2 Sample Raw Data Sheet. Math CBA.

TABLE 10-1 Sample Targets Behaviors and Instructional Aims

STUDENT	Academic Behavior Problems	Target Behavior/Aim
Tim	1. Slow Speed on add facts	1. Increase CR to 45 per minute; IR to 2 or fewer per minute for 3 days
	2. Low accuracy on problems requiring renaming	2. Increase accuracy on first type of renaming problem $\frac{nc}{+n}$ to 4 out of 5 correct for 3 days
Rick	1. Inconsistent performance on add facts	1. Increase CR to 45 per minute; IR to 2 or fewer per minute for 3 days
	2. Inconsistent performance on several problem types	2. Increase accuracy on a mix of other problem types assessed to 90% or above for 3 days
Sue	1. Difficulty generalizing renaming skills to problems requiring renaming in more than 1 column	1. Increase accuracy on $\frac{ncc}{+nnn}$ and $\frac{ccc}{+nnn}$ to at least 4 out of 5 for 3 days
Tom	1. Difficulty maintaining renaming skills	1. Increase accuracy on mix of renaming problems to 90% or above and maintain

data shown in Figure 10–3, Tom has maintained his ability to compute all types of addition problems except those requiring renaming.

After pinpointing the student's academic behavior problems, the teacher identifies target behaviors and determines instructional aims. Sample target behaviors and instructional aims for the students in our example are shown in Table 10–1.

As shown in our example, the teacher used the results of a CBA to pinpoint the students' academic behavior problems. Once each student's problems had been pinpointed, the teacher identified target behaviors and determined instructional aims for individual students to achieve. The same procedure can be used to evaluate pupil performance in other subject areas.

Name	Date	Addition Facts						No Renaming				Renaming				
		#C	#1	%C	Time	Cr	Ir	$\frac{nn}{+n}$	$\frac{nn}{+nn}$	$\frac{nnn}{+nn}$	$\frac{nnn}{+nnn}$	$\frac{nc}{+n}$	$\frac{nc}{+nn}$	$\frac{ncn}{+nn}$	$\frac{ncc}{+nnn}$	$\frac{ccc}{+nnn}$
Tom	4/4	97	3	97%	1:35	61.3	1.9	5/0	5/0	5/0	5/0	0/5	0/5	0/5	0/5	0/5
	4/5	96	4	96%	1:40	57.6	2.4	4/1	5/0	5/0	4/1	0/5	0/5	0/5	0/5	0/5
	4/6	98	2	98%	1:43	57.1	1.2	5/0	4/1	4/1	5/0	0/5	0/5	0/5	0/5	0/5

FIGURE 10–3 Tom's Raw Data Second Administration of Math CBA.

After administering a CBA, a teacher analyzes each student's performance and pinpoints their problems. Depending upon the way in which skills were measured on the CBA, one can identify students who have low accuracy, slow speed or whose performance was inconsistent. One can also make an educated guess as to the students' abilities to generalize their performance by evaluating their accuracy on related skills. To determine if students have difficulty maintaining their skills, the CBA must be readministered.

Analyzing Charted Data

In addition to analyzing CBA data to pinpoint academic behavior problems, one can also obtain useful information by inspecting charts. In the following example a number of charts showing hypothetical data are presented. By inspecting these charts the reader will become familiar with characteristic patterns which indicate students who:

1. *"Can't"* perform a skill very *accurately*
2. *"Can"* but *won't* or choose not to perform a skill
3. *"Can"* but do so too *slowly*
4. *"Can't"* *maintain* a previously learned skill
5. *"Can't"* *apply* learned skills to new situations

The data for students who "can't" or at least "don't" perform skills very accurately is characterized by low and stable performance.

A student who "can" but "won't," or who chooses not to perform, can easily be spotted by inspecting charted data. In our example it is apparent that the student "can" spell the words correctly, but that he does not do so consistently.

Looking at the data in Figure 10–6, it is easy to see that the student is quite accurate but that he reads very slowly.

The data in Figure 10–7 show that the student's performance during baseline was typical of a student who "can't." During the intervention,

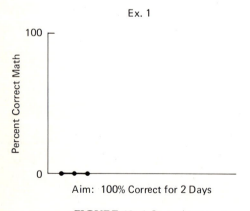

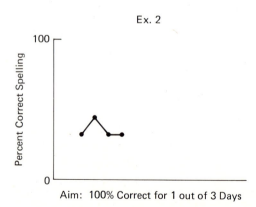

FIGURE 10–4 Low Accuracy.

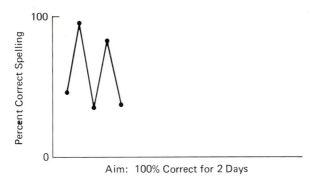

FIGURE 10–5 Inconsistent Performance.

the student demonstrated that he "could" master the words he was given to spell. On the first two weekly maintenance checks, the student's accuracy was quite high. However by the third weekly check accuracy had decreased to near the baseline level.

At first, the student's performance on both List 1 and List 2 as shown in Figure 10–8 indicated that he "couldn't" spell words containing "ee." The teacher intervened on List 1 words and measured performance every other day on List 2 words which also contained "ee." Even though the student was able to increase his accuracy on words which were directly taught, his performance on similar words did not improve. Hence the student failed to generalize his ability to spell "ee" words.

The data in Figure 10–9 show that the student could not compute his problems very accurately in either the resource or regular classroom. When the intervention was applied in the resource room, the student's accuracy increased in that setting. However, he failed to apply or generalize his skills to the regular classroom.

In this section we have discussed common academic behavior problems and suggested ways that teachers can pinpoint students' difficulties

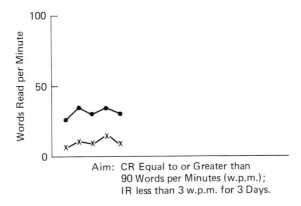

FIGURE 10–6 Slow Speed.

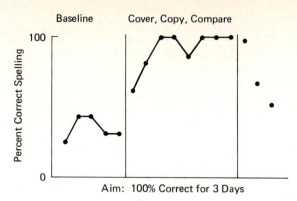

FIGURE 10–7 Failure to Maintain Performance.

by analyzing the results of CBAs and by inspecting charted data. By identifying behavior problems in the way we have described, teachers should be able to precisely pinpoint a student's problems. Rather than describing a student as having difficulty in math, a teacher could refer to a student's low accuracy, slow speed or difficulty in maintaining or generalizing computational skills. After a student's academic behavior problems have been pinpointed, attention could be focused on selecting and applying a teaching technique to improve the student's performance.

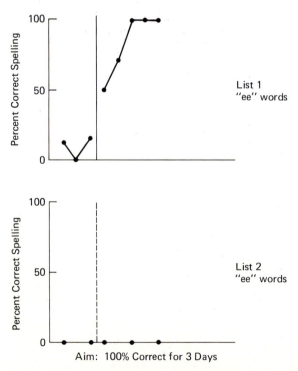

FIGURE 10–8 Failure to Generalize Skills to Similar Tasks.

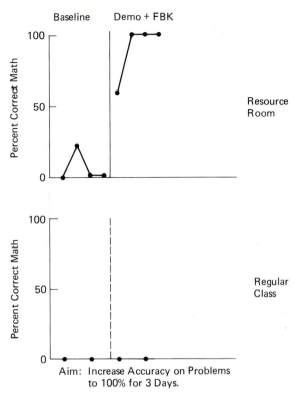

FIGURE 10–9 Failure to Generalize Skills to Different Settings.

INSTRUCTIONAL STRATEGIES

There really aren't any special techniques or magic formulas to improve performance. There are, however, some basic instructional strategies which have been shown to be effective in improving academic performance (Haring, Lovitt, Eaton, & Hansen, 1978; Lovitt, 1977; Sulzer-Azaroff & Mayer, 1977). These strategies include:

1. Instructions
2. Demonstration
3. Modeling
4. Discrimination Training
5. Drill
6. Practice
7. Prompts/Cues
8. Fading
9. Shaping
10. Feedback
11. Reinforcement
12. Contingencies for Errors

Research has and is continuing to focus on the effects of these strategies on improving students' accuracy, speed, and ability to maintain and generalize academic skills. At this time it is possible to make some general recommendations as to when teachers might elect to use one strategy over another. Each strategy will first be briefly described. Reference will also be made to research attesting to the effects of the various strategies presented. Finally recommendations will be made concerning the appropriate use of each instructional strategy.

Instructions

Teachers use verbal instructions to explain to their students how to perform a variety of academic tasks. Verbal instructions such as, "Remember to begin each sentence with a capital letter," or, "Keep your columns straight when adding" are routinely used by teachers. Instructions can and do exert a powerful influence on behavior. The effectiveness of written instructions on increasing computational speed was studied by Smith and Lovitt (1974). In their study seven learning disabled students were presented with a page of math problems on which the following written comment appeared, "Please do this page faster." This simple technique proved effective in increasing the student's computational speed.

While instructions can be very effective, there are certain instances in which one would choose not to use them. For example it would be quite tedious to try to explain to a student how to multiply fractions or how to tie his shoes. Rather than verbally explain one would probably demonstrate how to perform the behavior, perhaps while providing a verbal explanation at the same time. Similarly if a student lacked mastery of the necessary prerequisite skills to perform a behavior, one would not use verbal instructions. For example the verbal instruction, "Multiply these decimal problems and round your answer to the nearest tenth" would have little meaning to a student who has difficulty multiplying decimals or knowing what rounding means. In cases where it would be difficult to provide verbal instructions or when instructions are not effective, teachers rely on other techniques such as demonstration or modeling.

Demonstration

Teachers commonly show their students how to perform new academic tasks. For example a teacher may demonstrate how to solve a problem on the blackboard, or how to form the cursive letter *a* or how to conduct a simple science experiment. Demonstration is helpful in instances where it is easier to "show" rather than to "tell" a student how to perform a behavior. For example when teaching students how to measure length, one might demonstrate how to measure the length of a variety of objects in the classroom. Demonstration is often used to teach behaviors which consist of a series of steps such as those involved in using a calculator or putting paper into a typewriter. Demonstration techniques have been used to improve students' accuracy in math (Smith, 1973) as well as to improve performance in other subject areas.

Demonstration or the act of "showing" students how to perform a behavior is often combined with other techniques. While demonstration alone may be effective in increasing the performance of some students, others may require demonstration plus verbal instructions as well as feedback to acquire certain skills.

Modeling

Modeling involves imitating another's performance. When using modeling to teach a student how to compute a math problem, the teacher first demonstrates how to solve a sample problem. Following the demonstration the student is required to model the teacher's behavior by computing a similar problem. Modeling can also take a slightly different form. For example instead of requiring a student to immediately imitate the behavior of a model, a teacher can provide the student with a permanent model. This type of modeling strategy was used by Smith and Lovitt (1975) to improve students' computational accuracy. In their study the teacher first demonstrated how to solve a problem, while verbalizing the steps one would follow to compute the sample problem. A sample problem was left on each student's worksheets so that he could refer to it if necessary, as he completed his assignment. The technique of combining instructions with demonstration and leaving a permanent model proved effective in increasing the students' computational accuracy.

Modeling is also an important component in teaching other academic skills. For example Carnine and Silbert (1979) describe a correction procedure used in small group reading instruction which incorporates modeling. Their procedure, known as Model-Lead-Test, consists of the following steps: praise, model, lead, test, alternate and delayed test. When a student makes an error in saying a sound such as "/ŭ/" for "ŏoooo" the teacher:

1. Praises another student who responded correctly. (This procedure is used to discourage students from making errors to gain teacher attention.)
2. Models the correct sound ŏoooo.
3. Leads, or responds with the students.
4. Tests by asking all of the students to say the missed sound as a group without teacher direction.
5. Presents the missed sound and review sounds in an alternating pattern to which students respond as a group.
6. Individually tests the student on the missed sound at a later time in the lesson.

Modeling can be a very effective technique and one which can be readily combined with other techniques such as instructions, demonstration and feedback. Later in this chapter we will present some data showing how these instructional strategies were combined to improve students' accuracy in solving computational problems (Blankenship, 1978).

Discrimination Training

Discrimination training involves teaching students to respond in a particular way in the presence of certain stimuli, and not to respond in that way when those stimuli are absent. For example some students may respond to addition and subtraction problems in the same way. The trick is to get them to add when they encounter problems with a " + " sign and to subtract when they are presented with problems containing a " − " sign.

One technique which is based on discrimination training is focusing. This technique was used by Smith and Lovitt (1973) to remediate *b/d* reversals in spelling. Jacobi and Eaton (1975) also used this technique to remediate *b/d* reversals in reading. The student in the Jacobi and Eaton study was a fourteen-year-old girl described as being learning disabled. The student frequently reversed b's and d's when reading from word lists or her reader. After collecting baseline data, the teacher implemented the following intervention. The teacher wrote the word "bam" on a piece of paper and told the student "that she sometimes said 'dam' when reading 'bam.' She was asked to pay careful attention to her b's and d's" (Hansen & Eaton, 1978, p. 61). Within two days the student scored 100 percent on all b's and d's presented on her word list.

Discrimination training would also seem to be appropriate to use in teaching students who reverse numbers, or who have difficulty in math remembering when to borrow and when not. Reinforcement is often part of discrimination training. Correct responses are reinforced immediately and incorrect responses produce no reinforcement or are followed by further drill.

Drill

Drill "involves the opportunity to perform a task repeatedly until the quality and fluency of performance increase to a specified level" (Haring, 1978, p. 14). Teachers commonly drill students to improve their accuracy and speed on sight words and math facts. Drilling students on erred words appears to be a very effective way of improving their accuracy in oral reading (Eaton & Haisch, 1974; Lovitt & Hansen, 1976). Later in this chapter we will present a project in which a teacher used drill to increase students' accuracy in computing division facts.

Practice

The adage that practice makes perfect is not entirely true. Research conducted by Lovitt (1977) and his colleagues suggests that when students are initially acquiring skills, practice alone is not sufficient to improve performance. If a student doesn't know how to perform a skill, practice alone won't increase accuracy. This is not to say that practice activities do not serve a useful purpose during initial acquisition, or that practice is not effective at later stages of learning. During initial acquisition when a student is not performing a skill very accurately, it is important to provide appropriate practice activities following instruction. For example after a teacher has demonstrated how to punctuate a sentence, it is necessary to allow students to practice punctuating other sentences. After students have practiced their punctuation skills for a few days, the teacher can guage the effectiveness of instruction and determine whether other techniques such as feedback or reinforcement are necessary.

Even though practice alone may not be very effective during the initial stage of learning a skill, it may be somewhat effective in increasing students' speed (Lovitt, 1977). Practice may also be useful in maintaining students' skills, particularly when it is combined with other techniques such as feedback.

Prompts/Cues

Teachers sometimes find that students require further prompts or cues following instruction in order to respond correctly. For example in teaching reading a teacher may prompt the student in sounding out a word by making the sound of the initial letter. Hansen (1976) investigated the effect of a series of verbal cues ranging from "try another way" to "what sounds does '__' make" on students' ability to self-correct their oral reading errors. The results of her study showed that "'try another way' proved successful 40% of the time in correcting errors" (p. 73).

Sometimes visual cues are used to encourage correct responses. For example students are often provided with lined paper to guide them in making their letters the correct size. Teachers also direct students having difficulty with adding columns of numbers to draw lines separating the columns. Physical prompts, while used a great deal with severely handicapped students, are rarely used with students who have mild learning problems. Ordinarily it is not necessary to physically guide students as other previously discussed techniques prove to be effective.

Fading

Whenever prompts or cues are used they must be gradually withdrawn if students are expected to perform a behavior under natural conditions. Fading is a procedure in which "directions, imitative prompts, physical guidance, and other cues and prompts" are gradually withdrawn (Sulzer-Azaroff & Mayer, 1977, p. 516). Teachers commonly fade the use of instructional prompts. For example when initially teaching students how to solve multiplication problems a teacher may allow them to compute their problems using an abacus. Gradually the abacus is withdrawn and students are expected to compute their problems from memory. Textbooks also use fading techniques. For example handwriting programs commonly require students to trace letters, then to write letters following a dotted line, then to write letters when only the beginning points are provided, and finally to write letters when no extra cues are provided. Fading has been used to teach beginning reading skills to nursery school children (Corey & Shamow, 1972) and to increase computational accuracy (Haupt, Van Kirk, & Terraciano, 1975).

Shaping

While previously discussed techniques such as demonstration and modeling can be used to teach students new skills, there are times when skills must be broken down into small steps to facilitate learning. As the reader may recall from Chapter 9, shaping is a procedure in which successive approximations to some terminal behavior are reinforced. Just as one can shape social behaviors, for example by reinforcing a student for sitting in his seat for progressively longer periods of time, one can also shape academic behaviors. Shaping could be used, for example, to increase the legibility of a student's handwriting. To shape legible writing, a teacher might begin by reinforcing a student for producing letters which approximate the correct form. Gradually the teacher would adjust the criteria for reinforcement so that eventually only letters of the correct size, form and slant would result in reinforcement.

Shaping can also be used to increase accuracy and speed on academic tasks. Rather than reinforcing a student only if performance reaches the desired aim, a teacher could reinforce successive improvements toward the desired aim. At first a student may receive reinforcement for achieving a level of accuracy slightly above that attained during baseline. Once the student consistently performs at the desired interim aim, the level could be adjusted. By meeting each criterion level specified by the teacher, the student would gradually inch his way up to the desired level of performance.

Shaping is often combined with other instructional strategies such as demonstration, modeling and feedback. Shaping has been used to improve performance in reading comprehension (Hauck, Metcalfe, & Bennett, 1975) as well as to improve performance on a variety of other academic skills.

Feedback

Feedback or knowledge of results can take many forms. A teacher could choose, for example, (1) to return students' math assignments with correct and incorrectly computed problems noted, (2) to write the correct answer next to incorrect answers or (3) provide an explanation of how to solve erred problems. Blankenship and Lovitt (1974) conducted a study to determine the effects of these different forms of feedback on students' computational accuracy. All of the students in that study were performing at very low levels of accuracy. The results suggested that none of the feedback techniques investigated were effective in improving performance. Out of seven students, only one boy's accuracy improved when he was provided with the correct answers to erred problems. These results suggest that feedback alone may not be effective in improving accuracy when students are acquiring a skill.

Feedback appears to be more effective when it is combined with in-struction when teaching new skills, or after a student has acquired a skill and is striving to become proficient in it. Feedback can serve two important functions. First it can assist students in discriminating between correct and incorrect responses. Second it can serve to inform students of their progress and motivate them to do better.

Reinforcement

The reader is already aware of the effects of positive reinforcement on increasing desirable classroom behaviors such as completing assignments and following classroom rules. Reinforcement can also be used to increase academic performance. Reinforcement has shown to be effective in im-proving students' performance on a variety of skills, including: reading (Lovitt, Eaton, Kirkwood, & Pelander, 1971), computing math problems (Lovitt & Esveldt, 1970), spelling words (Evans & Oswalt, 1968; Karracker, 1971; Lovitt, Guppy & Blattner, 1969) and printing letters (Hopkins, Schutte, & Garton, 1971).

When students are initially learning a skill or are performing at low levels of accuracy, reinforcement does not appear to be effective (Blan-kenship & Korn, 1980; Smith, 1973). If a student "can't" perform a skill because he doesn't know how to, reinforcement alone will not improve performance. When students are initially learning or relearning a skill, specific instructions are usually required to improve their performance. Acquisition may be facilitated, however, by combining instruction with reinforcement.

Reinforcement can be very effective in increasing students' ability to consistently perform skills at a high level of accuracy. Similarly reinforce-ment can improve students' abilities to maintain and generalize their skills (Blankenship & Baumgartner, 1980). Later in this chapter sample projects will be provided which illustrate the effect of reinforcement on students' accuracy, speed, and ability to maintain and generalize previously learned skills.

Contingencies for Errors

When students make errors, a teacher may ask them to correct their errors, or correct their errors and practice the correct response "x" number of times. The effects of this error correction procedure, known as contingent drill, has been investigated by Hansen and Eaton (1978). In a spelling study conducted by Hansen, students practiced writing their words before taking a daily test. For students who failed to meet the desired aim through in-struction alone, a second intervention was arranged. Students were re-quired to practice their words as before and to write each word they missed on their daily test ten times. The combination of an instructional technique and a contingency for errors proved to be very effective in increasing stu-dents' spelling accuracy.

Contingent drill on errors has also shown to be effective in improving students' legibility in penmanship. In a study reported by Hansen and Eaton (1978) students were not told which letters were associated with drill. Actually the teacher chose for individual students five letters which they had difficulty forming. If on the daily assignment, a student formed any of the five letters incorrectly, he was assigned a practice page which required him to trace and copy the erred letter twenty times. When a letter was produced correctly for two out of three days, it was dropped and another difficult letter was added. With this system students never knew which letters would result in drill. Therefore they presumably took pains to write all of their letters legibly.

Contingent drill combined with instruction appears to be a very effective technique when students are initially acquiring skills. Other techniques which are aimed at reducing errors with students with inconsistent performance include reinforcing them for not making errors or for reducing their errors (Lovitt, 1978), and withholding special privileges for excessive careless errors (Lovitt & Smith, 1974).

Summary

In this section, we have discussed a number of instructional strategies which can be used to increase students' academic performance. These instructional strategies provide a basis for selecting and/or developing effective teaching techniques. In the following three sections, sample projects are presented to demonstrate how teachers can apply these strategies to improve the:

1. Accuracy of students who *"can't"*
2. Performance of students who *"can"* but *"won't"*
3. Speed of students who *"can"* but do so *too slowly*
4. Ability of students who *"can't"* *maintain* previously learned skills
5. Ability of students who *"can't"* *apply* their skills to new tasks or in different settings.

APPLICATIONS TO ARITHMETIC

Improving Accuracy

Teachers commonly encounter students who *"can't"* or who at least do not compute problems very accurately. In this section three sample projects are presented. The first project demonstrates the use of a Model-Lead-Test procedure. The second focuses on the use of demonstration, modeling and feedback. The third project illustrates the use of demonstration, contingent drill and reinforcement.

Classroom Application
Increasing Accuracy on Division Facts
(Voss, C., 1979)

Number of Students
    Three eight-year-old boys

Setting
    Regular classroom

Target Behavior/Aim
    Increase accuracy in writing answers to twenty-five division facts to 96 percent correct (24 out of 25 problems) for two days in a row.

Definition of Target Behavior
    A correct response was counted as a written answer which matched the correct quotient for each division fact presented on the worksheet. Incorrect responses included problems not attempted as well as incorrect quotients.

Materials
    Materials included division flash cards (Tables 6, 7, 8 and 9) and five worksheets containing twenty-five division facts from the same tables.

Observation System and Measurement Technique
    Permanent product recording was used to determine the number of correct and incorrectly answered problems per day. The boys' scores were converted to percent correct scores and their individual scores were charted daily.

Procedures
    During baseline the students were asked to complete a worksheet containing 25 division facts without any assistance or feedback from the teacher.
    Following baseline a Model-Lead-Test (Carnine & Silbert, 1979) procedure was used to drill the students on 50 division facts. The teacher then alternated quizzing the three boys on the flashcards. If a student responded correctly, the teacher verbally praised him.
    When an incorrect answer was given the teacher said the problem and gave the correct answer (Model), the student repeated the problem and answer with the teacher (Lead), and then the teacher presented the flashcard again to which the student was to respond with the correct answer (Test). The teacher separated the flashcards into two piles indicating correct and incorrect answers. After the 50 flashcards had been presented, the teacher drilled the students on those cards in the incorrect answer pile. The Model-Lead-Test procedure for practicing erred facts required the three boys to respond as a group.
    Following the Model-Lead-Test procedure, the students were asked to complete their worksheets. After the students completed their assignment, the teacher returned their papers with the number of problems computed correctly and incorrectly noted at the top of the page. Students who scored 96 percent or above were given a sticker on their worksheet.
    Weekly maintenance checks were scheduled during which the students were asked to complete their problems without drilling on the flashcards. Feedback as to the number of problems a student computed correctly and incorrectly was provided.

Results
    During baseline Tony averaged 58.5 percent, Jim 60.5 percent and Paul 88.2 percent correct. As can be seen in Figure 10–10, all three boys reached criteria within six days after drill began. On the maintenance check which occurred one week following the intervention, all three students achieved scores at or above criterion level.

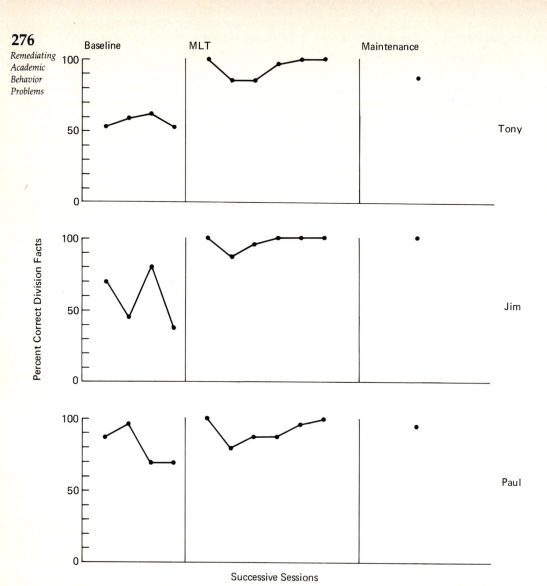

FIGURE 10–10 Students' percent correct scores on division facts. (Adapted from Christinia Voss, *The use of a model-lead-test procedure to improve children's ability to compute division facts*. Unpublished manuscript, University of Illinois, 1979. By permission of the author.)

Comment

This project demonstrates the kind of rapid improvement which is possible when a teacher precisely pinpoints deficit skills and then provides appropriate instruction, practice and reinforcement. Following the completion of this project, the teacher indicated that she planned to train peer tutors to use the Model-Lead-Test procedure.

Students make at least two types of computational errors, careless and systematic errors. The majority of errors made by students are of the careless variety (Grossnickle & Snyder, 1939). Careless errors are those which a student makes one day but not the next, whereas systematic errors are those which a student misses consistently due to the use of an incorrect computational procedure. Common systematic errors include failing to carry in addition, for example,

```
   37        48
 + 29      + 83
  ___       ____
  516       1211
```

and inverting the minuend and subtrahend in subtraction borrow problems, for example,

```
   37        48
  - 9       - 9
  ___       ___
   32        41
```

This latter type of error is known as a systematic inversion error. Systematic inversion errors are by far the most common type of systematic error made by students (Cox, 1975; Smith, 1968). The following sample project presents a remediation technique designed to increase the accuracy of students who made systematic inversion errors in computing subtraction borrow problems.

Classroom Application
Reducing Systematic Errors in Subtraction
(Blankenship, C. S., 1978)

Number of Students
 Nine students, age nine to eleven years. All students had been classified as learning disabled by their school district.

Setting
 Tutoring station within a school

Target Behavior/Aim
 To decrease systematic errors and to increase accuracy in computing subtraction borrow problems.

Definition of Target Behavior
 A student was said to have made a systematic inversion error when his/her answer contained an incorrect digit which corresponded exactly to the number one would obtain by subtracting the minuend from the subtrahend, for example.

```
   46       379       364
  - 8      - 94      - 87
  ___      ____      ____
   42       325       323
```

 While the majority of students made systematic inversion errors, one boy changed his error pattern from inverting the minuend and subtrahend to placing a zero in columns where borrowing was necessary, for example.

```
   46
  - 8
  ___
   40
```

The target behavior for this student was to decrease his use of zeroes in columns requiring borrowing.

Materials

Five sets of randomized forms, each containing nine different types of subtraction problems ranging in difficulty from problems of the type $\frac{37}{-9}$ to complex problems as $\frac{953}{-487}$ were developed. Each worksheet contained nine rows of five problems of each type for a total of 45 probems per set.

Five demonstration problems and five practice problems of the type $\frac{37}{-9}$ were placed on individual index cards to be used during the intervention period.

Observation System and Measurement Technique

Permanent product recording was used to measure the number of problems individual students solved correctly and incorrectly per day.

Procedures

During the baseline period neither instruction or feedback was provided. Each day during the intervention, the teacher placed a sample problem of the type $\frac{37}{-9}$ on the student's desk and proceeded to give the following demonstration:

$$\begin{array}{r} {\scriptstyle 2}\;{\scriptstyle 1} \\ \cancel{3}7 \\ -\;9 \\ \hline 28 \end{array}$$

"Let me show you how to figure out these problems. This is the ten's place (point), we have 3 tens. This is the one's place (point), we have 7 ones. This problem says, 'take 9 from 37.' We begin to subtract on the right side, but we see we can't take 9 ones from 7 ones—so, we have to borrow. We take 1 ten from the ten's place, that leaves 2 tens. We put that one ten in the one's place, that gives us 17 ones. 17 minus 9 is 8, 2 tens with nothing to subtract is 2 tens. So, 37 take away 9 is 28" (p.17).

Following the demonstration the student was asked to solve a sample problem. If the sample problem was solved correctly, the student was told that his answer was correct. If a student solved the sample problem incorrectly, the teacher told the student that the answer was wrong and then repeated the demonstration using another problem. As soon as a student solved a sample problem correctly, he was given his worksheet and told to work the problems in the same way as he had been shown.

Following the completion of the worksheet, the teacher corrected only the first row of problems (this row corresponded to the type of problems the students were instructed on). The students' papers were returned and they were told the number of problems they had solved correctly and incorrectly in the first row. No feedback was provided on the eight other rows of problems. This procedure was used to enable the teacher to determine if students could apply their newly acquired borrowing skills to more complex problems.

Two maintenance checks were conducted during which conditions were the same as those used during the baseline period.

Results

During baseline the students inverted between 70 percent and 100 percent of all digits which could be inverted. Their average accuracy during baseline was 0 percent correct. When the intervention was applied, systematic errors decreased and accuracy increased for all students.

Joe's daily data shown in Figure 10–11 represents the typical performance of students in the project. Like Joe most students were able to acquire, generalize and maintain their accuracy in computing subtraction borrow problems.

Comment

The technique of combining demonstration and modeling with feedback appears to be both effective and efficient in terms of teacher time. The demonstration took an average of thirty-five seconds a day per student and only a few minutes were needed to correct the students' papers and provide feedback. While this technique was only applied to two types of systematic errors, research in progress (Blankenship & Korn, 1980) suggests that this method is effective in decreasing other types of systematic errors in addition and subtraction.

Teachers commonly express concern over methods of teaching students how to solve arithmetic word problems. In the following sample project, a method will be presented for teaching students to solve word problems which incorporates demonstration, contingent drill for errors, and reinforcement.

**Classroom Application
Improving Performance in Solving Word Problems
(Blankenship, C. S. & Lovitt, T. C., 1974)**

Number of Students

Seven students participated in the project, all of whom were classified as learning disabled by the school district which referred them to the Curriculum Research Classroom, Experimental Education Unit, University of Washington. For the purposes of this example, data will be provided for one student whose performance was typical of the group.

Setting

Curriculum Research Classroom

Target Behavior/Aim

Increase accuracy in computing arithmetic word problems of the type $n - 9 = 3$ and $12 - n = 3$ to 100 percent correct for three days.

Definition of Target Behavior

Problems not attempted and wrong answers were counted as incorrect. Correct answers corresponded to the answer one would obtain by performing the computation presented in the word problem.

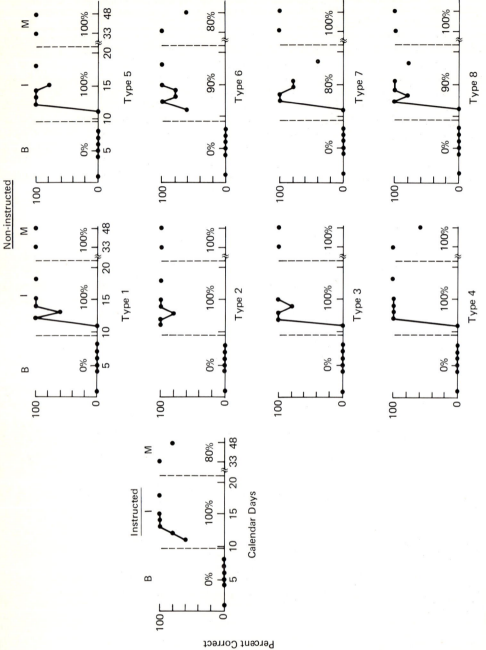

FIGURE 10–11 Joe's percent correct scores on all problem types. (From C. S. Blankenship, Remediating systematic inversion errors in subtraction through the use of demonstration and feedback, *Learning Disability Quarterly*, 1978, *1*, p. 21, By permission of the publisher.)

Materials

For each of four classes of word problems taught, the following materials were developed:

1. Demonstration Sheets—Five demonstration sheets, each containing two sample problems, one of each type to be instructed. A sample demonstration sheet for Class 4 word problems (n − 2 = 2 and 7 − n = 4) is shown in Figure 10–12.
2. Teacher Cue Sheets—Two scripts were written for each problem type to be instructed. A sample cue sheet for one type of Class 4 problem (n − 2 = 2) is shown in Figure 10–13.
3. Correct Sheets—Worksheets were developed which contained blank equation blocks and which were labeled to correspond to each type of problem taught.
4. Daily Worksheets—Five worksheets per class of problems were developed, each of which contained ten problems of each of two problem types to be instructed. The same problems were presented each day, but the number facts varied from one set to another. The problems were presented in a different order each day.

Demonstration Sheet
Class 4 Form a

Sam has 2 frogs. He has 2 more ducks than frogs.
How many ducks does Sam have? ____________

Size of Larger Group	Action	Size of Smaller Group		Difference
□	□	□	=	□

Mrs. Hill has 7 plates. She has 4 more plates than glasses. How many glasses does she have? ____________

Size of Larger Group	Action	Size of Smaller Group		Difference
□	□	□	=	□

FIGURE 10–12 Demonstration Sheet Class 4 Form a

Student reads orally the sample comparison addition problem. Teacher asks the following questions, supplies answers only if student cannot and directs the student to place numbers in appropriate spaces in the equation blocks.

1. What does the problem ask you to find? (size of larger group)
2. Do you know the size of the larger group (no)
3. So we leave this box blank.
4. Do you know the size of the smaller group? (   )
5. What is the size of the smaller group? (   )
6. We put the size of the smaller group right here.
7. Do you know the difference between the size of the larger group and the size of the smaller group?
8. What is the difference between the size of the larger group and the size of the smaller group? (   )
9. We put the difference between the size of the larger group and the size of the smaller group right here.
10. What is the action? Joining, separating, or comparing? (comparing)
11. What sign do we use for comparing? ($-$)
12. We put the minus sign right here.
13. Now let's solve the equation. (Student reads, teacher corrects verbally.)
14. To find the size of the larger group we add the size of the smaller group to the difference.
15. Please add the size of the smaller group to the difference.
16. What is the size of the larger group? (   )
17. We put the size of the larger group right here.
18. Student reads number sentence.
19. Is that number sentence true? (If not, student corrects it.)
20. Teacher reads problem question, student answers with noun and number.

Observation System and Measurement Technique

Permanent product recording was used to measure the number of problems answered correctly and incorrectly per day. The student's performance was also timed, thus enabling the teacher to record rate data. Both percent of problems computed per day and problems per minute were charted.

Procedures

During baseline in Class 4 problems, Toni was asked to compute twenty word problems as best he could. No instruction or feedback was provided. The first intervention consisted of the teacher demonstrating how to solve problems of the type $n - 9 = 3$ and $12 - n = 3$ using the appropriate Demonstration and Teacher Cue sheets. No feedback was provided to the student concerning his accuracy in computing the problems.

During the second intervention the demonstration was discontinued and the student was required to correct erred problems with the teacher. The student read each incorrectly answered problem and the teacher led him through the process by asking the questions contained on the Teacher Cue sheet.

The third intervention consisted of a combination of Technique 1 and 2. The demonstration was provided as in Technique 1 and the student corrected erred problems as described in Technique 2. During the fourth intervention, the student was given the opportunity to earn a notebook if he scored 100 percent correct for three days.

Teacher Cue Sheet
Class 4
Comparison Addition
$n - 2 = 2$

Student reads orally the sample comparison addition problem.
Teacher asks the following questions, supplies answers only if student cannot and directs
the student to place numbers in appropriate spaces in the equation blocks.

1. What does the problem ask you to find? (size of larger group)

2. Do you know the size of the larger group (no)

3. So we leave this box blank.

4. Do you know the size of the smaller group? (   )

5. What is the size of the smaller group? (   )

6. We put the size of the smaller group right here.

7. Do you know the difference between the size of the larger group and the size
   of the smaller group?

8. What is the difference between the size of the larger group and the size of
   the smaller group? (   )

9. We put the difference between the size of the larger group and the size of the
   smaller group right here.

10. What is the action? Joining, separating, or comparing? (comparing)

11. What sign do we use for comparing? (−)

12. We put the minus sign right here.

13. Now let's solve the equation. (Student reads, teacher corrects verbally.)

14. To find the size of the larger group we add the size of the smaller group to the difference.

15. Please add the size of the smaller group to the difference.

16. What is the size of the larger group? (   )

17. We put the size of the larger group right here.

18. Student reads number sentence.

19. Is that number sentence true? (If not, student corrects it.)

20. Teacher reads problem question, student answers with noun and number.

FIGURE 10–13 Teacher Cue Sheet,

Results

Toni's daily data is shown in Figure 10–14. During baseline Toni's accuracy ranged from 0 percent to 25 percent correct. His average accuracy during baseline and the first intervention was 14.2 percent and 11.7 percent, respectively. During the second intervention his accuracy ranged from 0 percent to 70 percent correct with an average of about 32 percent. After the first few days of Technique 3, his scores varied between 85 percent and 100 percent correct. By the sixth day of the fourth intervention, Toni reached the desired aim.

Comment

While a combination of demonstration and correction was effective in increasing Toni's accuracy, it did not result in his achieving the desired aim. Toni's performance during baseline and Technique 1 provides an example of what we mean by a student who "can't" or at least doesn't perform a skill very accurately. While Technique 2 originally looked promising, performance eventually leveled off. During Technique 3, Toni's performance is typical of a student who "can" but doesn't perform very consistently. In this case the chance to earn a notebook provided an appropriate incentive for Toni to master this class of word problems.

Although these techniques were used with individual students, the demonstration and correction procedures could easily be adapted to small groups of students.

Increasing Consistency

The performance of some students in math varies considerably from day to day. Teachers often explain such inconsistent performance on factors such as being tired or getting into a fight, or events at home which could be troubling a student. Although events outside the classroom can affect performance, very often inconsistent performance can be remedied by factors which teachers can control such as praise and access to free time.

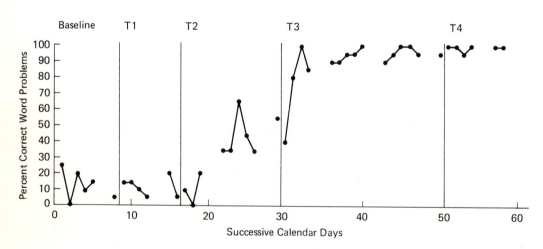

FIGURE 10–14 Toni's percent correct scores on word problems. (From C. S. Blankenship & T. C. Lovitt, *Story problem data collected in Curriculum Research Classroom, Experimental Education Unit, University of Washington,* 1974. By permission of the authors.)

In contrast to students who "can't", students who "can" but "choose not to" require very different teaching techniques. The following sample project illustrates the effects of reniforcement on improving the performance of a student whose accuracy in two subject areas was inconsistent.

Classroom Application
Using Contingent Access to Activities to Increase Accurate Responding
(Fowler, R. E., Thomas, L., & Santogrossi, D. A., 1977)

Number of Students
Eleven-year-old boy, Jack

Setting
Regular classroom (D. A. Santogrossi, personal communication, June 24, 1980)

Target Behavior/Aim
Increase accuracy on arithmetic and English assignments to at least 70 percent correct.

Definition of Target Behavior
Correct answers were counted as correct; wrong answers and items not attempted were counted as incorrect. When Jack failed to turn in an assignment it was recorded as 0 percent correct (D. A. Santogrossi, personal communication, June 24, 1980).

Materials
Curriculum materials used were not reported.

Observation System and Measurement Technique
Permanent product recording was used to measure Jack's percent correct scores on arithmetic and English assignments.

Procedures
During baseline presumably no contingencies were in effect. The first intervention involved the psychological consultant, the teacher and Jack who met to write a contingency contract. The contract specified that Jack could earn twenty minutes of free-reading time, provided he attained a score of at least 70 percent correct on his arithmetic assignment. No contingency was placed on accuracy on his English assignment.

Prior to the second intervention, the consultant, teacher and Jack met again to discuss the contract. At this meeting it was agreed that the contingency would apply to performance on both assignments. Therefore to earn his twenty minutes of free-reading time, Jack had to score at least 70 percent correct on his arithmetic and English assignment.

Results
As can be seen in Figure 10–15, Jack's accuracy on his arithmetic assignments varied considerably during baseline. When Jack was allowed to earn free-reading time based on his accuracy in arithmetic, his scores in that subject increased. Ac-

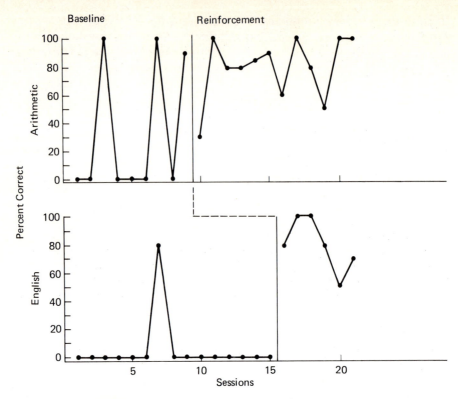

FIGURE 10–15 Jack's percent correct scores in arithmetic and English. (From R. E. Fowler, L. Thomas, & D. A. Santogrossi, Using contingent access to activities to increase accurate responding, *Education and Treatment of Children*, 1977, 1, p. 7.)

curacy on English assignments did not improve until the contingency was applied to performance in both subject areas.

Comment

Looking at Jack's baseline data, it is apparent that he "can" perform at the desired level, but that he does not do so consistently. Even when Jack's accuracy in arithmetic was consequated his accuracy in English did not improve. Jack therefore failed to generalize his increased accuracy to English. Only when he received reinforcement for achieving in both subjects was accuracy in English improved.

The authors' reported that the teacher also praised Jack on his performance. When using activities in the classroom to reinforce behavior, one would eventually decrease the amount of free time offered while continuing to occasionally praise the student's performance.

Increasing Speed

Some students compute their problems very slowly, seemingly taking hours to complete their assignments. Very often slow speed indicates lack of proficiency in computing basic facts. Teachers sometimes use drill to improve computational speed. Reinforcement has also been shown to increase computational rate (Lovitt & Curtiss, 1968). Instructions such as "Go faster," have also been used to increase students' computational speed (Smith & Lovitt, 1974). In the following sample project we will see the effect upon performance of simply telling a student the desired aim he is to achieve.

Classroom Application
Increasing Speed by Telling Peers' Rates
(Blankenship, C. S., & Lovitt, T. C., 1974)

Number of Students
Ten-year-old boy classified as learning disabled by his school district which referred him to the Experimental Education Unit, University of Washington.

Setting
Curriculum Research Classroom

Target Behavior/Aim
Increase correct rate on division facts to 33 problems per minute (p.p.m) and decrease incorrect rate to zero p.p.m. for three days.

Definition of Target Behavior
Incorrect answers included problems which were not attempted and wrong answers. Correct answers corresponded to the quotient one would obtain if the problem had been computed correctly.

Materials
The materials consisted of five worksheets, each containing the same twenty-five division facts presented in random order.

Observation System and Measurement Technique
Permanent product recording was used to measure the number of problems the student computed correctly and incorrectly each day. The student used a stop-watch to record the amount of time taken to complete his worksheet. The teacher used this information to calculate daily correct and incorrect rates which were plotted on a chart.

Procedures
During baseline neither instruction or feedback was provided. The first intervention consisted of requiring the student to complete a practice worksheet and check his answers on a calculator before doing his daily assignment. No other instructions or feedback was provided.
Prior to the second intervention, the teacher visited the student's regular classroom to obtain data on the computational rates of Bart's peers. Each student was given four division worksheets and allowed two minutes to work as many problems as they could. An analysis of the scores showed that the top 25 percent of the class computed the problems at or above 33 p.p.m. correct with zero to two errors. This information was used to determine a desired rate for Bart which was set at 33 p.p.m. correct with zero errors.

On the first day of the second intervention period, the teacher told Bart that the top 25 percent of the students in his regular classroom could do his problems at the rate of 33 p.p.m. with zero errors. The teacher encouraged Bart to aim for that rate. After the student completed his assignment, the teacher told him his correct and incorrect rates.

Maintenance checks were conducted every other day for a week and once a week for the next three weeks. During this time feedback was provided to the student as during the intervention period.

Results

The data in Figure 10–16 reveal that during baseline the student computed his problems at an average correct rate of 19.5 p.p.m. with 0 p.p.m. incorrect. During the first intervention, performance was quite variable and the student's average correct rate was 17.6 p.p.m. During the first three days of the second intervention, the student met the desired aim of 33 p.p.m. with zero errors. The maintenance data show that his correct rates decreased to about 10 p.p.m. correct. On the last weekly follow-up check before the end of the school year, Bart's correct rate again approached 30 p.p.m.

Comment

This project illustrates one way of determining desired aims for students receiving special services. By sampling the performance of a student's regular classroom peers, one can set realistic aims to ensure reentry into the regular classroom. In this case practice alone was not sufficient to improve speed. However performance improved when the student was told the desired aim and whether or not he achieved it.

Enhancing Maintenance and Generalization

Maintenance refers to the lasting effects of a behavioral change once instruction or reinforcement has been withdrawn. One type of generalization is said to occur when a student can apply previously learned skills to other tasks. Although very little research has investigated techniques to promote the maintenance and generalization of computational skills, the results of a study by Blankenship and Baumgartner (1980) suggest that:

1. Demonstration, modeling and feedback are often effective in increasing students' abilities to acquire, generalize and maintain their skills.
2. For some students reinforcement results in increased generalization; other students seem to require instruction on several types of problems before they can generalize their skills to computing other similar problems.
3. Maintenance can be improved by reinforcing accuracy on an intermittent or occasional basis.

Teachers are also concerned with generalization of skills from resource to regular classrooms. The following sample project illustrates the use of a technique to enhance generalization of computational skills from a resource to a regular setting.

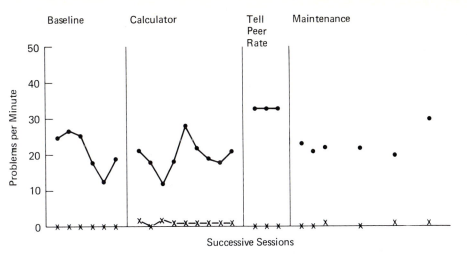

FIGURE 10–16 Number of problems Bart computed correctly and incorrectly per minute. (From C. S. Blankenship & T. C. Lovitt, *Computational arithmetic data collected in Curriculum Research Classroom, Experimental Education Unit, University of Washington*, 1974. By permission of the authors.)

Improving Generalization of Computational Skills to the Regular Classroom (Baumgartner, M., 1979)

Number of Students
    Nineteen students participated in this project. However for the purpose of our example, we will report data for only one student. All students were in regular fourth- or fifth-grade classrooms and all were receiving resource services for part of the school day.

Setting
    Resource-like setting and regular classroom

Target Behavior/Aim
    Increase accuracy in computing subtraction borrow problems.

Definition of Target Behavior
    Problems not attempted and those incorrectly answered were counted as wrong. Correct answers were those which corresponded to the answer one would obtain by performing the correct computation.

Materials
    Five sets of worksheets, each containing eight different types of subtraction borrow problems were developed. In addition for students who received small-group direct instruction, the teacher developed lesson objectives and scripts to use in teaching the following tasks: sign identification, place value, line counting and the borrow rule.

Observation System and Measurement Technique

Permanent product recording was used to measure the number of problems students computed correctly and incorrectly. Percent correct scores were graphed for individual students showing their performance in the resource and regular classroom.

Procedures

During baseline the students were presented daily with a worksheet containing ten subtraction borrow problems which they were to complete in the resource room. A comparable worksheet was given twice to the students during baseline to complete in their regular classroom. In neither setting were the students provided with instruction or feedback.

For those students who received small-group direct instruction, a fifteen-minute daily lesson was given which emphasized a Model-Lead-Test procedure. Following the lesson each student computed a sample problem. If the problem was computed correctly, the student proceeded to do this worksheet. If the sample problem was computed incorrectly, supplemental instruction was provided using the Model-Lead-Test procedure. No further instruction or feedback was provided as the students completed their assignment in the resource room. During the first intervention no instruction or feedback was provided to the students as they completed their assignment in the regular classroom.

Following the instructional phase an intervention was scheduled for students who had not generalized their performance to the regular classroom. For students who received small-group direct instruction, this phase consisted of having the regular classroom teacher provide the following reminder: "What was the borrow rule you learned in the resource room; do that here" (p. 49). No other instruction or feedback was provided. During the time when the students received the reminder in the regular classroom, they were provided with feedback and praise for their performance on their worksheets completed in the resource room.

During the no-reminder phase, the reminder was discontinued and students were given feedback and praise on the work they completed in the regular classroom. A follow up was scheduled five days after the last instructional condition. During this follow up praise and feedback were provided for work completed in the regular classroom.

Results

The data for the student shown in Figure 10–17 shows that accuracy increased substantially in the resource room when small-group direct instruction was provided. Performance did not, however, generalize to the regular classroom. When the reminder was in effect the student increased his accuracy in the regular classroom and managed to maintain his performance in the resource room. When the reminder was withdrawn, performance in the regular classroom maintained fairly well. The follow-up data reveal that the student computed his problems above 90 percent correct in the regular classroom.

Comment

This project emphasizes the importance of monitoring performance in the regular classroom when students are receiving special services in other settings. Although fourteen out of the nineteen students who participated in the project had no difficulty generalizing their computational skills to the regular classroom, a few students demonstrated an inability to do so. Of the five students who did not

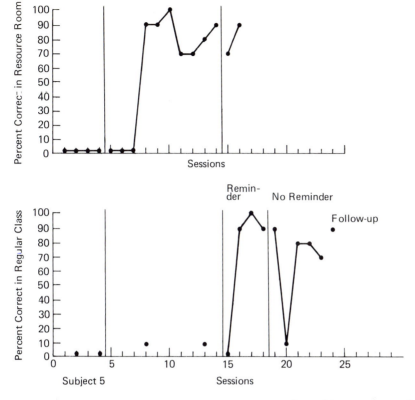

FIGURE 10–17 Student's percent correct scores on math problems computed in a resource and regular classroom. (From M. Baumgartner, *Generalization of improved subtraction regrouping skills from resource rooms to the regular class.* Unpublished doctoral dissertation, University of Illinois, 1979. By permission of the author.)

generalize, four of them were able to do so when a reminder was provided. For one student a reminder plus reinforcement was needed before his accuracy improved in the regular classroom.

Summary

In this section we have provided examples of teaching techniques which have been found to be effective in increasing students' accuracy, consistency, speed, and ability to generalize and maintain their computational skills. The techniques presented are just a sample of those which have been found to increase computational and problem-solving skills. While some of the projects were not conducted in regular classrooms, none of the techniques require an extensive amount of time. We encourage teachers to try these techniques and to adapt them to fit their own needs.

292
*Remediating
Academic
Behavior
Problems*

APPLICATIONS TO READING

Perhaps no other skill is deemed to be as important as reading. Many students with mild learning problems are referred for special education services based on difficulties in reading. In this section a number of projects are presented to illustrate techniques to improve students' reading skills.

Improving Accuracy

When students are initially learning how to read, a great deal of emphasis is placed on increasing their accuracy in saying sounds. In the following project, a Model-Lead-Test procedure was used to increase accuracy in decoding words which followed the pattern consonant-vowel-consonant (CVC), such as "fan" and "mat."

**Classroom Application
Improving Ability to Say CVC Words
(Caplan, S., 1979)**

Number of Students
   Seven-year-old girl, Jill

Setting
   Regular second-grade classroom

Target Behavior/Aim
   The teacher selected four decoding skills to remediate based on the student's performance on a CBA. For the purpose of this example, we will discuss performance on only one skill, sounding out CVC words, such as "mat" or "sap." The aim was to increase accuracy on saying ten CVC words selected from the student's reader to 100 percent for three days.

Definition of Target Behavior
   Words which were omitted or mispronounced were counted as incorrect. Only correctly pronounced words were counted as correct responses.

Materials
   Ten CVC words were selected at random from the student's reader and written on individual cards.

Procedures
   During baseline the student was asked to say the word presented on each card. No instruction or feedback was provided.
   During the intervention whenever the student omitted or mispronounced a word, the teacher modeled how to say the word, then said the word with the student and finally tested the student on saying the word by herself. Jill received drill on all of the words until she could say all ten of them correctly. After drill a daily measure was taken to assess Jill's ability to say the words without instruction.

During maintenance the student was asked to say the words under baseline conditions.

Results

    Jill's daily data in sounding out CVC words is shown in Figure 10–18. During baseline Jill could correctly pronounce five of the ten words. After the first day of the intervention, Jill consistently pronounced at least nine out of the ten words correctly. By the ninth day Jill had met the desired aim. The maintenance data, collected a few times per week over a two-week period, shows that Jill had maintained here ability to sound out CVC words.

Comment

    This project demonstrates that a simple technique which teachers have been using for years can increase decoding skills. After completing this project the teacher indicated that she was planning on using the same technique with small groups of students.

    Teachers are also concerned with improving reading comprehension skills. Sometimes students lack the ability to answer certain types of comprehension questions. Such was the case with Todd, a ten-year-old boy, who read fluently but had difficulty answering comprehension questions (Hauck, Metcalfe, & Bennett, 1975). Todd's data is shown in Figure 10–19. In commenting on the Hauck et al., study, Hansen and Eaton (1978) noted, "Todd was unable to answer comprehension questions unless he restated

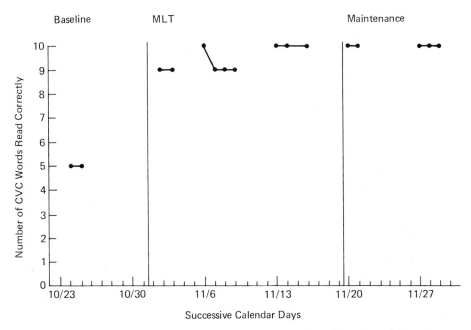

FIGURE 10–18 Number of CVC words read correctly by Jill. (Adapted from Susan Caplan, *Improving decoding skills.* Unpublished manuscript, University of Illinois, 1979. By permission of the author.)

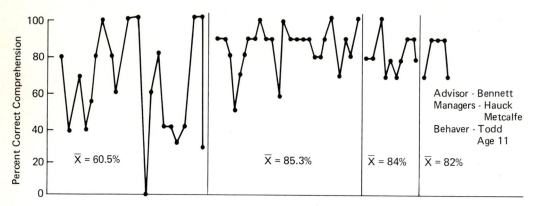

FIGURE 10–19 Todd's percent correct scores on reading comprehension questions. (From C. L. Hansen & M. D. Eaton, Reading. In N. G. Haring, T. C. Lovitt, M. D. Eaton, and C. L. Hansen (Eds.), *The fourth R: Research in the classroom*. Columbus, OH: Charles E. Merrill, 1978. By permission of the publishers.)

the text verbatim and could only perform at 80-100% when the teachers helped him find the appropriate response" (p. 68). In order to increase Todd's accuracy, his teacher simplified the task by focusing on one new type of question at a time. At first the teacher asked Todd only "what" questions such as, *"What* did the boy plan to do after school?" Later the teacher introduced "who" questions such as, *"Who* did the boy go to the game with?" As "who" questions were being introduced, the teacher continued to ask "what" questions based on the story Todd had read. Eventually the teacher asked Todd to answer three types of questions including "Who," "What," and "Where" questions.

Increasing Consistency

Not only are students expected to read accurately, but consistently as well. Oftentimes reinforcement contingencies can be used to increase students' consistency in reading at appropriate rates. Students can also demonstrate inconsistent performance in answering comprehension questions. Such was the case with Jill, whose performance on sounding out CVC words has already been discussed. In addition to practicing CVC words, Jill's teacher also asked her to read orally for two minutes each day. After Jill finished reading the teacher asked her five comprehension questions orally. As can be seen in Figure 10–20, Jill's comprehension scores during baseline varied between 20 percent and 80 percent correct. The intervention consisted of asking Jill to reread the passage and find the correct answer. As shown in Figure 10–20, by the third day Jill was able to correctly answer all comprehension questions the first time without having to reread the passage to find the correct answer.

Increasing Speed

Teachers are all too familiar with students who read slowly, seemingly stumbling over every word. Techniques which have been found to be effective in increasing oral reading rate include previewing, allowing a student to read or listen to a passage prior to reading it (Eaton, Lovitt, Sayre, & Lynch, 1974) and reinforcement contingencies (Lovitt, Eaton, Kirkwood, & Pelander, 1971; Roberts & Smith, 1980).

One technique, known as *contingent skipping*, was developed by Lovitt and Hansen (1976). The novel aspect of their technique is that a student is allowed to "skip" ahead in a reader based on meeting desired aims for correct and incorrect rates and comprehension. One of the benefits of skipping is that students who are performing from one to three years below grade level do not waste time reading books which are too easy. Instead they skip ahead to more difficult stories as soon as they have mastered easier material. While Hansen and Eaton (1978) have provided specific guidelines for implementing contingent skipping we will present the technique within a sample project.

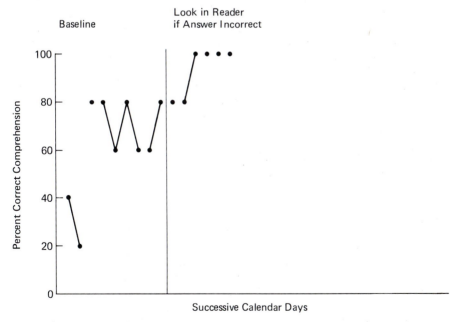

FIGURE 10–20 Jill's percent correct scores on reading comprehension questions. (Adapted from Susan Caplan, *Improving decoding skills*. Unpublished manuscript, University of Illinois, 1979. By permission of the author.)

**Classroom Application
Contingent Skipping
(Hansen & Eaton, 1978)**

Number of Students

Eight-year-old boy, Marty, who had been classified by his school district as learning disabled and referred to the Experimental Education Unit, University of Washington.

Setting

Curriculum Research Classroom

Target Behavior/Aim

The results of a CBA showed that Marty could read a 1^2 reader at forty to sixty words per minute (w.p.m.) correct with four to eight errors per minute and comprehend at least 50 percent of what he read. The aim was to have Marty read in a 3' reader at 56 w.p.m. correct, 2.9 or less incorrect w.p.m., and comprehend at least 79.3 percent of what he read. These aims were determined by multiplying Marty's "mean baseline correct rate and percent comprehension scores by 1.25 and the mean error rate by .75" (p. 81).

Definition of Target Behavior

The following oral reading errors were counted as incorrect responses: omissions, insertions, mispronunciations or substitutions, hesitations of more than four seconds, and words to which the student said "I don't know." Errors on proper names, places, repetitions and corrections made by the student were not counted as errors.

Materials

Marty read from the *Lippincott Readers* (McCracken & Walcutt, 1971), levels 1^2 to 3^1. A set of 30 comprehension questions were written for each 500-word passage Marty read. Comprehension questions included recall, sequence and interpretation questions.

Observation System and Measurement Technique

Event recording was used to count the number of words Marty read correctly and incorrectly each day during the first two minutes of reading a 500-word passage. The number of words read correctly and incorrectly were later converted to rate data. Permanent product recording was used to measure the number of comprehension questions Marty answered correctly and incorrectly per day.

Procedures

Before beginning the project, the teacher divided each book in the series into four sections having an equal number of stories. Following his placement into a reader based on CBA data, Marty was asked to skim through the first section of the book and decide the order in which he preferred to read the selections. Marty was then allowed to read those selections he indicated before other selections in that section. This procedure was used so that students would not try to avoid skipping because of their desire to read stories presented later in a section.

During baseline the teacher timed Marty's reading for the first two minutes. During this time the teacher recorded Marty's reading errors. The teacher supplied correct pronunciations for erred words, and occasional praise was given for accurate or fluent reading. Following the two-minute timing the student completed reading the 500-word selection out loud and the teacher provided correct pronunciations to erred words and provided occasional praise.

Following the completion of the 500-word segment, the teacher gave the student thirty written comprehension questions to answer at his desk. The student could request help in reading the questions, but he was not given other assistance or allowed to consult his reader. The student's comprehension questions were checked by the teacher and returned the same day.

Prior to the intervention the teacher told the student that he could "skip all remaining stories in a section of the book, if on the same day, his reading rates and comprehension scores equal or exceed" the criteria or desired aims (p. 81). If Marty didn't skip after four days in a section, one or more of the following techniques were used depending upon whether Marty's performance was:

1. Below Aim, Correct Rate—Orally read last 100 words from previous day's assignment until criteria is reached.

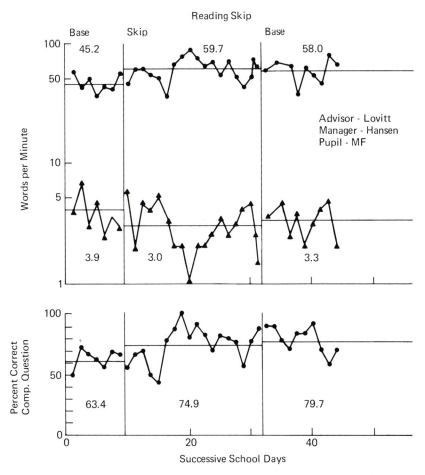

FIGURE 10–21 Marty's daily data in reading. (Lovitt, T. C., & Hansen, C. L. The use of contingent skipping and drilling to improve oral reading and comprehension. *Journal of Learning Disabilities*, 1976, 9(8), p. 486. By permission of the publishers.)

2. Above Aim, Incorrect Rate—Drill erred words embedded in phrases until all are read correctly.
3. Below Aim, Comprehension—Incorrect responses were checked by the teacher and the student had to reword his answers.

As soon as a student skipped he began reading in the next section on the following day. Drill was scheduled to occur if after four days in the new section the student failed to skip.

Results

As can be seen in Figure 10–21, Marty's average correct and incorrect rates in a 1^2 reader during baseline were 45.2 w.p.m. and 3.9 w.p.m., respectively. His average comprehension score during baseline was 63.4 percent. During the intervention, correct rate increased to 59.7 w.p.m., errors decreased to 3.0 w.p.m., and comprehension increased to 74.9 percent. When a return-to-baseline phase was scheduled, correct rate decreased slightly; incorrect rate increased a bit but comprehension remained high.

During this project Mary skipped seven times, averaging 2.7 days per section" (p. 82). Marty completed two readers and never required drill. By the end of the seventh week Marty was reading on grade level (3^1).

Comment

Hansen and Eaton (1978) noted that the opportunity to skip or to avoid drill appears to be sufficiently motivating to students. However some students they worked with required drill to improve their rates and/or comprehension scores. Contingent skipping and drilling has been used in both special and regular classrooms with great success.

Summary

In this section a number of techniques designed to increase students' oral reading rates and to improve their comprehension have been discussed. There are several other reading techniques, such as previewing and corrective feedback which are presented in *The 4th. R: Research in the classroom* by Haring, Lovitt, Eaton, and Hansen (1978), which teachers will find helpful in remediating reading difficulties.

To date there has been more emphasis upon investigating techniques to improve students' accuracy, speed and comprehension than on identifying techniques to promote maintenance and generalization of reading skills. As with other academic skills, techniques such as practice, feedback and reinforcement contingencies will probably assist students in maintaining skills. Generalization of reading skills could be determined by recording students' performance in the instructional text as well as occasionally measuring performance in other reading materials. By taking data in this manner, a teacher could determine whether a technique is influencing performance in both the instructional text and the other materials. By applying and evaluating teaching techniques using the data-based approach, teachers should be able to identify techniques which can assist students in generalizing their reading skills to a variety of materials.

There is no question that being able to express one's thoughts in writing is a very important skill. In the past few years, educators and parents have become increasingly alarmed by the fact that many students have difficulty expressing themselves in writing. The poor writing skills of students have received extensive coverage in newspapers, magazines and on television. Many colleges now require entering freshmen to take "bonehead" English to improve their writing skills.

Writing demands a number of skills, some of the most basic are the ability to spell words and to translate ideas into gramatically correct sentences. Of course in order to communicate effectively, one must also be able to write legibly or type. In this section we will focus on techniques to improve students' performance in such fundamental skills as spelling, penmanship and writing sentences.

Improving Accuracy

The traditional approach used to teach spelling consists of the following. On Monday students are assigned a list of words to study for the week. Workbook exercises are assigned which require students to fill in the blanks using their words, look up the meanings of words in a dictionary and write sentences using the words in that week's spelling list. On Wednesday a practice test is given. On Thursday more workbook pages are assigned and students are encouraged to study their words in preparation for the test on Friday. Friday comes and some students score 100 percent while others barely manage to spell more than a few words correctly. On Monday new words are assigned and the process is repeated. The outcome is that many students do not learn to spell very well. An alternative to this approach is provided in the following project.

Classroom Application
The Effects of Distributed Practice on Spelling Accuracy
(Reith, H., Axelrod, S., Anderson, R., Hathaway, F., Wood K., & Fitzgerald, C., 1974)

Number of Students
Thirteen-year-old girl, Delena

Setting
Junior high language arts classroom

Target Behavior/Aim
Increase accuracy in spelling words on a weekly spelling test

Definition of Target Behavior
A word was considered to be spelled correctly if it matched the spelling shown in the text.

Materials

Seventh-grade-level text *Basic Goals in Spelling* (Kottmeyer & Claus, 1968).

Observation System and Measurement Technique

Permanent product recording was used to measure the number of words spelled correctly and incorrectly on each weekly spelling test. The number of words was always twenty-two, so frequency of words spelled correctly was charted.

Procedures

During baseline Delena's teacher gave her twenty-two words to study. Throughout the baseline phase, the student completed workbook assignments which contained the words she was to study. At the end of the week the teacher gave Delena a spelling test covering that week's words.

Prior to the intervention, the teacher divided the twenty-two word spelling lists into four lists containing five or six words. Each day the teacher gave Delena one of the new lists containing five or six words and tested her on that list the following day. During this time the student continued to complete her workbook assignments. At the end of the week a spelling test was given on that weeks' words.

Two other conditions were arranged, including returning to baseline and intervention conditions. Procedures during those conditions were the same as those previously described.

Results

Delena's data on weekly spelling tests is shown in Figure 10–22. During baseline Delena averaged seven words correct out of twenty-two. When Delena was given five or six new words to study each day, her accuracy improved to an average of nineteen words correct per week. Her accuracy decreased considerably during the return-to-baseline phase when she was given all twenty-two words to study at the beginning of the week. When Delena was again presented with five or six new words per day, her scores improved on the weekly spelling tests.

Comment

The results of this project should cause teachers to reconsider the effectiveness of teaching spelling using the traditional method of assigning lists of words, requiring students to complete worksheets and taking a test at the end of the week. As Delena's performance shows, simply completing workbook assignments was not sufficient to improve her performance.

In commenting upon this study Axelrod (1977) pointed out that it is not possible to tell whether Delena's improvement was due to giving her shorter lists to study or daily testing. Based on other research conducted by Axelrod and his colleagues, which compared giving students lists of twenty words and lists of five words with and without daily testing, it appears to be "best to give shorter word lists with daily tests" (Axelrod, 1977, p. 153).

In the previous project conducted by Reith et al., specific instructional procedures were not used to increase spelling accuracy. Performance improved simply by reducing the number of words the student was required to study each day and testing her performance on a daily basis. Some students, however, may need to be shown an effective way of studying their words. A technique developed by Hansen (1974) known as *Cover-*

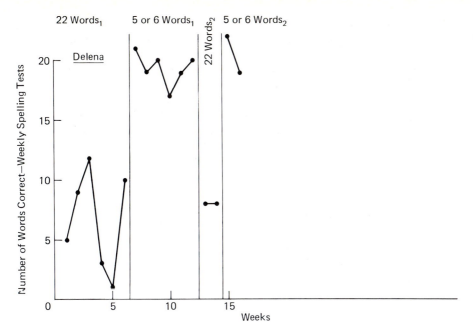

FIGURE 10–22 Number of words Delena spelled correctly on weekly tests. (From H. Reith, S. Axelrod, R. Anderson, F. Hathaway, K. Wood & C. Fitzgerald. Influence of distributed practice and daily testing on weekly spelling tests. *Journal of Educational Research*, 1974, *68*, p. 74. By permission of the publishers.)

Copy-Compare provides students with a strategy for studying their spelling words. The following sample projects illustrates the use of this technique.

Classroom Application
Improving Spelling Accuracy Using "Cover-Copy-Compare"
(Kessler-Futterman, A., 1979)

Number of Students
Two fourth-grade boys participated in this project; however for our purposes we will discuss only one student's data.

Setting
Regular classroom

Target Behavior/Aim
Increase accuracy in spelling words containing 'long a,' 'long e,' and 'long o' to 100 percent for two days in a row.

Definition of Target Behavior
"A word was considered to be correctly spelled if all necessary letters were included in the proper sequence" (p. 2). Incorrectly spelled words included words not attempted as well as words in which letters were omitted, inserted or were out of order.

Materials

Spelling words were selected from the fourth grade level text *Basic Goals in Spelling* (Kottmeyer & Claus, 1968). Multiple copies of a correction sheet similar to the one shown in Figure 10–23 were copied for use during the intervention.

Observation System and Measurement Technique

Permanent product recording was used to measure the number of words spelled correctly per day. A raw data sheet was used to record the exact words students spelled correctly and incorrectly each day. A total of ten words were dictated each day, so the teacher chose to graph the number of words spelled correctly.

Procedures

Based on the results of a spelling CBA, it was determined that John performed below criterion on words containing 'long a,' 'long e,' and 'long o.' The teacher decided to intervene first on 'long a' words, then on 'long e' words and finally on 'long o' words. As soon as John mastered the 'long a' list, baseline was schedule for the 'long e' list; when that list was mastered, baseline began on the 'long o' list. During baseline on each list, the student was provided with neither instruction nor feedback. The teacher dictated a word from the list, used the word in a sentence and then repeated the word.

When cover-copy-compare was scheduled, the student received a worksheet showing the correct spelling of words he had spelled incorrectly that day. The student first copied the word, saying each letter aloud to himself. The student then covered the word and wrote it from memory in the next column on the worksheet. Next the student compared the way he had written the word with the correct spelling of the word which the teacher had written on the first column on his worksheet. If the words didn't match, the student wrote the word correctly in the last column and then repeated the procedure until he could spell the word correctly from memory.

Maintenance checks were scheduled for the first two lists as the school year ended before John had mastered the third list. During maintenance the teacher decided that John would have to cover-copy-compare if he failed to spell at least eight out of the ten words correctly. This never occurred so the student received only feedback and praise during maintenance.

Results

John's data is shown in Figure 10–24. In looking at John's data it is apparent that the cover-copy-compare technique was effective in increasing his accuracy on

Word	Copy	Cover-Compare	Correction

FIGURE 10–23 Cover-Copy-Compare Correction Sheet.

all three word lists. John mastered the first two lists within six days after the technique was applied. Weekly postchecks on the first two lists indicated that the student had maintained his accuracy. Although there was not enough time to complete the intervention on the third list, the data indicate that performance on that list was increasing.

Comment

One way of adapting this technique to an entire class might be to group students together who were working on the same list. Each groups' words could be tape recorded using a word-sentence-word format. After the daily test students could either exchange papers or correct their own words using a colored pen. Students would then look up the spelling of incorrectly spelled words and practice them using the cover-copy-compare method. As soon as a student correctly spelled the words on the list for two days in a row, the student would be eligible for free time during spelling for the rest of the week. On Monday new lists would be given and the process would be repeated. Another intervention would have to be arranged for students who failed to master their list within five days after the cover-copy-compare technique was applied.

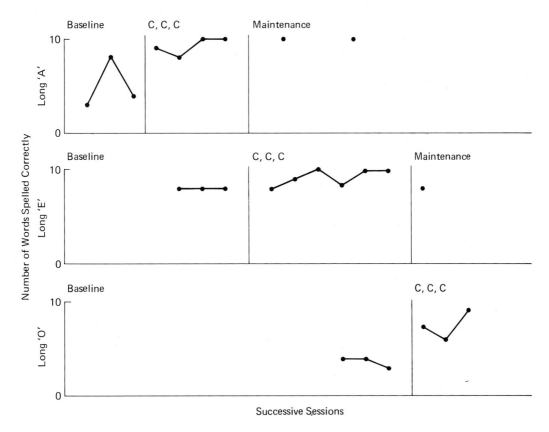

FIGURE 10–24 Number of words John spelled correctly. (Adapted from Anita Kessler-Futterman, *Improving spelling accuracy using "cover-copy-compare."* Unpublished manuscript, University of Illinois, 1979. By permission of the author.)

Penmanship also plays an important role in writing. If letters are poorly formed, the reader may have difficulty understanding the writer's message. While penmanship is no longer taught as an "art form," teachers still require students to write legibly. The following sample project illustrates the effect of a reinforcement contingency upon students' legibility.

Classroom Application
Improving Penmanship by Reinforcing Legibility
(Lovitt T. C., 1973)

Number of Students

Seven elementary age students participated in this project, all of whom had been classifed as learning disabled by their school district and had been referred to the Experimental Education Unit, University of Washington. Data will be reported for one student, Ted.

Setting

Curriculum Research Classroom

Target Behavior/Aim

Prior to the project data on the writing rates of normal peers were collected. Students in the top 25 percent wrote manuscript letters at the rate of 22 per minute correct with less than one error per minute. In relation to these scores, Ted's correct rate was at or above the rate of 22 letters per minute; however, his incorrect rates varied between five and ten symbols per minute.

Definition of Target Behavior

An error was said to occur when a student failed to copy a symbol correctly from a 500-word passage. Symbols included: letters, punctuation marks and spaces.

Observation System and Measurement Technique

Permanent product recording was used to measure the number of symbols students copied correctly and incorrectly per minute. The students used stopwatches to record the amount of time taken to complete their assignment. The teacher checked the students' work and calculated and charted their rates each day.

Materials

Students were provided with a different 500-symbol selection daily from a reader at their reading level.

Procedures

Prior to baseline the students were asked to copy their stories in manuscript one day and in cursive the next day. After a few days a determination was made, based on their performance, to focus on either manuscript or cursive writing. Ted was asked to write manuscript letters.

During baseline no instructions or feedback were provided. However the students were told that as soon as they had finished their assignment, they could play for the remaining minutes of the 30-minute period. Following baseline an intervention was arranged for students who were performing below the desired aim. As Ted was averaging 20.1 symbols per minute correct and 7.6 incorrect, he was told that he would have to correct his errors from the previous day after he completed the current day's assignment.

Following the intervention period, the students were told they no longer had to correct their errors. As during the previous baseline phase, the students could play for the remainder of the penmanship period provided that they had finished their assignment. Following the return-to-baseline phase the contingency was reapplied and administered as previously described.

Results

As shown in Figure 10–25 Ted had difficulty writing both manuscript and cursive letters prior to baseline. His performance on manuscript letters during baseline averaged 20.1 per minute correct and 7.6 per minute incorrect. When the intervention contingency was applied, correct rate increased and incorrect rate decreased. During the return-to-baseline phase Ted's correct rate increased gradually; however errors also increased. When the contingency was reapplied Ted's correct rate averaged 31.5 symbols per minute and his errors decreased to an average of 1.8 per minute.

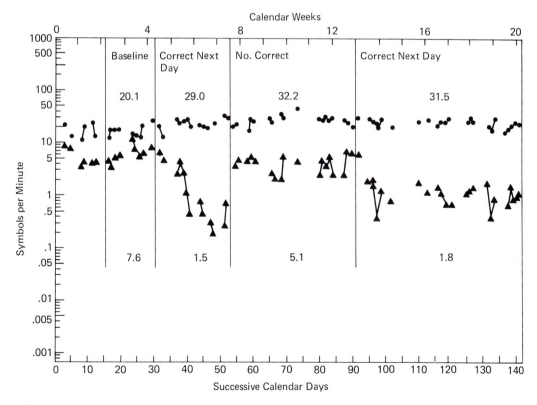

FIGURE 10–25 Number of symbols Ted wrote per minute. (From Lovitt, T. C. Applied behavior analysis techniques and curriculum research: Implications for instruction. In N. G. Haring & R. L. Schiefelbusch (Eds.), *Teaching Special Children*. New York: McGraw-Hill, 1976, p. 141. By permission of the publishers.)

Comment

This project is very similar to the Hopkins, Schutte, and Garton (1971) study which was discussed in Chapter 9. In the latter study students were allowed to play after they finished their penmanship assignment. As the project progressed, the students were allowed progressively less time to play. Even though no contingency was placed on errors in the Hopkins et al., study, the students' accuracy was not negatively effected by the free time contingency. The accuracy of the students in Lovitt's study, however, was better when free time was made contingent upon their accuracy. For four students, requiring them to correct their errors from the previous day effectively reduced their errors. The errors of two boys were reduced by requiring them to copy their mistakes twice. Errors for a third student decreased when he was required to correct his errors the same day.

Although students may not hurry through their work in order to play, some students may not be as careful as they should be when they are reinforced for work completion rather than accuracy. In light of Lovitt's results, accuracy rather than work completion should be consequated to encourage students to always do their best work.

Increasing Consistency

As in other academic subject areas, sometimes students "can" perform skills but choose not to do so. Sometimes students spell words correctly one day but not the next. Similarly the legibility of some students' handwriting varies from day to day. Leach and Graves (1973) noted the same kind of inconsistent performance among two junior high school girls whose accuracy in writing complete sentences varied from day to day. The procedures they used to increase the girls' accuracy in writing complete sentences are presented in the following project.

**Classroom Application
Increasing Accuracy in Writing Sentences
(Leach, D. M., & Graves, M., 1973)**

Number of Students

Two seventh-grade girls, Betty and Jane

Setting

Regular seventh-grade language arts class

Target Behavior/Aim

Increase accuracy in writing complete sentences

Definition of Target Behavior

A sentence was said to be correct if it contained at least five words, was punctuated and capitalized correctly, and had an identified subject and verb which were in agreement.

Permanent product recording was used to measure the girls' accuracy in writing complete sentences.

Materials

No specific materials were reported to have been used. Each day the teacher asked the girls to write ten sentences.

Procedure

During baseline the teacher graded the girls' assignments and returned them on the following day. When the intervention was applied the teacher immediately corrected and returned the students' pages. Following the intervention, a return-to-baseline phase was scheduled during which the girls' pages were returned the day after they completed them. The intervention was reapplied and the students again received immediate feedback as previously described.

Results

Data for Jane and Betty are shown in Figure 10–26. During baseline the performance of both girls was quite variable. Eventually, however, accuracy leveled

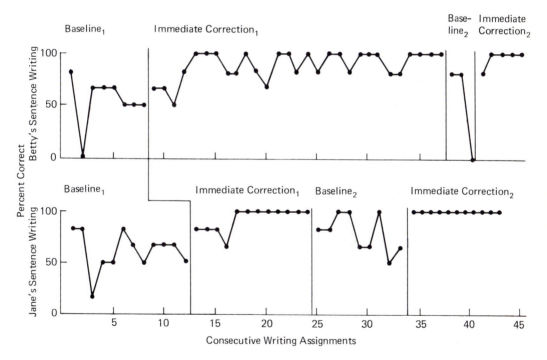

FIGURE 10–26 Percent of sentences written correctly by Betty and Jane. (Adapted from D. M. Leach & M. E. Graves, The effects of immediate correction on improving seventh grade language arts performance. In A. Egner (Ed.), *Individualizing junior and senior high instruction to provide special education within regular classrooms: The 1972–1973 research-service reports of the secondary special education project.* Unpublished document: Burlington, VT: University of Vermont, Department of Special Education, 1973, p. 17. By permission of Ann Egner Nevin.)

off to between 50 percent and 60 percent correct. By the fourth day of the intervention, both girls scored 100 percent correct. While Jane maintained this level throughout the intervention, Betty's accuracy fluctuated somewhat, though she averaged 90 percent correct. During the returning-to-baseline phase, the accuracy of both girls decreased. When the intervention was reapplied, the girls began to consistently turn in perfect papers.

Comment
This project demonstrates the effect feedback can have on performance when students "can" perform a behavior but choose not to do so. While immediate feedback is to be preferred over delayed feedback, sometimes teachers cannot manage to correct and return papers immediately. Bearing in mind the positive effects Lovitt (1973) noted when students correct their work the next day, teachers should not be unduly concerned about providing immediate feedback to students on every academic task they assign. For students who have a great deal of difficulty performing tasks, the more immediate the feedback, the better. For this reason teachers may want to enlist the aid of students and adult volunteers to correct papers.

Increasing Speed

In order to become proficient writers students must be able to generate ideas and translate them into sentences. In writing compositions, proper attention must also be paid to style, grammar and punctuation. The following project illustrates how a teacher was able to increase the number of words students wrote as well as to improve the quality of their writing.

Classroom Application
Increasing Rate of Words Written on Compositions
(Van Houten, R., Morrison, E., Jarvis, R., & McDonald, M., 1974)

Number of Students
The project was conducted in one second grade and two fifth grade classrooms. For the purpose of our example, we will present data for the 21 second graders who participated in the project.

Setting
Regular classroom

Target Behavior/Aim
Increase the rate at which students wrote words when asked to write a composition on a given topic.

Definition of Target Behavior
Each word in a sentence was counted unless a sentence was judged to be nonsensical or very repetitive. "A nonsensical sentence was defined as a random list of words not comprising a sentence and a repetitous sentence was defined as a sentence that immediately followed another in which all words were the same except for a noun" (p.548).

Materials

Prior to beginning the project, the second and fifth grade teachers made lists of composition topics which they judged to be of equal difficulty. Each day the teachers selected a topic randomly and assigned the students to write a composition on the topic chosen.

Observation System and Measurement Technique

Permanent product recording was used to measure the number of words students wrote during a ten-minute period. The average number of correct words per minute was charted for the class.

A graduate language student rated the quality of the pupils' compositions according to the following critera: (1) mechanical aspects, length, spelling, grammar and punctuation; (2) vocabulary, variety and word usage; (3) number of ideas; (4) development of ideas; and (5) internal consistency of the story" (p. 549). The graduate assistant was not aware that she was being asked to rate the students' papers as part of an experiment. Based on the previously mentioned criteria, the graduate student scored each student's compositions and assigned from zero to five points on each component for a total of twenty-five points per composition.

Procedures

During baseline the students were given ten minutes to write a composition on a topic chosen by the teacher. The students were not aware that their performance was being timed. The teacher told the students to try to write as many words as they could and to avoid writing repetitious sentences. No feedback was provided to the students during baseline.

On the first day of the intervention, the teacher called the students' attention to a chart on the board which showed the highest number of words each pupil had written on any previous composition. The students were told that they would be timed for ten minutes and the teacher encouraged them to try to beat their highest score. The teacher also told the students that "words that did not conform to good sentences and the repetitious use of sentences would not be counted" (p. 549). Examples of each type of sentence were provided.

After the ten-minute writing period, students were directed to correct their compositions using red pens. The students counted all words written and recorded their scores on the top of their pages. These counts were used to provide immediate feedback to students. The teacher actually scored and recorded their data. (Even though the students' scores were not used for recording purposes, the authors mentioned that the average agreement between pupil and teacher during both the intervention phases ranged from 80 percent to 95 percent). At lunchtime the teacher revised each student's new high point score, if necessary, and circled the scores of students who had exceeded their highest score. At the beginning of each writing period, the teacher told the student to look at the wall chart and see if they had beaten their previous top score.

During the return-to-baseline phase, the teacher told the class that they would no longer be timed but that they should continue to write as many sentences as they could. The teacher also reminded the students to try to avoid writing nonsensical or repetitious sentences.

The display chart was removed from the board and the students were told that they would no longer have to count their words and that their scores would no longer be placed on the chart. During this condition, students were timed for ten minutes although they were not aware that their performance was being timed.

When the intervention was reapplied, the procedures were the same as those previously described.

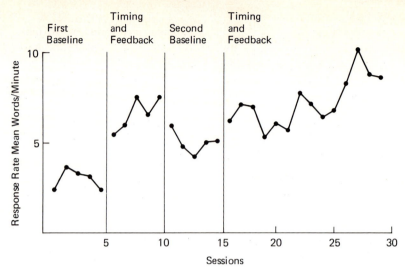

FIGURE 10–27 Number of words written per minute by a class of second-graders. (From R. Van Houten, E. Morrison, R. Jarvis, & M. McDonald, The effects of explicit timing and feedback on compositional response rate in elementary school children. *Journal of Applied Behavior Analysis*, 1974, *7*, p. 551. By permission of the publishers.)

Results

During baseline the students averaged about three words per minute as shown in Figure 10–27. When timing and feedback were originally introduced, the students' increased their writing rates. During the return-to-baseline phase when explicit timing and feedback were discontinued, the performance of the class decreased. When the intervention was reapplied, the pupils' scores continued to increase.

Comment

The authors noted that most students increased their writing rates during the intervention periods; however some students were effected more than others by the teaching technique. Quality ratings were also performed on the students' compositions. The mean ratings for the second-graders during Baseline 1, Intervention 1, Baseline 2 and Intervention 2 were: 6.4 (out of 25), 12.8, 10.1, and 12.7. The ratings agreed with the teacher's perception that the students' compositions were of a higher quality during the intervention periods.

This project demonstrates the effectiveness of a simple technique which teachers can use to increase their students' rates in writing compositions. Although the authors did not chart performance based on the students' counts, teachers might well do so and occasionally verify the accuracy of those counts by rescoring some of the students' assignments.

Summary

A number of teaching techniques have been presented to improve students' spelling, penmanship and writing skills. At one time some people questioned whether behaviors such as creative writing could even be taught. Research in this area has shown that it is possible to teach students to write creatively by reinforcing them for varying sentence beginnings, and for using different adjectives and adverbs (Maloney & Hopkins, 1973).

Very little emphasis to date has been placed on identifying techniques to improve students' generalization and maintenance of writing skills. For example we don't know whether certain cursive letters should be taught before others to enhance generalization or even if it makes a difference whether letters are taught in a given order. Similarly we don't know whether students who are required to spell words correctly for three days in a row necessarily maintain their accuracy better than students who move on to a new list once they score 100 percent. While specific techniques may be lacking to increase maintenance and generalization of writing skills, teachers can certainly begin to investigate techniques on their own. For example one could vary the order in which skills were taught or vary the number of days students are required to perform at criterion levels. By taking data on the effects of these procedures, teachers would be well on their way to identifying effective teaching techniques.

SUMMARY

Earlier in this chapter the authors stated that there really aren't any "special media or materials" or "special techniques" to improve academic performance. When you think about it, the basic instructional strategies recommended here have been used by good teachers for years. None require very much time to administer, nor are expensive materials necessary. On the contrary the teachers who conducted the academic projects used curriculum materials available in the classroom or developed their own materials based on sequences of skills they planned to teach. The reader might well ask, "What's so different about data-based instruction, if no special techniques or materials are used?" The answer is simply this—data-based instruction does not rely on the use of only certain techniques, rather it represents a strategy for dealing with social and academic behavior problems in a systematic way. Data-based instruction is far more than a collection of techniques which can be supported by research attesting to their effectiveness. It is a method which allows teachers to precisely measure behavior and evaluate the effects of techniques upon pupil performance. Our intent has not been to suggest that teachers should try to measure and record the behavior of all students in their class. Instead teachers should regard data-based instruction as a useful method to assist them in teaching students who have difficulty acquiring, generalizing, and maintaining social and academic skills.

SECTION 5

Mainstreaming Students with Physical and Sensory Impairments

Mainstreaming Students with Physical and Sensory Impairments

11

To this point the content of the book has focused on students with learning and behavior problems, students who have traditionally been labeled learning disabled, behavior disordered or educable mentally retarded. To be sure these students represent the vast majority of "special education" students who are being educated primarily in the regular classroom. There are, however, other groups of students who are increasingly integrated into regular education, including those who are visually impaired, hearing impaired and orthopedically impaired. These students are the subject of the present chapter, since they present unique instructional challenges to classroom teachers to whom they are assigned.

In discussing sensory and orthopedic problems of students, three terms must be distinguished: *impairment, disability,* and *handicap.* An *impairment* is a physical condition or limitation, such as reduced visual acuity or involuntary muscle contractions associated with spastic cerebral palsy. A *disability* refers to limited functioning resulting from an impairment. Thus, reduced vision might result in an adult not being able to drive a car, or spasticity might prevent a child from walking long distances without assistance. A *handicap* refers to educational, occupational or social effects of disabilities. Thus the visually impaired person might have limited opportunities to join adult clubs or attend social events because of the inability to drive, and the spastic child might be prevented from fully participating in school or scouting activities because of locomotive problems.

The distinction between *impairments, disabilities* and *handicaps* is important in our discussion, since educators often make handicaps out of impairments by the types of educational programs and facilities we offer. The expectations we have for students with sensory and physical impairments can turn physical problems into social problems. On the other hand many sensory and physical impairments can be overcome or sidestepped through proper teaching, educational planning and use of technology, so that disabling effects of certain conditions are minimized and increasing numbers of students can be educated appropriately in "normal" environments.

In this chapter information is presented concerning unique educa-

316

*Mainstreaming
Students with
Physical and
Sensory
Impairments*

tional characteristics of students with visual, hearing and orthopedic impairments. For each type of impairment, definitions and classification systems are described, educational implications of sensory and physical conditions are delineated, and suggestions for classroom teachers are presented. It must be pointed out that all of the techniques presented in Chapters 5 through 10 can and should be used with students who have sensory and physical impairments, since there is not a separate psychology of learning or teaching for these students. While occasional adjustments are necessary in content, teaching methodology, and ways of presenting and eliciting information from the student, students with sensory and physical impairments are much more *like* than different from nonimpaired students. Thus while the specialized information presented in this chapter can be helpful to teachers, it is not meant to overshadow the fact that students with impairments are first and foremost students, and should be taught as normally as possible.

VISUAL IMPAIRMENTS

Definition and Classification

Obviously students with visual impairments do not see as well as normal students. Unfortunately this statement provides us with no useful information. Vision is a complex human function, and there are a variety of ways in which visual performance can be impaired. Standard definitions generally cite three types of visual impairment.

1. *Visual acuity* may be limited, resulting in a person being able to see objects less clearly than the normal person;
2. *Field of vision* may be restricted, so that the angle at which one can see to each side is limited; and
3. *Color vision* is defective, resulting in an inability to distinguish among certain colors.

Of these three the one that will most often be encountered by the classroom teacher is limited visual acuity. Thus the remainder of the section will deal primarily with this type of visual impairment.

There are two approaches to defining visual impairment which are of interest here, the legal approach and the educational approach. Legal definitions are important because they are the most widely known and, to the general public, the most commonly accepted definitions. In legal terms, a person is "blind" whose vision in the *better eye, after correction,* is 20/200 or worse, while a "partially seeing" person has vision between 20/70 and 20/200 in the better eye, after correction. For example this means that using a standard measuring device, a person with 20/200 vision can see clearly at a distance of 20 feet what a normally seeing person can see clearly at 200 feet, while 20/70 vision indicates that the person sees at 20 feet what the normal person can see at 70 feet. Very few individuals cannot see at all, and the vast majority of legally blind persons have useful vision.

It should be noted that legal definitions of visual impairment are stated in terms of vision in the *better eye, after correction.* A person who loses one eye and has 20/20 vision in the other is not considered to be visually impaired, nor is the person for whom glasses brings visual acuity within normal limits.

A student with 20/200 vision or less in the better eye, after correction, is legally blind. Does this mean, as would be commonly assumed from use of the term "blind," that the child cannot see? For many years this assumption was made by educators for the blind, and legally blind students were taught to read *braille* and were given reading materials in braille. Since the early 1960's, however, the notion that educational decisions for students could be made on the basis of legal classifications of visual impairment has been put to rest. Using data collected in the annual census conducted by the American Printing House for the Blind, Jones (1961) reported that four out of five children with reported visual acuity of 20/200 (thus classified as legally blind) used print as their primary mode of reading, and large numbers of students with even worse visual acuity were reading print materials. This census has been repeated regularly over the last 20 years and, in general, the results indicate that increasing numbers of legally blind students are reading print rather than using braille. In the 1976 annual report of the American Printing House for the Blind, it was reported that nearly half of the legally blind students were reading large print, and less than one-fourth were relying on braille as their primary reading mode (Ward, 1979).

These studies, as well as increased attention to the benefits of *using* rather than preserving residual vision in children (Barraga, 1964), have led to an emphasis on *educational* rather than *legal* definitions of blindness. Legal definitions of blindness focus on deficits in students, while educational definitions stress "functional vision for educational purposes" (Ward, 1979, p. 338). The following *educational* definitions of the terms "blind" and "partially sighted" have been offered by Reynolds and Birch (1977):

> Educationally, children are considered to be blind when they must be taught to read by using braille, the Optacon, or other means that do not involve sight. Partially sighted students, for educational purposes, are those who have significant vision problems that require some special adjustments in instruction but, nevertheless, can be taught to read print of regular or large size. (p. 610)

Thus, for educational purposes, two students with the same level of visual acuity from a medical or legal point of view might be quite different in educational terms, with one reading braille and considered to be educationally blind, and the other reading large print and considered to be partially seeing. The emphasis in education of the visually impaired is to teach students to read print, if at all possible, for three primary reasons: (1) braille reading is slow and cumbersome; (2) braille materials are not easily and quickly available; and (3) reading print facilitates one's integration into normal school settings and the general society.

318

*Mainstreaming
Students with
Physical and
Sensory
Impairments*

It is important to note that students with visual impairments will not all have comparable types of vision problems. There are at least three different types of visual acuity problems which can be of concern to classroom teachers. First a student might have *myopia*, or "nearsightedness," in which near-point vision is sufficient but objects further away cannot be seen clearly. For this student reading might not present major problems, but playground activities or reading from the blackboard can be difficult. A second type of visual acuity problem is *hyperopia*, or "farsightedness," in which near vision is weak and distant vision is better. For these students extended periods of schoolwork demanding near-point vision can be fatiguing and difficult, and school learning problems can result. The third major type of vision problem in children, astigmatism, is an irregularity on the cornea or lens of the eye that distorts vision. Astigmatism is more diffuse in its effect and can result in limitations in both near vision and distance vision. Within limits each of these types of vision problems can be improved through use of corrective lenses, but for students with visual impairments, these corrections cannot bring vision into the "normal" range.

Students with moderate to severe visual impairments are usually identified at an early age, and classroom teachers do not play a role in initial referral and identification of the problem. Students with less serious difficulties, however, are often identified through the efforts of the school. Typically, in all school districts, periodic vision screenings are conducted to identify students who might have significant vision problems. The classroom teacher, however, cannot depend on these screening procedures to reliably identify all students whose vision might be defective and be interfering with school performance. Teachers must be observant in identifying students with possible vision problems and referring them for testing which goes beyond normal screening procedures. Calovini (undated) has provided the following list of behaviors which might signal existence of a vision problem:

Appearance
  Red rimmed eyelids
  Swollen eyelids
  Crust near lashes
  Frequent sties
  Red or watery eyes
  Eyes in constant motion

  Crosses eyes or one turning in and the other eye out
  Eyes that cross when the child is tired
  Eyes with pupils of different sizes

Behavior
  Blinks constantly
  Rubs eyes often
  Tends to have eyes crossed when reading
  Tries to brush away blur
  Seems overly sensitive to light
  Holds book too close or too far away when reading
  Frequently changes distance of book from near to far as he reads

  Reads only brief periods without stopping
  Shows reversal tendencies in reading
  Tries to guess words from quick recognition of a part of a word in easy reading material
  Tends to lose the place on the page
  Confuses o and a; e and c; n and m; h, n, and r; f and t
  Reads less well the longer he tries

Shuts or covers one eye when reading
Screws up face when reading
Frowns when trying to see distant objects
Thrusts head forward in order to see an object
Holds body tense when trying to distinguish distant objects
Becomes inattentive during reading lesson

Wants to play when he should read
Has short attention span when doing chalkboard, bulletin board or map work
Shows lack of interest during field trip discussion
Cries frequently
Becomes irritable over work
Has frequent temper tantrums (p.3)

Obviously, some of these behaviors (such as crying or temper tantrums) occurring in isolation would not lead one to suspect a vision problem. However if they consistently occur in combination with some of the vision-oriented behaviors listed, a referral for vision testing may be appropriate.

Educational Implications of Visual Impairment

Perhaps the best way to begin a section on educational implications of visual impairment is to describe some *noneffects* of limited vision. First visual impairment does not, of itself, result in lowered intelligence. Second with the exception of certain vision-based concepts, visual impairment does not adversely affect language development in children. Finally the social and emotional needs of visually impaired students are no different from other students of the same age.

While it is not possible to construct a "psychology of learning and development" for visually impaired students, a significant lack of visual skill can result in educational handicaps. Lowenfeld (1971) has pointed out that visual impairments can restrict the *range and variety* of experiences available to a student, as well as the student's mobility in the environment and the extent to which he/she controls the environment. Ward (1979) points out that a visual impairment can have educational implications in the following areas:

Cognitive Development—Restricted experience can result in difficulties in concept formation, language development, and vocabulary.

Motor Development—While motor development is essentially normal, difficulties in mobility can result in exclusion from family and school activities designed to build physical strength, ability, and stamina.

Emotional Development—While there are no emotional difficulties which could be tied directly to lack of vision, concerns and needs that sighted children have can be intensified when vision is limited, particularly for adolescents. Needs for independence, for respect and understanding, for mobility, for privacy, for feelings of accomplishments may seem at first more difficult to meet in the face of limited vision. (Ward, 1979, p. 347)

320

*Mainstreaming
Students with
Physical and
Sensory
Impairments*

None of the characteristics just listed will apply to all students with visual impairments. Factors such as degree of vision loss, age at onset, parental expectations and childrearing practices, and experiential background will all affect the cognitive, motor, emotional and social development of visually impaired students. The safest prediction to make is that visually impaired students whom we encounter in the schools will be as diverse as sighted ones and that "the similarities between visually handicapped children and so-called normal children outweigh the differences." (Ward, 1979, p. 346)

For students with moderate to severe visual impairments two educational implications are most important to discuss: (1) information input modes and (2) mobility. With regard to information input modes, as pointed out earlier, most visually impaired students can read normal print by bringing the print closer, by placing it in the range and position where it can be viewed, by magnifying it, or by having the size of the print enlarged. Also many visually impaired students and adults make considerable use of tape recorders, and learn to listen and comprehend at faster-than-normal rates.

For visually impaired students who do not learn to read print material, and for those with no useful vision, two primary options for reading a print format are available. The first and best known option is braille, a touch-print medium which uses embossed dots to stand for specific letters, numbers and contractions. Using a cell two dots wide and three dots high, each of the 63 possible dot combinations represents a letter, a number, a frequently used contraction or word, or a punctuation mark. The basic braille alphabet of letters and numbers is presented in Figure 11–1. Larger circles represent the location of the raised dots in the standard six-dot cell. Braille is read by touch, by moving the fingertips across the embossed dots in a left-to-right pattern.

Braille books are extremely oversized due to the space required to print braille characters and the thickness of pages. Also, braille reading rates are substantially slower than print reading rates, meaning that it takes more time to read a comparable quantity of material. Many blind students who read braille also use tape recorders and "talking books," which are records containing text, magazine and other book materials.

A second major mode by which blind students can acquire written information is through use of specialized equipment, most notably the *Optacon*. The term stands for "optical to tactile converter," and the Optacon is an electronic device which translates print into tactile sensations which are "imprinted" on the reader's index finger. Thus the reader can "feel" the print as it appears on the page. The Optacon is not a replacement for braille; rather, it allows blind individuals to read newspapers, bank statements and other print materials which are not typically available in braille.

In summary, for students with moderate or severe visual impairments, a classroom teacher should expect to encounter students using a variety of methods for learning written material. Most systems used by visually

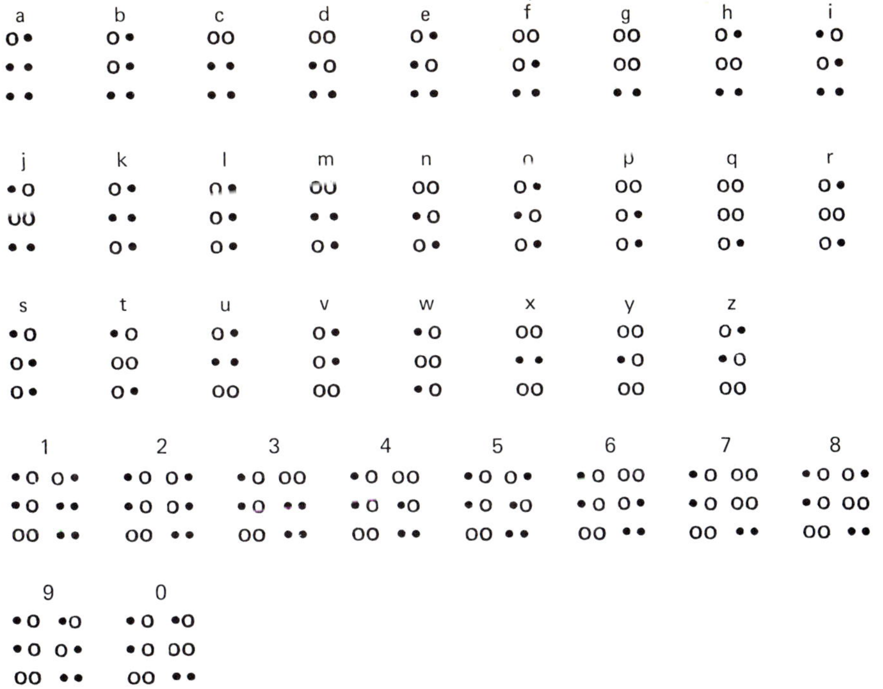

a b c d e f g h i

j k l m n o p q r

s t u v w x y z

1 2 3 4 5 6 7 8

9 0

FIGURE 11–1 The Braille Alphabet and Numbers. Reprinted from *Teaching exceptional children in all America's schools* by M. C. Reynolds and J. W. Birch, by permission of the Council for Exceptional Children.

impaired students tend to slow down reading rate and result in less efficient learning. It must be pointed out, however, that the *quality* of learning is not affected, only the rate at which information is acquired.

The second major limitation associated with visual impairment which will be discussed in this section is limited mobility. Students with very limited visual acuity will have trouble navigating in new environments, although many students will adjust very quickly if the physical arrangements are constant and predictable. A teacher should anticipate that a visually impaired student will need help in learning the layout of new surroundings, and on field trips or visits to unfamiliar parts of the school, a classmate can often be used as a sighted guide.

In general it is not considered the classroom teacher's responsibility to braille or tape record materials, or to teach orientation and mobility skills. Typically visually impaired students placed in regular classrooms will have available the services of a resource teacher and an orientation/mobility instructor to help in these areas. However it is important for classroom teachers to realize that the visual impairment might create the types of problems cited in this section. In the following section, suggestions will be provided to help classroom teachers to deal effectively with visually impaired students.

322

*Mainstreaming
Students with
Physical and
Sensory
Impairments*

Suggestions for the Teacher

The following list of guidelines for classroom teachers working with visually impaired students was compiled from various sources, and represents a composite listing of the suggestions deemed most important by these authors. Suggestions are provided under three general headings, *mobility, direct instruction* and *use of resource help.*

Mobility

1. The visually impaired student should be thoroughly introduced to the classroom and school space in which he or she will be working, with attention to permanent fixtures, movable fixtures and location of important rooms and places. The student must be helped to make a "cognitive map" of the school and classroom (Reynolds & Birch, 1977).
2. Arrangement of desks, work spaces and materials in the classroom should be kept as constant as possible, and the student made aware of any physical arrangement changes which occur (Calovini, undated).
3. Partially sighted students should be allowed to move about the room rather freely, to get a better view of teaching activities and demonstrations (Calovini, undated).
4. Blind students should be seated at the end of a table or row of desks to make mobility easier (Calovini, undated).
5. Emergency procedures should be established for fire alarms and other such occurrences. It is often helpful to designate a sighted student who will guide the visually impaired student to safety in case of emergency (Reynolds & Birch, 1977). Often the selection of a sighted guide will be simplified by observing friendship patterns or asking the visually impaired student to choose a helper.
6. The visually impaired student should, as much as possible, be expected to move about the classroom and school independently. Overprotection in matters of mobility must be avoided (Reynolds & Birch, 1977).
7. Allowances for vision problems should be made *only when absolutely necessary.* The student should be treated as normally as possible in all regards (Calovini, undated).

Direct Instruction

1. Sighted students in the classroom should be provided full and complete information concerning visual impairments, and should be prepared for the new student's arrival (Reynolds & Birch, 1977).
2. The curricular goals for visually impaired students should be the same as for sighted students. Teaching techniques should be changed only when absolutely necessary.
3. Lighting glare can be avoided by making sure that a student's desk does not directly face a major light source such as a window (Calovini, undated).
4. Teachers should be sensitive to the use of visual media such as the

blackboard and overhead projector, and should verbalize the material written (Reynolds & Birch, 1977).

5. The visually impaired student should be seated near the blackboard or the teacher when important demonstrations are done (Calovini, undated). This might require, as recommended above, a flexible seating arrangement.

6. The teacher should alternate close work involving near-point vision with work requiring distance vision, to avoid fatigue and loss of interest on the part of the student (Calovini, undated).

7. In some cases, such as art projects, the teacher should alter the task for the visually impaired student to insure successful performance.

8. Visually impaired students may use a variety of reading postures, and their faces may be very close to the reading material. This is not harmful to the student's eyes, and the teacher should encourage discovery of the *individual's* best posture for reading (M. Orlansky, 1977).

9. Large print materials should be used for reading only when absolutely necessary, since they slow down reading rate. It is preferable for visually impaired students to read regular print by either bringing the material closer to the eyes, or use of magnification devices (Calovini, undated).

10. The visually impaired student can often write best using dark-lined paper, and soft pencils or felt-tipped pens. (Calovini, undated)

11. At times allowing visually impaired students to work at the chalkboard helps them to write large and to have a change of pace from close desk work (M. Orlansky, 1977).

12. Teachers should encourage students to use typewriters in completing their work, particularly in cases in which typing skills are being or have been taught by the resource teacher (M. Orlansky, 1977).

13. Some blind students will engage in *"blindisms,"* which are repetitive, stereotypic movements such as rocking or playing with fingers. These generally decrease with age, and should not be a matter of undue concern for teachers (Reynolds & Birch, 1977). With the advice of the resource teacher, classroom teachers can devise ways of gently and consistently reminding students of blindisms and of praising students when they do not occur.

14. Visually impaired students should be taught to listen critically (Calovini, undated). Students with limited vision do *not* automatically develop good listening skills; they must be taught.

15. Many teachers, with or without visually impaired students in the room, have started tape libraries for the use of students who can learn best by both listening and reading. Some of the better readers in the room tape textbook material, and anyone who wants to can use the "listening center" for study purposes. This arrangement is, of course, very helpful for visually impaired students.

16. Visually impaired students should be provided with vigorous physical education activities and should, to the maximum extent possible, be encouraged to compete with sighted students (Reynolds & Birch, 1977).

17. When necessary visually impaired students should be allowed extra

324

*Mainstreaming
Students with
Physical and
Sensory
Impairments*

time to complete assignments. The allowance should be on completion time, not on quality of work to be done (Calovini, undated).

18. The teacher should generally expect the same standards of behavior and quality work completion expected of other students at a comparable skill level. Behavioral standards must be consistently enforced and work completion must be expected (Reynolds & Birch, 1977).

Use of Resource Personnel

1. Cooperation with the resource teacher is necessary in order to schedule resource sessions which do not interfere with important teaching periods in the classroom (Reynolds & Birch, 1977).
2. The resource teacher can acquire many specialized materials such as braille rulers, braille watches and raised maps, if aware that they are needed in the classroom. The regular teacher should communicate with the resource teacher concerning upcoming units and curricular emphases, so that such special needs can be anticipated.
3. The resource teacher should be a frequent visitor to the classroom and should be made to feel welcome by the classroom teacher.

HEARING IMPAIRMENTS

Definition and Classification

As with visual impairments the definition and classification of hearing impairments is a complex matter. Several factors must be taken into account in the definition itself. As with vision, students with comparable hearing losses will function and use their residual hearing quite differently. Thus this discussion is presented in *relative*, not absolute, terms.

Hearing loss is generally defined along two dimensions: (1) the *intensity* of sounds which can be heard is important and (2) the *frequency* of the sounds presented must be taken into account. *Intensity* of sounds is measured in decibels (dB), with zero decibels representing about the softest sound that can be heard by the normal human ear. Hearing losses are stated in dB levels, and the figures presented represent the lowest dB levels at which the individual could hear sounds presented. *Frequency* of sound waves which are presented must also be taken into consideration. Frequency is measured in number of cycles per second, and is expressed as hertz (Hz). For example, 1000 Hz means that the frequency of a sound is 1000 cycles per second. It is important to take frequency into account in defining hearing loss because speech sounds vary in their frequency, and because many hearing losses are not consistent across frequencies. In general the human ear can hear sounds at frequencies between 20 Hz and 20,000 Hz. However, nearly all *speech sounds* occur between 500 Hz and 2000 Hz, so this is the frequency range within which hearing impairments are usually defined (Lowenbraun and Scroggs, 1978).

In order to measure and define a hearing loss *audiometrically*, a pure-tone audiometric testing device is used. Sounds are presented to each ear independently, at varying decibel levels for varying frequencies, and the minimum decibel level at which the person can hear the sound is recorded for each frequency. For very young children or children who cannot readily signal when a sound is heard, testing procedures are available which measure automatic body changes in response to new sounds. For example minute changes in heart rate can be assessed to determine whether a subject is hearing a pure-tone sound.

There are two major types of hearing losses, each of which tends to produce different audiometric patterns. A *conductive hearing loss* involves some kind of blockage or malformation which prevents sound waves from reaching the nerve fibers which transmit the impulses to the brain. Conductive losses, which are sometimes amenable to correction by surgery, tend to produce comparable hearing loss across frequency levels. Conductive losses are also the most readily correctable through the use of hearing aids, since sounds are uniformly magnified by hearing aids at all frequency levels. A conductive hearing loss is shown in the *audiogram* presented in Figure 11–2.

The second type of hearing loss is a *sensori-neural* loss, which involves "damage to the sensors or nerve fibers which connect the inner ear to the

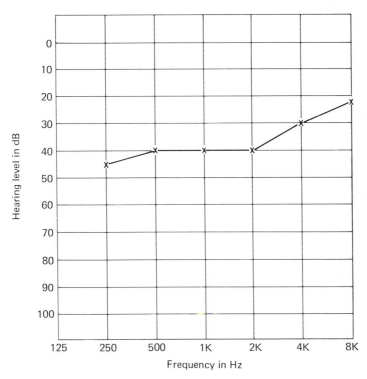

FIGURE 11–2 Pure tone audiogram of a child with a bilateral conductive hearing loss. From Lowenbraun, S., & Scroggs, C. The hearing handicapped. In N. G. Haring (Ed.), *Behavior of exceptional children.* Columbus: Charles E. Merrill Publishing Co., 1978.

326

*Mainstreaming
Students with
Physical and
Sensory
Impairments*

hearing center in the brain." (J. Orlansky, 1977, p. 14) Sensori-neural losses can often be traced to a number of hereditary and medical causes, and are generally irreversible. Also it is common for students with ***sensori-neural hearing losses*** to exhibit varying losses across speech frequencies. Thus a student might have a 50 dB loss at 500 Hz, and a 90 dB loss at 2000 Hz. A sensori-neural hearing loss is evident in the audiogram presented in Figure 11–3. This variability of hearing loss causes difficulty in the use of hearing aids to alleviate the hearing loss, since nerve damage can prevent conduction of sound no matter how much it is magnified. For this and other reasons, such as the distortion and pain which can occur with significant magnification of speech sounds, a few hearing impaired students cannot use hearing aids and must rely on other means of receiving auditory messages.

Thus far the focus of this section has been on audiometric definitions and classifications of hearing impairment. However as Reynolds and Birch (1977) point out, "it is not feasible to use the audiometric classification as a valid predictor of how an individual hearing impaired child might react to language instruction or achieve in school" (p. 532). As with visual impairment medical or legal classification must yield to educational classifi-

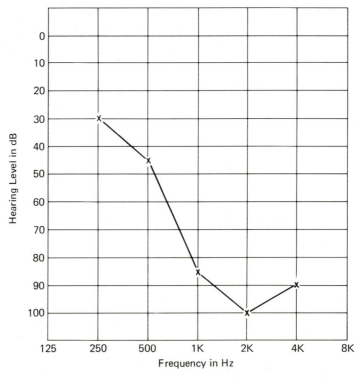

FIGURE 11–3 Pure tone audiogram of a child with a bilateral sensori-neural hearing loss that is more severe in the higher frequencies. From Lowenbraun, S., & Scroggs, C. The hearing handicapped. In N. G. Haring (Ed.), *Behavior of exceptional children.* Columbus: Charles E. Merrill Publishing Co., 1978.

cation. Hearing impairments are classified educationally in terms of *language learning*, since language development is the primary restriction associated with hearing loss.

Reynolds and Birch (1977) provide the following educational classification of hearing impairment:

> ... children with little or no hearing in the first or second years do not learn language in the natural, informal way most children do. They can be regarded as educationally deaf. The hard of hearing children are those who have significant hearing losses but who learn language in the usual way, though in some instances imperfectly. (P. 532)

Implied in this classification is a distinction between ***prelingual deafness***, which occurs at birth or at an early age, before language or speech is developed, and ***postlingual deafness***, which occurs following the development of speech and language. The age of onset of hearing impairments is important, since it generally makes a difference in the language and conceptual framework from which a student will operate.

As with visual impairment virtually all cases of moderate to severe hearing loss are discovered prior to the time a student reaches school age, and the classroom teacher will be asked to accept into the room a student who has already been identified and provided with substantial special education services. Also akin to visual impairment is the fact that some mild hearing losses are first noticed and reported by classroom teachers. J. Orlansky (1977) lists the following classroom behaviors which might be indicative of a hearing problem:

1. Difficulty following directions
2. Turning head to one side to hear better
3. Not paying attention
4. Hesitancy to participate in large groups, especially where a lot of talking takes place
5. Discrepancy between observed ability of child and test scores
6. Colds accompanied by earaches
7. Problems in understanding speech after cold subsides
8. Stubborn withdrawn behavior used ... to project feelings of insecurity or isolation. (pp. 86–92)

Observation of a combination of these factors in a given student can be sufficient cause for a teacher to refer the student for hearing testing.

Educational Implications of Hearing Impairment

Birch (1975) cites five factors which are the major determiners of educational effects of hearing loss:

1. The nature of the hearing defect, particularly whether the loss is in the range of speech frequencies
2. The degree of the hearing loss, since hearing aids are more helpful with mild hearing impairments

3. Age at onset of the hearing loss, since early deafness has a profound effect on language and speech learning
4. The hearing impaired student's intelligence, which is uncommonly difficult to assess, but which has a significant effect on the youngster's learning of language, speech and abstract thinking
5. The nature and amount of stimulation provided, since early, orderly and regular stimulation of language comprehension and communication can minimize the effects of hearing impairments and can maximize the constructive impact of special education. (Birch, 1975, p. 14)

Without doubt the most profound and pervasive effect of a moderate to severe hearing impairment is in the closely related areas of language and speech development. Language is developed orally, and in the preschool years, practically all communication takes place in the oral mode. Language is a system which involves both receiving and sending messages of an abstract nature, and both types of language activity are affected by a hearing loss.

With regard to receiving information, infancy and early childhood are periods of phenomenal conceptual growth. The young child learns to identify many objects, actions and feelings, and also learns that there are abstract labels, or words, which describe or "stand for" all of these things. Furthermore these words are strung together according to a complex set of rules which are mostly learned by the time a child reaches school. As Hatten (1979) points out, "luckily, the newborn infant has not been told how complex this task is and so proceeds to conquer the complexities of the language and the speech production process in a few short years" (p. 238). However, for a hearing impaired child, all the complexities of the process are apparent, and lack of the normal reception mode serves as a major hindrance to language and concept development.

Somewhat related to the receptive language problems of hearing impaired children are the difficulties in developing good expressive language, or speech. The young child learns to speak by a process of spontaneous babbling and vocal experimentation, hearing others and gradually approximating speech sounds. Of primary importance in this learning process are aural feedback on the child's own vocalizations and the ability to hear the speech of others. Limitations in both of these abilities make speech development for young hearing impaired children a difficult process.

The two primary alternatives to "hearing" the speech of others which have been developed for use by deaf individuals are *speech reading* and *sign language*. Speechreading has the advantage of allowing a deaf person to understand another person's speech by reading sounds from the movement of the other person's lips, tongue and face, so the speaker needs to know no special code or communication system. However as J. Orlansky (1977) points out, speechreading is not an exact process since many sounds have the same visual appearance and a number of sounds cannot be seen at all. The efficient speechreader sees only about 20 percent of what would be heard (Jeffers & Barley, 1971), and fills in many sounds and words through the use of contextual clues. Thus the level of concept development as discussed earlier in this section is a factor in determining the success a student has in learning speechreading skills.

As mentioned earlier the second popular communication alternative for the hearing impaired is the use of one of several available forms of manual communication, or "sign language." Signing and *fingerspelling* allow the deaf individual to both receive and send verbal messages through a system which uses gestures along with hand and finger movements. Several signing systems are currently in use in the United States, which means that not all deaf Americans are using the same language. Some use American Sign Language, also known as Ameslan or ASL; others use Manual English, and still others use Signing Exact English. There are definite and pronounced differences between these systems, with Signing Exact English bearing the closest resemblance to the syntax of spoken language. The least ambiguous manual communication method is finger-spelling, in which a unique hand position represents each letter and number, and words and sentences are spelled out a letter at a time. Practically all signing systems use fingerspelling for unfamiliar words or words for which signs are not available. The manual alphabet is presented in Figure 11–4.

For many years debate has raged among educators of the deaf concerning the use of manual systems of communication. "Oralists" have argued that manual communication separates the deaf person from the hearing world, and that allowing deaf students to sign will dampen their enthusiasm for the difficult task of learning speech and speechreading.

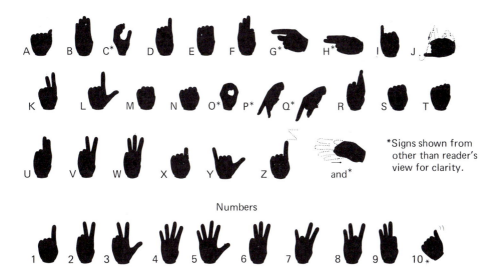

*Signs shown from other than reader's view for clarity.

Numbers

FIGURE 11–4 The American Manual Alphabet. (Used by permission. Copyright © 1976, Kathryn A. Licht.)

330

*Mainstreaming
Students with
Physical and
Sensory
Impairments*

Advocates of use of manual systems have stressed that conceptual development is critical for deaf children, and that early use of manual communication methods allows the student to acquire more information about the world than can be acquired through oral methods. While the debate still lingers, increasing numbers of deaf educators are using a "total communication" approach which combines oral methods with use of manual communication. The total communication approach has been summarized as follows by Lowenbraun and Scroggs (1978):

> Advocates of this approach believe that any and all means of communicating with a hearing impaired child should be used as early as possible. The goal is not to establish a specific language system but to establish basic communication pathways as quickly and efficiently as possible (p. 310).

The speech and language problems of hearing impaired students which have been described above have important educational implications. First, hearing impaired students tend to lag behind their hearing age-peers in academic achievement, with the difference greater for deaf than for hard-of-hearing children. Second, deficits in receptive and expressive language can produce a social isolation in which the hearing impaired individual is "alone in a crowd." Finally, as with the visually impaired, students with hearing losses can be restricted in their range and variety of experiences through the neglect or overprotection of the people around them.

All of these factors would seem to indicate that hearing impaired students have trouble adjusting to and succeeding in regular classroom settings. What is not taken into account in reaching this conclusion is that the range of individual differences among hearing impaired students is greater than the typical differences between students with and without hearing losses. There are large numbers of hearing impaired students who are excellent candidates for mainstreaming, and many deaf and hard-of-hearing students have been very successful participants in regular classroom activities. J. Orlansky (1977) points out that the hearing impaired students most apt to be considered for mainstreaming are those who have well developed speechreading, speech and language skills. Reynolds and Birch (1977) add that mainstreamed students should have academic skills comparable to at least some of their hearing peers in the regular class. The following section provides suggestions for classroom teachers in working with mainstreamed hearing impaired pupils.

Suggestions for the Teacher

Several lists of helpful guidelines for classroom teachers in working with hearing impaired students are available and the following represents a composite listing taken from three sources and the experiences of the authors. Suggestions are provided under three general hearings, *direct instruction, special equipment,* and *use of resource help.*

1. Hearing students in the class should be briefed on the arrival of a hearing impaired student, and all of their questions answered fully and directly (Reynolds & Birch, 1977).
2. Hearing impaired students should be seated near the teacher, and near the center of desk and table arrangements (J. Orlansky, 1977).
3. To the maximum extent possible, the teacher should maintain face-to-face contact with the students. The teacher should not talk when facing away from the student, and the student should be allowed to move around the room to get a better view of speakers' faces (Reynolds & Birch, 1977).
4. The teacher should talk to the hearing impaired student in complete sentences, avoiding single-word phrases and incorrect grammatic structures (J. Orlansky, 1977).
5. The teacher should speak to the student as much as possible, avoiding touching, tapping on the shoulder, and the like, to get the student's attention (Reynolds & Birch, 1977).
6. The teacher should use a natural, normal talking voice and use natural gestures, without exaggerating hand, arm or lip movements (Reynolds & Birch, 1977).
7. When the hearing impaired student is expected to speechread, the speaker should avoid standing in front of windows or other sources of direct light, since this shadows the face and makes speechreading difficult (Lowenbraun & Scroggs, 1978).
8. When talking about objects in the room, it is helpful to locate the object through pointing, touching or nodding (J. Orlansky, 1977).
9. Pictures and diagrams should be used whenever possible, and key words, outlines and assignments should be written on the chalkboard or an overhead projector (Reynolds & Birch, 1977).
10. Teachers should not hesitate to have hearing impaired students make oral reports in class, on topics of knowledge and interest to the student (Reynolds & Birch, 1977).
11. The level of work expected of a hearing impaired student must be closely monitored, since the student might be functioning at a lower academic level than most classmates, particularly in the language arts subjects (Reynolds & Birch, 1977). It is important to remember that academic problems of hearing impaired students are most often related to *language deficits,* not limited intelligence.
12. When hearing students are speaking to hearing impaired students, encourage them to speak naturally but clearly, and to maintain face-to-face contact (Reynolds & Birch, 1977).
13. It is helpful to "arrange" social interactions between a hearing impaired student and other students in the room through instructional groupings, group projects, games and organized activities.
14. The hearing impaired student should be "clued in" to slang words and phrases which are apt to be used by other students in the room (Reynolds & Birch, 1977).

332

*Mainstreaming
Students with
Physical and
Sensory
Impairments*

15. It is often helpful for hearing students to make extra copies of class notes for hearing impaired students, since the student with a hearing loss cannot be expected to write notes and watch the teacher's face simultaneously (J. Orlansky, 1977).

16. Tests should be given to hearing impaired students in formats and with time limits that allow the student to demonstrate knowledge without being unfairly penalized by the hearing loss.

17. For students who use sign language, the hearing students in the class are often interested in learning to sign. Sometimes a course in signing can be offered by a teacher of the hearing impaired.

18. For students who have interpreters, the seating arrangement should be such that the interpreter is near the hearing impaired student in full view (J. Orlansky, 1977).

19. Hearing impaired students should not be excluded from music and other school activities which seem to assume normal hearing (J. Orlansky, 1977).

20. Driver education is an appropriate school subject for hearing impaired students, since "hearing impaired people are usually very attentive and cautious drivers" (J. Orlansky, 1977).

21. Teachers should note audible alarm signals in the school, such as fire alarms and timers, and arrange methods by which hearing impaired students are made aware of the alarms when they sound (J. Orlansky, 1977).

22. For students with hearing aids, the general noise level in the room should be kept down as much as possible, since the hearing aid picks up *all* sounds, and background noises can be very distracting (Reynolds & Birch, 1977).

23. Because hearing impaired students are often not aware of noise levels, they must sometimes be reminded not to talk too loudly or create needless noise (Reynolds & Birch, 1977).

24. The teacher should occasionally direct questions to the hearing impaired student, to assure that he or she is attending to class presentations (Reynolds & Birch, 1977).

25. The same behavioral and work completion standards which are expected of all students should be expected of hearing impaired students (J. Orlansky, 1977).

Special Equipment

1. The teacher should become familiar with special equipment used by hearing impaired students, particularly hearing aids, and should help assure that the student is responsible in caring for the equipment. (Lowenbraun and Scroggs, 1978) Explanations of specific equipment can be obtained from a hearing specialist in the school system or from the student's parents.

2. The teacher should occasionally check the hearing aid, to assure that it is working properly (Reynolds & Birch, 1977).

3. It is often necessary to encourage the student to wear the hearing aid

and to keep it turned on, since students will sometimes choose to "tune out" the teacher and the classroom.

Use of Resource Help

1. It is a good idea to arrange to visit a teacher of the hearing impaired to observe techniques which might be used in the classroom (Reynolds & Birch, 1977).
2. If a resource person is working for part of the day with a hearing impaired student, it is important to coordinate activities so that instruction in the resource room complements instruction in the regular classroom.
3. Resource teachers can often be very helpful in obtaining captioned films and other specialized materials for use with hearing impaired students. By sharing lesson plans and upcoming instructional areas with the resource personnel, a classroom teacher can often obtain support materials which otherwise would not have been available.

ORTHOPEDIC AND OTHER HEALTH IMPAIRMENTS

Definition and Classification

Orthopedic and other health impairment as used in this chapter refers to both physical and health conditions which might create obstacles to normal functioning in a standard school or classroom. Hart (1979) points out that medical advances over the last twenty years as well as increases in accessibility of schools and classrooms have led to a change in populations of orthopedically impaired students served in special education. Students with crippling conditions which involve only the extremities (arms and legs) are less often regarded as candidates for special education, and students with more complex physical problems are, in many school districts, being integrated into regular classrooms to the maximum extent possible.

While the full range of medical conditions associated with orthopedic and health impairments cannot and should not be discussed in this chapter, the authors will present overview information on the following conditions which classroom teachers are apt to see in students integrated into the regular class setting: cerebral palsy, spina bifida, muscular dystrophy, sickle cell anemia and epilepsy. After descriptions of the conditions are given, we will discuss the inappropriateness of using these conditions as a basis for grouping students for educational purposes.

Cerebral palsy is "a neuromuscular disability that results from injury to the brain before, during, and after birth" (Hart, 1979, p. 205). Students with cerebral palsy have difficulty with certain motor movements, which "may vary from a mild involvement where walking, self-help, and communication are all affected, to a severe involvement where there is almost total incapacity" (Hart, 1979, p. 205). The majority of cases of cerebral palsy are mild, and these students have little or no difficulty succeeding in

334

*Mainstreaming
Students with
Physical and
Sensory
Impairments*

regular classroom settings. They may appear awkward or clumsy, or talk more slowly than other children, but when the teacher and classmates understand the condition, essentially normal functioning is possible. Students with moderate cerebral palsy are also often placed in regular classrooms, since the medical condition itself usually has no direct effect on the learning capabilities of the student. The three types of cerebral palsy which teachers are most likely to encounter are *spasticity*, which results in muscle tightness and difficulty in movement of limbs; *athetosis*, which involves uncontrollable rhythmic movement in the muscles; and *ataxia*, which entails muscular incoordination and lack of balance.

Spina bifida is a condition in which the spinal column is not fully developed and there is an opening which does not allow complete protection of the spinal cord. When there is no displacement or deformity of the spinal cord, the child encounters few problems. However if part of the spinal cord or spinal nerve roots protrude through the opening, orthopedic impairments can result. Some youngsters with spina bifida will miss considerable school because of operations, thus resulting in educational handicaps. Also spina bifida often produces motor impairments, as well as lack of bowel and bladder control. Many students manage well with bags for urine collection and handle these needs independently.

Muscular dystrophy is a progressive muscular disease which results in increasing muscle weakness and incoordination as students grow older. There are often periods of remission, but they are temporary and it can be expected that students with muscular dystrophy will gradually lose their ability to walk and perform other physical functions. Students who contract muscular dystrophy during the first few years of life have a limited life span, usually less than twenty years.

Sickle cell anemia is a genetic disorder which results in distortion and malfunction of the red blood cells, reducing the body's supply of oxygen and resulting in episodes of severe pain. During *sickle cell crises*, the pain is often "so severe that it cannot be relieved even when the child is in the hospital under pain-relieving drugs" (Hart, 1979, p. 209). The educational implications of sickle cell anemia relate to frequency of hospitalization and school absence, as well as occasional debilitating effects of the disease.

Epilepsy is a disorder of the brain which results in occasional periods of abnormal changes in electrical brain potentials, and subsequent *seizures*. During *petit mal seizures* there is a momentary loss of consciousness which is often either not noticeable or mistaken for a lapse of attention. *Grand mal seizures* involve a more extended loss of consciousness, accompanied by convulsive movements which can last several minutes. Many grand mal seizures are preceded by an *aura*, a warning sign which varies from one individual to another. Following the seizure the individual is drowsy and does not remember the seizure episode. Seizure patterns vary greatly. Some students will have a single seizure without a reoccurrence, others will have recurring seizures of varying frequency. Some seizures are associated with specific events, such as illness or a high fever, and in these cases the condition is not called epilepsy. Epilepsy refers to seizures of unknown origin and a pattern of recurrence. Medication is usually helpful in controlling seizures and, except for extreme circumstances, epilepsy itself should not be sufficient reason to remove a student from the regular education environment.

The conditions described above are all *medical* in nature, and while certain educational implications might be present, *none of these conditions should serve as a determiner of educational placement.* A physical impairment has nothing to do with how or how well a student learns, and special education groupings of orthopedically impaired students produce a far greater variance of ability and skill levels than is found in any regular classroom. This is the topic which forms the nucleus of the following section.

Educational Implications of Orthopedic Impairments

While orthopedic and health impairments do create situations to which classroom teachers must respond in a unique manner, the physical condition itself is seldom sufficient justification to remove a student from regular education. As Reynolds and Birch (1977) point out:

> From the point of view of instructional needs there is no justification for assembling children with crippling and health impairments into one group for schooling. Actually, no more heterogeneous array of pupils could be found, educationally speaking … What brought such youngsters together initially in special classes were noneducational considerations. First, many needed to be transported if they were to attend school at all. It was more convenient and economical to transport them all to one central place. Second, many required frequent and intensive occupational, physical, and speech therapy, plus medical consultation and nursing and dietary supervision. It proved more feasible to group those therapies and related health services in one place and to bring the pupils to them. Third, many of the pupils could not manage stairs and many used mobility aids such as crutches, walkers, and wheelchairs. To design and construct one school building to accommodate those factors seemed far less a problem than to make all existing and future school buildings barrier free." (pp. 402–404).

Special groupings of orthopedically impaired students for convenience and clustering purposes actually created many educational disadvantages, in which students with moderate or severe mental retardation were being educated in classrooms with bright students who had physical problems. Certainly mental retardation can accompany cerebral palsy or other orthopedic impairments, but in those cases the educational implications of moderate or severe retardation far outweigh the educational implications of the physical condition.

There are certain functional problems associated with orthopedic and health impairments which can have an effect on a student's educational opportunities. Perhaps the four most important of these problem areas are communication, mobility, self-help and social interaction. Each of these will be discussed separately.

Many students with orthopedic impairments have associated speech problems, and the combination of poor manual dexterity and unintelligible

336

*Mainstreaming
Students with
Physical and
Sensory
Impairments*

speech can often result in a student being able to share only a small part of his or her knowledge. For these students, receptive language is much better than expressive language, and we often assume they know less than they do. There are examples of cerebral palsied students communicating for the first time via specially equipped typewriters, and sending grammatically and syntactically complex messages when it was assumed they had little or no language understanding or skill. When students cannot communicate verbally or in writing, alternative communication systems are available such as electric typewriters or "communication boards," with which students can send messages by locating letters and common words on the board. In other words *communication* is not impaired if we can find alternate ways to communicate, and this is often done with the only limitation being the speed with which the message is sent.

Mobility in the classroom and school is also a common barrier to effective school participation by orthopedically impaired students. Generally students' means of mobility are determined by the time they get to school, and it is the task of the teachers and school personnel to adapt the school situation so that locomotion is possible. Often only experience can determine how a classroom should be arranged to accommodate a student in a wheelchair, and not all problems of mobility need to be solved before an orthopedically impaired student arrives at school. Initial flexibility is probably the most important factor in assuring that the school setting successfully adapts to the mobility patterns of the student.

Many physically impaired students do not have complete control over normal self-help activities such as toileting, dressing and eating. The students themselves must learn to help others know how to help them in certain situations, and teachers must guard against overprotecting these students. The goal should always be maximum independence in activities, and a dependent relationship with teacher and/or peers should be avoided. Although self-help limitations do not have direct educational implications, they can consume valuable learning and teaching time if ways of handling given situations are not routinized. Information from parents and/or school specialists can be helpful.

Because of the three problem areas just described, as well as a tendency for many able-bodied individuals to avoid contact with persons with physical limitations, many orthopedically impaired students experience social isolation in school and society in general. Sometimes it takes longer to carry on a conversation with a student with a speech problem, and many youngsters are not willing to take the time. Sometimes the presence of a physical handicap creates discomfort in the other person, and students often express a frustration in not knowing what to say to a physically impaired peer. Without some teacher attention an orthopedically impaired student can be an isolate in the classroom. On the other hand it is the experience of the authors that with a little encouragement, solid friendships can be and are formed between physically impaired students and their able-bodied peers.

These, then, are some *possible* educational implications of orthopedic impairment. As indicated throughout this discussion, these problems can usually be overcome with proper planning and use of adaptive equipment, and need not result in educational handicaps. In the following section, guidelines will be presented to assist teachers in preparing to work with orthopedically impaired students.

Suggestions for Teachers

Suggestions for classroom teachers will be presented in six categories: instruction, communication, mobility, self-help, social development and use of resource help. Because of the complexity and broad array of possible orthopedic and health impairments, some of the suggestions are specific to certain conditions and others are general and apply to most or all students with physical limitations.

Instruction

1. Regular class peers should be prepared for the integration of an orthopedically impaired student, using discussion sessions with complete answers provided to all questions. Students should be taught that certain behaviors such as drooling and slurred speech are a result of the physical impairment, not a sign of mental subnormality.
2. The orthopedically impaired student should be expected to learn standard curriculum material, with adaptations in teaching and response modes (Reynolds & Birch, 1977).
3. Orthopedically impaired students should be excused from class activities only when absolutely necessary. "Unless otherwise recommended, give students the opportunity to do what their peers do even though they might walk awkwardly, fall often, or seem uncoordinated" (Bigge & Sirvis, 1978, p. 384).

Communication

1. With students who have unintelligible speech, it should be assumed that they know more than they are telling you (Bigge & Sirvis, 1978). Major curriculum modifications should not be made for these students solely on the basis of formal or informal test results.
2. The teacher should gain a thorough understanding of all facets of the student's communication system, and should work with the resource teacher in seeking additional needed communication aids. Often explaining the classroom situation to a resource teacher will generate ideas for useful communication devices.
3. The teacher should not be hesitant to ask a student with poor speech to repeat a statement, or to paraphrase a statement to see if it was heard correctly (Bigge & Sirvis, 1978). It is not helpful to a student to pretend a message was understood if it was not.
4. Since orthopedically impaired students sometimes have labored speech, or use alternate communication systems, they should be given adequate time to respond to questions and instructions (Bigge & Sirvis, 1978).

338

*Mainstreaming
Students with
Physical and
Sensory
Impairments*

5. Test formats should be varied to allow the physically impaired student ample opportunity to demonstrate his or her knowledge. A popular approach to special testing situations is to allow peers to administer tests orally, or to use volunteers, resource teachers or aides to record the student's responses to test questions.

Mobility

1. The teacher should be flexible with classroom arrangements, and assume that the initial arrangement will need to be changed once the student has been in the room for a while. Experimentation is the best way to assure that a proper physical setting is attained.
2. Class schedules for orthopedically impaired students should be individually arranged to assure that room changes, floor changes, and the like are possible within the time limitations.
3. At times when speedy transitions are necessary, or in special cases such as field trips, help from peers or volunteers should be arranged to assure successful participation by orthopedically impaired students.

Self-help

1. Students should be encouraged to be as independent as possible in completing all self-help activities (Bigge & Sirvis, 1978).
2. Parents, resource teachers and the students themselves should be consulted to assure that self-help activities are handled in the classroom in a fashion similar to procedures used in other settings.
3. Other students in the room should be taught to ask before they assume that physical assistance is needed.
4. In situations in which assistance is needed, it should be routinized as to who helps, in what circumstances and to what extent.
5. In all cases in which physical assistance is provided, care should be taken to assure that an atmosphere of dependence and overprotection is not provided. Whenever possible assistance should be provided in a teaching format, with the eventual aim being independent performance.
6. The teacher should determine from parents and resource personnel whether special safety precautions or activity restrictions are necessary. In general students should be expected to monitor their own behavior in this regard (Bigge & Sirvis, 1978).

Social Development

1. The teacher should encourage peer relationships and support the orthopedically impaired student in attempts to initiate peer interaction. Usually the teacher is aware of certain students in the room who are more likely "friendship candidates" than others and, where possible, these relationships should be facilitated.
2. Orthopedically impaired students should be included in group learning situations, and be given opportunities to participate to the fullest extent

possible. For students with communication or mobility problems, this might involve asking direct, short-answer questions or providing physical assistance (Bigge & Sirvis, 1978).

3. Teachers should include orthopedically impaired students in small groups formed to do class projects or plan class activities.
4. If an epileptic student has a grand mal seizure at school, the teacher should react calmly, remove surrounding furniture and other dangerous objects, turn the student's head to the side, and let the seizure run its course. No objects should be placed in the student's mouth. After the seizure the student should rest for a while before returning to class activities. However the rest period should be only long enough to regain orientation and teaching should go on as normal. Often with students who have auras, the seizure will be predicted and arrangements can be made. This is a brief period of time, however, and an aura is helpful only if preplanning has been done. It is important to discuss seizures with other students in the class and to explain that they are not harmful to the student and are not typically indicative of more serious problems. For students who have recurrent grand mal seizures, an extra set of clothing should be kept on hand, since urination or defecation sometimes occurs during a seizure.

Use of Resource Help

1. It is important for the classroom teacher to identify times when extra hands will be needed in the classroom, such as when tests are being given or special projects are being done. At these times volunteers, aides and resource teachers should be requested to provide the necessary extra help.
2. It is important to coordinate scheduling for orthopedically impaired students, who often receive supportive services such as physical therapy during school hours. Teachers should work cooperatively with support personnel in establishing these schedules, and should assure that students are not missing key instructional sessions in the classroom, such as reading or math, on a regular basis.
3. Resource teachers, physical therapists and occupational therapists can be of substantial help in locating or creating adaptive equipment which can be useful to a student in a regular classroom. When a classroom teacher encounters a problem for which current equipment and techniques are not working, these persons should be contacted for ideas and assistance.

CONCLUSION

This chapter has discussed children with visual, hearing and orthopedic impairments, with a focus on how they can be helped to succeed in the regular classroom. It should be noted that in each section on suggestions

340

*Mainstreaming
Students with
Physical and
Sensory
Impairments*

for teachers, a subsection was titled, "Use of Resource Help." It is our belief that growing numbers of special education students should be integrated into regular class settings, and that when such integration occurs, the role of the special educator changes. In addition to teaching students, special educators must act as resource persons to classroom teachers. Further, classroom teachers should expect this resource help in carrying out many of the suggestions listed in this chapter. The authors believe that education is entering a new era in which regular and special educators are expected to pool their talents and work *together* to educate students. This is an exciting prospect. Developments in this direction will be of substantial benefit to both students and teachers. In this book we have attempted to quicken the pace of this movement, by communicating with regular classroom teachers. No one, regular or special, should do the job alone. All must continue to learn to work together.

GLOSSARY

Glossary

Activity reinforcer A preferred classroom activity which follows a behavior and results in increasing the behavior.

Assessment A process in which a student's performance is measured for the purpose of making an educational decision.

Astigmatism Irregular curvature of the cornea or lens which results in blurred or distorted vision.

Audiogram A standard graph which provides a visual depiction of hearing ability at varying sound frequencies.

Automatic recording Use of a mechanical apparatus to record a student's responses as they occur.

Baseline data Student performance measures collected prior to intervention, to establish a standard for determining student progress.

Behavior disorder A category of special education services intended for students who consistently exhibit school behavior which is considered by others to be inappropriate or unacceptable.

Blindism Repetitive, stereotypic movements, such as rocking or playing with fingers, sometimes exhibited by visually impaired students.

Braille A touch system of reading and writing which uses patterns of embossed dots in a six-dot cell to stand for specific letters, numbers and contractions.

Cerebral palsy Neuromuscular impairment resulting from brain injury before, during or after birth; may or may not be associated with learning problems.

Chart A visual representation of student performance data on targeted academic and/or social behaviors.

Conductive hearing loss A blockage or malformation in the outer or middle ear which prevents sound waves from reaching the inner ear nerve fibers which transmit the impulses to the brain.

Contingency contract A written agreement specifying desired behavior and consequences for behavior, made between a teacher/parent and a student.

Contingent observation A procedure in which a student is placed a few feet away from others contingent on inappropriate behavior, thus being able to observe but not participate in the reinforcing activity.

Continuous recording A recording system in which one attempts to write down all of the behaviors exhibited by a student within a certain period of time.

Criterion-referenced test Test designed to measure a student's ability to perform a particular set of skills with reference to a stated level of performance, or criterion.

Curriculum-based assessment (CBA) Assessment based on direct and frequent measures of a student's performance, on a series of sequentially arranged objectives which are derived from those contained in the curriculum used in the regular classroom.

Data-based instruction (DBI) Instruction based on systematic and continuous measurement of student progress toward specific instructional aims.

Demonstration The act of "showing" a student how to perform a behavior.

Diagnosis Identification of conditions which are thought to affect a student's learning and/or social behavior, often based in large part on formalized evaluation procedures.

Disability Limited functioning resulting from an impairment.

Discrimination training Teaching students to respond in a particular way in the presence of certain stimuli, and not to respond in that way when those stimuli are absent.

Drill Repetition of a task to increase a student's proficiency in performing the task.

Due process procedures Specified procedures for guaranteeing informed consent and resolving disputes between parents and school personnel regarding provision of special education services for individual children.

Duration recording Recording procedures designed to measure the amount of time a student engages in a behavior.

Edible reinforcer Preferred food which is given contingent on appropriate behavior, and which results in increasing the appropriate behavior.

Educable mental retardation A category of special education services designed to serve students who exhibit school learning and behavior problems, and who perform poorly on tests of general intelligence and adaptive behavior.

Epilepsy A disorder of the brain which results in occasional periods of abnormal changes in electrical brain potential, and subsequent seizures.

Event recording Data collection procedures designed to count the frequency of discrete behaviors as they occur over a specified period of time.

Extinction An instructional procedure in which the reinforcement for a previously reinforced inappropriate behavior is discontinued.

Fading Gradual withdrawal of prompts or cues, intended to produce independent performance.

Fingerspelling A manual communication method in which a unique hand position represents each letter and number, and words and sentences are spelled out a letter at a time; often used in combination with sign language.

Generalization Application of learned behavior to other settings and skills.

Group contingency An instructional procedure in which individual reinforcement is contingent on group performance.

Handicap Educational, occupational or social limitations associated with disabilities.

Hearing impairment A physical condition which limits effective use of the auditory mechanism, and which may result in disability or handicap.

Hyperopia Farsightedness; a visual impairment in which near vision is poor and distant vision is better.

Impairment A physical condition or limitation, such as reduced visual activity.

Individualized education program (IEP) A written instructional program which must be developed for each student who receives special education services, and which contains at least the following components: (1) present levels of educational performance; (2) annual goals; (3) short term objectives; (4) educational services to be provided; (5) participation of the student in the regular education program; (6) date for initiation and anticipated duration of services; and (7) procedures for evaluating progress toward instructional objectives.

Instructional objective (**aim**) An explicit statement of the expected outcomes of instruction, which includes the expected performance and the criterion for success.

Intelligence test A standardized, norm-referenced test which is designed to assess an individual's general ability level and to predict performance on cognitively oriented tasks.

Interval recording A data collection procedure which involves *continuous* observation of a student's behavior during a series of specific time periods.

Latency recording A data collection procedure which measures the time between the onset of a stimulus and the initiation of a response.

Learning and behavior problems School performance difficulties which lead teachers to refer students for special education services; a noncategorical description for students *traditionally* labeled learning disabled, behavior disordered, or educable mentally retarded.

Learning disability A category of special education services intended for students who exhibit school learning problems, who perform adequately on tests of general intelligence and adaptive behavior, and who do not exhibit other handicapping conditions (see page 7 for a discussion of traditional definition of the term *learning disabilities*).

Least restrictive environment A principle for delivery of special education services which stipulates that all children have a right to normal school experiences, and that a student should be removed from the standard educational program *only* when it is essential to meeting his/her educational needs. Such removal should be for as little as possible of the school day, and the use of separate educational settings should be minimized.

Mainstreaming Education of children with "handicaps" in the regular classroom, for all or part of the school day.

Maintenance The lasting effects of a behavioral change once instruction or reinforcement has been withdrawn.

Mean The average of a set of scores.

Median The middle score in a set of scores which have been rank ordered from lowest to highest.

Mediation procedures Informal procedures for parents and school district personnel to negotiate disagreements during the special education placement and planning process, designed to alleviate the need for formal due process hearings.

Mildly handicapped See "learning and behavior problems."

Modeling Demonstration, or provision of examples of, correct performance for a student, followed by student performance of the task.

Muscular dystrophy A progressive muscular disease which results in increasing muscular weakness and incoordination, and an abbreviated life span (often less than 20 years).

Myopia Nearsightedness; visual impairment in which near vision is sufficient but distant vision is poor.

Negative reinforcement A process in which removal of an object or event following a behavior serves to increase or maintain the behavior.

Nondiscriminatory testing Use of assessment procedures which do not systematically discriminate against specific subsets of the student population, such as those of low socioeconomic status or members of minority groups.

Norm-referenced test Test in which scores of a particular student can be "referenced" or compared to the scores obtained by a similar sample of students on whom the test was standardized.

Observational recording Measurement of classroom behavior which is transitory in nature and must be observed as it occurs.

Optacon An electronic device which translates print into tactile sensations which are impressed against the reader's index finger.

Orthopedic and other health impairments Physical conditions which limit one's motor performance and/or ability to consistently perform school tasks, and which may result in disability or handicap.

Permanent product data Data obtained from a performance "product," such as a work sheet or tape recording, which can be measured after the behavior has occurred.

Phase line An entry on a chart, in the form of a solid vertical line, which indicates that the conditions under which the data are being collected have changed.

Placement, instructional Assignment of a student to instructional levels in academic subjects, preferably on the basis of the outcomes of a curriculum-based assessment.

Placement, special education Determination that a student is eligible for special education, and specification of types of special education services to be provided.

Positive reinforcement A process in which the presentation of an object or event following a behavior serves to increase or maintain that behavior.

Postlingual deafness Deafness which has its onset following the development of speech and language.

Prelingual deafness Deafness which occurs at birth or at an early age, before language or speech is developed.

Premack principle A principle of behavioral change which states that high-frequency behavior can be used to reinforce low-frequency behavior.

Public Law 94-142 Federal legislation enacted in 1975 which established the right of all handicapped children to a free, appropriate public education in the least restrictive environment. The law establishes principles upon which special education services are to be based, and provides funds to assist state and local education agencies in providing these services.

Punishment A process in which the removal of a reinforcing event or presentation of an aversive consequence following a behavior serves to decrease that behavior.

Range The difference between the lowest and highest scores in an array of scores.

Referral A process by which teachers, parents and others involved in a student's education formally indicate that the student is having difficulty and might be in need of special education services.

Reliability The consistency of data collected by different observers judging the same student behaviors; also, the extent to which test scores are consistent for a given subject from one testing session to another.

Resource room A form of special education services for students with learning problems. Students are removed from the regular classroom for certain periods of the school day and provided supplementary instruction in areas of difficulty.

Resource teacher A special education teacher who provides supplementary instruction for students with learning and behavior problems. In addition, resource teachers often provide consultative help to classroom teachers to help solve students' academic and behavioral difficulties in the regular classroom.

Response-cost A process in which a predetermined amount of available reinforcers are withdrawn contingent upon an inappropriate behavior, resulting in a decrease of the inappropriate behavior.

Screening A procedure in which large numbers of students are given low-intensity evaluations, for the purpose of identifying potential problems which warrant further assessment.

Self-recording A process in which students record their own performance for the purpose of modifying their behavior.

Sensori-neural hearing loss A hearing loss resulting from a lesion in the inner ear or in the 8th nerve which leads to the hearing center in the brain.

Shaping A procedure in which successive approximations to some terminal behavior are reinforced.

Sickle cell anemia A genetic disorder found almost exclusively in the black population, which results in distortion and malfunction of the red blood cells, reducing the body's supply of oxygen and resulting in episodes of severe pain.

Sign language A form of communication used primarily by the hearing impaired, in which verbal messages are sent and received through a system which uses gestures along with hand and finger movements.

Social reinforcement Use of praise, smiles and other "natural" rewards mediated by another person, contingent upon appropriate performance.

Special class A type of special education service in which a student spends the majority of the school day in a self-contained classroom, apart from the regular education program and apart from nonhandicapped peers.

Special education The provision of educational services, either in addition to or instead of regular classroom instruction, designed to meet the educational needs of students whose school learning is either hindered by handicapping conditions or significantly above or below school standards.

Speechreading A method through which hearing impaired individuals understand speech, by "reading" sounds from the movement of the other person's lips, tongue and face.

Spina bifida A condition in which the spinal column is not fully developed and there is an opening which does not allow complete protection of the spinal cord. Spina bifida may result in orthopedic impairments, as well as inconsistent bowel and bladder control.

Staffing A meeting involving parents, school personnel and, when appropriate, the student, for one or more of the following purposes: (1) determination that a student is or is not eligible for special education; (2) determination of special education placement; (3) development of an IEP (may happen in a staffing or a separate IEP meeting); (4) significant change in a student's special education placement or services; and (5) termination of special education services for an individual student.

Tangible reinforcement Use of toys, stars, school supplies or other items as contingent events for appropriate performance, resulting in increased appropriate performance.

Target behavior The behavior which is to be changed.

Teacher consultation A form of special education services in which the special educator works with classroom teachers to facilitate the solution of learning and behavior problems in the regular classroom. Teacher consultation is often used by resource teachers in combination with direct instruction for students.

Time sampling A form of data collection in which the observer notes the presence or absence of the target behavior within specified, uniform time intervals.

Visual impairment A physical condition which limits effective use of one's vision, and which may result in disability or handicap.

References*

Anastasi, A. *Psychological testing* (3rd ed.). London: MacMillan, 1968.

Anderson, S. B., Bogatz, G. A., Draper, T. W., Jungleblut, A., Sidwell, G., Ward, W. C., & Yates, A. *CIRCUS*. Princeton, NJ: Educational Testing Service, 1974.

Arter, J. A., & Jenkins, J. R. *Differential diagnosis-prescriptive teaching: A critical appraisal* (Tech. Rep. No. 80). Urbana, IL: University of Illinois, Center for the Study of Reading, January, 1978.

Arter, J. A., & Jenkins, J. R. Examining the benefits and prevalence of modality considerations in special education. *The Journal of Special Education*, 1977, *11*, 281 –298.

Axelrod, S. *Behavior modification for the classroom teacher*. New York: McGraw-Hill, 1977.

Ayllon, T., & Roberts, M. D. Eliminating discipline problems by strengthening academic performance. *Journal of Applied Behavior Analysis*, 1974, *7*, 71 –76.

Barraga, M. C. *Increased visual behavior in low-vision children*. New York: American Foundation for the Blind, 1964.

Barrish, H. H., Saunders, M., & Wolf, M. M. Good behavior game: Effects of individual contingencies for group consequences on disruptive behavior in a classroom. *Journal of Applied Behavior Analysis*, 1969, *2*, 119 –124.

Baumgartner, M. *Generalization of improved subtraction regrouping skills from resource rooms to the regular class*. Unpublished doctoral dissertation, University of Illinois, 1979.

Bigge, J., & Sirvis, B. Children with physical and multiple disabilities. In N. G. Haring (ed.), *Behavior of exceptional children*. Columbus, OH: Charles E. Merrill, 1978.

Bijou, S. W., Peterson, R. F., & Ault, M. H. A method to integrate descriptive and experimental field studies at the level of data and empirical concepts. *Journal of Applied Behavior Analysis*, 1968, *1*, 175 –191.

Birch, J. W. *Hearing-impaired children in the mainstream*. Reston, VA: Council for Exceptional Children, 1975.

Blankenship, C. S. Remediating systematic inversion errors in subtraction through the use of demonstration and feedback. *Learning Disability Quarterly*, 1978, *1*, 12 –22.

Blankenship, C. S., & Baumgartner, M. *Acquisition, generalization, and maintenance of arithmetic borrowing skills*. Unpublished manuscript, University of Illinois, 1980.

Blankenship, C. S., & Korn, J. *The differential effects of antecedent and consequent events on two types of arithmetic errors*. Unpublished manuscript, University of Illinois, 1980.

Blankenship, C. S., & Lilly, M. S. Essentials of special education for regular educators. *Teacher Education and Special Education*, 1977, *1*, 28 –35.

Blankenship, C. S., & Lovitt, T. C. *Computational arithmetic data collected in Cur-*

*From *Mainstreaming Students with Learning and Behavior Problems*, by Colleen Blankenship and M. Stephen Lilly. Holt, Rinehart and Winston, 1981.

riculum Research Classroom, Experimental Education Unit, University of Washington, 1974.

Blankenship, C. S., & Lovitt, T. C. *The effects of three types of feedback on three levels of acquisition in arithmetic.* Unpublished manuscript, University of Washington, 1974.

Blankenship, C. S., & Lovitt, T. C. *Story problem data collected in Curriculum Research Classroom,* Experimental Education Unit, University of Washington, 1974.

Bracht, G. H. Experimental factors related to aptitude-treatment interactions. *Review of Educational Research,* 1970, 40, 627−645.

Broden, M., Hall, R. V., & Mitts, B. The effect of self-recording on the classroom behavior of two eighth-grade students. *Journal of Applied Behavior Analysis,* 1971, 4, 191−200.

Brown, L., Wilcox, B., Sontag, E., Vincent, B., Dodd, N., & Gruenwald, L. Toward the realization of the least restrictive educational environment for severely handicapped students. *AAESPH Review,* 1977, 2, 195−201.

Buckholt, D. R., Ferritor, D. E., Sloane, H. N., Della-Piana, G. M., Rogers, K. S., & Coor, I. F. *Classroom & instructional management: A teacher training program in behavior analysis.* New York: CEMREL, 1975.

Buros, O. K. (ed.). *The seventh mental measurements yearbook* (8 vols.). Highland Park, NJ: Gryphon Press, 1972.

Buros, O. K. (ed.). *Tests in print: A comprehensive bibliography of tests for use in education, psychology, and industry.* Highland Park, NJ: Gryphon Press, 1973.

Bushell, D., & Burgess, R. L. Some basic principles of behavior. In R. L. Burgess & D. Bushell (eds.), *Behavioral Sociology: The experimental analysis of social process.* New York: Columbia University Press, 1969.

Cain, L., Levine, S., & Elzey, F. *Cain-Levine Social Competency Scale.* Palo Alto, CA: Consulting Psychology Press, 1963.

Calovini, G. (ed.). *Mainstreaming the visually handicapped.* Springfield, IL: Office of the Superintendent of Public Instruction, undated.

Cantrell, R. P., Cantrell, M. L., Huddleston, C. M., & Woolridge, R. C. Contingency contracting with school problems. *Journal of Applied Behavior Analysis,* 1969, 2, 215−220.

Caplan, S. *Improving decoding skills.* Unpublished manuscript, University of Illinois, 1979.

Carlson, C. S., Arnold, C. R., Becker, W. C., & Madsen, C. H. The elimination of tantrum behavior of a child in an elementary classroom. *Behavior Research and Therapy,* 1968, 6, 117−119.

Carnine, D., & Silbert, J. *Direct instruction reading.* Columbus, OH: Charles E. Merrill, 1979.

Chinn, P. C., Drew, D. J., & Logan, D. R. *Mental retardation: A life cycle approach.* St. Louis: C. V. Mosby, 1975.

Clark, M. *Reinforcing task completion.* Unpublished manuscript, University of Illinois, 1978.

Clasey, D. *Contingent coloring as a reinforcer to improve in-seat behavior.* Unpublished manuscript, University of Illinois, 1979.

Coleman, R. A. A conditioning technique applicable to elementary school classrooms. *Journal of Applied Behavior Analysis,* 1970, 3, 293−297.

Cooper, J. O. *Measurement and analysis of behavior techniques.* Columbus, OH: Charles E. Merrill, 1974.

Corey, J. R., & Shamow, J. The effects of fading on the acquisition and retention of oral reading. *Journal of Applied Behavior Analysis,* 1972, 5, 311−315.

Cox, L. S. Systematic errors in the four vertical algorithms in normal and hand-icapped populations. *Journal for Research in Mathematics Education*, 1975, *6*, 202−220.

Craig, H. B., & Holland, A. L. Reinforcement of visual attending in classrooms for deaf children. *Journal of Applied Behavior Analysis*, 1970, *3*, 97−109.

Cratty, B. *Perceptual-motor behavior and educational processes.* Springfield, IL: Charles C. Thomas, 1969.

DeBriere, T., Spellman, C., & Aronhalt, R. *Multi-graph paper.* Lawrence, KS: H & H Enterprises, 1975.

DeVault, M. V., Frehmeyer, H., Greenberg, H., & Bezuska, S. J. *SRA mathematics: Learning system text.* Chicago: Science Research Associates, 1978.

Diana v. State Board of Education. Civil No. C-70, 37 RFP (N.D.CA, Jan. 7, 1970).

Dinkmeyer, D. *Developing understanding of self and others (DUSO): A program to promote children's social and emotional development.* Circle Pines, MN: American Guidance Service, 1970.

Doll, E. *Vineland Social Maturity Scale.* Circle Pines, MN: American Guidance Service, 1964.

Douglas, J. *Teacher's edition to accompany secret spaces-good news.* New York: Macmillan, 1975.

Dunn, L. M. *Exceptional children in the schools: Special education in transition* (2nd ed.). New York: Holt, Rinehart & Winston, 1973.

Dunn, L. M., & Markwardt, F. C. *Peabody Individual Achievement Test.* Circle Pines, MN: American Guidance Service, 1970.

Durost, W. N., Bixler, H. H., Wrightstone, J. W., Prescott, G. A., & Balow, I. H. *Metropolitan Achievement Tests.* New York: Harcourt Brace Jovanovich, 1971.

Eaton, M. D. Data decisions and evaluation. In N. G. Haring, T. C. Lovitt, M. D. Eaton, & C. L. Hansen (eds.), *The fourth R: Research in the classroom.* Columbus, OH: Charles E. Merrill, 1978.

Eaton, M., & Haisch, L. *A comparison of the effects of new vs. error word drill on reading performance.* Working paper No. 23, Experimental Education Unit, Child Development and Mental Retardation Center, University of Washington, 1974.

Eaton, M., & Lovitt, T. C. Achievement tests vs. direct and daily measurement. In G. Semb (ed.), *Behavior analysis and education - 1972.* Lawrence, KS: University of Kansas Press, 1972.

Eaton, M., Lovitt, T., Sayre, E., & Lynch, V. *The effect of previewing on oral reading rate.* Working paper No. 22, Experimental Education Unit, Child Development and Mental Retardation Center, University of Washington, 1974.

Egner, A., & Lates, B. J. The Vermont Consulting Teacher Program: Case presentation. In C. A. Parker (ed.), *Psychological consultation: Helping teachers meet special needs.* Reston, VA: Council for Exceptional Children, 1975.

Evans, G. W., & Oswalt, G. L. Acceleration of academic progress through the manipulation of peer influence. *Behavior Research and Therapy*, 1968, *6*, 189−195.

Fantasia, K. Personal communication, February 3, 1980.

Federal Register, Vol. 42, No. 163 - Tuesday, August 23, 1977. Department of Health, Education, & Welfare, Washington, D.C.

Forness, S. R. Implications of recent trends in educational labeling. *Journal of Learning Disabilities*, 1974, *7*, 445−449.

Foster, G. G., & Salvia, J. Teacher response to label of learning disabled as a function of demand characteristics. *Exceptional Children*, 1977, *43*, 533−534.

Fowler, R. E., Thomas, L., & Santogrossi, D. A. Using contingent access to activities to increase accurate responding. *Education and Treatment of Children,* 1977, *1,* 5 –8.

Franks, D. J. Ethnic and social status characteristics of children in EMR and LD classes. *Exceptional Children,* 1971, *37,* 537 –538.

Frostig, M., & Horne, D. *The Frostig program for the development of visual perception: Teacher's guide.* Chicago: Follett, 1964.

Frostig, M., Lefever, D., & Whittlesey, J. *The Marianne Frostig Developmental Test of Visual Perception.* Palo Alto, CA: Consulting Psychology Press, 1964.

Fry, E. *Fry's Readability Scale.* Providence, RI: Jamestown Publishers, 1977.

Gallagher, J. J. The special education contract for mildly handicapped children. *Exceptional Children,* 1972, *38,* 527 –535.

Gearhart, B. R. *Learning disabilities: Educational strategies.* St. Louis: C. V. Mosby, 1973.

Ginn 360 reading program. Boston, MA: Ginn & Co., 1969.

Goldman, R., Fristoe, M., & Woodcock, R. W. *Goldman-Fristoe-Woodcock Test of Auditory Discrimination.* Circle Pines, MN: American Guidance Service, 1970.

Goldstein, H., Moss, J., & Jordan, L. J. *The efficacy of special class training on the development of mentally retarded children.* Urbana, IL: University of Illinois Press, 1965.

Goodman, L., & Hammill, D. The effectiveness of the Kephart-Getman activities in developing perceptual-motor cognitive skills. *Focus on Exceptional Children,* 1973, *9,* 1 –9.

Graubard, P. S. Children with behavioral disabilities. In L. M. Dunn (ed.), *Exceptional children in the schools: Special education in transition* (2nd ed.). New York: Holt, Rinehart & Winston, 1973.

Grossman, J. J. (ed.). *Manual on terminology and classification in mental retardation.* Washington, DC: American Association on Mental Deficiency, 1973.

Grossnickle, F. E., & Snyder, J. Constancy of errors to basic facts in the fundamental operations in arithmetic. *Journal of Educational Research,* 1939, *33,* 336 –344.

Haffner, L. *Using contingent observation to reduce "monopolizing" a conversation.* Unpublished manuscript, University of Illinois, 1979.

Hall, R. V. *Managing behavior, Part 1: The measurement of behavior.* Lawrence, KS: H & H Enterprises, 1971. (a)

Hall, R. V. *Managing behavior, Part 3: Applications in school and home.* Lawrence, KS: H & H Enterprises, 1971. (b)

Hall, R. V., Axelrod, S., Foundopoulos, M., Shellman, J., Campbell, R. A., & Cranston, S. The effective use of punishment to modify behavior in the classroom. *Educational Technology,* April, 1971, 24 –26.

Hall, R. V., & Fox, R. G. Changing criterion designs an alternative applied behavior analysis procedure. In B. C. Etzel, J. M. Leblanc, & D. M. Baer (eds.), *New developments in behavioral research: Theory, method, & application in honor of Sidney W. Bijou.* New York: Halsted Press, 1977.

Hall, R. V., Fox, R., Willard, D., Goldsmith, L., Emerson, M., Owen, M., Davis, F., & Porcia, E. The teacher as observer and experimenter in the modification of disputing and talking-out behaviors. *Journal of Applied Behavior Analysis,* 1971, *4,* 141 –150.

Hall, R. V., Lund, D., & Jackson, D. Effects of teacher attention on study behavior. *Journal of Applied Behavior Analysis,* 1968, *1,* 1 –12.

Hallahan, D. P., & Cruickshank, W. M. *Psychoeducational foundations of learning disabilities.* Englewood Cliffs, NJ: Prentice-Hall, 1973.

Hammill, D. D. Training visual perceptual processes. *Journal of Learning Disabilities,* 1972, *5,* 552—559.

Hammill, D. D., & Larsen, S. C. The effectiveness of psycholinguistic training. *Exceptional Children,* 1974, *41,* 5—14. (a)

Hammill, D. D., & Larsen, S. C. The relationship of selected auditory perceptual skills and reading ability. *Journal of Learning Disabilities,* 1974, *7,* 40—46. (b)

Hammill, D. D., & Wiederholt, J. L. Review of the Frostig Visual Perception Test and the related training program. In L. Mann, & D. A. Sabatino (eds.), *The first review of special education* (Vol. 1). Philadelphia: JSE Press, 1973.

Hansen, C. L. *The generalization of skills and drills vs. corrective feedback to the independent reading performance of intermediate aged learning disabled boys.* Unpublished doctoral dissertation, University of Washington, 1976.

Hansen, C. L. *Program for individualized spelling instruction.* Program Project quarterly report, University of Washington, Fall 1974.

Hansen, C. L., & Eaton, M. D. Reading. In N. G. Haring, T. C. Lovitt, M. D. Eaton, & C. L. Hansen (eds.), *The fourth R: Research in the classroom.* Columbus, OH: Charles E. Merrill, 1978.

Haring, N. G. Research in the classroom: Problems and procedures. In N. G. Haring, T. C. Lovitt, M. D. Eaton, & C. L. Hansen (eds.), *The fourth R: Research in the classroom.* Columbus, OH.: Charles E. Merrill, 1978.

Haring, N. G., Lovitt, T. C., Eaton, M. D., & Hansen, C. L. (eds.). *The fourth R: Research in the classroom.* Columbus, OH: Charles E. Merrill, 1978.

Hart, V. Crippling conditions. In M. S. Lilly (ed.), *Children with exceptional needs: A survey of Special Education.* New York: Holt, Rinehart & Winston, 1979.

Hatten, J. Oral communication disorders. In M. S. Lilly (ed.), *Children with exceptional needs: A survey of Special Education.* New York: Holt, Rinehart & Winston, 1979.

Hauck, B., Metcalfe, J., & Bennett, P. *Teaching early comprehension skills: A case study.* Unpublished manuscript, Experimental Education Unit, Child Development and Mental Retardation Center, University of Washington, 1975.

Haupt, E. J., Van Kirk, M. J., & Terraciano, T. An inexpensive fading procedure to decrease errors and increase retention of number facts. In E. Ramp and G. Semb (eds.), *Behavior analysis: Areas of research and application.* Englewood Cliffs, NJ: Prentice-Hall, 1975.

Hawkins, R. P., & Doebs, R. W. Behavioral definitions in applied behavior analysis: Explicit or implicit. In B. C. Etzel, J. M. LeBlanc, & D. M. Baer (eds.), *New developments in behavioral research: Theory, method, and application in honor of Sidney W. Bijou.* New York: Halsted Press, 1977.

Hendricks, G. *Increasing the percent of time on-task & completion of assignments.* Unpublished manuscript, University of Illinois, 1979.

Hobbs, N. *The future of children: Categories, labels, and their consequences.* San Francisco: Jossey-Bass Publishers, 1975.

Homme, L. E. Human motivation and the environment. In N. Haring and R. Whelan (eds.), *The learning environment: Relationship to behavior modification and implications for special education.* Lawrence, KS: University of Kansas Press, 1966.

Homme, L. E., Csanyi, A. P., Gonzales, M. A., & Rechs, J. R. *How to use contingency contracting in the classroom* (Rev. ed.). Champaign, IL: Research Press, 1977.

Homme, L. E., DeBaca, P. C., Devine, J. V., Steinhorst, R., & Rickert, E. J. Use of the Premack principle in controlling the behavior of nursery school children.

Journal of the Experimental Analysis of Behavior, 1963, *6*, 544.

Hopkins, B. L., Schutte, R. C., & Garton, K. L. The effects of access to a playroom on the rate and quality of printing and writing of first- and second-grade students. *Journal of Applied Behavior Analysis*, 1971, *4*, 77–87.

Howell, K. W., Kaplan, J. S., & O'Connell, C. Y. *Evaluating exceptional children: A task analysis approach.* Columbus, OH: Charles E. Merrill, 1979.

Hughes, F. & Gregerson, G. Reduction of irrelevant talking-out in a first grader through the use of magic (slate). In R. V. Hall, *Managing behavior, Part 3: Applications in school and home.* Lawrence, KS: H & H Enterprises, 1971.

Illinois primer on individualized education programs. Springfield, IL: Illinois Office of Education, 1979.

Jacobi, C., & Eaton, M. *The remediation of b-d reversals in oral reading.* Unpublished manuscript, University of Washington, 1975.

Jansky, J., & de Hirsch, K. *Preventing reading failure.* New York: Harper & Row, 1972.

Jastak, J. R., & Jastak, S. R. *Wide Range Achievement Test.* Wilmington, DE: Guidance Associates, 1965.

Jeffers, J., & Barley, M. *Speedreading.* Springfield, IL: Charles C. Thomas, 1971.

Jenkins, J. R., & Pany, D. Standardized achievement tests: How useful for special education? *Exceptional Children*, 1978, *44*, 448–453.

Johnson, D., & Mykelbust, H. *Learning disabilities: Educational principles and practices.* New York: Grune & Stratton, 1967.

Jones, J. W. *Blind Children: Degree of vision, mode of reading.* OE-35026. Washington, DC: U.S. Government Printing Office, 1961.

Jones, R., & Kazdin, A. Programming response maintenance after withdrawing token reinforcement. *Behavior Therapy*, 1975, *6*, 153–164.

Jones, R. L. Labels and stigma in special education. *Exceptional Children*, 1972, *38*, 553–564.

Karracker, R. J. Token reinforcement systems in regular public school classrooms. In C. E. Pitts (ed.), *Operant conditioning in the classroom.* New York: Thomas G. Crowell, 1971.

Kazdin, A. E. *Behavior modification in applied settings.* Homewood, IL: Dorsey Press, 1975.

Keogh, B. K., & Becker, L. D. Early detection of learning problems: Questions, cautions, and guidelines. *Exceptional Children*, 1973, *40*, 5–11.

Kephart, N. C. *The slow learner in the classroom.* Columbus, OH: Charles E. Merrill, 1960.

Kessler-Futterman, A. *Improving spelling accuracy using "cover-copy-compare."* Unpublished manuscript, University of Illinois, 1979.

Kimmell, G. M., & Wahl, J. *Screening Test for Auditory Perception.* San Rafael, CA: Academic Therapy Publications, 1969.

Kirk, S. A. *Educating exceptional children.* Boston: Houghton Mifflin, 1972.

Kirk, S. A. Research in education. In H. A. Stevens and R. Heber (eds.), *Mental retardation.* Chicago: University of Chicago Press, 1964.

Kirk, S. A., & Kirk, W. D. *Psycholinguistic learning disabilities: Diagnosis and remediation.* Urbana, IL: University of Illinois Press, 1971.

Kirk, S. A., McCarthy, L., & Kirk, W. D. *Illinois Test of Psycholinguistic Abilities* (Rev. ed.). Urbana, IL: University of Illinois Press, 1968.

Knieriem, S. *Remediating "talk-out" behavior in the regular classroom.* Unpublished manuscript, University of Illinois, 1979.

Kottmeyer, W., & Claus, A. *Basic goals in spelling.* New York: Webster Division, McGraw-Hill, 1968.

Landsman, M., & Dillard, H. *Evanston Early Identification Scale*. Chicago: Follette, 1967.

Larry, P. v. Riles, 41 U.S.L.W. 2033 (U.S. June, 21, 1972).

Larsen, S. C., & Hammill, D. D. The relationship of selected visual-perceptual abilities to school learning. *The Journal of Special Education*, 1975, *9*, 281–291.

Larsen, S. C., Rogers, D., & Sowell, V. The use of selected perceptual tests in differentiating between normal and learning disabled children. *Journal of Learning Disabilities*, 1976, *9*, 85–90.

Leach, D. M., & Graves, M. E. The effects of immediate correction on improving seventh grade language arts performance. In A. Egner (ed.), *Individualizing junior and senior high instruction to provide special education within regular classrooms: The 1972–73 research service reports of the secondary special education project*. Unpublished document. Burlington, VT: University of Vermont, Department of Special Education, 1973.

Lee, E. *Increasing the on-task behavior of a nine-year-old girl*. Unpublished manuscript, University of Illinois, 1978.

Lerner, J. *Children with learning disabilities*. New York: Houghton Mifflin, 1971.

Leydorf, M. Physical-motor factors. In B. K. Keogh (ed.), *Early identification of children with potential learning problems*. *The Journal of Special Education*, 1970, *4*, 313–320.

Lilly, M. S. (ed.). *Children with exceptional needs: A survey of special education*. New York: Holt, Rinehart & Winston, 1979.

Lilly, M. S. Evaluating individualized education programs. In S. Torres (ed.), *A primer on individualized education programs for handicapped children*. Reston, VA: Council for Exceptional Children, 1977. (a)

Lilly, M. S. A merger of categories: Are we finally ready? *Journal of Learning Disabilities*, 1977, *10*, 115–121. (b)

Lilly, M. S. A training-based model for special education. *Exceptional Children*, 1971, *37*, 745–749.

Lovaas, O. I., Berberich, J., Perloff, B., & Schaeffer, B. Acquisition of imitative speech by schizophrenic children. *Science*, 1966, *162*, 705–707.

Lovitt, T. C. Applied behavior analysis techniques and curriculum research: Implications for instruction. In N. G. Haring & R. L. Schiefelbusch (eds.), *Teaching special children*. New York: McGraw-Hill, 1976.

Lovitt, T. C. Arithmetic. In N. G. Haring, T. C. Lovitt, M. D. Eaton & C. L. Hansen (eds.), *The fourth R: Research in the classroom*. Columbus, OH: Charles E. Merrill, 1978.

Lovitt, T. C. *In spite of my resistance . . . I've learned from children*. Columbus, OH: Charles E. Merrill, 1977.

Lovitt, T. C. Team I Report. *A program project for the investigation and application of procedures of analysis and modification of behavior of handicapped children*. University of Washington, Experimental Education Unit, Child Development and Mental Retardation Center, July 1973.

Lovitt, T. C., & Curtiss, K. A. Effects of manipulating an antecedent event on mathematics response rate. *Journal of Applied Behavior Analysis*, 1968, *1*, 329–333.

Lovitt, T., Eaton, M., Kirkwood, M., & Pelander, J. Effects of various reinforcement contingencies on oral reading rate. In Ramp & Hopkins (eds.), *A new direction for education: Behavior analysis*. Lawrence, KS: University of Kansas Press, 1971.

Lovitt, T. C., & Esveldt, K. A. The relative effects on math performance of single versus multiple ratio schedules: A case study. *Journal of Applied Behavior*

356   *Analysis,* 1970, *3,* 261−270.

Lovitt, T. C., Guppy, T. E., & Blattner, J. E. The use of free-time contingency with fourth graders to increase spelling accuracy. *Behavior Research and Therapy,* 1969, *7,* 151−156.

Lovitt, T. C., & Hansen, C. L. Round one—Placing the child in the right reader. *Journal of Learning Disabilities,* 1976, *9,* 347−353.

Lovitt, T. C., & Hansen, C. L. The use of contingent skipping and drilling to improve oral reading and comprehension. *Journal of Learning Disabilities,* 1976, *9,* 481−487.

Lovitt, T. C., & Smith, D. D. Using withdrawal of positive reinforcement to alter subtraction performance. *Exceptional Children,* 1974, *40,* 357−358.

Lowenbraun, S., & Scroggs, C. The hearing handicapped. In N. G. Haring (ed.), *Behavior of Exceptional Children.* Columbus, OH: Charles E. Merrill, 1978.

Lowenfeld, B. Psychological problems of children with impaired vision. In W. M. Cruickshank (ed.), *Psychology of exceptional children and youth.* Englewood Cliffs, NJ: Prentice-Hall, 1971.

Maccarone, S. *Teacher's edition to accompany Beginnings-Endings.* New York: Macmillan, 1975.

MacMillan, D. L., Jones, R. L., & Aloia, G. F. The mentally retarded label: A theoretical analysis and review of research. *American Journal of Mental Deficiency,* 1974, *79,* 241−261.

Madden, R., Gardner, E. R., Rudman, H. C., Karlsen, B., & Merwin, J. C. *Stanford Achievement Test.* New York: Harcourt Brace Jovanovich, 1973.

Madsen, C. H., Becker, W. C., Thomas, D. R., Koser, L., & Plager, E. An analysis of the reinforcing function of "sit down" commands. In R. K. Parker (ed.), *Readings in educational psychology.* Boston: Allyn & Bacon, 1970.

Mager, R. F. *Preparing instructional objectives.* Belmont, CA: Fearon Publishers, 1962.

Maginnis, G. A. Readability graph and informal reading inventories. *The Reading Teacher,* 1969, *22,* 516−518.

Maloney, K. B., & Hopkins, B. L. The modification of sentence structure and its relationship to subjective judgments of creativity in writing. *Journal of Applied Behavior Analysis,* 1973, *6,* 425−433.

Mann, L. Perceptual training: Misdirections and redirections. *American Journal of Orthopsychiatry,* 1970, *40,* 30−38.

McCracken, G., & Walcutt, C. *Lippincott's basic reading.* Philadelphia: Lippincott, 1966, 1971.

Mercer, J. R. A policy statement on assessment procedures and the rights of children. *Harvard Educational Review, Reprint Series No. 9,* 1974.

Mills, R. E. *The teaching of word recognition.* Fort Lauderdale, FL: The Mills Center, 1964.

Mills vs. Board of Education of the District of Columbia, 348 F. Supp. 886 (D.D.D., 1972).

Myklebust, H. R. *The Pupil Rating Scale: Screening for learning disabilities.* New York: Grune & Stratton, 1971.

Myklebust, H. R., & Boshes, B., Olsen, D. A., & Cole, C. H. *Final report: Minimal brain damage in children.* M. S. Public Health Service Contract 108−65−142. Evanston, IL: Northwestern University Publications, 1969.

Nihira, J., Foster, R., Shellhaas, M., & Leland, H. *Adaptive Behavior Scales.* Washington, DC: American Association on Mental Deficiency, 1969.

O'Connell, C., & McManman, K. *Charting and precision teaching: Adult acquisition rates.* Working paper No. 14, Arizona State University, Tempe, AZ, 1977.

O'Leary, K. D., Kaufman, K. F., Kass, R., & Drabman, R. The effects of loud and soft reprimands on the behavior of disruptive students. *Exceptional Children,* 1970, *37,* 145−155.

Orlansky, J. Z. *Mainstreaming the hearing-impaired child.* Austin, Texas: Learning Concepts, 1977.

Orlansky, M. D. *Mainstreaming the visually impaired child.* Austin, Texas: Learning Concepts, 1977.

Patterson, G. R. An application of conditioning techniques to the control of a hyperactive child. In L. P. Ullman & L. Krasner (eds.), *Case studies in behavior modification.* New York: Holt, Rinehart & Winston, 1965.

Paulsen, S. S. *Improving accuracy on reading assignments.* Unpublished manuscript, University of Illinois, 1978.

Pennsylvania Association for Retarded Children v. Commonwealth of Pennsylvania, 334 F. Supp. 1257 (E.D. PA, 1971).

Popham, W. J. *Criterion-referenced measurement.* Englewood Cliffs, NJ: Prentice-Hall, 1978.

Porterfield, J. K., Herbert-Jackson, E., & Risely, T. R. Contingent observation: An effective and acceptable procedure for reducing disruptive behavior of young children in a group setting. *Journal of Applied Behavior Analysis,* 1976, *9,* 55 −64.

Premack, D. Toward empirical behavior laws: 1. Positive reinforcement. *Psychological Review,* 1959, *66,* 219 −233.

Prescott, G. A. Criterion-referenced test interpretation in reading. *The Reading Teacher,* 1971, *24,* 347 −354.

Prillaman, D. An analysis of placement factors in classes for the educable mentally retarded. *Exceptional Children,* 1975, *42,* 107 −108.

Proeger, B. B. The Pupil Rating Scale: Screening for learning disabilities. *The Journal of Special Education,* 1973, *7,* 311 −317.

Reese, E. P., & Johnson, K. R. *Observing, defining, and recording behavior: A first step toward accountability. Part I.* Unpublished paper, Mt. Holyoke College, 1976.

Reger, R. Resource rooms: Change agents or guardians of the status quo? *Journal of Special Education,* 1972, *6,* 355 −359.

Reimers, H., & Hall, R. V. Reduction of nail-biting and increasing speed of doing dishes through reinforcement (experiment 2). In R. V. Hall, *Managing behavior, Part 3: Applications in school and home.* Lawrence, KS: H & H Enterprises, 1971.

Reith, H., Axelrod, S., Anderson, R., Hathaway, F., Wood, K., & Fitzgerald, C. Influence of distributed practice and daily testing on weekly spelling tests. *Journal of Educational Research,* 1974, *68,* 73 −77.

Reynolds, M. C., & Birch, J. W. *Teaching exceptional children in all America's schools.* Reston, VA: Council for Exceptional Chidlren, 1977.

Risley, T. R. Spontaneous language and the preschool. In J. C. Stanley (ed.), *Preschool programs for the disadvantaged: Five experimental approaches to early childhood education.* Baltimore: Johns Hopkins University Press, 1972.

Roach, E. F., & Kephart, N. C. *The Purdue Perceptual-Motor Survey.* Columbus, OH: Merrill, 1966.

Roberts, M., & Smith, D. D. The relationship among correct and error oral reading rates and comprehension. *Learning Disability Quarterly,* 1980, *3,* 54 −64.

Robinson, N. M., & Robinson, H. B. *The mentally retarded child.* New York: McGraw-Hill, 1976.

Rubin, E. Z., Simon, C. B., & Betwee, M. C. *Emotionally handicapped children and the elementary school.* Detroit: Wayne State University Press, 1966.

Sabatino, D. A. Auditory perception: Development, assessment, and intervention. In L. Mann & D. A. Sabatino (eds.), *The first review of special education* (Vol. 1). Philadelphia: JSE Press, 1973.

Salvia, J., & Ysseldyke, J. *Assessment in special and remedial education.* Boston:

358   Houghton Mifflin, 1978.

Santogrossi, D. A. Personal communication, June 24, 1980.

Schmidt, G. W., & Ulrich, R. E. Effects of group contingent events upon classroom noise. *Journal of Applied Behavior Analysis*, 1969, 2, 171–179.

Schmidt, J. A. *Using contingency contracts to increase work completion.* Unpublished manuscript, University of Illinois, 1980.

Schutte, R. C., & Hopkins, B. L. The effects of teacher attention on following instructions in a kindergarten class. *Journal of Applied Behavior Analysis*, 1970, 3, 117–122.

Science Research Associates. *Level placement and chapter placement tests for the SRA mathematics program, 1978 Edition.* Chicago: Science Research Associates, 1978.

Sedlak, R. A., & Weener, P. Review of research on the Illinois Test of Psycholinguistic Abilities. In L. Mann & D. A. Sabatino (eds.), *The first review of special education* (Vol. 1). Philadelphia: JSE Press, 1973.

Senf, G., & Comrey, A. State initiative in learning disabilities: Illinois' project SCREEN, Report 1; The SCREEN early identification procedure. *Journal of Learning Disabilities*, 1975, 8, 451–457.

Simon, E. A. *Improving work completion and accuracy in the regular classroom.* Unpublished manuscript, University of Illinois, 1979.

Slingerland, B. H. *Slingerland Screening Tests for Identifying Children with Specific Language Disabilities* (2nd ed.). Cambridge, MA: Educators Publishing Service, 1970.

Slosson, R. L. *Slosson Oral Reading Test.* East Aurora, NY: Slosson Educational Publications, 1963.

Smith, C. B., & Wardhaugh, R. *The new Macmillan reading program, series r.* New York: Macmillan, 1975.

Smith, C. W. *A study of constant errors in subtraction and in the application of selected principles of the decimal numeration system made by third- and fourth-grade students.* Doctoral dissertation, Wayne State University, 1968.

Smith, D. D. *The influence of instructions, feedback, and reinforcement contingencies on children's abilities to acquire and become proficient at computational arithmetic skills.* Doctoral dissertation, College of Education, Area of Special Education, University of Washington, 1973.

Smith, D. D., & Lovitt, T. C. The educational diagnosis and remediation of *b* and *d* written reversal problems: A case study. *Journal of Learning Disabilities*, 1973, 6, 356–363.

Smith, D. D., & Lovitt, T. C. *The influence of instructions and reinforcement contingencies on children's abilities to compute arithmetic problems.* Paper presented at the Fifth Annual Conference on Behavior Analysis in Education, University of Kansas, October, 1974.

Smith, D. D., & Lovitt, T. C. The use of modeling techniques to influence the acquisition of computational arithmetic skills in learning-disabled children. In E. Ramp and G. Semb (eds.), *Behavior analysis: Areas of research and application.* Englewood Cliffs, NJ: Prentice-Hall, 1975.

Smith, R. M., & Neisworth, J. T. *The exceptional child: A functional approach.* New York: McGraw-Hill, 1975.

Smith, S., & Sherwood, B. D. Educational uses of the PLATO system. *Science*, 1976, 192, 344–352.

Sontag, E., Burke, P. J., & York, R. Considerations for serving the severely handicapped in the public schools. *Education and Training of the Mentally Retarded*, 1973, 8, 20–26.

Starlin, C. *The use of daily and direct recording as an aid in teaching oral reading.*

Unpublished doctoral dissertation, University of Oregon, 1970.

Sucher, F., & Allred, R. A. *Sucher-Allred Reading Placement Inventory.* Oklahoma City: The Economy Company, 1973.

Sulzbacher, S. I., & Houser, J. E. A tactic to eliminate disruptive behaviors in the classroom: Group contingent consequences. *American Journal of Mental Deficiency,* 1968, *73,* 88‒90.

Sulzer-Azaroff, B., & Mayer, G. R. *Applying behavior analysis-procedures with children and youth.* New York: Holt, Rinehart and Winston, 1977.

Terman, L., & Merrill, M. *Stanford-Binet Intelligence Scale, 1972 norms edition.* Boston: Houghton Mifflin, 1973.

Thomas, D. R., Becker, W. C., & Armstrong, M. Production and elimination of disruptive classroom behavior by systematically varying teacher's behavior. *Journal of Applied Behavior Analysis,* 1968, *1,* 35‒46.

Tiegs, E. W., & Clarke, W. W. *California Achievement Tests.* Monterey, CA: CTB/McGraw-Hill, 1970.

Van Houten, R., Morrison, E., Jarvis, R., & McDonald, M. The effects of explicit timing and feedback on compositional response rate in elementary school children. *Journal of Applied Behavior Analysis,* 1974, *7,* 547‒556.

Vollrath, F., & Clark, M. Effects of reinforcement procedures on talking frequency in a slow-reading group. In R. V. Hall, *Managing behavior, Part 3: Applications in school and home.* Lawrence, KS: H & H Enterprises, 1971.

Voss, C. *The use of a model-lead-test procedure to improve children's ability to compute division facts.* Unpublished manuscript, University of Illinois, 1979.

Walker, J. E., & Shea, T. M. *Behavior modification: A practical approach for educators* (2nd ed.). St. Louis: C. V. Mosby, 1980.

Wallace, G., & Larsen, S. C. *Educational assessment of learning problems: Testing for teaching.* Boston: Allyn and Bacon, 1978.

Ward, M. Children with visual impairments. In M. S. Lilly (ed.), *Children with exceptional needs: A survey of special education.* New York: Holt, Rinehart & Winston, 1979.

Wechsler, D. *Manual for the Wechsler Intelligence Scale for Children—revised.* New York: Psychological Corporation, 1974.

Weintraub, F. J. Legislation—initiation and implementation (Part III). In S. A. Kirk & J. M. McCarthy (eds.), *Learning disabilities: Selected ACLD papers.* Boston: Houghton Mifflin, 1975.

Wepman, J. M. *Auditory Discrimination Test* (Rev. ed.). Chicago: Language Research Associates, 1973.

Wheeler, A. H., & Fox, W. L. *Managing behavior, Part 5: Writing instructional objectives.* Lawrence, KS: H & H Enterprises, 1972.

White, O. R., & Haring, N. G. *Exceptional teaching.* Columbus, OH: Charles E. Merrill, 1976.

White, O. R., & Liberty, K. A. Behavioral assessment and precise educational measurement. In N. G. Haring & R. L. Schiefelbusch (eds.), *Teaching special children.* New York: McGraw-Hill, 1976.

Wiederholt, J. L. Historical perspectives on the education of the learning disabled. In L. Mann and D. Sabatino (eds.), *The second review of special education.* Philadelphia: JSE Press, 1974.

Wilcox, B., & Pany, D. *Use of group contingencies in classroom management: A review and evaluation of research.* Unpublished manuscript, University of Illinois, undated.

Willerman, J. *The remediation of off-task behavior in the regular classroom.* Unpublished manuscript, University of Illinois, 1979.

360   Williams, C. D. The elimination of tantrum behavior by extinction procedures. *Journal of Abnormal and Social Psychology*, 1959, *59*, 269.

Willis, J. W., Hobbs, T. R., Kirkpatrick, D. G., & Manley, K. W. Training counselors as researchers in the natural environment. In E. Ramp & G. Semb (eds.), *Behavior analysis: Areas of research and application*, Englewood Cliffs, NJ: Prentice-Hall, 1975.

Wolfson, D. *The use of checklist to monitor a student's daily completion of in-class assignments in a middle school setting.* Unpublished manuscript, University of Illinois, 1979.

Wooley, K. *Remediating "off-task" behavior in the regular classroom.* Unpublished manuscript, University of Illinois, 1979.

Name Index

Subject Index